Hollywood

Hollywood
Recent Developments

edited by

Christian W. Thomsen
Angela Krewani

with contributions by

Robert Blanchet
Dietmar E. Fröhlich
Jean-Pierre Geuens
Randi Gunzenhäuser
Vinzenz Hediger
Kay Hoffmann
Angela Krewani
Claudia Liebrand
Gudula Simone Moritz
Volker Pietsch
Karen A. Ritzenhoff
Pamela C. Scorzin
Christian W. Thomsen
Frederick Wasser
Celeste M. Williams

Edition Axel Menges

Printed with support by the University of Siegen

© 2005 Edition Axel Menges, Stuttgart / London
ISBN 3-932565-44-4

Prepress image processing: Jörg »Hipp« Thomsen
Printing and binding: Daehan Printing and Publishing Co., Ltd., Sungnam, Korea

Editorial supervision: Dorothea Duwe
Design: Axel Menges

Contents

Christian W. Thomsen / Angela Krewani
Preface

I, Christian Thomsen, started cherishing a particular liking for the cinema when I was about ten years old. As a youngster in post-war Germany in the late 1940s and 1950s visiting our local movie theater cost about a dime. I loved westerns and those American films where beautiful cars cruised along Californian beaches. I tried to imitate the sheriffs' walk with large-caliber colts at their hips, always on the alert and ready to draw.

But one thing puzzled me from very early on. I had no idea about editing techniques and wondered how film music was created. I first imagined camera crews being accompanied by bands of musicians. It became more puzzling with symphonic orchestras. Enjoying films with African scenarios, jungles, adventure stories in exotic settings, I wondered how on earth film producers could make us believe that there are whole orchestras playing in a humid tropical environment while an expedition is searching for hidden treasures or gangsters are hunted on a river. Just think about sensitive string instruments and their tuning!

Getting more knowledgeable I thought this highly unrealistic, even absurd and ironic. Music and action for me often fell apart; the sole function of film music seemed to me the creation of dramatic emotion – a poor surrogate for something that should have been told in moving images, with the art of acting and sounds suited to the action. What I wanted – even in early student days – was an integrative sound concept as part of an overall aesthetic concept for the mixed medium of film. This should consist of visual, auditive and body languages as well as of environmental texts of setting, architecture, nature etc. I had to wait a long time for this and even today old mistakes of a mere supporting background of film music are frequently repeated.

Meanwhile, my notions about sound tracks have considerably deepened. Reflecting on the most characteristic and noteworthy developments of Hollywood since the early 1990s, I think that – together with the rapid growth of an entire CGI industry and their ever more spectacular effects – it is the quality of sound that has improved most. The creation of sound worlds, the immersion into an organically composed whole of visual and auditory experiences has dramatically changed our perception of Hollywood films.

Today, sound worlds – of which music is only a part – are at least as important as special effects. Born from the tradition of 19th century European symphonic music as I still remember it from my youth, film music and sound tracks have grown into a multi-sensory experience. They support actions, emotions, moods and ideological contents of movies as well as deeply influencing our aesthetic and intellectual facilities – via subconscious levels – without illustrating and explaining visual levels in the sense of program music.

The »director of sound« has been upgraded comparable to the former cameraman who has risen to the status of »director of photography«. The film's director ranks equal with the leading actors at least.

In a star-oriented – even star-possessed – Western culture they all tend to become stars and entrepreneurs of their own. Only the script writer's role still seems to be underrated. But: without scripts, no movies. And without sound and music much of the visual experience becomes pretty banal.

The extreme proliferation of sound ties in with a general impact of today's cinematic visual systems that turn cinema into a »cinema of visual and aural effects«: Besides the upgrade of sound systems the reception of film is optimized through special effects, usually being produced digitally. Although a digital cinema could offer new and fantastic worlds to explore, special effects are employed to augment the viewer's immersion into the film. This tendency goes along with a highly developed cinematic architecture, which also points to the notion of cinema as »special event«.

As counterpart to these developments stands the televisualization of most parts of the film production: Recent figures evidence that about 50% of the revenues emerge from the video and DVD home market – in this respect the filmic experience is vanished in favour of the completely different involvement of watching TV. And TV itself has been developing new formats that constantly undermine the cinematic experience it historically had tried to achieve.

As another consequence of the televisualization of film production occurs the transnationalization of film production. Since productions for television are somewhat smaller in production costs and Hollywood itself has ventured into global corporate culture, executives turned to European broadcasting stations intending joint projects: This brought the international heritage genre into being. This genre feeds on literary adaptions of canonical novels, generally by eminent literary figures such as Henry James, Jane Austen or Charles Dickens, just to name a few. These films set out to recreate an authentic experience of times gone by through elaborate mise-en-scène, romantic landscape and period costumes. But over the last years the genre has branched out into more contemporary settings as well: Although not being period pieces movies such as *Bridget Jones' Diary*, *Notting Hill* and *Chocolat* sport images of contemporary France and England. Especially the films referring to France allude to French national film culture without being French at all. Thus national film cultures are incorporated into Hollywood, which – in return – becomes increasingly globalized.

Whereas the reference to European tradition plays a minor role within Hollywood film production, the integration of Asian films and their aesthetics has been pivoting over the years. Especially Hong Kong films and their martial arts scenes have highly affected Hollywood film production as it can be watched in Ang Lee's *Crouching Tiger, Hidden Dragon* or in the *Matrix* series. Particularly *Crouching Tiger, Hidden Dragon* is a seminal example for a new but steadily increasing form of transnational or global cinema referring to a set of national traditions and being closely affiliated with Hollywood. The film was made with a relative modest budget of $ 15 million and it earned more than $ 200 million worldwide. It earned $ 128 million in the movie theaters and an additional $ 112 million on the video and DVD market. Although the film was not directly produced within Hollywood, but shot on location in China, it displays the global aspects of film production, which are also quite common within recent production structures. Much of the money came from the various divisions of Sony – being itself one of the major players in Hollywood at one time. Funds were provided by Columbia Film Productions Asia, Sony's Hong Kong branch that was set up in order to produce films for the Asian local markets, Sony Picture Classics in New York bought the US distribution, Columbia Pictures in Hollywood endowed the rights for Latin America and Sony Classical provided the funds for the soundtrack. (Klein, 2004, 18–19)

As mentioned above, the film was shot on location in China, the soundtrack was recorded in Shanghai, the post production took place in Hong Kong and the film finally was edited in New York. Thus the production and screening of *Crouching Tiger* provides the perfect example for the new, globalized movie, which cannot be traced back to an authentic cultural situation or even to a certain pattern of national film production. Thus Christina Klein concludes her essay on *Crouching Tiger* with some remarks on the global characteristics of this film which also very easily can be understood as a delineation of the trends towards globalization within Hollywood. »*Crouching Tiger* stands as an exemplary instance of transnational cinema. ... The production and consumption of these films take place on a multinational rather than a national scale, and the aesthetic affiliations they make cross multiple cultural boundaries. Thus, the national-cultural identity of these films is surprisingly fluid; it changes depending on whether one looks at studio ownership, sources of financing, production locale, the ethnic or legal identity of the cast and crew, audiences, narrative and cinematic style, or thematic concerns. The emergence of this cinema makes it vitally important to develop critical tools that enable us to read films from a transnational perspective.« (Klein, 2004, 37 f)

Although the *Matrix* alludes to martial art movies as well, it also tempers with the tradition of the Japanese manga and anime: It is well known that the narrative forerunner to *Matrix* is an anime called *Ghost in the Shell*. But Japan has not only entered Hollywood economically, but it is shaping filmic narratives as well, either in the form of fascination with a foreign culture and as fear of being outmoded by this strong economy and culture. Whereas Ridley Scott's *Black Rain* and Michael Bay's *Pearl Harbour* voice the fear of being overtaken by Japan, Edward Zwick's *The Last Samurai* delivers an unabridged fascination with ancient Japanese culture. In a somewhat critical vein American manhood and American values are depicted as degenerated comparable to Japanese codes of honor, fighting and masculinity. As Barbara Wyllie notes, American masculinity seems to be in a big crisis, up to a point where it erases all other concerns. (Wyllie, 2003, 181) In order to conquer the crisis in masculinity, the superheroe re-enters the screen: Letting the 1990s pass there is an overwhelming collection of male superheroes, The Terminator and all the other fighters overstress their masculinity in order to cover up the fear of female dominance as it is expressed in Ridley Scott's *G.I. Jane.* This development may correspond to the upsurge of academic masculinity studies in the US. (Mosse, 1996; McLaren, 1997)

The construction of gender identities has experienced a change over the last years. While *Thelma and Louise* weren't allowed to leave male culture and patriarchal relationships, women today can do as they want to. Maybe *G.I. Jane*'s entrance into the military world is not everybody's cup of tea, but comedy in particular seems to overturn established gender relationships. Diane Keaton in *Something's Gotta Give* favors a younger lover, even if she ends up with the old, Viagra driven friend, played by Jack Nicholson, who steps around the role of the super hero by giving the old fool instead. The remake of the *Stepford Wives'* functions in a similar fashion, being a black parody on the 1950s family values: In this case even well-educated women are not allowed to take up professional careers but are – with the help of nanotechnology – turned into perfect, Barbie-like housewives. This film opposes the intentions of a political right-wing movement of returning to the outlived family values of the 1950s.

Talking about the theory of the short story, Edgar Allan Poe always emphasizes unity and totality of effect which should form the aesthetic core of a story. We are concerned that it is exactly this quality, the artistic and technical unity of effects, which – apart from all the other developments dealt with in this book – counts most when we discuss positive achievements of recent Hollywood films.

We are fully aware that our book does not cover the entire range of recent developments in the film industry. But we are optimistic that it will contribute substantially to an ongoing discussion on a number of important aspects. We are grateful to all contributors and the international cooperation which is stimulating and mind-enhancing.

Nonetheless, we think this book turned out much more homogeneous than we imagined this experiment could be. We thank our secretary, Anne Weber, »Hippo«, Kevin and all the other student assistants, who helped to turn manuscripts and pictures into data packages. Where would we be without them?

After all, even if we are critical we love Hollywood. We owe much of our interior landscapes to the visions, the characters and the stories of that most characteristic ingredient of American culture. And, of course, to the people who earn their living by creating those complex products resulting in contemporary movies. We hope for fruitful response from our readers.

Christian W. Thomsen
9/11. Before and after

Before

»The Plot of the Event of September 11 – the destruction of the twin towers of the World Trade Center by terrorists – might have been written by Hollywood, or by Baudrillard. So fantasmatic, so familiar was the scenario that it fitted seamlessly into the manichaen agenda of the Pentagon hawks planning the next American war and the next. Indeed, a perfectly plausible paranoid response reads this plot as a plot on the part of those who have most thoroughly benefited from it.«[1]

Here we will ask about the role of Hollywood, and its interdependence with the events around 9/11. Even if we know that a fully satisfactory answer to so complex a question cannot be given, it remains a key question to be researched when dealing with Hollywood's developments in the early 21st century.

Did Hollywood anticipate, conjure up, contribute to 9/11? What was its reaction to 9/11? Has anything changed in Hollywood's mainstream treatment of 9/11 related topics like terrorism, war, interior and external politics, disasters, the science-fiction treatment of aliens, extraterrestrial events? These are the questions to be discussed in short in this contribution.

There certainly were greater catastrophes in human history, but never before has a nation – a world power – received a more traumatic blow and shock.

In early November 2001, film director Robert Altman argued that the current wave of violent movies had »created the atmosphere« that »set the pattern«, in which terrorists could plan and execute acts of mass destruction. Yet, »in the American imagination these fantasies have been around for a long time«.[2] And, indeed, even when we concentrate on only a few films released in the decade preceding 9/11 it cannot be overlooked that »it was prepared by years of ideological work which created a ready-made explanatory framework« and that »it is precisely now when we are dealing with the raw Real of a catastrophe that we should bear in mind the ideological and fantasmatic coordinates which determine its perception«.[3]

The latter have to do with language and sets of images spread by literature, films and other media creating fragments of reality consciousness in our mind. When uttering such a constructivist position I remember my Vietnamese friend Thien with whom I studied in London in the years 1964/65 at the height of the Vietnamese war. Thien, who was later to become President of the University of Saigon and cruelly tortured by the Vietcong, came from a 4000 year old Vietnamese family. His thesis was: »The Americans will lose this war.« Asked why, he replied: »Because they hardly know any conjunctive. They only know black and white, yes and no. But we«, he continued, »we have seven different varieties of conjunctive in our language, henceforth in our mind oscillate seven shades of grey between black and white, seven possibilities of perhaps between yes and no.«

That war, almost as unjustified and false in its causes as the present disaster surrounding the Iraq politics of the George W. Bush administration and the reasons given for the war, is still a haunting trauma in the American psyche. It still offers ammunition for election campaigns and inexhaustible material for the film industry. Iraq and the false pretenses surrounding possible connections with 9/11, as it will turn out, might last even longer. The roots are deep and have grown from a distant past. Just to mention a few stages in an ongoing process: rigid Calvinism and its inhuman double moral standards as exemplified in Hawthorne's *Scarlett Letter* (1850); sectarian Christian fundamentalism of many Bible Belt preachers ready for self-righteous crusades in the name of an unrelenting god of their own making; arms fetishism glorified through a pioneer period and as skillfully as unscrupulous, exploited by the NRA and the various lobbies of the arms industry; the deep seated fear that foreign or even extraterrestrial invasions might devastate the New World, the New Found Land, the earthly paradise of the chosen people of WASP origin; McCarthyism and other related campaigns to puff up political opponents from mere scapegoats into gigantic dimensions of Satan incarnate: Milosevich, Saddam Hussein, Bin Laden, to name the most recent ones. And who will be the next?

In the age of moving images the film industry is deeply involved in the creation of a set of collective mind patterns from the very beginning. Fritz Lang's *Metropolis* (1926) still lurks behind every movie-skyscraper demolition. *King Kong* (1932/33) and all its filiations in their fantasies of rape and destruction still testify how much the world is turned around by »sex and bananas«, by exotism and commercialism, by power games, by dreams of adventure and heroism. Doomsday

1–8. *Independence Day*, directed by Roland Emmerich, 1996.

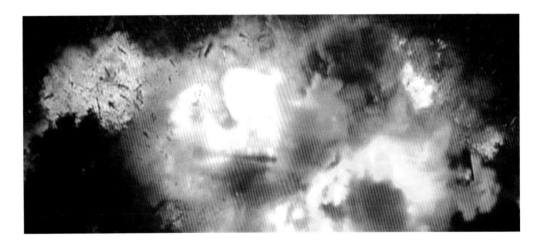

fantasies, terror, fear, xenophobia excite the nerves of cinema audiences even long before Orson Welles succeeds in evoking mass hysteria by a mere radio play: *The War of the Worlds* (1939), based on George Orwell's science-fiction novel from 1898. From then on an endless chain of body snatchers, ugly aliens, mad scientists, megalomaniacal criminals, religion-motivated revengeful terrorists, sadistic lunatics try to simultaneously tickle our nerves, to entertain and spread the paralyzing mildew of horror over our souls until »the culture becomes an echo chamber of speculative doom«.[4]

As an antidote, myths have been created which in their structure are similar to the fetishism of animistic indigenous societies, but which also overlap with fairy tales, religious folklore, romantic fantasy genres and which altogether fulfill the major function of stabilizing a societal system which by its very nature is heterogeneous. Continuous worship and displaying of the American flag is one such symbol, the steady invocation of a personal god who may support, bless and protect America, even a comet, if about to destroy the entire planet in 24 minutes, is another. The adoration of fire arms, with all its sexual undertones of super-masculinity, in the firm belief that problems of all sorts can be solved by shooting, finally by fist-fighting, is common to all American action-, war-, terror-, science-fiction-movies, to a degree where peaceful solutions are almost excluded and specific target groups (14–29 year old males) are conditioned to permanent aggressive militarism.

And up their sleeve they frequently have the ultimate threat of the big bomb. Such proceedings are a mirror reflex of official politics. The United States administration makes it clear on every occasion it thinks suited that they will use nuclear arms if they think it necessary, whereas, of course, such warfare is strictly forbidden for everybody else. Not to speak of Hiroshima and Nagasaki, where hundreds of thousands have been killed, documents published 25 years after the Cuban crisis made evident that the Joint Chiefs of Staff, Army, Navy, Air Force recommended to President Kennedy, even asked for it, to attack the Soviet Union with H-bombs. If that had happened, none of us would be alive.

The aesthetics of brutality and violence in mainstream Hollywood movies find their counterpart in Japanese and Indonesian films. But there violence and killing are more ritualized in the tradition of Asian martial arts although a blending of the two traditions is fully under way and Quentin Tarantino's *Kill Bill* (2004) finally shows that now women are emancipating in the fine art of killing as one of the most popular sport disciplines of the American movie industry. All that goes together with an almost total neglect of foreign cultures, other ethnicities, other value systems, even if the United States are multi-ethnic themselves. American protagonists suffer, love, have individual biographies and individual deaths. When the moments of the great killings have arrived in war or science-fiction movies members of other ethnicities or of those the Americans have declared their enemies are killed nameless, by the hundreds, mere cannon fodder or meat for crocodiles. From an outside perspective, when watching American demigod-superheroes, one is reminded of Shakespeare's bitter comment in *King Lear*: »As flies to wanton boys, are we to the gods: They kill us for their sport.« (IV. i. 36)

No wonder that Islamic nations remember medieval crusades when watching films which, after all, are produced for America *and* international markets.

Which brings us to the most characteristic figure, the American superhero, Batman, Spider-man, Superman, Neo, who are immediate derivatives of the comic industry, but ultimately derive from the idea of the romantic medieval knight and the classical demigods of Greek mythology. The typical American twist in this chronology is the suggestive lore that everybody, everyman may become a superhero, usually the asthenic boy from next door, who is shy with women, afraid of women, but out of desire, frustration and suppressed sexuality develops superhuman powers to save at least the world, if not the entire universe. The heroes in disaster movies are usually not that great, but they develop from everyday characters or odd eccentrics defending their families into heroic figures serving their nation and finally all mankind at the risk of their own life.

Neo, the Messiah, we will deal with later. But the myth of the superhero is, of course, in accordance with other American standard clichés like the »from rags to riches« myth. Since that, after all, can happen – usually more on business levels, with persons like Bill Gates and the Google brothers Larry Page and Sergey Brin – it is an eminent thriving, fermenting force in American society.

American film directors contribute to visualize group fantasies, to create categories of perception, which make the general public familiar with violence, terror, horror, »angstlust«, and an overall climate of constant threat combined with the impending doom of the apocalypse. That is, by no means, a new development in the years preceding 9/11. But it culminates in the 1990s with

9–12. *Godzilla*, directed by Roland Emmerich, 1998.

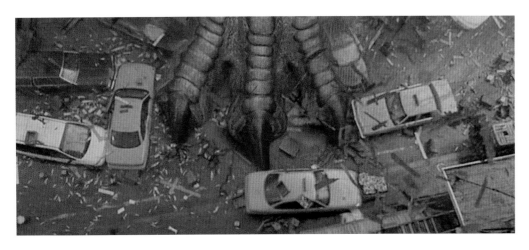

13–18. *A. I. Artificial Intelligence*, after an original idea by Stanley Kubrick, directed by Steven Spielberg after Kubrick's death, 2001.

This machine was trapped under the wreckage before the freezing.

CGI and other new technologies for yet unknown special effects, soaring budgets and the steady increase of psychological inhibitions and thresholds.

The fictitious threat grows cosmic and universal in the 1990s with films like *Independence Day* (Roland Emmerich, 1996), *Air Force One* (Wolfgang Petersen, 1997), *Armageddon* (Michael Bay, 1998), *Deep Impact* (Mimi Leder, 1998), *Godzilla* (Roland Emmerich, 1998), and it may even come from within as in Tony Scotts *Enemy of the State* (1998). Two German Hollywood directors, Roland Emmerich and Wolfgang Petersen, play important parts in this development. They exceed each other in grandiose imagery, but also in dripping pathos, banal dialogues and chauvinistic patriotism. And one is tempted to ask, whether that is a tribute paid to compensate their German origin, political mimicry or a deeper kind of Teutonic-American congeniality of spirits?

In a country and a culture, where, as in the case of Janet Jackson (2004), one bare female breast causes a major media uproar and high fines, paranoia and schizophrenia are institutionalized. The most atrocious and barbaric slaughters and killings are part of the daily diet of movies, TV programs and video games, while on state level thousands of nuclear warheads, inhuman splinter bombs – ironically called »Daisy Cutters« – and thousands of tons of chemical weapons are taken for granted as the legitimate arsenal ready for use to deal with anybody who might threaten state interests.

Accordingly there is a growing tendency for severe criticism of governmental institutions and politics (cf. *Armageddon*, *Enemy of the State*, *Outbreak*) to be found even in mainstream Hollywood movies which distinctively differs from movies of the 1980s and early 1990s like *Star Trek. The Motion Picture* (1979), *Star Wars* (1977) or *Stargate* (1994) and their many filiations. In the end they usually beat their way back into the arms of harmony, democracy and the restoration of order and security, fairy tales for children and adults alike.

What still baffles an outside viewer's mind is, how in anticipation of post 9/11 legislature, in many 1990s movies in any state of crisis civil rights and democratic powers are readily cut back or even cancelled while the military and the secret services take over and the country is put more or less under martial law. Such proceedings are obviously taken for granted. Yet, there usually is a lonesome hero who fights and finally succeeds in winning civil rights back. A sad impression prevails in the certain feeling that again the latter solution belongs to the fairy tale level of all those movies. Therefore, part of the pre-9/11 atmosphere of many Hollywood movies is a growing awareness that the United States are heading towards a »Big-Brother-is-Watching-You«-society of continuous and networked surveillance.

In connection with 9/11 two more major topics are of importance for showdown scenarios. On the one hand is the figure of the president as the true leader and tribal chief in the original sense who like Bill Pullman as President Thomas J. Whitmore in Emmerich's *Independence Day* or Harrison Ford in the role of President James Marshal in Petersen's *Air Force One* grow from rather mild, reluctant, imperfect party politicians into genuine leaders who, at the risk of their own lives, lead their people through valleys of humiliation and doom to glory and freedom. Pathos and clichés abound, but its intentions are good!

Hollywood is known as *the* dream factory. Such epitheta turn into nerve-tickling nightmares, when the other pre-9/11 scenario comes into view: the destruction of New York. NYC is at least the symbolic capital of the Western world, its skyline the most picturesque and best known. Its towers incorporate symbols of power, elegance, sex, engineering, of the entire value system capitalist America stands for. King Kong up on the Empire State Building, the wriggling white woman in his claws, became an icon of pop culture. Chrysler Building, Empire State Building and the twin towers of the World Trade Center are the most prominent figure heads of the NYC skyline, consequently film scenarios of the 1990s compete for their most spectacular destruction. Roland Emmerich might win the title of master destructor with *Independence Day*. In Steven Spielberg's *A. I. Artificial Intelligence* (2001), released a few months before 9/11, we find a totally different scenario of the end of New York. Pictures of great aesthetic beauty: ironic, poetic, melancholic. In the far distant future, when the human race is extinguished, the ruins of the once Megalopolis like Angkor Vat or those of pre-Aztec cultures tell the story of a bygone world from an era long ago which is rediscovered by pale, transparent, semi-virtual aliens, in the end even the dream of the Blue Fairy crumples and dissolves.

While blockbuster disaster movies of the 1990s set the general pattern of gloom and doom, remember those huge flying saucers in *Independence Day*, modeled after Jonathan Swift's oppressive flying city Laputa in *Gulliver's Travels* (1726), there are also many films which deal with actual terrorist attacks and show plenty of parallels with TV documentations of the 9/11 events. To mention but a few, the now classic *Airport* (1969) is the prototype for movies dealing with airplane hijacking. Terrorists use nerve gas to hijack a jumbo jet in *Executive Decision* (1995), *Speed* (1994) centers around the attack on a regular bus, *Flaming Inferno* (1974) shows plenty of burning and collapsing highrise buildings. In *Project Peacemaker* (1997) terrorists intend to explode a dirty nuclear device in Manhattan.

There is one film, yet, which makes you shudder in retrospect because of its complexity, realism and its storyboard qualities for terrorists with numerous parallels to the actual 9/11 and post-9/11 events and that is Edward Zwick's *The Siege* (1998), which characteristically enough was no particular box-office success and met with plenty of negative criticism. *The Siege* takes place in the present of the late 1990s in New York.

American secret service agents kidnap and question Sheik Achmed Bin-Talal because they suspect him of being the puppetmaster behind an attack upon a US military base in the Near East. In response to that a number of suicide attacks on targets in New York begin: first on a public service bus, then on a Broadway theater and finally on the FBI headquarters. Special agent Anthony Hubbard (Denzel Washington) is in charge of the case.

Soon he realizes that other services investigate as well but try to cover up certain aspects. He meets Elise Kraft a. k. a. Sharon Bridger (Annette Bening) who works for the CIA, obviously with a lot of background knowledge. Their cooperation does not really go along very well and it gradually dawns on Hub that Elise / Sharon, torn between Arab and Western culture, is personally deeper involved in the case than he presumed. After having destroyed the infra-structure of the FBI special anti-terror unit on One Federal Plaza the president declares a state of emergency for New York. General William Devereaux (Bruce Willis) takes command in Brooklyn with a heavily armed division because Brooklyn is the quarter of New York with the largest population of Arab background. His methods of fighting terrorism are those of military dictatorship, total surveillance, mass arrests, concentration camps, brutal interrogations, torture. FBI agent Hub has no chance to officially oppose this system yet tries to further investigate the case on his own under the rule of law. Elise / Sharon first stands in his way collaborating with Devereaux. Later on she cooperates with Hub when realizing that military strategy does not lead to any satisfactory success. Now she tells Hub the entire story. The terrorists have been trained by the CIA a couple of years ago in Iraq to overthrow the Saddam regime. But the CIA suddenly decided to break off the operation. Sharon managed to provide the group with student visa for the US to escape their own regime's henchmen. When the CIA had kidnapped the sheik, a high-ranking ayatollah, they began to use their knowledge about infiltration strategies against the USA, committing suicide bomb attacks. As »sleepers« they formed independently operating cells in New York. After having eliminated several of the cells Elise / Sharon wants to contact the last, decisive cell in order to end terror.

As contact person she uses her intellectual lover Samir (Sami Bonajila) who arranges a meeting with this last cell in a Brooklyn public bath. Meanwhile New Yorkers protest with massive demonstrations against the administration and the military. All ethnical groups of multicultural New York unite for »No Fear«-demonstrations. Elise / Sharon meets the last cell in that public bath and has to realize, what the audience was already dimly aware of, Samir himself is this last cell. He plans a suicide assassination on the demonstrators to kill as many as possible. With ritual washings he prepares his final deed. Hub intervenes and tries to stop Samir which is only possible when Elise / Sharon sacrifices herself. The film ends with special agent Hubbard arresting General Devereaux for torture and murder and the end of the state of emergency.

The Siege operates on complex psychological levels using carefully chosen contrasting characters. Anthony Hubbard as personification of law and order in every positive sense with a firm belief in the ultimate power and strength of democracy, using all available high technology of investigation methods. General Devereaux, his antagonist, as personification of military power, authoritarian stubbornness with a final tendency for dictatorial megalomania. Elise / Sharon as the cultural in-between, trying to mediate between the cultures and religions, getting lost and blinded in her emotions. Samir Nazhde, who embodies the threat-the-West experiences through intelligent fundamentalist Islamists whose belief in the power of religion, subversive tactics, simple but effective weapons makes them extremely dangerous.

It goes without saying that a Hollywood movie like this cannot fully avoid clichés. After all it has to tell a mass audience within a balanced structure what the reasons and motives are which urge terrorists to their deadly plots, how their individual psychology merges with religious and cultural group fantasies of their ethnic background in clash with western standards, convictions, ways of life. On the other hand it looks into the rivalry of secret services and the military, into the psychological difficulties and methods of investigation to understand the psyche of terrorists and to uncover their cells. Religious, psychological, political and military discourses overlap and intertwine with personal motivations of characters who are much more rounded and convincing than in the average films of the genre.

The Siege is anything but one-sided and critics who condemned the film as »unrealistic, stupid and full of clichés«[5] still had ahead of them the experience of 9/11 and what came after it. When Hub, in a blazing speech, rejects torture and defends the basic rules of democracy and the American constitution, critics who blamed Zwick for too much pathos had not experienced the Iraq war and the events of Abu Ghoreib yet. With exactly the same methods and justifications as shown in the film representatives of America lost the last bit of moral reputation the nation may have had in the Near East, did immense damage to Western civilization as a whole and betrayed their own constitution. It is pathos, indeed, what Hub brings forth, but without our sticking to those ideals we will experience a new age of barbarism.

The awareness that the enemy much more likely comes from within than by transatlantic or transpacific invasion against which you have to build up an immensely expensive star wars defense system with uncertain reliability is also demonstrated in another psychologically complex and convincing late 1990s movie, namely *Arlington Road* (1999), which deals with the Unabomber affair.

Dramaturgically and aesthetically fascinating in *The Siege* is a technique which becomes more and more common in recent movies, the cross-referentiality and intertwinement of different media[6] in order to gain a high amount of authenticity. The film uses TV images and the off-voice of news anchormen to achieve an outside perspective and commentary level. This procedure blurs boundaries between different levels of reality, contributes to a new understanding and definition of reality when showing in the parallel montage news scenes with speeches of the »real« President Clinton side by side with the film's protagonists. This staged authenticity shall provide an increased potential of identification with the protagonists. It is also the decisive stimulus for the present wave of docu-fiction films. It has far reaching consequences for all of us insofar as we can observe how this blurring of boundaries between »real« and fictitious, virtual reality in many sectors of everyday and artistic life. Even in a field which seemingly is a stronghold of firmness and stability like architecture world famous representatives of their profession like Toyo Ito meanwhile characterize their own work as »blurring architecture«.[7] This is a direct result of living in a media and information culture. Therefore science-fiction author Brian Aldiss' witty statement »nobody knows what ›real‹ really means«, has become a keypoint of insight for the analysis of the human condition in the early 21st century.

9/11

September 11, 2001 is the best documented day in human history. Countless news, special reports, interpretations, documentations and documentaries on documentaries have been produced and given this terrorist attack a world-wide media coverage which exceeded everything heard and seen before. In one gigantic masterstroke the terrorists had tried to achieve with comparatively moderate means what no army in any previous war had succeeded in, namely to eliminate at one blow the symbolic and actual centers of the enemy nation's political, military and economic power, with a symbolic significance reaching far beyond that nation. This is a war. And a new kind and quality of war. No wonder the US administration reacted the way it did in immediate response. The questionable aspects emerge in the further political and military treatment of the event.

As far as our present topic is concerned we can once again refer to Brian Aldiss' play on words »nobody knows what ›real‹ really means«. Everybody was taken by shock and surprise and people's first reaction on what they saw on their TV screen was: »This is like a Hollywood movie scenario« or »This really is a Hollywood movie«, fiction and not reality. But it was real.

From that point of view it was only consequent that Pentagon officials met with Hollywood script writers to discuss possible scenarios with people who were used to think big in cinematic disaster formats.

»After the event of September 11, 2001, the Pentagon arranged a conference with Hollywood directors, screenwriters and producers to find ways to think ›outside the box‹ of conventional security thinking. Chris and Janet Morris were recruited to the Department of Defense's Nonlethal Weapons Program by a former CIA intelligence director who had read their thriller *The 40-Minute War*, a story about Arab terrorists flying a plane into the White House.«[8]

In this and other subsequent meetings patriotic lines of approach were agreed upon.[9] The international image of America should be improved and understanding as well as support for the government's fight against terrorism should be called for.[10]

How did Hollywood, Hollywood taken as a generic term, react? On the day of doom many cinema chains closed their theaters and multiplexes. Theaters which stayed open were almost totally empty. The major Hollywood studios, TV stations and agencies closed and the production of films, series and TV shows came to a standstill.[11] The Hollywood studios of AOL Time Warner, Warner Bros, Sony Pictures up to Vivendi International sent their employees home. Only the New York offices of AOL Time Warner, Sony, News Corp and Vivendi/Universal stayed open, not for work, but to offer safety, food and communication facilities to their employees.[12]

The huge United Artists Megaplex on Union Square was changed into a shelter. Loew's Cineplex announced to take similar steps for its Manhattan theaters. Times Square and Rockefeller Center were closed for safety reasons, and even the General Electric Building, home of NBC broadcasting, was evacuated.

The most important film festival on the American continent, that in Toronto, interrupted its shows, to be continued on the following Wednesday.[13] The LA Gala planned that very night for the celebration of the Latin Grammy Awards was cancelled.[14]

A quick reaction of the studios consisted in the postponement of at least 15 movies which showed thematic overlappings with 9/11. The most prominent of those was the Schwarzenegger film *Collateral Damage*, the release date of which was pushed back from October 5, 2001 for four months to January 2002.[15] In this, one of the weaker Schwarzenegger movies, yet with production costs of about 100 Million dollars, an LA fire fighter loses his family in a terrorist attack on a skyscraper. He starts his own campaign of revenge and chases the terrorists in Columbia. There is also an US embassy bombed by terrorists.

On the other hand was the nationwide wave of patriotism not only commercialized by firms producing flags, but also by Columbia and Twentieth Century Fox, the former starting Ridley Scott's Somalia war epic *Black Hawk Down* in December 2001 instead of March 2002, the latter bringing forward the start of *Behind Enemy Lines* from January 2002 to November 2001.

Black Hawk Down, based on a book by journalist Mark Bowden (1999), is the deeply gripping story of the debacle American elite forces met in Mogadishu, Somalia, in October 1993.

»As a rash of pure cinematic spectacle, *Black Hawk Down* is undeniably breathtaking«,[16] shattering the dream work of psychic escapism so often employed in war movies. In the paperback edition of the book, published in 2000, Bowden ventured a single editorial comment. »The lesson our retreat taught the world's terrorists and despots is that killing a few Americans, even at the cost of more than five hundred of your own fighters, is enough to spook Uncle Sam.«[17]

Tom Doherty explains how *Black Hawk Down* reveals tactical crises of American warfare and grinds traumatic wounds of the American psyche:

»In generic, if not geopolitical terms, *Black Hawk Down* exemplifies a popular subset of the combat film, the extraction film. Its genesis and basic template is a schematic expression of the martial impotence felt during the Iranian hostage crisis: trapped by hostile, usually Arab-coded depredators, Americans must be rescued by the tactical brilliance and dauntless courage of the elite military forces, fulfilling in fantasy a scenario that ended in catastrophe when rescue helicopters crashed in the sands of Desert One in 1980. All the more anguish, then, when the expert extractors in the Delta Forces and the Army Special Ranger not only failed to extricate primitive warlords but then also require emergency extraction themselves. On the soundtrack Jimi Hendrix's ›Voodoo Child‹ kicks in as the helicopters take off for downtown Mogadishu. This is not a good omen.«[18]

This technically brilliant film demonstrates the shortsightedness of American politics as well as that of filmmakers. »Cinema is a space involved in the process of actively forgetting and actively producing history.«[19] If we accept this thesis then *Black Hawk Down* showing patriotism and a lot of sympathy not for the government but for courageous, suffering soldiers and their esprit de corps, fails completely in comprehending and visualizing of what is going on on the other side, of trying to understand the political as well as the cultural and individual situation of those peoples who are attacked by American forces. Terrorism changed the nature of war. The Second World War is finally over. No *Saving Private Ryan* battles will be fought anymore and consequently war tactics and war films have to change as well.

American military reactions in Somalia, Afghanistan and Iraq still remember that of dinosaurs gnashing their teeth, thrashing their huge tails and with an extravagant amount of technical equipment (air force, air craft carriers, high-tech reconnaissance) they may well destroy the infrastructure of any country. But in the long run dinos cannot win, because their brain capacity is too small to win the hearts. What was proved in Vietnam was repeated in Somalia and will repeat again in Afghanistan and Iraq unless there is a complete change of approach on the American side. The new forms of war, forced upon the West by terrorists, knows no fixed armies, no nationalities, no boundaries, combines low-tech with high-tech, achieves terror of the soul and immense economic damage with small means. It begins to dawn on military minds that this requires definite changes in their tactics. But as long as they only fight the symptoms and rarely the causes and origins terrorism is based upon, they cannot win this war which consequently is very ill and vague defined by President Bush with no foreseeable end.

Behind Enemy Lines, in all other respects a bad film, is a good example for that wrong approach. The true story behind the movie script is that of two American jet fighter pilots who were shot down over deep forests in the Bosnian war. They managed to survive undiscovered in the woods until a special forces rescue team picked them up and brought them back to their aircraft carrier. They were flown back to the United States and received by President Clinton who called them true American heroes who behaved just like those in Hollywood war films. The president himself blurs and blends levels of reality, equates illusion, wishful thinking, Hollywood dream reality with »real« reality, which underlines the model character movies take for »real« action.

Dripping with chauvinism *Behind Enemy Lines* documents one side of Hollywood's reaction to 9/11, increased patriotism, regardless of analytical insight and multiperspective interpretation. In the immediate aftermath of 9/11 many films were delayed in their release or were cut for scenes which showed the Pentagon or the WTC towers.[20]

Martin Scorsese's *Gangs of New York* was pushed back for almost a year because of brutal fighting scenes between 19th-century rival Irish and Italian gangs in New York, MGM's remake of *Rollerball* was delayed for months and Robert Redford's *Spy Game*, with gigantic destructions in the Near East, was cut for its Pentagon aerial photos. Rupert Murdoch's Sky Channel took all their terror movies out of its programs while CBS cancelled two episodes of the series *The Agency* produced by Wolfgang Petersen, one showing a bomb attack of Osama Bin Laden's, the other a case of anthrax. Patriotic war films and light entertainment with comedies, CGI monster and fantasy-films dominated Hollywood's output in the months immediately following 9/11. The major studios cut back their production considerably. PR campaigns and trailers (*Spider-Man*) were changed, but *Harry Potter* and *The Lord of the Rings* offered thrilling escapism from a somber political reality.

That may suffice for a sketch of Hollywood's immediate response to 9/11. The question remains to be answered whether this political singularity caused some genuine aesthetic and thematic changes in Hollywood's further treatment of 9/11 related scripts and production output or whether, after a while, it just went back to »business as usual«.

After

Answers to 9/11 can be found on many levels: political, military, social, economic, religious and psychological ones. They are all interrelated. Psychology and psychoanalytic interpretation may help to comprehend and understand motives of political and military action and reaction.

Howard F. Stein in a brilliant, multifaceted essay tries to shed light from a psychoanalytical perspective on both sides of the conflict, his main thesis being »that political beliefs and the real world actions that follow them ... are fed by irrational motives«.[21]

He states that »the overreaching theme is that of boundaries: their permeability, their violation, their collapse, their re-affirmation«.[22] And he continues with his analysis: »It is as if there are inchoate narratives that precede events, poised to claim and to fill them with projected meaning ... And behind these narratives lie group fantasies of unconscious motives of desire and defense. What on one level was already known in fantasy at another level constituted a devastating surprise attack upon unsuspecting innocence.«[23]

Coming closer to our present topic Stein quotes an analysis of Carlo Rotella: »We have been rehearsing the events of September 11 ... – quintessentially in the action movies that have perfected the formula of explosions, collapsing buildings, malign perpetrators and special-effects bystanders sent pinwheeling by gouts of orange flame. The action movies of the 1980s and 1990s stink of hubris and ingratitude; in retrospect, they seem to suggest that a whole culture was asking for it (which is not the same thing as deserving it when it happens).«[24]

19–22. *Terminator 3*: *Rise of the Machines*,
directed by Jonathan Mostow, 2003.

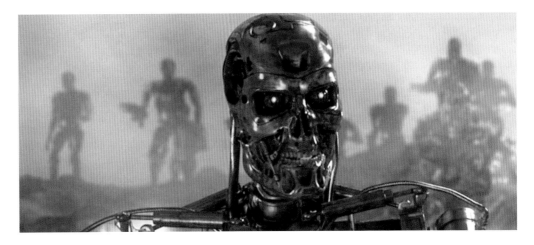

Stein points to the total change of chosen battle fields in comparison with former wars. Instead of open fields or rocky mountains they are now highly symbolic-charged work-places. America's behavior on the international scene provoked and created enemies who may not have become active without the Bush administration's withdrawing from and rejection of many international agreements. »The counterpart of terrorist paranoia was America's hysterical denial.«[25]

In classical psychoanalytical manner he describes underlying sexual motives for the terrorist attack as »an immense rape scene, the two jets as vicious phallic thrusts piercing vulnerable tissue. Yet the Twin Towers were themselves proud, audacious American phallic thrusts into the technological New York City and American skyline. Symbolically, it felt as if the attacks (instruments of projective identifications) were intended to turn symbolic American ›maleness‹ into ›femaleness‹, and in turn to transform the feminized adversaries of America into potent, triumphant males. The collapse of both towers into a mass grave shows how far the symbolism of (national) castration or emasculation can go.«[26]

Stein proceeds to analyze the reasons for the immense hatred mainly Islamic terrorists carry against America, making responsible the exploitive, destructive, abandoning foreign policy of the United States coupled with the catastrophic cultural consequences of modernization and economic globalization upon Islamic and other tradition-bound peoples. As psychologist he points to the mutual dependence of both sides and to the underlying Oedipus conflict and religious as well as social similarities. »Behind the public mask of patriarchy lies the motor. Father religions have mother churches.«[27] Basically the result of his analysis is a recommendation for sincere communication instead of violent action which only will lead to further bloodshed.

In the light of Stein's thesis let us have a look on a number of post-9/11 films, to see whether any noteworthy changes have taken place.

Terminator 3 (2003), the last action movie of California's new governor, may serve as an example for a certain ambiguity. At first glance it looks as if nothing had changed. Again the doom of the apocalypse, the future of mankind is at stake. They will not do it for less. As it is a rebellion of the machines and the Terminator himself is a machine this serves as an excuse for utmost brutality, an orgy of killing and destruction. The film is licensed for the age of 16, so just remember the uproar about one bare female breast! One could wonder and ask Howard Stein about the sexual motivation in the American predilection to utterly destroy architectures of all kinds from room interiors via single houses to highrise buildings and entire cities. Is it because architecture provides shelter, safety protection? Is it because architecture is a genuine, archetypical representative of civilization?

At second glance this film is corroded from within by a high amount of irony and self-irony. Don't take it too serious, Schwarzenegger seems to say, let me just one more time live up to my childish pranks and fantasies and then I will turn into a serious politician. This, of course, is not a solution to the threatening apocalypse and therefore *Terminator 3* remains a kind of technically brilliant video game where one imagines hundreds of skilled and extremely creative special-effects experts to be at work, busy as bees, to achieve all those effects of demolition and destruction. The message of the film is clear, not new but reflective: mankind, and that means mainly America, may destroy itself with weapons it constructed to defend itself, weapons which eventually might take over and turn against their creators.

It is not pure coincidence that the third part of the *Matrix* trilogy, *The Matrix Revolutions* (2003) also deals with the final showdown of the man-machine war. *Matrix* may have its faults, but it is indefinitely richer and more complex than *Terminator*. Once again Americans are trained for the apocalypse and living in the cavernous underworld of Zion is pretty depressive and rough.

At the end of the Christian apocalypse the New Jerusalem is visioned and erected. The longing for a savior and redeemer is age-old, as old as religion, and it is inextricably interwoven with the recognition of the dual nature of man. Thus *The Matrix* is more than the simple story black vs. white, good vs. bad, retold for the umpteenth time. It is multifaceted and tries to achieve an amalgam of central ideas of the great religions of the world, be they of Christian-Judaic or Tibetan and Zen-Buddhist origin. In a time of growing globalization it tries to offer a worldwide acceptable mix of classical and modernized epistemological positions spiced and freshened up with such of quantum mechanics, Jungian psychology, Postmodernism, science fiction, Hong Kong martial arts movies, fragments of computer sciences, virtual reality concepts and other sources.[28]

Although the Neo figure is modeled in many respects after Jesus, including virgin birth, he is by no means a purely Christian Messiah. »According to orthodox Christian belief, Jesus was a sinless Godman who brought salvation to the world, not through violence and power, but through his sacrificial death and resurrection. Neo, by contrast, is a more human being; he is far from sinless; he employs violence to achieve his ends (including arguably, the needless killing of the innocent); and although he may bring liberation from physical slavery and mental illusion, he does not bring true salvation.«[29] Whatever that may be one is tempted to ask. A blockbuster action and science-fiction movie is neither a philosophical nor a religious treatise. The film succeeds in externalizing and transforming inner conflicts, basic psychological structures into visual experiences and images never seen before. Simultaneously, it is struggling along with computerized and virtual reality-enhanced concepts of Plato's »Allegory of the Cave« and Renaissance considerations about the true character of reality.

At least it is a bold attempt and it will find a place in film history for its spectacular effects and philosophical complexity. The blurring of different levels of reality is intensified as never before. It breathes a certain spirit of humanity and racial tolerance. The machines on the other hand are inhuman swishing technical-spermatozoon-like creatures of monstrous ugliness. The *Matrix* trilogy oscillates between martial arts, high-tech and virtual reality fantasies and the search for a philosophical-religious solution for the problems of our time. In that it fails and ends in pure mysticism. On the socio-political level of post-9/11 filmmaking one may ask the question whether America is really in such a need of a redeemer, a Messiah? If yes, the country must be in a pretty bad condition, because the solution offered is an absolute illusion of wishful thinking and as such an evasion from the actual problems. That means, after all it is new style good / bad old Hollywood escapism.

Blockbusters with budgets of more than 100 Million dollars are major financial enterprises, businesses of their own. To judge them by art-house cinema critical standards would be nonsense. Roland Emmerich qualified as master patriot in the 1990s, thereby camouflaging his German origin. With *The Day After Tomorrow* (2004) he displays post-9/11 chameleon qualities and turns into a real Bush-basher. To achieve this within Rupert Murdoch's Twentieth Century Fox is a mystery of its own. The scientific background of his new Ice-Age story is not absolutely absurd, but owns a certain theoretic possibility. Emmerich was much criticized for his speeding up and compressing a long-term development into just ten days where global superstorms howl over the continents and turn the northern hemisphere into ice-fields.[30] Time-lapse-technique is the dramaturgic privilege of the artist. Shakespeare does nothing else in plays like *Macbeth*. For Emmerich the Ice-Age club serves as an instrument to attack environmental politics of the Bush administration who refused to sign the Kyoto climate agreement and to warn Americans that after 9/11 they cannot say that nothing is as before, but go on with exactly the same way of life as before, exploiting the planet's resources as they were used to do, destroying the atmosphere with gigantic CO_2-emissions. But above all the Eco-Armageddon serves him as an ideal opportunity to stage his favorite scenario, the apocalypse of New York. The background story around climatologist Jack Hall (Dennis Quaid) and his father-son relation with son Sam (Jake Gyllenhaal), including a schmaltzy love story, may be lousy. Emmerich is forgiven for everything except his unique New York images.[31] New York, the open city, open towards the sea and towards the people from all around the world, the storms, the floods, the tidal wave. Huge swarms of birds cross the city fleeing from the icy storms, swarms of NYC-cabs block the streets of Manhattan. The shock when the tidal wave arrives between the skyscrapers. We have seen this before, but never so beautifully filmed. They built a one-million liter tank in their Montreal studio, flooding the streets of movie-NYC, to shoot these scenes which find their absolute climax when a Russian freighter tumbles and joggles down Fifth Avenue. The image of New York's frozen skyline with the icebergs in front, Caspar David Friedrich gone West. Unforgettable. Here Emmerich's film is really grand cinema.

And his subversive ideas and images are not too bad either; an inefficient president, soon drifting out of action; the vice-president taking over, looking and speaking like Dick Cheney; the famous Hollywood sign swirling through the air; the Americans fleeing across the Mexican border looking for safety and shelter in reversal of what actually happens for many years the other way round where refugees are sent back across the border night by night by American border police.

And Michael Moore? The Academy awarded him an Oscar for the best documentary in 2002. *Bowling for Columbine* became a worldwide success which is still continuing. *Fahrenheit 9/11* (2004) brought Moore the Golden Palm in Cannes, the world's most important film festival, the first time a documentary received the award for the best film. Both successes presumably would not have happened without the events of 9/11.

Moore is a passionate, aggressive comedian and filmmaker sending out messages. After the amok killings at Columbine High School he decides to start a campaign against what he thinks one of the greatest faults in American society – its arms fetishism – with the result of more than 12.000 people killed annually in the USA by hand guns and more than 250.000 severely wound-

23–30. *The Day After Tomorrow*, directed by Roland Emmerich, 2004.

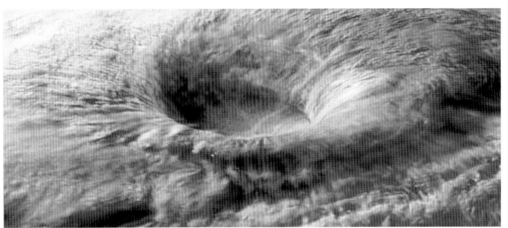

ed. He tries to reveal causes, expose backgrounds and not only blame symptoms. For that, he develops his own documentary style which makes use of the camera and of editing in two separate ways: tactful restraint where his sympathies lie as in the case of the mother of the six year old boy who killed a classmate without really knowing what he did. The camera in the second method proceeds with sly friendliness with which he lures himself into the confidence of people like NRA chairman-president Charlton Heston whom he wants to unmask. Then he suddenly changes into the obtrusive and obsessive hunter spirit of the comedian-gone investigative journalist. As such he becomes personal, subjective, manipulative, entertaining through his editing technique of creating a montage of highly suggestive shots. The funniest thing, when he acquires a rifle in a bank, the most touching, when he succeeds in his campaign against the sale of ammunition in a chain of retail stores by not only using one of the now handicapped student victims of the Columbine shootout, but by using the media as pressure group, thereby revealing how the American system works. The most embarrassing scene for me that, where he compares two cities, Detroit and Windsor, both lying, opposite each other, on the same river, one American, the other Canadian. Both speak the same language, read the same books, see the same films and videos, own the same amount of fire arms, one with a breathtaking crime rate and many murders, the other with a very low crime rate and hardly any murders at all. Where in Detroit people barricade their houses with safety locks at night while the people on the other side of the river leave their doors open, even if occasionally cases of burglary occur. What is the reason for such a basic difference in mentality and social behavior, Moore asks? For him, the fault lies with the general climate of threat, anxiety, frustration and apocalyptic fear produced by sensationalism in the news coverage. Throughout politics and the media; run and controlled by those who want to manipulate society to their own profit. After 9/11 the government uses this climate to install surveillance systems, building up a new bureaucracy of control not unlikely to what Eastern European countries were used to when still under communist regimes. While the administration was all the time talking of democracy and freedom, people's civil rights were being restricted.

Which brings us to *Fahrenheit 9/11*, Moore's contribution to the 2004 presidential election campaign. A documentary with well over 100 Million dollars box-office intake in a few weeks is an absolutely new phenomenon, compared with six Million of production costs.

Moore always personalizes history. That may be very American, but it is only half or an unknown percentage of the truth. Looking closer *Fahrenheit 9/11* is composed of two films, two major story lines. The first consists of his personal feud against the Bush clan and their involvement with the Bin Ladens, Saudi oil magnates, princely investors who own 1/7 of America. The second is his attack on the Iraq politics of the George W. Bush administration and its war on Iraq. In his eyes the war is not only unjustified, but a deliberate misleading of the public and betrayal of the American nation, their constitution, the ideals of democracy and the people themselves. Moore takes his material from private and public archives, news, documentaries and from his own camera work. The latter being considerably higher in the second part of the movie.

Politically interested people have seen most of the archive material and all of the news material before, some of it repeated many times. But it is the montage technique, the way he connects images, chains of pictures, the narrative style with which he starts associations in the viewer's head, which makes it so effective. There are Condoleeza Rice and Colin Powell talking about the ineffective Iraqi army which has no weapons of mass destruction and is of no danger to America during the election campaign. Then he shows Powell as foreign secretary reading a 17 pages paper to the United Nations' security council which consists of 10 pages copied from a 10 year old British student paper and 7 pages of unproven speculations about weapons of mass destruction, showing computer simulations and passing them off as genuine photos or pictures which were published years ago in the European press, posing them as recent material from air reconnaissance. A person who lies so openly to the world and its representatives loses all his credibility and ruins his country's international reputation, which is the worse if he happens to be the foreign secretary of the only remaining world power.

Or we see and hear Donald Rumsfeld who with a down-toned melodious voice talks about »the care and the humanity that goes into our targeting«, a quote which Moore combines with pictures of destroyed Iraqi homes, killed civilians, mutilated children, wounded American soldiers.

Or the most ridiculous scene of all, the staged arrival of President George W. Bush in a jet fighter pilot's uniform aboard an aircraft carrier, trying to imitate as top gun the president in *Independence Day* and announcing to the world »Mission Accomplished« all the while looking like a gawky clown. With that very day the second part of a war, that may lead to similar results as the Vietnam War, begun, this part costing many more American lives than the first.

The decisive scene of the film is the one, filmed by a teacher, where President Bush sits in a Florida classroom, receiving the message of the terrorists' attack on WTC. Seven minutes he sits there without saying a word, no button in his ear that tells him what to do, a picture of utter help-lessness. Then he absentmindedly starts leafing through a children's book. Body language is treacherous and Moore should have left it at that. Instead he mounts with his own voice and pic-tures of his own an interior monologue of George W. deciding to shift the entire blame to Saddam Hussein, in order to take people's minds off his own connections with the Bin Laden family. Here Moore leaves all accepted standards of documentarism, hits below the belt and turns his political documentary into demagogic docu-fiction.

Moore regains credibility in his second part with the story of Lara Lipscomb, lower middle-class mother of an American soldier whose Black Hawk helicopter was shot down two weeks af-ter his arrival in Iraq. Reading the last letter of her son Lara, the woman burning with patriotism, turns into a suffering mother who begins to look through the machinations of politicians, who use their citizens as canon fodder in a war game for their own profit. Congressmen asked in front of and evading Moore's camera while hurrying into parliament, whether their own sons would not enlist for the Iraq war, underline this impression.

The Bush administration achieved what no previous American government achieved before. In trying to fight terrorism – but mixing this with other political and economic interests within two years after the events of 9/11 – they managed to turn around a sympathetic pro-American world opinion by 180 degrees into distrust and anti-Americanism. They did immense damage to world economy and world security, proving that gigantic arming does not make the world safer.

Moore's conspiracy theory, of course, is that they did this in the interests of the men behind them, a mafia consisting of oil, arms and communication industry representatives and other re-lated businesses, as never before an American government was that much intertwined with par-ticular economic interests.

What did Michael Moore contribute to the development of post-9/11 film? He heightened the interest in documentaries. He made them entertaining and finally successful. He created a new genre of documentary film journalism not unlike Tom Wolfe's »New Journalism« in the 1960s. He shifted documentarism into docu-fiction with methods already used, for instance, by William Shakespeare in writing history like *Richard III* and *Macbeth*, the montage of document material, spiced with slight but decisive personal comments, speeded up with time lapse technique.

As usual, there are two sides to the coin. The entertaining one, thereby gaining people's atten-tion for politics, historical analysis and an insight awareness of what's going on. And then the ma-nipulative, seductive side, where it becomes extremely difficult to decide what's what. To once again speak with Brian Aldiss' words: »Nobody knows what ›real‹ really means.« That blurring of reality concepts is a world-wide process of our media and communications society.

And post-9/11 Hollywood movies beyond Michael Moore? At least some of them have be-come less one-sided, more critical, integrating differing points of view. To enjoy the apocalypse, the end of the world, from the comfortable seat of a multiplex cinema, immersed into the acoustic inferno of Dolby Surround is as entertaining as disturbing and goose-pimples producing. Does it change our attitudes and reality consciousness? To certain degrees yes and often unconsciously. Do movies help to cure causes and not only symptoms? Hardly. Unfortunately the possibilities that the laws of human inertia and self-righteousness will prevail are overwhelmingly great. And until the next 9/11 it will be mainly: »business as usual.«

Karen A. Ritzenhoff
On the cutting edge. New visual languages in film-editing conventions in Hollywood

As a professor of mass media who teaches TV production and courses in film theory at a State University, I have witnessed over the years the growing impact of an emerging new visual language in our students' work. Video productions are far less oriented towards building sophisticated meaningful narratives; rather students try to impress by using a magnitude of digital effects, graphics, fast-paced edits, unconventional camera techniques, multiple layers of visual stimuli. There are at least two conditions of media production and socialization that may be driving these changes. One is the impact of new digital editing technology, now broadly available and affordable. A second is the cultural ubiquity of Hollywood, and the impact of Hollywood practices and editing conventions on those modeling the work they see. But another influence also seems apparent in contemporary student work: the impact of independent filmmakers who are testing the boundaries of Hollywood convention. Cross-influences among those innovations in visual representation practices that characterize the »indie« movement, along with mainstream conventions that continue to persist in so much commercial filmmaking seem to jostle in similar ways across commercial television, cable programming and advertising.

Despite exciting new approaches in the independent American film scene at the beginning of the 21st century, television in general seems to adhere to an increasingly conservative visual trend, a cheapening effect. The production value of sitcoms and reality TV shows is rather low. This essay is not interested in the haphazard visual direct cinema technique, commonly used now in reality TV shows on US television where producers quickly throw together lengthy, tedious programs, shot and edited in digital format. These melodramatic programs build on suspense, with such titles as *Temptation Island, Big Brother, Joe Millionaire, Who Wants to Marry My Dad, Extreme Make-Over, Real World, Bachelor* etc. and mostly regurgitate coupling rituals that unfold with uncanny dullness. Once the outcome of the specific tease is revealed in the last show, there is hardly any incentive to watch the program again and it has little re-run value (different from films that can become classics). It seems as if standard television is reverting to a style of editing and production so lacking in imagination that it offers little variation of style and form. Redundancy of narrowly defined and standardized representational conventions unites all varieties of the same theme. The impact of this haphazard visual style of television on the »indie« and also conventional Hollywood style cannot be ignored. The visual language of mainstream TV, the intentional suturing of commercial programming with regular content, impacts not only the pace of editing but also the representational norms of digital filmmaking. This article will focus on trends in independent filmmaking which allow new aesthetics of visual languages to transform the repertoire of seeing while critically engaging with dominant television formats.

Interdependence between TV and film

This being said, it is quite typical in media studies to differentiate between film analysis and television production. Studying film and dissecting the structural building blocks of chosen examples seemingly requires more theoretical rigor than looking critically at television programs. Whereas film studies are taught in American academe often by distinct schools or in separate cinema studies departments or offered (as in the case of my university) by faculty in English, television production is generally taught in the communication field. If hands-on shooting and editing is involved, film is sometimes included in a school of communication (for example the Department of Radio-TV-Film at Northwestern University). One main reason could be the difference in production value: Shooting a film used to require a comparatively large budget to support not only the film crew but the film stock, price of developing and printing. Television production, however, is cheap, once equipment is in place. What has happened with the explosion of digital media is the opportunity for a younger generation of directors to burst into the field of visual expression. In a training environment such as the International Film and Television Workshops in Rockport, Maine, an international forum for those interested in the production of visual media that was founded almost thirty years ago, the course offerings embrace television, digital media, film and high-definition television (HDTV, since summer 2003). Almost all projects are united, though, once they go into the editing phase: the prevalent format for post-production is non-linear editing, computer based, digital processing. As Richard Barsam explains in his 2004 textbook, *Looking at Movies: An*

1. *Requiem for a Dream*, directed by Darren Aronofsky, 2000.

Introduction to Film: »The advantages of nonlinear editing with digital equipment are thus considerable: it is faster, saves money both by reducing steps in producing the workprint and requiring a smaller crew, provides easier access to the material, offers modern working conditions, and makes it possible to preserve different versions of the movie, to transmit images or
the entire movie via satellite or the Internet, and to easily integrate electronic special effects into
the movie.«[1]

It comes as no surprise, then, that it may be increasingly difficult to differentiate between the
so-called low production value of television and the high production value of film because the
boundaries are blurred. This observation is at the heart of this article: the cutting edge of visual
language may still be developed in the independent, marginal scene surrounding Hollywood. But
film cannot be thought of independently from television. Both are interdependent: there is a dialogical dependence from one to the other. It is quite literally the case that more and more film directors tend to work in the television industry and are no longer shunned for working for a different medium. But it is also the case that the generation of film directors who produce films are dependent on the visual aesthetics of television, having consumed its products since early child-
hood. Many filmmakers who have come to fame in independent filmmaking on small budgets,
later get co-opted into the studio system (i. e. Quentin Tarantino, Steven Soderbergh, the Coen
Brothers, Julie Dash, Agniezska Holland) and TV productions where larger budgets set the tone.

This essay attempts to reflect on the rapid changes in the film industry in terms of media aesthetics. It also explores the dialogical relationship between TV vs. movie productions and how
film enunciates the more popular medium of broadcasting. In doing so, the main focus will be on
Requiem for a Dream (2000) by Darren Aronofsky, a provocative and innovative film about heroin
and drug addiction: it can be used to highlight existing trends in emerging editing conventions.
The pace of the editing in this film, the sensation of a visual rush related to the consumption of
heroin, the powerful representation of images cannot be looked at isolated from the existing effect
of television consumption. Aronofsky recapitulates the TV experience. It is not so much the actual
convention of representation used in individual shows, but the overall effect of being stimulated
by an avalanche of sensations while looking at TV excessively, as many children tend to do, that
Aronofsky articulates.

The stimulus threshold for children who have, for example, Attention Deficit Disorder (ADD) has
gone up. The extent to which a person is affected by ADD can not be detected similar to an ail-
ment like cancer where a patient either has it or not, best described as a dichotomy of symptoms. Instead, ADD is more and more regarded as a dimension, similar to the variable of intelligence, measured by an IQ test. Television consumption causes viewers to respond by developing
distinct mechanisms to think, because television is more stimulating than real life. Therefore spectators have to »down-regulate« when being over-stimulated by the rapidly changing imagery on
the television set and the attention system is responding increasingly differently to the sensitive
stimuli that surround us in real life. The actual TV program format may be dull (such as reality TV
shows mentioned above) but the acceleration of exposure to visuals through the habit of zapping
between channels and channel surfing between commercial breaks, leads to the phenomenon of

multiple image platforms. Attention becomes a nodal point in consumption. This observation is a key to understanding new visual languages in film editing: directors respond to the social need for stimulation and accelerated visual flow to reflect a state of mind. It is as if the mental map in the average consumer is changing and image producers accommodate this increasing trend, catering to a fragmented and truncated view of reality with extreme close-ups and a rush of edited images.

Directors of the TV generation

The history of different editing styles will be discussed briefly in this paper to provide a quick overview and build a context for the film analysis. Issues such as narrative and the construction of visual culture will be touched upon. The main focus, however, lies on the actual analysis of the filmic text to illustrate the »cutting edge« that is engaging and challenging the media mainstream.

As film scholars Bordwell and Thompson explain at the end of a chapter on »The New Hollywood and Independent Filmmaking«: »At the end of the century, many of the most thrilling Hollywood films were being created by a robust new generation, born in the 1960s and 1970s and brought up on videotape, videogames, and the Internet. Like their predecessors, these directors were reshaping the formal and stylistic conventions of the classical cinema while also making their innovations accessible to a broad audience«.[2]

Aronofsky sees himself as a product of a youth culture, raised by watching excessive amounts of TV. When asked about his »new visual style«, he explains: »If anything it came from eight hours of TV a day. I was a TV junkie as a kid. I am the Sesame Street Generation. 1969, I was born the year Sesame Street was launched and that was the year my mom plopped me in front of the TV and said, don't cry anymore. And I think 17, 18 years later, after eight hours of TV a day, I think that's the culture I come from.«[3]

The critique of standard television and its repetitive narrative structure informs Aronofsky's work in very concrete ways. One of the key sequences in *Requiem for a Dream* shows one of the four protagonists, Sara Goldfarb (Ellen Burstyn), in front of the TV, watching a talk show program. The middle-aged woman subjectively responds to the tube and her transformation in the process of constructing meaning is powerfully depicted. Initially, she detects her alter ego, a star version of herself, on the screen: the television Sara wears big hair, ample make-up, a red dress and is entirely artificial and glamorous. Her desired self appears on celluloid as a distorted mirror effect. While the original Sara is addicted to diet pills, hallucinating, her hair unkempt, her outfit worn, the television identity promises to be glorious. In the subsequent segment, the admired talk show host and her fantasy media twin are beamed out of the space of the television box and join her as digitized figurines in her living room.

Sara's world implodes as the television personalities start to talk to her, mocking her shabby apartment and her state as a spectator. Even the audience in the original TV studio turns towards her, reverting the gaze and they all keep on screaming in a loud voice »feed me Sara«. This collectively voiced demand is alluding to the fact that the protagonist has gotten to this stage of media transference by taking diet pills to fit in the red dress that her broadcast alter ego is now wearing. She ends up being indeed the center of attention while her apartment is converted into a movie set despite her objections. The safe distance between the TV and the spectator collapses and is erased, leaving a vacuum to be filled by the animated personnel of the earlier talk show.

Aronofsky criticizes the addiction to television in this scene that leads his protagonist into mental despair and a personal abyss. Even though the actual phenomenon of hallucination is linked to the amphetamines that she takes in order to lose weight and be eligible to perform on the TV show, the initial desire to be seen as a spectacle begins her lonely descent into mental sickness. The described scene starts with a »high« as Sara Goldfarb watches her fetishized image on the TV screen. Her de-naturalized alter ego is even speaking to the fictive studio audience, praising her son Harry and remembering her late husband Seymore. It is as if the authentic Sara in her TV reclining chair is satisfied and pleased by what she sees. As she continues to take more pills, her over-stimulated state of mind changes and her perceptions are continuing to be off balance. The speed contained in the diet pills leads her into delusion and manic hysteria. She starts to »crash« and have an onset of depression, visualized by Aronofsky's idea of bringing the TV personalities like silhouettes and static images into her living room. The psychotic state induced by the amphetamines is pictured in a climactic scene where audience and a group of young women in a

Conga line burst into sensual moaning to voice the call for being fed. Aronofsky finds a creative visual way to depict the rush and crash of drug consumption, even more extremely when he shows the heroin addiction of the three young protagonists of the film.

In Aronofsky's world, a society impacted by the need to saturate the mind via drugs and television will necessarily have to be disappointed because there is the built-in consequence of being split from reality. As the protagonists fail, their addictions get more pronounced and the potential satisfaction through consumption no longer holds true!

Discussing the paradigms of visual representation allows us to critically look at the future challenges for a consumer society, caught in the highly manufactured media web.

Digital editing

Whereas some films are still spliced together on the editing table in an old-fashioned, linear way, most commercial work in post-production is assembled first in an off-line version in the digital format, then sent to on-line editing companies who work with footage digitized at a higher resolution. It is also increasingly common for directors to start projects in a digital context for the off-line edit and then transfer the editing decisions to film. If one stays in the digital realm entirely, in and out points of edits can be listed down to frames and get fed into a computer which then selects those chosen sequences from raw footage and even does the actual editing automatically – without manual human intervention necessary. It is also common knowledge that journalists who covered the American invasion of Iraq in spring 2003 shot and edited their own footage on location, working with Final Cut Pro computer software or its equivalent in the field. The signal was fed back via satellite, allowing an international audience to gasp at desert footage, at times badly transmitted and broken up. The image quality of digital transmission is still evolving. The supposed authenticity and immediacy of the footage, caught during the Iraqi invasion, remained unquestioned, possibly also due to the rawness of the material quality. The »rawness« in film used to be due to the graininess of the image and shaky hand-held cameras. Another feature new to the digital realm is the fact that the image itself is broken up, once the transmission of the signal fails. (One example is the disrupted coverage on recent hurricanes at the Florida coast where journalists reported live about the damage. While they were talking, the screen with their image would suddenly be frozen into a static mosaic, disintegrated into small digital pieces.) On the cusp of an entirely digital age, new features in visual aesthetics can be detected.

Advertisement producers or independent directors have the opportunity to save on budgets by doing some of the off-line editing themselves. New production companies come to life quickly because students and hobby videographers can now afford to have their own editing base at home. When I recently started teaching basic TV production, five of twenty beginning students had Final Cut Pro systems at home and worked extensively with editing. TV stations allow amateur footage to be aired such as video work shot during the 9/11 attack on the World Trade Center. It is astounding as a teacher to see how accelerated the access to technology has become and how the industry is embracing these changes. Even middle and high schools can afford to purchase their own production units and offer enrichment classes in video production. As contributing faculty to an institute for media literacy that works with mostly public school teachers in Connecticut, the River Valley Institute of Media Education, I have witnessed first hand how schools have changed over the past five years. The explosion of technical opportunities had been anticipated by producers and critics alike in the mid nineties already.« (*American Cinema: American Culture*, »The Edge of Hollywood«, 1995) One of the interviewees, producer Jim Stark, encourages viewers as an epilogue to the 50-minute program to go out there and try to shoot and edit a project themselves: »As the technology changes«, he says in the tape, »it is going to be easier and easier to make these very cheap films for someone like … who has got that much talent.« And Todd McCarthy, film critic at *Variety* magazine, claims on that same tape: »If you are determined to make a film now, I am convinced that you can find a way to make it, whether you shoot it on video and get it transferred or you get everyone and the equipment for free. Or you save up for two or three years. All those ways now are possible whereas before it was completely out of the question.«[4]

Digital editing has made the art of editing accessible for the everyday consumer: whereas one had to spend $ 15 000 to $ 20 000 on a low-end digital editing system by Avid or Media 100 only five years ago, videographers and novice filmmakers can enter the field by buying the latest version of Final Cut 4, an industry standard competitor to the Avid software that is much cheaper,

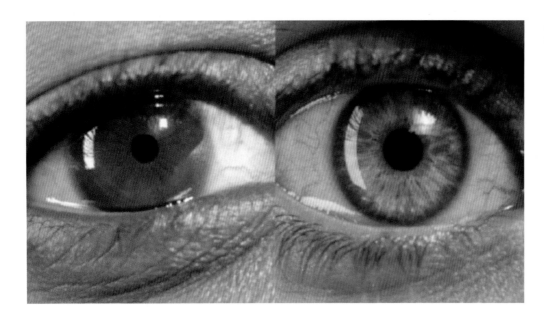

2. *Requiem for a Dream*, directed by Darren Aronofsky, 2000.

loading it onto a Macintosh computer with a strong hard drive and memory – and $ 3000 later they are in business. Final Cut Pro 4 came out in August 2003, advertised as »Apple's dynamic and powerful non-linear editing package«. (Apple Pro Training Series, 2004) In the introduction, Apple promises: »Whether you're a seasoned veteran or just getting started in the editing field, Final Cut Pro 4 can serve all your editing needs.«

Final Cut Pro is based on a set of windows which provide the »interface«: Timeline, »Browsers«, »Viewer Window« that plays back the edited clip and »canvas« where the chosen edited clip is revealed. The juxtaposition of two main windows in which the clip and the edited version of the scene are displayed concurrently, resurfaces in the major film example that will be used in this paper to demonstrate the new visual language in film editing: In *Requiem for a Dream*, director Darren Aronofsky has edited a film sequence to describe heroin addiction that will surface throughout his film like the refrain to a musical score. In that refrain you will recognize the juxtaposition of two windows in a split screen, similar to the editing software, Final Cut Pro is promoting.

In the editing »lingo«, video clips are captured, digitized, copied and pasted into a timeline. The manipulation of the footage has increasingly varied possibilities. Whereas non-linear editing systems, prevalent until only eight years ago, relied on the basis of one video and two audio tracks that were merged and blended to create different layers of meaning, this new software can edit up to 99 video tracks on top of each other and an endless amount of audio tracks. Clips can be inserted, overwritten, replaced, or superimposed with the click of a mouse. Images can be easily animated and altered. Effect possibilities are at one's finger tips. At the end of a short segment on »nonlinear digital editing with computerized equipment«, Richard Barsam concludes: »Some editors still prefer the tactile pleasures of working with a Moviola or flatbed, both of which remain available. Within the next decade, however, the ›film‹ cameras, processing and editing equipment, and projectors used for professional filmmaking will in all likelihood be completely replaced by digital equipment, and the film stock itself – the celluloid material that has for more than one hundred years passed through this equipment – will disappear from productions.«[5]

The trajectory to learn about editing for most classic film students in institutions of higher learning is still the rigorous study of the »Masters«, be it the American born »Film School Generation« or the »indie« generation of directors who have been influenced by the Hollywood directors but mostly by an international independent film scene. Of course, the French New Wave (1959–64) played a major part in impacting American filmmakers in the second part of the 20th century. Jean-Luc Godard, François Truffaut, Claude Chabrol, Jacques Rivette and Eric Rohmer have left a lasting impression on film students. »The novelty and youthful vigor of these directors led journalists to nickname them ›la nouvelle vague‹ – ›the New Wave‹. Their output was staggering. All told, the five central directors made 32 feature films between 1959 and 1966«.[6] Barsam argues that New Wave filmmakers »challenged the conventions of narrative cinema (particularly what they saw as a stultified French cinema, as opposed to freer American movies) through discontinuity editing and other ›experiments‹, often juxtaposing standard techniques with newer manipulations. They showed that onscreen invention could help viewers interpret and draw meaning from cinematic images and sounds.«[7] On-location shooting, natural sound recording, erratic camera movement, loose plot construction and ambiguous film plots are among the characteristics for style and form of these films.

Another big impact on American directors and film scholars were the theories of French cultural studies, eminent in the writing of these filmmakers in the *Cahiers du Cinema* as well as the scholarship of Deleuze and Guattari, Christian Metz or the work of semiotician Roland Barthes. The connection to the early theories of Russian directors/theoreticians such as Sergey Eisenstein, Vsevolod Pudovkin, Dziga Vertov and Lev Kuleshov also have to be taken into account, especially when discussing *Requiem for a Dream*.

Theories of editing

Montage

In his classic text, *The Major Film Theories: An Introduction* (1976), Yale film historian J. Dudley Andrew coined the main trends in scholarship to the mid 1970s, based on the work of Sergey Eisenstein, Rudolf Arnheim and André Bazin. In his section on »cinematic means: Creation through Montage« he discusses the central concept of montage as a »collision of attractions«.[8] Andrew argues that Eisenstein developed his concept of montage as a response to theories on dialectical thinking, prevalent among intellectuals at the beginning of the 20th century. The cognitive process of viewers is being evaluated and how they respond to shots with different themes being juxtaposed to create their own meaning. Eisenstein practiced his theories by concentrating on mostly static images, similar to Darren Aronofsky's key montage in *Requiem for a Dream* when he depicts visually the rush of heroin intravenous injection. As Andrew explains about Eisenstein: »He preferred to shoot static fragments of an event, energizing them with a dynamic editing principle«.[9] Andrew continues to take one of Eisenstein's films, *Strike*, as an example to explain the concept of collision: »In his film *Strike*, for example, Eisenstein didn't hesitate to juxtapose bizarre images, like the face of a man and the picture of a fox, or the picture of a crowd and one of a bull being slaughtered. These images, each providing a strong stimulus, remain meaningless until the mind creates the links between them through its metaphoric capabilities. The story itself emerges from numerous such metaphors, the mind creating an interplay between specific workers struggling against a specific managerial system. Before the end of the film the spectator begins synthesizing the controlling ideas of the film, ideas about capital and labor. The film achieves its effect when the spectator realizes the conclusion (or synthesis) of the collision of such major ideas«.[10]

Richard Barsam (2004) chooses a short key sequence from Aronofsky's film, which will be discussed in greater detail in this essay, to illustrate techniques of editing. He labels the effect of juxtaposing different images that are sutured in parallel windows as »split-screen« editing and calls it a »contemporary demonstration« of the Kuleshov effect. The idea of the Russian master was to experiment on the »aesthetic effects of montage«: »To demonstrate the power of juxtaposition and context, Kuleshov interspersed the unchanging and expressionless face of the great Russian actor Ivan Mosjukhin with unrelated shots of different emotional values: a child playing, a plate of soup, a dead woman. Through the power of montage, the audience thought they saw Mosjukhin change his facial expression according to the juxtaposed event. The montage had engendered what Kulosheov called ›artificial landscape‹, a ›creative geography‹.«[11]

Kuleshov's combination of one shot of an individual man with an indifferent facial expression with several different shots led the spectator to read different meaning into the combined shots, imposing meaning, even though the original shot never changed The montage effect that Lev Kuleshov evoked proved the point that the inference of the viewer overrides the actual source, constructing meaning that can be suggested through specific editing conventions, employed by the filmmaker and editor. Barsam explains: »As pictures are juxtaposed, literally placed side by side, the meaning of one affects the meaning of the other. That is, together the shots influence our creation of their meaning – and their combined meaning then affects how we see the following two halves, whose meaning undergoes a transformation similar to that of the first two, and so on. This interpretative process goes on through the sequence, into the following shot, the following sequence, and ultimately the entire movie. Our creation of meaning proceeds from increment to increment, though at a much faster rate of calculation than this caption can convey«.[12]

Despite Barsam's thesis that Aronofsky used an already established convention, this essay will argue that his editing technique is not only a quote of montage technique, developed at the beginning of the 20th century but can only be understood in the context of more recent digital video aesthetics that affect the work of emerging filmmakers.

In a recent film critique, published in the *New York Times* Movie section, David Kehr points at the unusual editing effect of the American remake thriller *Wicker Park* (2004) by Paul McGuigan. In »eerie shots a la ›Vertigo‹, but no sign of Stewart«, Kehr explains the supposedly innovative style of a »split-screen« and says about the director: »He has clear talents as a filmmaker. He employs an interesting split-screen effect, using digitally blurred borders instead of the standard hard matting to compare multiple points of view, and there are a couple of eerily elongated shots of empty corridors that Hitchcock might have appreciated.«[13]

This may further substantiate the argument that editing styles, employed by Aronofsky to depict his protagonists' imagination and inner most feelings in complex montage sequences, are indeed emerging in other visual texts.

Continuity editing

The prevalent Hollywood editing convention is still »continuity editing«. It is a major factor of the classic Hollywood style. In one of the ten educational video tapes on *Amercian Cinema* (1994) that deals with the »Hollywood style«, a seasoned editor who learned her trade in the height of the studio system, talks about »seamless editing«. She describes the fact that edits were supposed to be unnoticeable by the audience, creating a sense of reality that was highly conventionalized in its narrative functions. Starting with an establishing shot, editors had to work their way into a scene with shots, reaction shots, close ups, medium shots and re-establishing shots. She illustrates this style by looking at the final moments in *Casablanca* (1942) where Ingrid Bergman and Humphrey Bogart say good-bye – the editing in this scene is highly conventionalized.

Bordwell and Thompson see the role of editing being closely related to the overall »film's stylistic system«: »An ordinary Hollywood film typically contains between 1000 and 2000 shots; an action-based movie can have 3000 or more. This fact alone suggests that editing strongly shapes viewer's experiences, even if they are not aware of it. Editing contributes a great deal to a film's organization and its effect on spectators«.[14]

Bordwell and Thompson describe the sensation of a film for the audience: »As viewers, we perceive a shot as an uninterrupted segment of screen time, space, or graphic configurations. Fades, dissolves, and wipes are perceived as gradually interrupting one shot and replacing it with another. Cuts are perceived as instantaneous changes from one shot to another«.[15] This explanation is based on the notion that editing is indeed seamless and »graphically continuous«. Discontinuous editing where time and space do not coalesce as the directors of the French New Wave practiced it, or many independent American directors experiment with (Quentin Tarentino in *Pulp Fiction*, 1994, for example or the German director Tom Tykwer in *Run, Lola, Run*, 1998, editor: Mathilde Bonnefoy), directs the viewer's attention to the act of editing. These practices have more in common with the montage approach than the classic Hollywood style.

The polished surface of movie making at the height of the Hollywood style does not allow the audience to experience the breaks that truly exist in the editing. The seamless flow of shot to shot that follows a set of conventions and rules, makes this style prevalent to an illusion, the illusion that one is watching reality unfold. As the film scholar David Bordwell has stated in the *American Cinema* tape: »The style becomes illusionistic.« The supposedly invisible style of Hollywood filmmaking is replicated in the way standard blockbuster movies are still shot and edited today. One typical example is Cameron's *Titanic* (1997): it follows the previously described Hollywood style and seamless editing.

A short discussion of a chosen film sequence may help to illustrate this point. The scene is from the first half of Cameron's melodrama and follows the interaction between the two main protagonists, Leonardo DiCaprio and Kate Winslet. As they walk down the deck of the ocean liner »Titanic«, they engage in conversation. Highly artificial in its building blocks, it is nevertheless supposed to adhere to the seamless editing style, where cuts are made invisible by their conventionality. The camera seems to dance around the two protagonists. The scene starts, similar to what the editor described about *Casablanca*, with an establishing shot of the deck, a long shot and then moves into a closer shot of the protagonists. As they talk to each other, we switch from medium shots to reaction shots and a few close-up shots, before the scene is re-established in a wide shot.

As Herbert Zettl explains about conventionalized editing: »*Continuity editing* concentrates on the structuring of on-and-off-screen space and on establishing and maintaining the viewer's mental map. When driving to a specific location, you are establishing a mental map that you follow on the way back. You do the same when watching television or a motion picture. The *mental map* helps you to make sense of where things are, where they are going, or where they are supposed to be in on-and off-screen space. Continuity editing concerns itself primarily, but not exclusively, with the clarification of an event«.[16]

Other prevalent examples to illustrate the convincing power of continuity editing, related to the conventionality of high-action drama, are films with the Austrian superhero and new California governor, Arnold Schwarzenegger. The recent film *Collateral Damage* (2002) draws its name from the fact that terrorists claim that civilian casualties in terrorist acts are »collateral damage«, nothing more. In the aftermath of 9/11, the destruction of the World Trade Center in New York where almost 3000 civilians lost their lives, this film release was stalled. Schwarzenegger plays a fire fighter, the true American hero, who seeks revenge for the senseless killing of his wife and son. The movie starts with a high-action scene that establishes Schwarzenegger as the lead protagonist of the film. He is shown as the savior of a trapped victim who is in the midst of a fire blast. The outstanding features of this film clip are quick edits, dramatic music that enhances the sense of danger and urgency, extreme close-ups of the fire ax, boots, lights on the fire helmets, different sources for natural sound such as the breathing of the fire fighters mixed with non-diegetic sound of trumpets and horns when danger lurks, anticipating impeding horror. The camera work produces the sense of high-action and drama.

The focus on the job of a fire fighter that sets the tone of the film establishes Schwarzenegger as the icon of American heroism: like the fire fighters who entered the Trade Towers to save innocent lives, the protagonist rescues the helpless. To further accentuate that fact, a key moment in the opening scene of the film is shown in slow motion. It turns out that Schwarzenegger's wife was dreaming this high-energy scene and she awakes to the peaceful sounds of her husband building (ironically) a war airplane with their son. Soon thereafter, mother and child will be killed in a terrorist act of destruction, while father Schwarzenegger watches them perish. This will be the motivation for him to seek revenge and fight an international ring of Columbian terrorists quite single handedly. The conventional editing style, the seamless editing and illusion of reality provides the viewers with a high-energy action drama that mobilizes the ideology of American heroism, a message not uncommon to many stereotypical Hollywood blockbuster dramas.

It is by no means accidental that Arnold Schwarzenegger was prominently featured as a stark supporter of the American President George W. Bush during the Republican Convention in New York in early September 2004. The location of the convention was chosen to exploit the role of the president in the aftermath of the attack on the Twin Towers in Manhattan. Visual proof of how the president reacted to the national crisis when the towers fell, a moment that has imprinted on Americans a sense of visual trauma, anteceded the president's speech. A video showed how he talked to firefighters on Ground Zero. This is another example where television and film narratives intersect and even affect real politics, trying to sway voters to re-elect a president by interpellating his past record, captured on video with the power of visual imagery.

Complexity editing

Complexity editing, in contrast to continuity editing, undermines this cognitive mental map. Instead it is used »to intensify an event and reveal its complexity«.[17] When Herbert Zettl describes the different facets of the so-called complexity editing functions he distinguishes between »metric montage«, »analytical montage« and »idea-associative montage«. The latter best describes the editing convention of the Russian montage theorists. »The strength – but also the weakness – of the montage is that it is filmic in nature; that is, it is a purposely synthesized event. This means that idea-associative montages are a deliberate juxtaposition of fixed event elements, or cells, in order to produce a specific effect or energy level.«[18]

The conventionalized narrative structure of the classic Hollywood style is in stark contrast to more experimental US and foreign films where montage mechanisms are more common. At the extreme, no editing takes place. This is the case in the international independent film, *The Russian Ark* from 2002, a European-Russian co-production. It provides a unique example for an entire film, shot without a single edit. There are two narrators who allow the story to flow independent of any editing. As you will be able to tell if watching the sequence from the beginning of the movie, there is a narrator who seems to be able to comment what happens in front of the camera lens from the privileged point-of-view of the knowing observer. The male voice never has a body:

it is an intimate voice, though, that talks directly to the audience. He introduces the second narrator, the host of the movie, a film character who is crafted after a French court official. That protagonist whom we see in the second half of the clip speaks Russian and seems to be asking the same questions that the audience asks – where are we, why is everybody speaking Russian, in which century do we move? Some of the questions will be answered in the course of the film, others will not, giving the movie a surrealist quality. The fact that there is not any editing taking place highlights this unusual journey through the ages of the Hermitage museum in St. Petersburg, Russia. The embodied narrator walks through the ages, transgresses from room to room, and casually introduces the audiences to the courtly life under the czar and the communist era. The film is a masterpiece and the quality of its construction lies in the endless continuity of its endless shot design.

The opening scene begins with guests dressed in 18th century clothes who enter the »Hermitage« museum, talking in loud voices. Then the scene grows more silent as we are introduced to the actual narrator of the movie who allows us to peak into other parts of the Hermitage. The camera moves in and out of spaces and the natural sound follows the action of the camera direction.

Another example to illustrate independent filmmaking is the opening scene from the Coen brothers' film, *O Brother, Where Art Thou?* (2000). It combines the visual elements of the *Russian Ark* and *Collateral Damage* and *Titanic*. Joel and Ethan Coen have worked independently, outside the Hollywood mainstream. The opening scene sets the tone of the film about three refugees from a grueling prison camp, with a long, uninterrupted pan from right to left, where the setting is established. Contrary to the action driven, intense opening sequence of the Schwarzenegger film, this scene begins with muted colors and sounds. It almost seems as if the setting is shot in black and white at the very outset that helps to make the viewer believe, we are traveling back in time. The very first impression provided by the film is the natural sound of hammers and voices, stemming from the line of prisoners who are working on breaking stones with their heavy hammers while chanting along the rhythm of their work. As the shot starts to introduce characters such as the prison guards on horseback, it changes into color. Then the Coen brothers use extreme high- and low-angle shots to show the actual laborers on the prison line. The film fades to black and the first intertext is displayed with the title of the movie. The use of intertitles is reminiscent of the era of silent films.

After a fade to black, the viewers are introduced to the three protagonists of the film, escapees from the prison line who duck in the adjacent cornfields while escaping the slave labor. As the camera remains still in the foreground, the three actors are coming closer. This scene is also deprived of any editing. It is obvious that the Coen brothers resist fast cuts to establish a mood of tranquility. Then, the film cuts to a more agitated sequence, when the three fugitives try to catch a chicken at an adjacent farmhouse. The camera moves again to an extreme perspective: the floor. We see the shackles on the legs of the prisoners as they try to walk in unison. The clip ends with a crane shot as the camera establishes the location of the scene. The use of editing accelerates the action, for example, when the prisoners are chasing the chicken, the camera takes on a hand-held quality. But there is nothing unusual per se in their visual language.

New visual languages

Herbert Zettl explains a broad spectrum of editing conventions in a chapter on »Structuring the Four-Dimensional Field: Complexity Editing« in his textbook classic, *Sight, Sound, Motion: Applied Media Aesthetics* (1999). He ends with the notion that »visual dialectic« is the term that best describes collision montage and the visual conflicts that arise with it: »Eisenstein juxtaposed shots in a dialectical manner (colliding opposite ideas to create a synthesis – a *tertium quid*) and also scenes and entire sequences. The whole film, then, represents a complex visual dialectic«.[19] When studying several chosen scenes in Aronofsky's *Requiem*, one can detect Eisenstein's montage techniques as well as the homage of the filmmaker to animation that have influenced his creative imagination.

The film starts with a reference to television. The first few shots depict the talk show host, »Tappy« who leads through his show »The Month of Fury«. The program is religiously watched each day by the protagonist Sara Goldfarb. Her ritual of seeing the show is rudely interrupted when her only son Harry unplugs the set to walk it to a pawn shop on Brighton Beach. The 20 dollars in cash that he receives are immediately spent on drugs that he consumes with his friend.

Already in the opening scene Aronofsky employs the split screen device to illustrate initially the distance between mother and son who cannot communicate. (He will use the same device later during a love scene between Harry and his girlfriend who touch each other affectionately but are also separated by the two screen images.) Although they are in the same apartment, mother and son are separated by a door; they are also separated by the split screen. The two separate screen images depict the same event from two different perspectives. Sara follows her son's actions while having locked herself in and the spectator sees her subjective view of her son dismantling the television set and rolling it out the door still attached to the TV table while she peaks through the key hole. The second split screen device is used when the two friends consume heroin. This is the refrain used throughout the film: in a quick succession of images, shots that last only a few frames are edited together to a five second unit. In this case, the image is not split yet, a device that Aronofsky will employ later in the film for the same depiction of drug consumption. This first introduction of the onset of heroin is shown with increased sound effects that highlight first the ripping of a bag with the drug, then the sigh of relief when the drug hits the blood system.

The visual narrative for the refrain has certain elements that are repeated throughout the movie: extreme close-ups of body parts, for example the mouth and teeth tearing open the sachet of heroin, a lighter that heats the drug, the bubbling of fluid, an extreme close-up when the drug is pulled into the syringe, another extreme close-up of the iris in an eye dilating and a mouth exhaling in relief. A drop can be seen falling into a container, metaphoric for the drug hitting the blood stream. Little cells are advancing through arteries. These images are edited in quick succession and can barely be isolated. The abstract juxtaposition of disconnected visual elements is reminiscent of the Russian montage technique of producing the sensation of collision.

There are three short sequences, chosen from Darren Aronofsky's *Requiem for a Dream* to demonstrate this key feature in the film. Each one of the clips is unusual due to a provocative and unique editing style. Fast paced, redundant, confusing at times and surrealist, Aronofsky connects with traditions from the French New Wave or filmmakers such as the French director Chris Marker whose legacy of *The Jetty, La Jetée* (1962) can be traced in the first sequence to be discussed. The first of the three selected sequences from *Requiem for a Dream* involves all four protagonists: Jared Leto plays a young white male, Harry Goldfarb, whose heroin and drug addiction is followed in the course of the film. His mother, played by Ellen Burstyn, falls victim to the lure of cheap entertainment, especially a talk show where she has hopes of being cast as the middle aged, successful »Sara Goldfarb from Brighton Beach« in a bright red dress. In order to fit into the dress of her dreams that signifies better times with her family, she starts taking diet pills and gets addicted to this drug. Her dependence on the pills casts her into a mental breakdown, depicted in the third clip. Two other protagonists are played by Jennifer Connelly as Marion Silver, the young female lover of the son, and his African-American dealer friend and equally heroin addicted fellow victim, Tyrone Love, played by Marlon Wayans.

Requiem for a Dream is the story of four people on the fringes of society, away from the limelight of the metropolis, who all lose their footing due to drugs and the lures of popular culture and a capitalist consumer oriented society. The film is based on a 1978 novel by the late Hubert Selby Jr. Aronofsky became acquainted with Selby's work while attending Harvard University as a freshman, and claims that the writing style inspired him to translate the prose into film language. The desire for visual storytelling then led him to LA film school. The director was attracted by Selby who wrote about Brooklyn where Aronofsky was born in 1969. Hubert Selby, whose original text is written in a surrealist, staccato-like prose, similar to Aronofsky's editing style, ended up collaborating on the screenplay for *Requiem* as a co-author. It is a merciless tale of failure and mental demise, signified through an aggressive and unique editing and camera style, a new visual language that breaks norms and conventions.

In one of the first dream sequences of the film, Harry waits for his friend to bring back a bag of heroin. Both have the dream of marketing the drug to double the profit and assure each other »let's do it right«. While Harry is anticipating his friend's return he suddenly sees his girlfriend Marion outside his bedroom window: she is standing in a red dress at the end of a jetty and turns around as he approaches her, smiling at him. There is no natural sound, despite the fact that the spectator can see Harry calling out her name. This vision of Marion on the jetty will appear again at the very end of the film but the girlfriend will not longer be waiting. The sound in this scene is not synchronous with the action. The audio tracks seem disconnected from the video track as if, figuratively speaking, the editing system had mixed up its »synch« between the tracks. (There is such a control as »un-synch« in digital editing.) As Marion turns around and looks at Harry, the

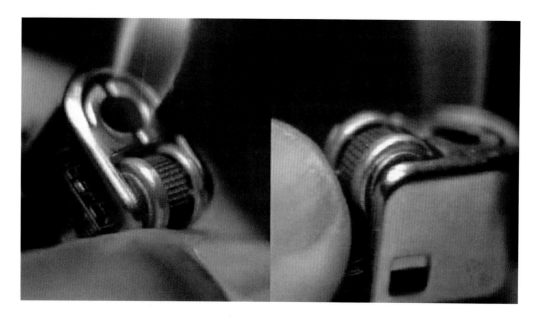

sound blends back and forth. When a disconnected sound cue occurs, the scene reverts back to the little room in the protagonists' apartment where his friend Tyrone enters the door and brings the first dose of heroin that both consume. This leads to the key sequence of *Requiem for a Dream*, the refrain of addiction that is symbolic of the entire movie. It depicts the ritual of heroin injection, administered through the veins, by creating a short sequence: a spoon, a syringe, the passage of blood and the dilation of the pupil are represented in rapid, energetic imagery. This time two screens are shown with the same visual elements, but slightly phased off. It is as if Aronofsky depicted the parallel consumption of the two protagonists who follow the same ritual of drug intake.

The rhythmic cutting has a strong emphasis on sound design. It depicts the rush of heroin and the on-set of the »high«, a phenomenon that drug addicts describe as an overwhelming sensation of comfort and warmth that provides a motherly feeling of relief and joy as if the addict has arrived at »the other side of the door«. The intensely uncomfortable sensation of withdrawal leads the addict to develop an overwhelming desire for the next »trip«. Aronofsky shows withdrawal with the bodily signals of sweat, nausea, muscle cramping, tenseness throughout his film in great detail. The actual high is always represented with the almost identical rush of images. The filmmaker also uses the slow fade to white as a means to impress the sensation of comfort and light due to the drug. In one scene where Marion takes drugs by herself, she stands half naked in front of a mirror. After she has taken heroin, the screen slowly fades to white as she lifts both arms towards the sky in a gesture of triumph and happiness.

When the two frames are edited side by side in a split screen during the drug intake, the effect is reminiscent to the images an editor sees on parallel monitors when constructing a narrative. The frames are all extreme close-ups of details surrounding heroin consumption and the brief »refrain« ends with the iris of the same eye enlarging suddenly, indicating the drug high. This sequence will be repeated in a similar manner throughout the film, providing a continuous visual device that is similar to a musical theme that returns. It's a fitting parallel because the title of the movie is »requiem«, a mass for the dead, commonly performed at funerals.

The sequence that describes the mother's drug addiction to diet pills is similarly composed as the montage for the drug high: unnatural sound heightens the sense that she eats pills instead of regular food; this slowly drives her onto the verge of nervous breakdown. The second part of the film focuses on the mother and her fall. It starts quite literally with the intertext »fall«, leading up to the last and final episode of the film structure, »winter« with a scene that will conclude this discussion. In the »fall« segment of *Requiem*, we see the African-American protagonist, Marlon Wayans, fleeing from a brutal murder scene where potential new dealers have been slaughtered in front of him. As he runs away from the crime scene, the police follow him and he is arrested. The camera style is erratic as if the camera were hand-held: Aronofsky uses a special camera rig, a »snorry cam«, that attaches to the actor's body. He uses this device also in the scene where Ellen Burstyn runs down a street after her mental collapse. The desperateness of the protagonists' situation is heightened by hectic sounds, hectic camera movements, subjective points-of-view and the use of extreme close-ups.

3, 4. *Requiem for a Dream*, directed by Darren Aronofsky, 2000.

Three parallel actions strands are shown in the course of this »fall« segment: the arrest, the mother's drug addiction and her son's heroin trip with his girlfriend. The drug consumption of the mother is indicated by merciless repetition of the same act of swallowing a pill: the sound that accompanies the edits is extremely loud as she gulps down one pill after the other. She is being shown in her little apartment at Brighton Beach, ready to watch her favorite television show and in her fantasy she starts seeing her TV alter ego in a red dress who is being introduced by the talk show host as the new star of the program. The audience cheers her on. Meanwhile, the refrigerator turns into a gaping animal, roaring menacingly. The redundancy of TV consumption is reflected in her redundancy of taking pills. The consumption is parallel to the repetitiveness of TV programming where the same visuals are played over and over again. The »sameness« of American popular culture lies in its repetition and Aronofsky signifies that message in his editing style as well. Ellen Burstyn sits in front of her TV set and is depicted with a fisheye lens: her apartment is expanding and gains surreal dimensions.

The refrain sequence for the heroin addiction of her son repeats in the same pattern as previously seen. As a contrast to the fast-paced extreme close-ups that make up this sequence, the following frame of the two protagonists on a heroin high is shot in an extreme high-angle shot: the camera circles above them as they lay on the floor, surrounded by fashion snapshots, belonging to the girlfriends deteriorating business. She ends up prostituting herself to support their joint addiction, descending into the abyss as the other characters in *Requiem* do as well. The scene cuts back to the prisoner and then to the mother's living room where she is shown calling a doctor's office to inquire about the effect of the pills. »Nothing to worry about, Ms. Goldfarb«, replies the polite voice of the doctor's office assistant on the phone. As the mother takes more pills, she admires her well-groomed alter ego on the TV set. The refrigerator, symbol of consumption, starts acting up, a feature that will become more prevalent in the third and final scene.

In this final example from *Requiem for a Dream*, the dreams of the four protagonists are destroyed completely. They have reached the abyss of society. Director Aronofsky symbolizes this descent into madness for the mother's character with a stunning sequence: the TV reality is folding into her perceived »normalcy« in front of the TV set. With the use of special effects, Aronofsky transplants the TV personalities, the Goldfarb TV alter ego (dressed in the red dress, dolled up) and the talk show host into the living room of the Goldfarb apartment. Sara Goldfarb herself is shown in a state of deterioration: seated in her red dress, she remains in the same position in front of the TV, the hair is undone, her face puffed up by the drug consumption. The fridge starts to roar like a wild animal. The visuals on the TV are repetitive and identical to the previous TV scenes. As the celluloid images emerge in her apartment, the mother excuses herself: »I am old, alone, you don't understand, please, I'll explain.« Instead, the formerly desirable TV world turns against her: the audience on the screen point fingers at her, roaring with laughter. Suddenly, the walls of her apartment go up and it turns into a studio set, where a make-up artist approaches her chair and gives her a countdown indicating that she will also be on TV. Her desire to be on the screen turns into a farce, a satire of representation.

Her world deteriorates and in a bucolic scene that is reminiscent of an orgy, the TV audience and formerly desirable TV host turn against her. In a frantic appeal »feed me, Sara« the audience yells at the mother, demanding to be fed: Aronofsky ridicules TV consumption by turning the effect of popular culture upside down. Instead of consuming the TV content, the spectator is consumed herself; in the end, the fridge opens up to devour her, pulling her into hell. The only thing left of her, is an empty, shrill reference tone in an abandoned apartment. The disconnectedness with reality is signified in the final scene as Sara Goldfarb runs down a street: only her red dress has any color, the fellow pedestrians are only shadows passing by as she has lost track of her world. She is completely disconnected from everyday life.

In the final segment of the film, Aronofsky uses rhythmic editing and montage to show the parallel descent of the four characters: Tyrone is in prison experiencing »cold turkey«, withdrawal symptoms to heroin; Harry is in a hospital where his infected left arm is amputated with a saw; Marion prostitutes herself in an voyeuristic decadent orgy, surrounded by men in suits, to get money for another dose of heroin and Sara Goldfarb receives electroshocks in a mental institution after refusing to take any food. The four lives are connected through the editing; images flash up and are replaced, accumulating in a climatic rush of distorted visuals. The rhythmic cutting is motivated by a strong emphasis of sound design, provided by the pounding sound of the orgy, the physical labor of Tyrone when he works in the prison's kitchen (in this shot the author Hubert Selby plays the prison guard), the administered electroshocks to Sara Goldfarb's temples in the hospital and the gory amputation of Harry's arm in a different clinic. The rhythmic sound and rapid, energetic editing binds the four desperate fates together. After this orchestrated finale, all four characters curl up in a fetal position on their beds in four different locations: Marion is caressing the bag of heroin on the couch in her run down studio apartment, Tyrone dreams about being held in his mother's arms while falling asleep in the prison, Sara Goldfarb is still fantasizing about the TV show host while confined to a narrow corner in the mental institution, and Harry curls up in his hospital bed, day dreaming about seeing Marion again on the now empty jetty. The camera pulls out each time to a high-angle shot. In the music world a requiem is meant to provide comfort, repose and rest. All four characters come indeed to rest in the final shots of the film but their dreams remain unfulfilled. James Berardinelli (2000) describes the ending in his movie review: »*Requiem for a Dream* certainly isn't the first recent motion picture to offer an unpleasant picture of what happens when an individual becomes hooked on drugs, but its quadruple character study is unsparing. This is in large because of the brilliant final fifteen minutes which is a tour de force of directing and editing. Employing hundreds of cuts, Aronofsky careens back and forth between his four main players, showing their increasingly dire circumstances and allowing those to escalate to a brutal climax. This is easily the most startling and memorable extended sequence in any film this year, and, for raw power, it exceeds any scene I can recall from other films about addiction. *Requiem for a Dream* gets under your skin and stays there.«[20]

Director Darren Aronofsky shows in his film how four protagonists slide into a hellish state of consumption: drug addiction and TV addiction are connected and become intertwined. He says about his own film: »You know, I think it's a modern horror film. We always saw this as a monster movie except that the monster was invisible. The creature was invisible. It was addiction living in the character's heads and the only other difference is that the creature wins.« The visual language of television with its merciless repetitiveness and redundancy is mirrored in his particular editing style that breaks conventions of Hollywood narrative storytelling. This new visual language is chosen by Aronofsky to highlight the grotesque nature of contemporary popular culture on American TV. Everyday life and fiction are blended in layers of meaning that merge into one large hyper-real scenario. This is a satire of the representation of reality – on TV and the film screen. Aronofsky does not use empty effects but deliberately introduces a provocative new style of editing and storytelling to unmask American consumer culture.

Conclusion

Similar to the other lead characters in *Requiem*, the personal becomes political, a reflection of contemporary American society, because all four protagonists represent varying degrees of personal demise through addiction. In Aronfosky's rationale the dependence on TV is equally as destructive, if the identification and fetishizing is taken to an extreme, as the addiction to drugs. His means of showing this interdependence is visual. Consumption of images in the digital age is excessive, Aronofsky argues in his motion picture. The consumption of heroin leads his three young protagonists into crime, prostitution, before all three collapse, unable to function in society anymore. Mental institutions, prison, hospital and ultimately the possibility of death overshadow the ending of Aronofsky's grim, bleak tale of human destruction.

The widely spread phenomenon of addiction in society is rarely represented in images. Aronofsky has found a way of creatively reflecting the brutality of personal destruction by challenging the status quo of seeing. His visual tale is so compelling and deeply confusing because it takes the viewers on a roller coaster ride of visuals, the staccato of his narrative, the rush of shots, the hectic pace of editing all accumulate in his last section of the film, »winter«, when the characters can not be saved any more. Aronofsky does not provide hope. This may be the most unrelenting feature of his film. The hopelessness that he foresees for society is captured in his cinematic style, in a film that »gets under your skin« as Berardinelli put it. The visual memory of this motion picture is equally as disturbing as the actual viewing.

Aronofsky has created a new style of representation, fitting to the mental state of a society at the beginning of the 21st century, geared towards image consumption, at all cost. This is one way of interpreting the visual refrain of the film when heroin is injected into the veins of the protagonists: images appear in quick succession in the split screen that capture in extreme close-ups what the sensation of a high may feel like. Drug addicts too are exposed to an excessive amount of images that impacts their mental visions, parallel to the »diet« of excessive TV watching. The iris widening due to drug consumption is similar to the shock of being exposed to the rush of visuals on television – a sensation, Aronfosky replicates in his filmic language. These effects which were necessary to telling the story would have been tremendously expensive to produce just a few years ago, because film effects are much more costly than rendering video effects. Aronofsky would not have been able to afford these effects in a non-digital world. The recent ability to use digital editing technology to create many effects helps independent filmmakers to make this type of alternative storytelling affordable and possible.

When the climax in Sara's media transference is reached and her television alter ego kisses the talk-show host and turns to her, luring her with her claw-like hands by screaming »feed me Sara«, the protagonist is sliding into utter despair. She has visions of her refrigerator taking on a life of its own. It is approaching her television comfort chair and opens its freezer compartment like a gaping mouth, devouring her, an ugly beast of her imagination. For the longest time thereafter, a high pitch sound can be heard. This is the beep of the television signal when the programming has ended and only the color bars remain. The chair of the protagonist is empty because she has fled her own apartment, a last attempted flight that will end in a mental institution where she is subjected to electroshocks to zap her out of her state of obsession. Aronofsky's filmic conclusion is captured in this image, also displayed on the official web site of the distributor: when the frantic succession of images finally stops, the chair is empty. There is no programming worth seeing and nobody left to watch. The irony of this argument is that one can hardly encounter that high-pitch reference tone with the color bars on American television any more, even though it is still familiar to many European audiences. In the American mainstream, hundreds of cable channels make sure that the show always keeps on going.

Kay Hoffmann
The digital cinema dilemma. Obstacles to digitalizing the movie screens

»The digital cinema will come. But nobody knows exactly when.« This phrase has been true at least since the mid-1990s, when the digitization of film production had its breakthrough and the first high-quality video projectors were introduced by the industry. John Chittock, chairman and founder of the British research institution and trade magazine *Screen Digest* wrote as early as 1996: »Improvements in the quality of video projection have now reached a point where the results on a cinema-size screen can be indistinguishable from 35 mm film. Video projection systems have generally relied upon the use of three cathode ray tubes (red, green and blue) as their light and image source, but new systems have been developed which are no longer limited in their light output by the use of television tubes; in particular, a completely new technology employing microscopic mirrors is now yielding screen brightness to rival conventional film projection. By repeating the scanning lines of the video picture (›line doubling‹), the familiar line structure of a television picture can be made almost invisible, and other systems are now using high-definition television with line structures as high as 1250, replacing (in Europe) the standard 625 lines of television.«[1] He predicted that video projection would begin to appear in new auditoria by the turn of the millennium, and in existing cinemas within the next ten years if not less. Chittock was right with that prognosis, but the general roll-out has not yet occurred. Of the around 150 000 cinemas worldwide as of summer 2003 only 169 screens in 142 cinemas have been equipped with high-end digital projection systems,[2] as a study by the magazine, *Screen Digest* found out. By end of June 2004, this number had only risen to 250 projectors around the world.[3]

A short survey of technical breakthroughs

That will change of course, because »digital technology is the same revolution as adding sound to pictures and the same revolution as adding color to pictures. Nothing more and nothing less«,[4] as George Lucas pointed out in 1997. For him it seems anachronistic that in the USA alone several thousands prints are still being packed in cans and shipped all over the continent, as it was done the last hundred years. But the breakthroughs in film technology he mentioned also show that it always takes around 25 years from the first presentation to general introduction on the market.[5] And not always the best technologies succeeded. The so-called silent film was never really silent, and pioneers like George Eastman or Oskar Meester in Germany attempted to synchronize gramophone music and sound to film very early on. Between 1903 and 1913 around 1500 »Tonbilder« (sound-images) were produced in Germany[6] and ran quite successfully in around 500 theaters. The optical sound system Triergon[7] had its premiere at the Alhambra Theater in Berlin on September 17, 1922. It was developed by Joseph Masolle, Joseph Engel, and Hans Vogt, but even though it worked well, it did not make it on the market. In many film histories, the premiere of *The Jazz Singer* in October 1927 is described as the official start of the sound-era, and nearly all the cinemas in North America und Europe were converted to be able to show talking pictures between 1930 and 1932. The process of introducing color film took even longer, stretching almost from the beginnings of film in 1895 into the 1930s. It was also a process in which many people were involved. The same is true for the introduction of television and video technology, which both took decades to reach a breakthrough.

The idea of an »electronic cinema« also has a long history, reaching back to the 1920s. In 1955, Albert Abramson, an American historian of technology who worked for CBS Hollywood, already predicted the death of celluloid: »The cinema has entered the electronic age. The electronic motion picture is reality. Motion picture production is changing from a mechanical process to an electric one. The film camera is being replaced by the electronic television camera. Motion picture film is superseded by magnetic tape. Even the motion picture projector is giving way to the large screen electronic reproducer.«[8] Ampex had just introduced its two-inch video machine as a stationary system, which worked with open reels. A tape with a running time of 90 minutes weighed 22 pounds and was only usable in TV studios. The Hollywood studios stayed with film as the production medium and took a wait-and-see position. They earned their money by selling their movies to television and producing TV programs in their studios, but preferred not to start experiments with electronic production. Such a system tends to be very conservative, or as Robert Sullivan, a vice president at Avid Technology, the maker of one of the most widely used digital film-editing machines, which was introduced 1991, said: »Hollywood is a lot like Detroit. It's probably a 60- to 70-year-old business and it still sticks to a certain way of making its products.«[9] At the end of the 1970s, Francis Ford Coppola postulated that the time for electronic cinema had now definitely come. At the Academy Awards Ceremony in 1979, where he won an Oscar for his Vietnam epos *Apocalypse Now*, he proclaimed: »We're on the eve of something that's going to make the Industrial Revolution look like a small out-of-town tryout. I can see a communication revolution that's about movies and art and music and digital electronics and satellites, but above all, human talent – and it's going to make the masters of the cinema, from whom we've inherited this business, believe things that they would have thought impossible.«[10] He was right with his vision, but much ahead of time. The attempts to revolutionize film production with his American Zoetrope studio and to bring back more power to the filmmakers with the help of computers and perfect planning of production failed. But he had the vision of a digital cinema, which has come true by now. The computer is at the center of production, collecting and combing all the information from the script, the story board and the calculation up to the first rehearsals, photos, and finally the shots all the way through the final phases of production. »Coppola's film *One from the Heart* was to have been the prototype of this innovative movie-making. But at a cost of over 30 million $, the production was neither cost efficient nor particularly successful at the box office, taking in only 1 million $ worldwide. The dream of an electronic cinema had fallen flat once again.«[11] His frustrating experience with the Zoetrope system for the production of *Hammett* (1982), which proved more the new power of the producer Francis Ford Coppola than the director Wim Wenders, is analyzed in Wenders's brilliant black-and-white film *Stand der Dinge* (1982).

Renaissance of the cinema

Beside some technical experiments with wide-screen-systems like Cinerama or Cinemascope, the projectors in movie theaters have not changed very much since the introduction of the talking movies at the end of the 1920s. In the 1970s, two inventions were made, which enables the rise of the multiplex cinemas in the 1990s. One is the Dolby noise reduction system, which was first introduced by the Dolby Laboratories in September 1973. Four years later, they presented a revolutionary optical sound system, which used the two soundtracks on film for a four channel sound system in the theaters. Loudspeakers were not only positioned behind the screen anymore, but a fourth effect channel surrounded the spectators in the theaters. So it was possible to create a sound design with dialogues, music, and sound using space and making it part of the story. In 1977, the first films to be distributed with this new sound system were George Lucas's *Star Wars* and Steven Spielberg's *Close Encounter of the Third Kind*. In 1986, Dolby SR (Spectral Recording) was introduced, in 1991 Dolby Digital. It became the general standard and in Germany, for instance, half of the theaters are equipped with Dolby systems. Another system is THX, which George Lucas introduced in 1982. But that is not technical hardware, but a set of requirements for optimal image and sound quality in the theaters, which are accurately controlled to keep the THX distinction.

The second innovation came from Germany. The movie theater owner Willi Burth had developed an endless-loop-system for his theater as early as 1954, but did not make it public until he presented it at the Photokina in 1968.[12] Up to that time, the films were screened with two projectors, which alternately showed the acts or reels of film. So every eleven minutes, the projectionist had to start the other projector and change the reels. Willi Burth's invention was to splice the film together and lay it on one plate. From there it runs through the projector and is wound up on another plate, from which it can immediately be started again. The projectionist does not have to be present all the time or can be responsible for a number of screens at once. In 1988, Willy Burth received a Technical Oscar for his invention, which became an international standard in the cinemas and was one of the fundamental technologies of the multiplex theaters.

This was a new type of theater, which emerged in the early 1990s. It is a huge building with at least eight screens and 1500 seats and state-of-the-art projection technology. Multiplexes combine movies with gastronomy and other leisure-time activities.[13] They have attracted many spectators and forced the traditional houses to invest in their theaters as well. In Germany the cinema audience rose from 102.5 millions (1990) to 177.9 (2001), but then dropped again to 149.0 (2003).[14] The multiplex theaters very often have enormous screens and ascending, comfortable seat rows (stadium seating). They represent the change to the »event-society«, a term brought into the public discussion by the sociologist Gerhard Schulze.[15] He considered that the event value has become more and more important and that many people orient their leisure time toward that new goal. For the film historian Knut Hickthier, the adoption of the general industrial standards of the media business to cinema by multiplex theaters was overdue.[16] In the multiplex buildings, elements of event and consumption were integrated, which were long approved in shopping malls and leisure parks. The audience is searching for a thrilling, bombastic film experience. That explains the success of the Imax format. It was developed in the 1960s and had its premiere at the Expo in Osaka 1970. The image on the 70 mm film is turned 90 degrees and is stored longitudinal to the direction of film transport. So the image is 15 holes long instead of 5 holes as with conventional 70 mm film. That means it is three times bigger than the normal 70 mm film image and ten times bigger than the 35 mm image, thus letting it provide a sensational viewing experience. During projection, the large film surface of the image has to be sucked to the lens by a vacuum to keep projection sharp all over. The Imax theaters were first built next to museums and in amusement parks and screened mainly documentaries on expeditions, wildlife, and the secret of life these films had an average length of under one hour. They boomed in the 1990s, leaving other special film projection system like Showsan – developed by effect specialist Douglas Trumbull (*2001: A Space Odyssee*) in 1976 – far behind. By 1995 there were already 128 Imax theaters worldwide, and in the meantime many have been opened, drawing millions of spectators a year. Beside the classic Imax projection, you now find the Imax Dome, where the film shot with a 180-degree fish-eye lens is projected in a dome over the spectators, as well as very efficient 3-D projection. James Cameron shot a 3-D documentary on his Titanic excursions and Jean-Jacques Annaud presented with *Wings of Courage* the first 3-D Imax movie in 1995. It is obvious that these mega productions with huge and heavy cameras are the extreme antithesis of a light digital production.

Electronic production

Meanwhile the digitization of film production has become a general standard. There is hardly any production that does not use digital postproduction and effects, which meanwhile have become nearly invisible for the spectators and even for FX specialists.[17] The tremendous use of special effects has again made the mainstream productions into a »cinema of attraction«, a term introduced by Tom Gunning[18] to describe the early cinema of 100 years ago. But in the view of George Lucas, creator of the six *Star Wars* episodes and with his Skywalker Ranch one of the patrons of new film technology, the studios have missed the point by using digital tools mainly for editing and effects. »In his eyes, digital technology, by reducing the need to shoot on exotic locations, build expansive props and film certain scenes over and over, is a practical tool, a means of telling stories on as grand a scale as a director wants, but on a reasonable budget. ›They don't get it, they're about five years behind. I don't think they understand what I do here‹, Mr. Lucas said of the big studios.«[19] Pixar, Dreamworks and finally also Disney produced some breathtaking animated blockbusters in 3-D like *Antz, A Bugs Life, Toy Story I+II, Monster Inc., Finding Nemo* or *Shrek I+II*. The images are made in computers, but the success is not based on using the new technology, but in strong and emotional stories, as many in the animation business point out in nearly every interview. An unprecedented number of movies have been shot digitally with different electronic high-definition cameras from Sony, Thompson, and Panasonic. Very often the electronic camera uses an adapter to make it possible to shoot with the traditional film lenses to give the electronic image a film look. Digital cameras were first used for independent productions and documentaries. In the year 2000, 40 % of the movies and 50 % of the documentaries at the Independent Film Market in New York[20] were shot digitally. At the Cannes Film Festival in 2003, five of the films running in the main competition were shot with the new Sony CineAlta HD camera: the winner *Dogville* by Lars von Trier, *The Matrix Reloaded* by Larry and Andy Wachowski, *The Moab Story: The Tulse Luper Suitcase Part 1* by Peter Greenaway, *La Petite Lilli* by Claude Miller, and *Bright Future* by Kiyoshi Kurosawa. In his film, Peter Greenaway wanted to shoot with a multiple viewpoint with up to ten different perspectives at once, an idea long suggested by Cubism. In a glossy magazine published by Sony, he praised the possibilities of developing a new language of film: »You need to continually reinvent the medium of the moving image, and it is fascinating to try to put every aspect of the new visual possibilities into one major work – to provide, if only at first primarily for oneself, a bench-mark product, to use the information age technology not just for storing and retrieving and collating information but for creating a new aesthetic world.«[21] That is an interesting approach, to create really something new, but one that not many people are interested in. Another pioneer was George Lucas, who shot *Star Wars: Episode II* partly with Sony's electronic camera and the third part completely with five 4:4:4 CineAlta cameras.[22] In the last five years 156 titles were distributed also for digital projection, starting with *Star Wars: Episode I*. The possible digital distribution of the third part in 2005 could become an indicator for the acceptance of digital cinema. In digital technology optimists see the chance to produce films more individually and outside the studio systems. This could have tremendous effects, as Gundolf Freyermuth pointed out: »The hopes for a cinema beyond Hollywood that George Lucas and other pioneers of digital moviemaking have repeatedly expressed and – as well the CGI movement on the Internet – point towards such individualization and democratization of the medium. Regarding the process of film production, it would transform and dissolve, in the Hegelian sense, the industrial division of labor. Lucas, the avantgarde billionaire, demonstrates in this respect a future of filmmaking, in which all the creative decisions are made by the cinematic narrator alone. Empowered by the computer, he will be script writer, producer, and director as well as set designer and character painter; the role left to the studios will be at best reduced to that of a publishing house or an art gallery. Such an individualization would have, of course, far-reaching aesthetic consequences for the production and reception of movies. In the history of the arts, subjectivization almost always was accompanied by marginalization.«[23] The idea of the democratization of media was already a driving force of the video movement in the 1970s, but they turned out to be Beta testers for the industry and were rolled over by the commercial introduction of the video market in the 1980s.[24] The idea of film production without celluloid could be a false conclusion similar to the office without paper.

Electronic projection

In March 2002, the seven Hollywood studios Disney, Fox, MGM, Paramount, Sony Pictures Entertainment, Universal and Warner Bros. formed the Digital Cinema Initiative. »DCI's primary purpose is to establish and document voluntary specifications for an open architecture for digital cinema that ensures a uniform and high level of technical performance, reliability and quality control. DCI will also facilitate the development of business plans and strategies to help spur deployment of digital cinema systems in movie theaters.«[25] With this initiative they seek to avoid the confusion that has plagued the TV industry by establishing clear standards for digitization. In the summer of 2003, the traditional Pacific Theater on Hollywood Boulevard, where the premiere of the first official talking movie *The Jazz Singer* took place in 1927, was converted to a digital film laboratory and test bed, where screenings with different projectors and systems could be carried out to define standards. The tests were being conducted by the Digital Cinema Laboratory, an organization set up by the University of Southern California's Entertainment Technology Center, which was to test the different systems for the DCI group.[26] In November 2003, DCI published their Technical Specifications Version 3.0. The press release said: »By a unanimous vote, all seven DCI Member Studios approved pursuit of a hierarchical architecture approach for digital cinema, which defines a 4K (4098 by 2160) delivery system that will be compatible with both 4K projectors expected to be available in the near future and with 2K projectors available today. DCI is continuing to encourage manufacturers to develop 4K projectors and related technology for DCI testing and evaluation.«[27] This decision for the 4K option could mean that the digital roll-out for digital cinema may take even longer that some expect. It is reaching for the stars with the highest technical standard. The amount of data required is 6.5 times higher than the European TV standard with 625 lines, and even with a 2K rendering for visual effects, the computers quickly reach their limits. On the other hand it could be a reaction on the booming home market, where good video projectors are already offered for under $6000. So the cinema has to offer something better.

But the electronic industry is already producing the first digital cinema systems and projectors, not waiting for the definite standard set by DCI. On June 3, 2004, the Sony Corp. presented its »Digital Cinema System«, which is based on silicon crystal reflectors and laser technology, at the Pacific Theater.[28] This system already works with a 4K resolution. Participants were impressed not only by the quality of the image, but also that Sony presented a prototype and very openly discussed which problems have to be solved regarding contrast, brightness, color, and the huge amount of data involved. Sony developed the GLV technology (Grating Light Valve) using three electronically controlled lasers in red, blue, and green, which combine to produce a white light. It should be possible to screen an image of 10 x 50 meters and according to the *Daily Variety* the projector should cost between $ 50000 and $ 80000, depending on its efficiency. The official start is planned for the World Exposition in March 2005. JVC's D-ILA chip projector and the

Barco projector already exist for some time, since both were already presented at the European Film Institute (EIKK) conference »Cinema of the Future« in Karlsruhe, Germany in November 1996.[29] The D-ILA chip is, for example, used by the Kodak Digital Cinema System,[30] which was presented in 2002, but is still waiting for the digital roll-out. Texas Instruments developed the DLP chip, which works with digital mirrors and reaches a resolution of 2K. The company now has an efficient DLP cinema projector on offer. At the ShowWest in Las Vegas in 2004 Dolby Laboratories, famous for their developments of sound systems for theaters, also announced their plans for a digital cinema system of their own, which is to be designed in accordance with the open standards of the Digital Cinema Initiatives (DCI) and is to be on the market by the end of 2004.[31] So films are produced digitally, projectors are on the market. What is the problem with converting the theaters? That has, of course, economic reasons. A high-resolution system with projector, computer, data management and so on costs between $ 150 000 and $ 250 000 per screen and is four times more expensive than analogue projection systems. The question is who will have to pay for that. New business models have to be developed. The movie theater owners have no direct advantage from digital projection and have had to invest a lot of money in modern technology and new multiplex theaters in recent years. The fact that digital projection leads to cost reduction effects is always an argument, because the distributors do not have to produce the prints anymore. On the one hand that is true, but on the other hand an average Hollywood production costs 60 million $ and another 30 million $ for marketing, while the costs for the prints are only around 3 million $ or 3.7 %, as Patrick von Sychowski[32] from *Screen Digest* pointed out. So the cost reduction seems not to be such a strong argument either, but the financing is important. At the ShowWest, the distributors discussed starting a fond with Wall Street money to finance the roll-out. But then the question still remains who owns the projector and whether movies from another studio or an independent production can be shown with a projector financed by a certain studio. The relation between the studios, the distributor and the theater owners will change for sure in the digital age, but nobody knows yet what form these business plans will take.

Beside the question of who will pay for the innovation, the other important issue is the threat of film piracy – even if it is not openly discussed by the industry. It was also a phenomenon of the 1990s that very close to the official start in the States or even after preview or press screenings, pirated copies of movies appeared in the Internet and could be downloaded. It forced the Hollywood studios to change their distribution policy and to have a movie started on the same day worldwide if possible. Otherwise the pirates had the advantage of a few months after the American premiere. This caused damages of billions a year to the film industry, and the companies joined forces worldwide to fight against it and to criminalize the pirates with arrests and hard punishment. Press screenings are controlled very intensely and even mobile phones are not allowed, because they could tape the synchronized sound. The audience is controlled with night-watch glasses to see if somebody is taping the film from the screen with a small DV camera. But many examples have proved that this is a more amateurish side of video piracy. Most professionals have contacts in the business and try to organize getting a print at the different stages of distribution. The Academy of Motion Picture Arts and Science wanted to stop sending out videocassettes for the Oscar nomination in 2004, because they also soon appeared in the Internet. The academy pays a reward of $ 500 for each convicted delinquent who taped a movie in a theater. So, one of the advantages of digital cinema, the worldwide networking in a globalized market, is also its biggest disadvantage in the era of global piracy.

Everybody can imagine how risky it would be to distribute not only analogue tapes, but digital masters via satellite to the theaters. Cracking the scrambling and other security technologies would be a challenge for every hacker and pirate. A digital master would make it possible for the pirate to replicate the movie as often as he wants without any loss of quality. Much money is being invested to find ways to prevent piracy. Microsoft, for example, developed a special digital rights management system with their Media Player 9 version, where the film data are compressed and the computer has to ask online for permission before each screening. The projectionist has to enter a special code, which the management system sends directly by phone. One has to see if Microsoft or other companies will succeed with their systems and if they can convince the studios that the protection is worthwhile.

Meanwhile, digital cinema is being realized in two fields, which are very typical for the installment of new technologies; commercials and public supported distribution of art and documentary films in Europe are again driving forces. For example Kodak presented their Digital Cinema System at the Cinema Expo in Amsterdam in 2002. When the digital roll-out for the movies did not take place, they concentrated on distributing the system for use in screening commercials, trailers or special events in the theaters. »With the screening of commercials in the cinema we changed to the fast lane«,[33] as Denis Kelly, Kodak's Digital Operation Manager for Europe, pointed out. In 2004, Cinema Screen Media (CSM) ordered the Kodak system for another 900 screens in the States, which means that over 1200 screens now show commercials digitally. This system works with a less expensive LCD projector (3500 Ansi Lumen), which costs $15 000, but it can be changed to a high-end 2K projector, which still costs around $60 000, if the digital roll-out takes place in two or three years, as the film industry is expecting. Kodak's Cinema Operating System (COS) is based on IBM technology and »will provide a digital backbone to theaters, equipping them with the storage, scheduling, and playback capability they need to upgrade pre-show advertising content today, and eventually to show digitally-projected movies and other entertainment. This is the infrastructure cinemas will need to take full advantage of the promise and potential of digital cinema.«[34] Each installation is checked online every 15 minutes and mistakes are corrected automatically. The system should be connected to the ticket computer of the theater to give the information, how many visitors the screening had. This gives Kodak a new kind of control, too. In some other countries, efforts are being undertaken to develop systems to screen commercials digitally that would make it very easy to shape the precise structure for the different screenings or to change commercials from one hour to another. At the moment, the commercials have to be screened the whole week. This flexibility is attractive in particular for the agencies.

Another experiment, funded with public money from the European Media Programme, started in March 2005. 175 cinemas in eight European countries (Austria, Belgium, Germany, Netherlands, Portugal, Scotland, Slovakia, and Spain) will be combined in the European Docu-Zone (EDZ) network. EDZ will finance the installation of low-resolution projectors (with 1.3 K output) and the cooperating cinemas will only have to screen a documentary or another program at a fixed schedule each week for the next five years. The simultaneous projection of the documentary once a week will be followed by a live discussion with the director after the show to create a special event. The model for EDZ was the Netherlands, where producer Kees Ryninks established the DocuZone project with twelve theaters, to avoid the costly transfer from tape to 35 mm film.[35] There it worked very well on a small scale; on the average, 26 moviegoers attended each screening. The EDZ is coordinated by Björn Koll from the German arthouse distributor Salzgeber, and for him it is important to establish an independent venue and not to wait for standards set by the majors. A technical test will be a European documentary film festival by EDZ from November 12–14, 2004, which the already connected cinemas will show in morning and afternoon screenings. In Great Britain, the UK Film Council will install 250 high-tech digital projectors in 150 cinemas by the end of 2004, using 23 million $ of lottery money. John Woodward, UK Film council chief, said: »The aim of the network is to use state-of-the-art technology to cut the cost of distributing films.«[36] He hopes that the move will it make easier for film lovers to see arthouse films. In China, the state is also planning to order 200 high-end digital projectors and servers soon. The president of the European Digital Cinema Forum (EDFC), Ase Kleevland, also sees the option of projecting TV programs like sports or concerts in the digitally equipped theaters. But the head of the German theater owner association, Andreas Kramer, warns that it would be a wrong move to install lower resolution beamers now and not to wait for the international standard and high-end resolutions with at least 2K or 4K. »Digital cinema has to be more than television on a huge screen.«[37] One has to keep in mind that in many countries outside Europe and North America the transition has already taken place on a low-resolution level, a fact that is often overlooked and underestimated.

One has to ask what the impact will be if the transition to digital cinema is finally made. Many Europeans hope that it will give arthouse films, documentaries, and independent productions better chances to be screened not only in the major cities, but in the countryside as well, and that it will break the Hollywood dominance in most of the markets. From their perspective, digital projection will turn the mainstream oriented film business into a real film culture again. In my opinion, that vision is questionable. Because if all the screens will become digital cinemas and are connected via satellite or broadband some day, the studios will be tempted to start an expected blockbuster on all the screens of a multiplex in order to break new records on the first weekend. Especially if the major studios own the projection equipment it will be ridiculous for them to screen arthouse films instead. So the market could even become more strongly integrated than it already is.

Internet as a new platform?

It is an open question whether or not movie theaters will keep their role of being the locomotive for the marketing campaigns in all the other media afterwards. In 2003, a study of the American Motion Picture Association, in which most of the major studios are organized, came to the result that the movie theaters were only responsible for 25 % of the revenues worldwide, while the home entertainment sector reached 56 % for the first time, and the rest came from television. That indicates the increasing importance of DVDs, which achieved sensational growth in all markets, in spite of the economic crisis in many countries. In the future, the Internet – already a popular and established platform for short movies and animation – could become an important medium for delivering movies on a pay-per-view basis, like the film pirates already practice today. The music industry just went through this experience, and the studios take that threat very seriously. In an interview, James Cameron, who was one of the first directors to use digital effects in *The Abyss* (1989) and *Terminator 2* (1990), was asked if he thinks digital delivery over net and filmmakers with their own file servers will revolutionize distribution: »I think they will revolutionize an individual's ability to get the work seen, as opposed to having to work as an indentured servant for many years to get that opportunity, and in meantime you've completely lost touch with your audience. [Laughs.] You're going to have people making short pieces – call them films, call them anything – sticking them out there, getting immediate feedback. And possibly you'll find a better crop of young filmmakers to choose from, further down the line. But does it change the big smokestack film industry system? Probably not very much, simply because we have more films than we have people going to see films.«[38] But the predictions of the future of film and Internet is another issue that cannot be discussed in detail here.

Future perspectives

Experts predict that the digital cinema will become reality in the next three to ten years. These are figures that we have heard since the 1990s, but perhaps they are more realistic today in view of all the technical developments. The general question is whether the digital cinema will succeed, if it only delivers the same quality and content that a 35 mm print already offers. Media history shows that a new medium has better chance if it brings something new or adds at least some additional value for the user. Not too many people think in that direction, considering what the new qualities of the digital cinema could be – visual, aesthetic, economic, or as a service for the spectators. Peter Freyermuth said: »Future works of digital story telling will have to find an innovative structural fluidity. The equivalent to analog-serial montage permitting the weaving of narrative structures that are simultaneously interactive and immersive has yet to be invented. Not until then will it be possible to realize the aesthetic potential of digital technologies and to fully express the complementary experiences of the digital age: the opposing sensations of being nowhere and being everywhere, of radical individualization and global conformity, of isolating fragmentation and networked complexity.«[39] Instead, most of the discussions concentrate on the comparison between film print and digital, how to reach a film look or how the disadvantages can be treated. To imitate the old is the usual reaction when starting new technologies on the market. But to be successful, you need visions and perspectives of what the new medium can do. In regard to digital cinema, such perspectives seem to be totally lacking at the moment. That is even more surprising because the whole film industry is convinced that digital cinema will soon be here.

Jean-Pierre Geuens
The digital world picture

Not so long ago many of us were still denying what today is a certainty: the demise of film and its replacement by digital technology. Of course we grudgingly recognized that the new medium made editing faster and more exciting, sound recording more malleable to postproduction changes, and visual effects simply astounding, but somehow we still held firm to the notion that the rich texture and the shading palette of the film image could never be overtaken. No longer so: it is now clear that, under the relentless drive of George Lucas and some electronic firms, all remaining »film« aspects of cinema, from the origination of the material to its projection in theaters, will soon be propelled into the digital age – ready or not, and sooner rather than later.[1] However, the final triumph of the new technology should not be perceived as anything more than icing on the cake. For all practical purposes, the revolution is already upon us, and we should therefore not shy away from discussion – wild speculation, even – about its impact on the art of cinema.

Certainly the literature associated with the movie industry constantly deluges us with thousands of pages in which we are told of digital breakthroughs that push the envelope further and further.[2] At the same time though, what is said is carefully couched so as not to frighten those who fear being left behind.[3] In *American Cinematographer*, for instance, Lucas himself goes out of his way to reassure cameramen that »aesthetic decisions still have to be made« and »that the essence of what they do – which is to frame a shot and to make sure the lighting is beautiful or appropriate – will always remain the same«.[4] Rather than making the members of the technical crew redundant or displacing a part or all of their labor onto a new set of workers operating exclusively behind computers, the new technology is generally presented as just another tool that will, in the end, enhance the creative control of all the parties concerned.

This view severely understates the radical discontinuity at the core of the digital revolution, insofar as it has in its power to shatter the long-standing arrangements that regulate how movies come into being. As for theorists, they have been slow to challenge the industry's steady-as-she-goes message, mainly because they have been absorbed by flashier aspects of the technological takeover, and especially everything related to the hypertext.[5] So here I hope to determine the ways by which digital moviemaking changes the rules of the game. I will then attack what I perceive to be the nihilistic tendencies of the new medium; and I will conclude by bringing to light a different use of the technology – one that might take us back from the abyss. In any event, what is presently going on in the field is already shaking our very understanding of what a »film« is.

Changing the rules of the game

In »The Question Concerning Technology«, Martin Heidegger's main argument is that »technology is no mere means« but rather »a way of revealing« what we then take to be the world.[6] By this Heidegger is suggesting that the kind of technology we use circumscribes our view of the world, earmarking our access to it, ultimately shaping what we make of it. On a lesser scale, it follows that different means of production are not interchangeable either, that new empowering devices do not simply provide a better, more efficient way of doing the same thing. On the contrary, each interjects a distinct filter, an engineered mediation that regulates the labor of those who use it. At the same time, different devices also direct attention toward specific features of the work at hand, channeling expectations toward a desired computer output and thus modulating the final outcome. It should not surprise us that digital moviemaking is not only refashioning our behavior during the entire creative process but also urging us toward certain objectives rather than others.

To understand what is taking place in the shift from film to digital, one first needs to remember what made shooting with film such a unique experience. It was never like any other job. From the start, there was the eeriness of the setting: the cavernous hall with its sacred relics – the hard-shelled camera resting heavily on a solid tripod, the lights with their barn-doors craning down at awkward angles from suspended cat-walks, the small microphone perched at the very end of a long pole, the tracks on the floor that started abruptly and led nowhere, the smoke spewing in the air like incense. As for the actual filming, it looked and felt like a ritual whose formalized arrangements had been set long ago. Has anyone ever stood in that setting without being mesmerized by the choreographed ballet involving actors and crew or by the seemingly endless repetition of the exact same lines of dialogue? No wonder then that even hardened veterans felt a sense of awe every time the director called: »Action!« For all realized that something magical was bound to take place, and one held one's breath until the call: »Cut!« echoed out. Reality had been exorcised somehow and, if all had gone well, shards of that reality ended up on the surface of the celluloid. At the end of the day, one was exhausted – physically, to be sure, but also mentally – the kind of depletion one feels when something truly transcendental has taken place.

None of this was easy, either, for one was constantly reminded of the dumb opacity and the brute materiality of the medium. For 40-some years, for example, because of the parallax issue in the old cameras, operators could not be certain, until they saw the dailies a day later that their framing and focusing had been up to par.[7] Lighting too was done blind, and it took years of apprenticeship with experienced directors of photography for newcomers to understand the exact relationship between foot candles and relative levels of exposure in the final image. Even editing, as Walter Murch wistfully recalls, could not be treated lightly in the old days because of the potentially explosive nature of the film's nitrate base.[8] And today still, irrespective of all the technological refinements we take for granted in our modern Arriflex and Panavision cameras, anything can go wrong at any time: witness, for instance, the despair of Andrey Tarkovsky and Sven Nykvist when their principal camera jammed during the shooting of the last, most important, and most expensive scene in *The Sacrifice* (1986).[9] Finally, despite all precautions, a hair on the gate, a light leak in a magazine, or inexplicable mishaps at the lab can still destroy hours and hours of hard work. Yet none of this has ever deterred film crews. In fact, it has always spurred them on, as if they were all measuring their professional worth by going up against these obstacles, learning to overcome them only through meticulous preparations followed by a continuous exercise of exacting craftsmanship. The very difficulty of shooting a film thus brings pride in one's work: much was demanded, it got done, and now one feels good about it. That in a nutshell is what demarcates film work: the sense of magic that permeates the shoot and the sense of accomplishment that comes from working out miracles in the face of incredible odd.

By radically simplifying the nature of the shooting process, by bringing transparency to it, digital technology pensions off these heroic features of film. The image for one is there from the start. It doesn't have to be imagined, produced, begged for, cajoled into existence. It is given immediately. It makes no demands, requires no work. No incantation or rite is necessary to bring it about. It is always already there, once and for all, accessible at all times, and even visitors on the set can make suggestions for its enhancement. Beyond this, it is also cheap, which means that one can easily become careless, shooting endless takes of an action instead of figuring out which one actually works. Even though the work on the set proceeds in more or less the same manner as before, there is a sense that the shoot is too easy, that digital technology demands very little of you and can now be accomplished even with second-rate personnel.[10] So, whereas film heightens everyone's attention and sharpens the work, a lackadaisical response is often the reaction whenever a digital camera makes its appearance.[11] Actors and crew lower their expectations accordingly. The full intense involvement that is the mark of a film shoot has given way to a dispassionate, half-hearted effort on everybody's part.

My second point has to do with the focus inherent in the two technologies. Professional film cameras – the old Mitchells, for instance – were designed to be simple, offering relatively few options beyond the basics. Once speed and shutter had been selected and the various elements of the lens determined, all eyes were meant to concentrate on the action taking place in front of the camera. For that is where the scene is shaped, the material articulated, the film made. Understood this way, motion picture cameras were never more than expensive recording devices.

Digital cameras could not be more different. From the start they beg the operators to try the myriad of options they make available. The exposure can be immediately adjusted to any light level, brightening up even the darkest areas. The colors can be programmed to match whatever light sources are being used or can be extravagantly tweaked for all sorts of expressionistic effects. Tone, grain, contrast, and density can be altered to provide a specific look. Shutter adjustments can be refined to produce stunning visual effects in any movement. Fades and dissolves can be adjusted on the spot for maximum impact. A black-and-white look can be substituted for color at any time, and different composition ratios are equally available at a moment's notice. Other filters of lesser appeal stand ready to implement yet other transformations of the image.

Professionals who got their training years ago may regard all this tweaking as gimmicky but, for the tens of thousands of students who are now learning their skills with the help of these cameras, there is no turning back: this is what moviemaking is all about. In the same way that a Moviola feels prehistoric after one has learned editing on an Avid, one cannot be expected to go back to an unadorned scene once filmmaking has been experienced through optical options. Classical film shooting construes the action itself as the focal point of the crew's activity, but digi-

tal moviemaking refracts that attention back to the camera. The scene itself is no longer the primary focus; what matters most is the visual mesh that shapes what is going on. Moviemaking has now become a question of looks.

For Lev Manovich, more is involved here than mere attention to the surface of the text: »While previously the great text of culture from which the artist created her or his own unique ›tissue of quotations‹ was bubbling and shimmering somewhere below the consciousness, now [the entire creative process] has become externalized (and greatly reduced in the process).«[12] In other words, whereas it might have taken years for someone like Mikhail Kalatozov to develop the extraordinary visual style that became his hallmark, today »style« can be purchased from day one by activating a switch on a gizmo. However, these electronic filters have already been processed by the culture at large, hence the very real danger that they could displace or eliminate the less visible, more fragile influences that normally compete in one's artistic development.[13] For Anne-Marie Willis, this may already have taken place, with the consequent result that »imagination becomes reduced to imaging«.[14] No longer originating from a filmmaker's head, visual motives are now dependent on the largest hype from the world of cool media imagery.

Then there is digital wizardry per se. Because the pixel revolution made it possible to manipulate any part of the image without loss of resolution or impact on the surrounding area, new image formations suddenly became possible. At first, the digital intervention was subtractive in nature: television antennas were removed from rooftops in historic epics and wires from bodies in stunt work. More dramatic things also occurred: Gary Sinise's leg, for instance, was neatly erased from the rest of his body in *Forrest Gump* (1994). By nature, though, such work always involved the pasting of fresh material onto the blotted-out area, eventually spelling out the full potential of image compositing. All at once, threatening clouds replace the dull sky that greeted actors and crew during the shot. And, to the delight of cost experts everywhere, a small crowd is magically duplicated to fill an entire stadium. In yet more extraordinary breakthroughs, President Kennedy addressed Mr. Gump, John Wayne came back to life, and Fred Astaire was seen dancing with a vacuum cleaner. Finally, *Who Framed Roger Rabbit?* (Roger Zemeckis, 1998), *Terminator 2: Judgment Day* (James Cameron, 1991), and *Jurassic Park* (Steven Spielberg, 1993) pushed the boundary of the new technology even further, convincing all, filmmakers as well as audiences, that nothing stood beyond its reach.[15] Indeed, in *What Dreams May Come* (Vincent Ward, 1998), the world itself could be remade to reflect the vision of a Timothy Leary on a bad day. From this point on, the filmic image of old with its umbilical cord to the world lost its original primacy. Parts of the image could still originate in a traditional setting, but they could no longer be differentiated from the added photographic layers or the surrounding plastic elements.

Nihilistic tendencies

The luxuriousness of the new images should not, however, blind us to the underlying disjunction at the core of such projects. To construct a coherent picture out of material gathered from radically different sources (straight photography, composited pictures, computer-generated images, other animated material of one kind or another, etc.) involves redeployment away from the traditional source of the medium – the world of everyday life. For, even though the turbo-charged images have all the earmarks of a believable ensemble when pasted together, what we see never existed as such. In fact, for Jean Baudrillard, the whole point of the new technology is to substitute »signs of the real for the real itself«, with the benefit that »never again will the real have to be produced«.[16] And indeed, George Lucas prides himself on having disconnected the medium from »all that real stuff« that repels him so much.[17] So when he and his team digitally alter, animate, or composite people, objects and landscapes, more than an aesthetic effect is involved. What we face here rather is a deep distrust of the everyday world, the sense that the »real stuff« is no longer good enough to do the job that is now envisioned for the cinema. By the same token, there is also the fear that any unadorned view might, by its very presence, give the lie to the artifact of which it is asked to be a part. The goal then, in maintaining the integrity of the discourse and in keeping it well-ordered, monologic, and sovereign, is to regulate every bit of reality that is let in so as to erase what doesn't fit and to replace it with more suitable material.

The green screen is at the core of the digital studio. Here actors say their lines and rehearse their moves before being pasted against a pictorial environment of some sort. Today the actors who share a scene generally perform it together, but pick-ups and inserts are most often done solo. The technique in fact no longer requires the simultaneous presence of all the participants, and it is thus doubtful that traditional blocking will survive, as it makes more sense economically to shoot one actor at a time, not just for some exceptional shots, but for all the scenes of a particular actor. To understand the true nature of the process taking place, one needs to imagine the actor standing alone in front of a large screen, facing camera and crew. There is no furniture around, no other decor or background, and the light that floods the set is not naturalistically motivated. As for the performance, it is addressed to no one, with expressions and gestures without immediate cause or impact. Certainly the author would have been told beforehand how this particular bit will fit once other players, furniture, light, and backdrop are added to the final plate, but, at this very moment, the continuity and the interaction with the living environment which, in John Dewey's eyes, provide us with our sense of identity and our ability to act in the world are simply not there. Indeed for Dewey, in any life experience »there is never any ... isolated singular object or event. ... There is always a field in which observation of this or that object or event occurs«.[18] Thus for an actor to stand alone in an empty space is very unlike sharing a room with others, being able to take their measure as well as being aware of the exact shape of the furniture, the feel of the carpet, the color of the walls, and the spatial location of every object in relation to one's own body. Most importantly, when we engage another human being, it is not someone in general whom we encounter, a generic personality, but a living body whose unique look, expression, and behavior contribute to our own response. As human beings then, we continuously interact with each other and our surroundings, probing at one moment, reacting at another. In fact, to have what Dewey calls *an* experience, there must be a »complete interpretation of self and the world of objects or events«.[19]

Admittedly the alienating procedure of the green screen may not be particularly troubling to actors accustomed to working in films. They have always had to adjust to the idiosyncrasies of the medium: bringing up their characters piecemeal instead of all at once, being replaced by stunt experts when the action got rough, and addressing lines of dialogue to a vacant point next to the lens instead of a human being. Moreover, as Walter Benjamin pointed out, because »the film actor lacks the opportunity of the stage actor to adjust to the audience during his performance«, the acting often turned out to be less than thrilling.[20] As a matter of fact, the lack of context and continuity imposed by the new technology could be used to advantage in another kind of cinema, Godard's for instance, to help deconstruct the actor's usual baggage (the sense of the character's identity, the backstory, the wants and the needs, the knowledge of what's happening, and the consciousness of the main obstacle to one's objective).[21] Here, however, the intention remains trite. The idea is not so much to probe the dialectical struggle between the actor and the character as to generate conventional movie characters. At the very least, with the green screen, the job of the traditional actor is made more difficult. Something important may be left behind. Can one truly expect great performances in such conditions?

Compositing can also infiltrate the very fabric of everything it shows us. Certainly the concept is not new. Henry Peach Robinson, for instance, more than 100 years ago, used combination printing »to avoid the mean, the bare and the ugly ... to avoid awkward forms and to correct the unpicturesque« in his photographs.[22] Similarly today, a filmmaker can assert control over all the accidental missteps that inevitably slip in during the shooting of a picture and then permeate the very fabric of the text. »Now«, Lucas boasts, »you can adjust all that«.[23] For Scott McQuire, typical examples would include »a momentary look on an actor's face, a chance configuration of light and shadow, a random juxtaposition of objects ...« And he concludes: »It is the realm of contingency that the digital threshold overtakes.«[24]

To understand what is truly going on here, we need to take a closer look at Lucas' pioneering work in *Star Wars: Episode I – The Phantom Menace* (1999). For it is in that film that we see rehearsed for the first time the technological moves that, for better or worse, will redefine our understanding of moviemaking in the not-so-distant future. In one shot, for instance, the dialogue is edited out of an actor's lips by morphing his mouth shut. In a reverse example, dialogue is added to a performance by shooting »someone else's lips ... and match(ing) [these] lips to new lines of dialogue recorded by the actress«.[25] A third situation involves a shot with two actors for which the director »prefer[ed] each actor's performance in different takes«.[26] No problem: a brand-new shot is created that combines the separate performances. In yet another scene, the actress (Natalie Portman) was supposed to have looked first at the young Anakin and then at the floor, but unfortunately these actions were reversed in the take finally chosen as the best. The obvious solution involved running some of the footage backwards but, in doing so, some steam rising in the background now appeared to go in the wrong direction. So a further trick was called upon to make the steam rise within the new (reversed) image. Finally, in a digital experimentation that »actually brought tears to my eyes«, Martin Smith, the editor of the film, points to a shot in a hangar that takes place before the racing sequence. First, Lucas didn't like the time it took for Anakin to turn his head before reacting to another character's entrance, »so Smith skip-printed some of the boy's head-turning motion and smoothed it out«. Then, still in the same shot, because the actress didn't look up to respond to another character's lines, some new footage of her doing so was glued in. But that is not all. Now Lucas wanted to include R2-D2 and C-3PO to the scene and increase the size of the hangar. Again, no problem: »The camera now makes a synthetic ›pan‹ to the left to reveal the hangar's enormity, the two famous robots entering, and Anakin's racing pod being towed in. ILM had to create the rest of the hangar's dusky interior, with busy robots going about their duties, people waking across frame and a very large hangar opening in the background through which the desert planet's harsh sun light now glares.«[27]

The difficulty here involved not so much the added material per se, but the production of a convincing change in the perspective on the characters and the background of the original footage to make them fit the camera's added synthetic pan.

In the face of such tours-de-force, the tendency is to sit back and applaud the technicians who made it possible. More to the point, the surfeit of digital tampering can also suggest the emergence of a radically new »camera« which, to quote Manovich again, no longer »functions as a material object, co-existing, spatially and temporally, with the world it [is] showing us«.[28] Put somewhat differently, the brilliant ILM demonstration forces us to rethink the traditional arrangement that gave preeminence to the shoot for the gathering of the core material of the finished film – editing and the rest of postproduction being used merely to fine-tune the work. For Smith, this way of working is »now out of the window«.[29] Instead, all phases involving the making of a movie have now merged into one. Not only can one edit and create special effects while on location, one can also rewrite, restage and reshoot – essentially think the film anew – while editing. The discrete operations have combined into one general interface where all facets of the story as well as of the moviemaking process are accessible and revisable at any time.

The tendency to micromanage every detail in the picture has other ramifications that need to be addressed as well. In hindsight, it was probably inevitable that the actors' faces, bodies, and performances were going to be digitally modulated and enhanced (for our viewing pleasure of course) once compositing work became routing enough. At the very least, the practice displayed in *The Phantom Menace* puts an end to the idealistic notion that the performance we are watching originates with an identifiable human being. At the same time, even though we may not truly be aware of the difference, does not something change in our appreciation of the work once we know that words can leave a person's mouth without ever having entered that person's head, that faces can be altered to meet the exact nuances of the text, and that bodies can be made to enact actions that they never initiated? In other words, what happens to our emotional involvement with characters once we know that the »performing« on the screen owes everything to the talent of a digital animator? Can simulatory reality ever supply the sense of the soul under the skin? Milli Vanilli, anyone?

To shed yet more light upon George Lucas's grand project in the ILM factory, we better return to Heidegger. Indeed, for the German philosopher, »the fundamental event of the modern age is the conquest of the world as a picture«.[30] By this Heidegger does not allude to photography, but to our exacerbated drive to »set whatever is, itself, in place before oneself«.[31] The notion thus expresses Heidegger's view that late twentieth-century western civilization has taken a turn for the worse insofar as we now, with the help of technology, believe ourselves to be the exclusive »relational center[s] of that which is as such«.[32] In other words, our power to make things happen in the world has been boosted to such an extent that we no longer consider people and other entities in nature as others, in their distinctness, with their own underlying reasons, but as objects made to serve us, material to be used at will. The worker is merely a provider of labor; the river a source of energy. In our greedy search for »unlimited power for the calculating, planning, and molding of all things«,[33] and the irresistible pleasure that goes with it, we forget, that »that which is does not come into being at all through the fact that man first looks upon it«.[34] All in all, for Heidegger, to adopt the technological world view is to wish insatiably to master, control, and dominate whatever is set before us.

Surely, for Heidegger, the instrumental thinking at the core of Lucas's ideas would be a clear example of a nihilism run amuck, one possible also »involv[ing] a pathology of the will to power«.[35] Appropriately, the *American Cinematographer* [36] article where the director discusses the future of moviemaking is called »Master of His Universe«. And in a »Sixty Minutes« segment, Lucas himself is seen in his large screening room, surrounded by a gang of computer animators, pointing a laser beam toward the screen and asking them to realign his army of drones: »Why don't you take this guy and stick him over there?«[37] Clearly such work points to a new protocol for directors working in the electronic factory, one where anything can be artificially produced or retrieved from an ever-expendable digital backlot, then made to perform exactly as desired. Such directors, no longer embroiled in the complexity, the otherness, and the resistance of the everyday world, would become truly omnipotent, their power absolute.

I thus believe that a dangerous ethos permeates the entire *Phantom Menace* project. In fact, Lucas's drive to lord over everyone and everything in his images, to make them conform to his wishes and to mil every bit of surplus value out of them, is reminiscent of a similar labor performed by the less savory characters of the Marquis de Sade, who also made mincemeat of their victim's bodies, seeing in them but human matter to be played with as long as pleasure was ultimately attained. Certainly, to make use of Marcel Hénaff's thoughts on the subject, there is a »continuity between shattering the organic body, systematically dividing it up, and quantifying it, on the one hand, and methodically rendering it profitable and subjecting it to industrial exploitation on the other«.[38] In a similar vein, in Lucas's grandiose enterprise, the integrity, grace, and dimensionality of a human body is responding to the surrounding living environment as systematically leveled as its body parts are forced to perform independently of one another just like any other raw material that is mined and apportioned with cold and calculated efficiency. If Reinhard Heydrich were alive today and a filmmaker, he would not proceed any differently.

Back from the abyss

Having warned us against the potential ravages of modern technology, Heidegger concludes his essay on a surprisingly optimistic note. Quoting a few lines from the poet Hölderlin, he suggests that »the essence of technology must harbor in itself the growth of the saving power«.[39] By this he means that, regardless of how dominant and overwhelming technology appears to be at first, it inevitably contains within itself seeds that could again make us confront the essential mystery of being in the world. With this in mind, I now suggest that the digital revolution in the movies also provides us with some effective antidotes. Three countermeasures appear to me to have the most potential in this regard: the emergence of a fresh shooting spirit as a result of the miniature cameras now on the market; the development of storytelling techniques that were not possible with film; and the creation of radically new visual treatments for the image.

First, let's examine how the pint-sized digital cameras available everywhere can contribute to producing a new kind of filmmaking.[40] I would like to recall »The Caméra-Stylo«, Alexandre Astruc's celebrated manifesto, written some 50 years ago, in which he called for a cinema where »the filmmaker/author writes with his camera as a writer writes with his pen«.[41] That line can be interpreted in two ways. On the one hand, there is an appeal for a new relationship between writing and image-making, one where direction would go beyond merely »illustrating or presenting a scene« – a proposal that was to a large extent answered by the New Wave directors.[42] On the other hand, the sentence also suggests the need for more discreet equipment: a smaller camera that could be held personally by the director. In the end, for both Astruc and the New Wave directors, the reality of production in their days – the heavy equipment, the bulky cameras, the large crews needed to make a film, etc. – was just too much to overcome. Quite reasonably, a caveat ended his piece: the realization that »although we know what we want, we do not know whether, when, and how we will be able to do it«.[43]

But we know the answers. Today it is finally possible to implement the creative arrangement he proposed back then – that of a writer carrying pen and paper in a café. Liberated from the weight of the gear and »the pressure of this $20 000-an-hour crew that's had their breakfast and is waiting just outside the door«.[44] The artist is now able to face the world in a novel way, thinking on the spot and »writing« with his or her camera. Jon Jost, to take a single example, thrives in this new environment because his tiny camera allows him to shoot his movies unnoticed insofar as people »think that you're shooting home movies or something ... I told the actors«, he said, »we are just going to go into this café, and you're going to sit down here and there, and we'll shoot this thing ... and could you go and ask them to turn the music down a little lower?«[45] Because there are no big cameras around, no celebrities to fuss about, no cops, no crew, no lights, no boom, no stunts, no obvious rehearsals, no »Action!« and no »Cut!«, a different protocol emerges.[46] What is lost – careful compositions, harmonious lighting, exacting camera movements, etc. – is more than compensated for by the authenticity, restlessness, and unpredictability of a real-life situation.

Another redemptive move can be observed in Mike Figgis's ambitious digital project *Time Code* [47] (2000). While long takes were always used to great effect, they were necessarily limited by the size of the magazine attached to the camera. In this project, however, capitalizing on the time advantage made possible by digital video, Figgis shot four stories in simultaneous long takes of 93 minutes. Motivating the whole operation was Figgis's desire to bring back »the sustained power of a theater performance to film«, a move that puts him in flat opposition to about everybody working professionally today.[48] Additionally, even though Figgis shot the entire event (the four concurrent stories) 15 times and coached actors and crew at screening sessions at the end of each day, the nonstop action in different locations severely limited his ability to influence the specifics of each take. »To discourage any attempt at cross-editing«, he even encouraged »the actors to wear different clothes every day«.[49] So, in contrast to Lucas, who wants to micromanage every detail under his command, Figgis puts himself in a situation where he had to trust his actors and crew to do the best they could each time they went out. Sure, things went wrong at times, but happy accidents showed up as well. By letting the dice roll where they would, Figgis demonstrated in no uncertain terms that indeterminacy in a project can infuse it with surprising rewards. Far from being perceived as flaws, mishaps by actors and camera operators in fact heighten our involvement in the nonstop event.

Finally, the digital apparatus was made to subvert the conventional pictorial space that regulated painting for four centuries and has dominated film since its origin. One only has to look at Raúl Ruiz's *Time Regained* (1999) to have a taste of what could be achieved (with more ease) through the new medium. In his attempt to find a visual equivalent to Marcel Proust's elaborate writing style, Ruiz decided to place people and objects on moving platforms and propel them this way or that in the midst of a shot, changing the perspective of each scene in the process.

To our eyes, the result is marvelously fresh as Picasso's *Les Demoiselles d'Avignon* must have been to its own audience in 1907. Beyond this, one could also make use of compositing while rejecting the conventional approach that seeks only to »reterritorialize« (to use Gilles Deleuze and Pierre-Félix Guattari's notion in »Anti-Oedipus«) the discrete components into a new image that looks just as organic and homogeneous as any ordinary picture. Here, instead, the individuated parts could be used to comment on one another in the same manner as different voices and styles of speech combine to create the power of James Joyce's *Ulysses*.[50] By celebrating its manifold potential, the new compound would thus openly challenge the monadic image. Although video artists have explored this kind of image-making almost from the beginning, they have for the most part handled it in a painterly fashion, not as a dramatist would. The daunting challenge will be to make this complex, constructivist, multi-imaged panorama around the characters work dramatically for the story.

In the *Phantom Menace*, the most extraordinary digital accomplishment leads to a shot that nobody notices in the theater. Indeed, it would have been much cheaper to film the expanded scene at the time of the shoot had Lucas known then what he truly wanted. For him, however, the point is moot: what matters is to move moviemaking away from the world to a digital back lot with all the controls it implies. If Lucas is successful, and the rest of the business follows, all the talk of a renaissance in the art, the democratic opening of the medium to a new brand of filmmakers, the possibility of expanded, less restricted distribution channels, etc., will have been for naught – a situation Benjamin characterizes as the »phantasmagoria« of progress.[51] Is the whole affair no more than a sideshow, an offshoot of Sony's corporate challenge to Eastman to become the number one company in the business? If that's the case, the present disruptions in the system will eventually ease up, and the same movies as before will once again be made – with large, high-definition electronic cameras maybe, but with the same talent and crew, the same high budget, and with the »monopolistic stranglehold ... of the distribution marketplace« intact.[52]

Whoever wins in the end though, there's no escaping the fact that Lucas's proposal for the future remains at bottom thoroughly conventional, for in the product he envisions, the visual world is reconstructed along the same specifications as the old one, and so we end up with a 19th-century story dressed up in 21st century garb. Furthermore, Raúl Ruiz is probably right when he suggests that »technological overload leads nowhere«.[53] To imagine the future of a vital and creative digital camera, we better look elsewhere. Whether directors choose to write, shoot, and edit a movie entirely on their own, conceive of the project as a throw of the dice, a Nietschean becoming where the result cannot be known in advance, or think of radicalizing the image of old, it is just possible that the medium finally has the chance to venture into avenues we never thought possible. To be able to do so after one hundred years of cinema should reassure us that, indeed, we ain't seen nothin' yet.

ALEXANDRE ASTRUC

DU STYLO À LA CAMÉRA...

... ET DE LA CAMÉRA AU STYLO

Ecrits (1942-1984)

Vinzenz Hediger
Making movies is like making cars, only more fun

No Hollywood marketing campaign is complete without a »Making of« film. In this contribution, I would like to discuss the »Making of« in terms of what I propose to call the consumer interface of the film. I would like to define the consumer interface of the film as a set of images, sounds, writing and spoken language that circulates – in movie theaters, in broadcast and print media and on the internet – in order to inform potential customers about a particular film. The consumer interface of the film consists of advertising, publicity, and journalism. Furthermore, the consumer interface includes information originating from the consumers, such as recommendations in chat rooms and other forms of word-of-mouth. For the most part, control over the consumer interface of the film rests with the producer-distributor companies who pay for most of the advertising. However, the commercial fate of a given film depends on what consumers contribute to the consumer interface, i. e. word-of-mouth in its various forms.[1]

The »Making of« film is one of the crucial elements of the consumer interface. »Making of« are usually first shown on television and the resurface on video and DVD editions. »Making of» are pseudo- or mock-documentaries (Kernan, 1991), i. e. advertising films that pose as journalism. In this contribution, I would like to discuss yet another aspect of the »Making of«. I would like to argue that the »Making of« should best be understood as an industrial film, i. e. a form of utility films that serves a practical purpose in the production and circulation of goods, and that the genre they most closely resemble is indeed the so-called image film, or the consumer-oriented industrial film. I will first give a brief outline of the history of the »Making of«, from the first decades of the last century up until recent years. In a second step, I will discuss industrial films in relation to the »Making of«. In conclusion, I will argue that »Making of« films perform two particular services for the film industry. First, they intensify the audience's emotional and cognitive involvement with, or, if you will, investment in films. »Making of« films multiply the opportunities for involvement and posit the film as an object of fascination as well as a program for entertainment. And second, »Making of« films establish what you might call a balance between irony and immersion in the audience's attitude towards the film. The fictional worlds of Hollywood invite immersion, but they also require irony, that is a play of knowing and pretending not to know that these worlds are artificial and constructed. »Making of« films tell us how the virtual worlds of Hollywood are made, and they provide a knowledge about the production process that is much more comprehensive than the knowledge suppressed in what has come to bee known as the »willing suspension of disbelief«.

In March 1912, Edison offers to exhibitors a ten-minute film called *How Motion Pictures are Made and Shown*.[2] While this film is not a »Making of« in the sense that we now understand it – it's not about the production of an individual film, but rather about the technical processes of movie making and movie projection in general –, it clearly belongs to the genre of films about the making of films. Neither is it necessarily the first »Making of« in the history of cinema. It is simply the earliest one that I could locate. The film belongs to a public discourse about the technical aspects of filmmaking that also included popular science books such as Frederick A. Talbot's 1912 publication *Moving Pictures. How they Are Made and Worked*, which includes a chapter on special effects (Talbot, 1912) and articles in newspapers and magazines. Indeed, the *Motion Picture World*, the trade paper that announces the release of the Edison film, describes it »as an exceptionally fine treatment of an always popular subject«. As early as 1912, then, the divulging of »behind the scenes« knowledge is part and parcel of film promotion. Tom Gunning has spoken about the period from 1907 to 1913 as a period of »narrative integration« in American cinema. In the years to 1913, films develop complex narratives with elaborate characters, coherent chains of action and reliable moral horizons – in short, fictional worlds that invite immersion. (Gunning, 1991) The »Making of« discourse emerges along with the process of narrative integration, which is perhaps no coincidence. Apparently, immersion requires the counterbalance of »behind the scenes« knowledge, a point that I will return to later.

Initially, the main focus of the »Making of« discourse is on the technical apparatus of cinema and the marvels it performs. In the early years of cinema, the film technology fascinated audiences at least as much as the films themselves. Continuity editing carefully conceals the apparatus of cinema, as film theorists of the 1970s liked to point out. One could argue, however, that the apparatus, the invisible machinery of the visibility of film, resurfaces in the peripheral discourse of the »Making of« the moment continuity editing becomes standard with the introduction of the feature film. In that sense, the »Making of« discourse of the early 1910s continues the audience's fascination with film technology even as the feature film comes to dominate film distribution and exhibition. What is new about the »Making of« discourse of the early 1910s is another element: the movie star. In fact, the »Making of« discourse could be said to emerge at about the same time as the star discourse, and in alliance with it. As Janet Staiger points out, American production companies began advertising the names of their featured players as early as 1909. (Staiger, 1991) Richard DeCordova suggests that film stars proper, i.e. popular screen actors whose private lives are the object of public interest and media discourse, emerge around 1914. (DeCordova, 1991) In 1913, Francis X. Bushman, one of the most popular screen actors of the 1910s and 1920s recently released from his contractual obligations to the Essanay studios, goes on a lecture tour throughout the United States. As one trade paper reports: »Mr. Bushman is giving a brief talk on how moving pictures are made, after which a picture showing himself (sic) is thrown upon the screen and he proceeds to elucidate it with interesting remarks and dramatic lines.«[3]

The star acts as a »bonimonteur«, a film lecturer who not only explains the film's contents and supplies the missing dialogue (thereby completing his own on-screen performance, but who first recounts how the film was made from a technical point of view. In Bushman's lecture, star performance and »Making of« discourse coalesce into a form of entertainment that survives to this day. Star interviews with actors talking about the technical aspects of their work and of filmmaking in general have long been a staple of Hollywood film publicity, and some »Making of« films even use the film's star as a narrator. In a »Making of« for *Independence Day* (USA, TCF, Roland Emmerich, 1996), Jeff Goldblum takes the audience on an inside tour through a »top-secret« research lab that turns out to be the set of the film.

Throughout the 1910s, »Making of« footage regularly appears in trailers. In addition, production companies promote the audience's knowledge about the production process through films and through magazine and newspaper articles courtesy of the studio's publicity department.[4] One such film, entitled *A Trip Through the World's Greatest Motion Picture Studios*, was released in 1920 by the Ince studios. As a trade paper article suggests: »... contrary to all precedents, *A Trip Through the World's Greatest Motion Picture Studios*, sidesteps the casual star and player ›snapshot‹ glimpses found in some magazine and special supplements devoted to ›behind the scenes‹ moments. The Thomas H. Ince production is distinct and original in that it presents in conventional story and continuity form, the full day's work in a representative American cinema institution, from sunrise to sunset, as the personages arrive in the early morning, through the complete schedule of studio functions to the final departure at eight.«[5]

If previous »Making of« films combined star gossip and fascinating glimpses of cinema's machinery of visibility, the Ince film is up to something rather more serious (at least if we are to believe the trade paper; unfortunately, no copy of the film survives): a comprehensive analysis of an »American institution«, the film studio as a factory. Ince studios were the first company in Hollywood to taylorize their production. Thomas Ince introduced scientific management and the division of labor into film production in the late 1910s, adopting models from other industries such as the car industry. (Staiger, 1979) By 1920, the factory model had become industry standard, and *A Trip Through the World's Greatest Motion Picture Studios* reflects that process. *A Trip* introduces a third important layer into the »Making of« discourse: as much as about stars and technology, »Making of« are about the representation of film production as an industrial process. It is important to note that the trade paper report calls the studio an »American institution«. Insistence on the industrial character of film production serves a specific propagandistic goal. Through the representation of the studio as a factory, Hollywood tries to establish itself as just another hard-working American industry emblematic of the (protestant) work ethic that made America great. A number of such films were produced throughout the 1920s. *MGM Studio Tour* from 1925 for instance, with a running time of ten minutes, establishes a full inventory of all departments of the Metro-Goldwyn-Mayer studios, created the year before through a merger of Metro and Goldwyn studios at the behest and under the ownership of New York cinema tycoon Marcus Loew.

Most channels for divulging information about films were in place by 1915, from advertising in newspapers, trailers, posters, handouts, publicity and »exploitation«, event marketing. (Staiger, 1990) Right away, film companies use these channels to divulge information about the production of films. When Cecil B. DeMille rebuilt ancient Egypt in the desert near Palm Springs for *The Ten Commandments* in 1923, numerous illustrated magazine articles covered the building activities. At times, the volume of behind-the-scenes information led to complaints from exhibitors. R. Gordon Hudson, owner of the Alden Theater in Safety Harbor, Florida, an exhibitor who claims he »has a hard time making ends meet at the box office«, is a case in point. In a letter to the *Motion Picture News* from 1928, he questions the industry's wisdom in divulging information about the making of films: »I firmly believe that a lot of inside info has been put out by the periodical movie magazines that really hurt the industry … An audience would not enjoy a stage play viewing it from the rear and seeing all the trick lights and devices that produce the effects. The same applies to revealing all the secrets of the studio in pictures taken behind the set showing the fake snow storm or the fake rain. To live and enjoy the picture, the audience must feel that the cloud-burst covers a vast area and not just perhaps a tank of 20 feet times 20.«[6]

The reference to the theater is particularly interesting. From the early 1910s the film industry tried to rival and surpass the legitimate theater. In 1912, the year that Talbot published his book and Edison released *How Motion Pictures are Made and Shown*, New York entrepreneur Adolph Zukor founded Famous Players, later to become part of Paramount studios. As the name indicates, the company hired famous stage actors to play film roles. Stage actors were attractive for film producers because they carried cultural legitimacy and promised to broaden the audience base of the film industry to include the middle classes. In many important points, the film industry departed from the model of the theater. For instance, film programs in most cinemas ran continuously rather than at fixed hours throughout the classical period. Also, the theater industry remained safely positioned in the realm of art, while the film industry, as Hudson rightly points out, aggressively advertised the fact that it was indeed an industry. The theater still was a normative ideal for the film industry well into the 1920s, however – how else could the Florida exhibitor take the film industry to task for departing from the practices of the theater?

The three basic layers of the »Making of« discourse – technology, stars, and industrial process – are in place by 1920. »Making of« films in the sense of filmed entertainment about the production of individual films – emerge in the early 1930s. In 1934, MGM produces a short film called *Happy Days Are Here Again*. Again the film presents the studio as a factory, but the focus is one specific film, Ernst Lubitsch's version of *The Merry Widow*. As one trade paper writer describes the film: »A plane zooms in the sky, the MGM plant is pictured and then nose-diving down, ›The Merry Widow‹ is mentioned for the first time. There is shown the effort devoted to research in set architecture, costuming, etc. Then a camera crane and its crew are depicted photographing one of the colorful sequences, follows a trip on a camera car and the manner of making long shots and close-ups, revealed, next an explanation of the microphone and the sound-control room, and a seamstress working on the costumes and their modeling. Franz Lehar, writer of the music, is introduced and the stars and the elaborate spectacle are presented.«[7]

The film was apparently so successful that audiences applauded after each showing of the film in some Los Angeles theaters. »Nine minutes in running time«, the trade paper correspondent concludes his report, »this special trailer is a genuine departure in entertainment and showmanship salesmanship.«

The other studios soon followed suit and came out with ten-minute short films on virtually every major production. Paramount, for instance, advertised Cecil B. DeMille's 1934 *Cleopatra* with a short film called *The Hollywood You Never See* about the preparation and research that went into the production of the film. Soon known as »featurettes«, these short films served multiple purposes. First and foremost, they were advertising films, drawing the audience's attention to important new films in the making. Second, they served educational purposes. *Hollywood Extra Girl* for instance, a featurette for Cecil B. DeMille's *The Crusades* (Paramount, 1935), reports the story of the film's production by following the daily travails of an extra girl. The film shows that life is very hard in Hollywood for aspiring starlets; the unmistakable message is that small town beauties should think twice before hopping on the bus to Hollywood in the hope of becoming movie stars. *Hollywood Extra Girl*, is both an advertising and a »social engineering« film, addressing a pressing social problem of the 1930s: the influx of aspiring movie actresses into the film city. Finally, featurettes were meant to make money. Produced by the studios' short film departments, featurettes were rented to theaters at regular short film rates. In the classical era, advertising was a source of income for the studios: trailers and posters, too, were rented to exhibitors rather than simply distributed along with the film.[8]

In the 1950s, featurettes found a new outlet in television, where they were shown mostly by local and regional television stations outside of network programming schedules. Trying to adapt to the new medium, the featurettes of the 1950s often posed as news reports, TV documentaries or educational films. A featurette for *Teahouse of the August Moon* (USA, MGM, Daniel Mann, 1956), a comedy starring Marlon Brando, shot in Japan, shows how Japanese and American personnel work together in perfect harmony – a model of new-found friendship between former enemies.[9] The posing strategy points to one of the particularities of the »Making of« film. »Making of« films are a weak or, if you will, parasitical format. Throughout their history, their function basically remains the same: they divulge information about the production of films. As media environments change, so does the look and style of »Making of« films, however: they adapt to the media environment in which they are shown and pose as short films in the 1930s, as TV news reports in the 1950s etc. It comes as no surprise, then, that in the mid to late 1960s many featurettes emulate the look and sound of »direct cinema« documentaries. Additionally, particularly in the late 1960s, when auteur criticism had found its way to America courtesy of the New York critic Andrew Sarris, »Making of« start to focus on the director, on the film's »auteur«, rather than on the star, the special effects or production values (let alone the industrial structure of the production pro-cess). The tendency is particularly pronounced in featurettes for imports, such as Claude Le-louch's *Vivre pour vivre* (France / Italy, United Artists, 1967). The featurette begins with a shot of the director and the following commentary: »His name is Claude Lelouch. His profession is directing motion pictures. His specialty is love.«

The auteur-centered vérité style transpires in featurettes for US studio productions, too. The featurette for *Mr. Buddwing* (USA, MGM, 1966), a crime film starring James Garner and directed by Delbert Mann, focuses on the director's relationship to the city of New York, where the film is set. As the narrator informs us: »Delbert Mann approaches New York as he would a leading lady. Studying her movements, her poses, her nuances, and judging the emotions they would transmit through the eye of a camera.«

The director is an expert in film as a technology of seduction: the featurette's definition of Mann the auteur still resembles that of the director in the classical studio system: the director's job is to make the leading lady shine. Similarly, in the featurette for *Grand Prix* (USA, MGM, 1966), director John Frankenheimer is an expert in handling high-powered movie stars in high-powered racecars.

Famous directors appeared in advertising materials even before the 1960s. Most notably, Cecil B. DeMille was considered to be the equivalent of an important star in terms of drawing power. The director, who had become an American household name as the presenter of the weekly »Lux Radio theater« show, which aired from 1936 to 1944, personally appeared in most of his trailers and in all of his featurettes. In the classical period, there were only few directors who were known to the mass public, however. According to one Gallup poll from the 1940s, these included Ernst Lubitsch, Howard Hawks, Sam Goldwyn, David O. Selznick and Alfred Hitchcock. Other directors and even screenwriters would appear in trailers of the 1950s, but Hitchcock with regular advertising appearances until the mid-1960s. Even Hitchcock's career as an advertising spokesperson for his own films only really took off after the TV show »Alfred Hitchcock presents« became a hit in 1955/56, however. (Hediger, 2003)

»Making of« films of 1960s that focus on comparatively unknown or young directors such as Delbert Mann or John Frankenheimer introduce a new layer in the rhetoric to the »Making of«: the auteur discourse. While Mann and Frankenheimer are still cast as experts, as engineers rather than artists, the auteur-as-artist emerges in the featurettes of the 1970s. One Warner Bros. featurette from 1972 begins with a quasi-documentary description of – once again – New York City, but this time, the director is an insider, and his insider status assures the authenticity of his artistic vision:[10] »One of the wealthiest and most sophisticated cities in the world, [New York] also has a great number of little neighborhoods. And recently, one filmmaker who comes from a small neighborhood, called »Little Italy«, made some of his own experiences there into a movie. His name is Martin Scorsese and he is the director of the motion picture, *Mean Streets*.«

It would be wrong to assume that the introduction of the auteur into the »Making of« discourse of the late 1960s came at the expense of the star. *Mia and Roman,* the featurette for *Rosemary's Baby* (USA, Paramount, 1967) focuses on Roman Polanski, the »young European director«, and his work with Mia Farrow, »already a popular personality without pushing for the limelight«. Clearly, the aim of the featurette is to broaden the audience base for what is basically a horror thriller: by introducing a young star and a young director-auteur to American audiences, and particularly to sophisticated urban audiences. In their choice of vocabulary, the closing lines of the voice-over commentary suggest as much: »Mia and Roman. They met to make a movie. From the fusing of these two distinct talents came the discovery of a superb actress and a philosophy of love and understanding.«[11]

While featurettes were still distributed to theaters in the 1960s, the demise of the short film program in the 1970s limited the possibilities for theatrical exhibition. The advent of cable television opened up new venues for featurettes. HBO uses the »Making of« format to promote upcoming Hollywood films, particularly those in which the company or its parent Time Warner has a financial interest. Just like film advertising in general, »Making of« increasingly target specific audience groups.[12] Recent featurettes focus on director, star or special effects technology according to the target audience. One »Making of« for *Godzilla* (USA, Columbia, Roland Emmerich, 1998) combines all the established registers. Posing as a news report presented by a noted TV personality (parasitical posing), it discusses the film's »star«, the computer generated monster lizard, in terms of acting and stardom (star discourse; Godzilla is introduced, tongue in cheek, as a Japanese star who now finally makes his Broadway debut) and in terms of special effects (technology), but also focuses on the producer/director duo of Roland Emmerich and Dean Devlin (auteur discourse).

Of particular interest in terms of audience address is the presentation of Emmerich and Devlin as popcorn-movie-auteurs. Yes, Devlin and Emmerich are artists, the featurette suggests, yes they have a vision, but, as Devlin says: »We make popcorn movies. We love popcorn movies. And if you love popcorn movies, chances are that some of that passion transpires to the audience.« In other words: Devlin and Emmerich are directors who are also fans. Two scenes early in the featurette show director Emmerich reacting to a video monitor. The monitor shows special effects scenes as they are being shot, the destruction of the Madison Square Garden building among them. Emmerich is clearly overwhelmed by what he sees, i.e. by the wizardry of his own team. »Wow!« he exclaims, as if he were already sitting in a theater and sharing an audience reaction. Janet Staiger argues that film advertising differs from conventional advertising in that it fails to directly represent the consumer and his experience of the product. (Staiger, 1990, 22–23) One explanation for this is that film advertising has no need of representing the consumer because it does not speak *to* the consumer and *about* the consumer but, supposedly, *from* the position of the consumer (it speaks the consumer, to phrase it in vaguely Lacanian terms). In a way, film advertising has always tried to emulate fan discourse, and talked about films the way enthusiastic audiences would. (Hediger, 2001, 225 f.) In other words: Film advertising, that part of the consumer interface of the film that the producer/distributor companies control, is a virtual fan discourse. As such, it strategically tries to anticipate and influence word-of-mouth, i.e. that part of the consumer interface that eludes the producer/distributor's control. If the »Making of« films of the 1960s and early 1970s absorbed the oppositional notion of the auteur as artist into the advertising discourse of the industry, the *Godzilla* »Making of« goes one step further and repositions the auteur as the speaking subject of the virtual fan discourse: the producer/director as fan. Ideally in the blockbuster era, the *Godzilla* featurette suggests, auteur, producers and consumer fans are all but the same.

Finally, the DVD has opened up new avenues for the distribution and established new modes of consumption for »Making of« films. Virtually every DVD now contains some kind of bonus material. »Making of« on DVDs still advertise the film, albeit only indirectly. Bonus materials have become a crucial feature for product differentiation. When DVDs were first introduced, the studios tried to market DVD editions like video editions. DVDs only contained the film and some trailers for upcoming releases. Soon, however, DVD buyers began to use the Internet to warn each other against DVDs that, according to their taste, did not contain enough bonus materials. In time, the consumers managed to enforce the same standards of edition for the DVD that were current for the Laser Disc, an earlier digital home movie format particularly appreciated by movie buffs and film collectors. Just like Laser Discs, DVDs now have to contain featurettes and other bonus material, including director's commentary, interviews and picture galleries.

Viewed on DVDs, »Making of« films primarily serve an informational purpose. It is to a discussion of this purpose that I would like to turn to now.

As I've tried to show, »Making of« films have been a crucial element of the culture of Hollywood film consumption even before the feature film emerged as the standard format of film distribution in the mid-1910s. Also, »Making ofs« are a weak and parasitical format: They adapt to the media environment in which they are shown both in style and theme. This adaptability, or parasitical quality of the »Making of« may be traced to the multiple purpose of these films: They advertise the film and supposedly educate and inform the audience. Given their parasitical nature, it is perhaps not surprising that »Making of« films have been critically discussed as pseudo- or fake-documentaries by scholars such as Lisa Kernan. I propose a reading of »Making of« films that focuses less on their supposedly manipulative nature. Rather, I propose that the pliability of the »Making of« is a playful way of adapting to the format's function in changing media environments. In order to better understand that function I would like to discuss the »Making of »as a sub-genre of the industrial film.

Research on industrial film has so far been limited to specific industries and geographic areas[13]. At this point, it is possible to discern four basic types of the industrial film, however: The research film, which is used in research and development; the training film, which is used to instruct workers and other personnel in the processes of producing and marketing a certain product; the product or advertising film, which explains the particular features of a given product to the prospective customer; and the image film, which serves to construct a public image for a particular company or for an entire industry. I will define an industry as a group of competing companies engaged in the production and marketing of the same product.

Most »Making of« films are image films according to this typology, even though they are also used to advertise individual films. The *MGM Studio Tour,* for instance, closely follows the conventions of the representation of factories and factory personnel in the publicity materials of other industrial enterprises. Much like conventional industrial films, the *MGM Studio Tour* features a shot of the staff of a particular department at the end of each segment. It has been one of the important achievements of the revisionist, or »new« film historians of the 1970s and 1980s to point out to what extent the Hollywood studio system was actually a modern industry organized according to Taylorist principles. Revisionist film history helped to debunk the myth of Hollywood as a glamorous movie colony dominated by scandal, intrigue and luxury that had formerly dominated film historical accounts of the American film industry. What an analysis of the peripheral discourses of film consumption, and particularly of the »Making of« helps us understand is that Hollywood never made a secret of the fact that it was actually a modern factory system. Quite to the contrary: as a film such as *MGM Studio Tour* shows, the studios actually went to great pains to actively promote such an image with the American public.[14]

The *MGM Studio Tour*, just like so many industrial films, was not particularly entertaining. The list of departments is comprehensive, and the ten minutes it takes to enumerate the full list are ten long minutes. The featurettes of the 1930s are more successful in that they entertain, and work as image films. Featurettes are »entertainments in themselves«, as one studio executive put it at the time. One type of featurette, produced in several versions by Warner Bros. in the late 1930s and the early 1940s, uses the musical format to convey the message that the studio is actually a modern factory. A singing and dancing guide leads a group of visitors through the production facilities of Warner Bros. and delivers her explanations in song.

Even in their more entertaining format, these featurettes may still be seen as industrial image films, however: they attempt to create a particular public perception of the business of movie making, as much as they promote individual films. This is particularly true for the early 1930s. In the early 1930s, the industry had come under serious economic pressure due to the depression, and under political pressure from the Legion of Decency, which prompted the enforcement of the production code, originally written in 1930 but largely ignored by the industry, in 1934. (Black, 1996) Film advertising had been subject to regulation since the early 1930s. (Haralovich, 1982, 1984) When the entire industry came under pressure, the featurette films were part of the studios' reaction. While the Legion of Decency depicted the film industry as a decadent purveyor of filth, the industry countered by representing itself as a healthy, clean, disciplined, in short: all American industry. The featurette was one of the privileged instruments of that image campaign. According to one featurette for Cecil B. DeMille's 1938 film *The Buccaneer*, Hollywood is a place where people work from 18 to 20 hours a day. In the opening scene we are shown how DeMille returns from a twelve-hour day at the studio only to spend the rest of the night watching foreign films in a relentless search for new faces and talents. Nor is such rhetoric specific to the 1930s. *A Trip Through the World's Greatest Motion Picture Studios* already focused on »the full day's work in a representative American cinema institution, from sunrise to sunset«, which implies long working hours.

Even today, »Making of« films never tire of stressing the fact that Hollywood is not only a place of fun, but first and foremost a place of very hard work. Stars appearing in featurettes will always point out how hard they worked on a particular film, but also how much fun they had making it. Stars will also tend to repeat the same kind of statement in their interviews with journalists, an indication of the degree to which »Making of« films are part of a fully integrated and coordinated consumer interface.

The »Making of« rhetoric of work as pleasure again links the genre to the industrial film. One early American industrial film from the tobacco industry in 1914 aimed to attract potential workers to a new cigarette factory in North Carolina by showing that working in a factory was actually better than working in agricultural jobs. As one trade paper reports: »It was an entertainment and the workers thereabouts flocked to be entertained. But they went away persuaded. And when the new factory opened, the films had brought about a complete reversal of local opinion on the factory question. Instead of the dreaded dearth of workers, by far more workers applied for jobs than were required and the new institution started off with flying colors, a success from the very start.«[15]

If one of the initial purposes of the industrial film was to persuade viewers that work and pleasure can go together – many industrial image films feature representations of leisure time facilities provided by the factory –, the »Making of« certainly continues in that tradition. »Making of« films, by reiterating that work and pleasure go together, also feed back into similar discourses in other films.

Industrial films from the steel industry or the car industry render the production processes in great detail. »Making of« films can be seen as industrial films also in that they satisfy the same kind of curiosity in the details of the production process. In the trade paper article quoted at the beginning, the trade paper journalist encourages exhibitors to book the Edison film about the making of films with the following argument: »There is too much mystery thrown about the making of a picture and anything that satisfies curiosity is worth [promoting].« »Making of« films, then, are useful because they satisfy a certain curiosity about the details of the production process. It would be interesting to write a cultural history of that particular affect, the curiosity about industrial production processes. But such a history of course exceeds the limits of this article. My guess would be that it is a specifically modern affect that can be traced by at least to some of the illustrations in Diderot's and D'Alembert's *Encyclopédie*, which explain how certain consumer goods are manufactured. Much like »Making of« films, these illustrations serve no immediate practical purpose. They are not instruction manual illustrations; rather they simply produce, and circulate, knowledge about production processes. They make production processes visible.

Contrary to what the Florida exhibitor cited above assumed, our interest in a product actually grows, rather than diminishes the more we know about how it was made. This goes for fictional films, too. With some exasperation, historian Daniel Boorstin noted in the early 1960s that our fascination with illusory worlds grows with every effort to debunk it. (Boorstin, 1987, 194) »Making of« films benefit from this psychological dynamic. They turn the film from a mere program for entertainment into an object of fascination by satisfying the specifically modern curiosity in the details of the industrial production process. Through this, »Making of« films intensify the involvement of the audience with the film in a Foucauldian sense: the aim to increase a particular film's share of the audience's attention, time and money.

Finally, with regard to the individual film, I would like to argue that »Making of« films contribute to what you might call a balance of immersion and irony in the audience's attitude toward films. »Making of« films are industrial image films in that they convey a certain image of the industry as a whole, and they are industrial advertising films in that they feed into a dynamic of curiosity. I would like to argue that one of the main goals of the Hollywood film industry is the creation of immersion experiences, through films, but increasingly more so also through a whole chain of entertainment opportunities, linking the film in a chain of programs with video games, theme park rides etc. As I've tried to argue in my discussion of the Edison film from 1912, the film industry has been producing irony about immersion along with immersion ever since it has been making narratively integrated fiction films. Irony and immersion may thus be seen as the two main facets of industrially produced entertainment programs, with the »Making of« films taking providing much of the irony: they provide knowledge about the construction of the fictional world that one can pretend not to possess when watching the film. Given the wide availability of »Making of« films on DVD, one could argue that irony has become, if anything, more important in the last decade: to the extent that industrially produced immersion experiences have become more perfect and more widely available, the need for irony provided through industrial films has increased, too.

Frederick Wasser
The transnationalization of Hollywood

Hollywood is booming, while the American film industry weakens. A transnational Hollywood is sucking all the oxygen out of its own national cinema as it does the same to the German film industry, the French film industry, the Brazilian film industry, the British film industry, and others. The American film industry once made movies in the United States with American money, for an American audience. It made movies and that was all it made. However, transnational Hollywood exists on a different, more fabled level altogether, making many things including movies, music records, television shows, theme park rides, videos for the world; without much competition, or viable alternatives. Perhaps Bollywood[1] and Hong Kong might aspire to the status of Hollywood, but their global popularity, industrial organizations and powers are secondary or tertiary, and only serve to highlight the transcendent power of Hollywood.

Hollywood may well be the international capital of culture, its location in the southwestern corner of the United States a mere accident. Indeed, is it located in that corner? Transnational Hollywood's financing and corporate structures are everywhere. It films everywhere, takes its ideas, its stars and its talent from everywhere, and it is shown everywhere.

Film has always been international, particularly in distribution. However, I distinguish this condition from the current phenomenon of a transnational Hollywood. In this chapter, I will trace the transition from international to transnational by proceeding on parallel lines between aesthetics and economics. All media industries are divided in their activities between production, distribution and exhibition. While exhibition must always be local, dedicated to a specific audience, production and distribution can be either local or global and it is within the matrix of production and distribution that the transition to transnational occurred.

History

In the first decade after the invention of motion picture technology, the French film industry developed more rapidly than the US companies, largely because of the international ambition of Pathé Frères. Its American branch became part of the Motion Picture Patent Company (MPPC), when Thomas Edison put this patent pool together in order to control the movie industry in 1908. However, the French quickly lost the comparative advantage. In general, the Europeans showed less willingness to exploit films than the Americans. They built less movie theaters per capita (*New York Clipper*, January 20, 1912, 12, and January 27, 1912, 5) and had fewer film showings per day (*New York Clipper*, February 3, 1912, 5). By 1915, World War One effectively curtailed the activities of French and other European film studios. The US has dominated ever since.

The Americans had learned to earn large profits from round the clock film showings, seven days a week. The demand was so great that new independents continually thwarted the MPPC's attempt to monopolize production, distribution and exhibition. Independents, who wished to get into the film industry despite the restrictions of the MPPC, initially built their revenues by distributing foreign films in the US. The MPPC was effectively broken up in 1915, bringing these independents to the fore. The new film distributors came from a different class and ethnic backgrounds than Edison and his associates. Either they were immigrants themselves or first generation Americans and almost all traced their roots to the Jews of Eastern and Central Europe. The development of the American film industry by immigrant business people is critical for understanding the international appeal of Hollywood.

Edison, himself, thought of cinema as little more than an amusement park novelty. His associates resisted the cost of putting together movies that were longer than ten minutes (one reeler).[2] They invested amounts that were appropriate to an amusement industry. We can hypothesize that they were too situated in the American hierarchy of culture to think that expensive lavish movies could capture the public imagination and make large returns. One of the successful immigrant film producers, William Fox, said that Edison and the MPPC »made up their minds that this [film] was not an industry or art but that it was a mechanical occupation and that it required no brains«. Fox went on to state that it was the foreign-born part of the American audience that enabled the early »motion picture business [people] ... to enlarge their scope until the industry ... had a right to expect the respect of the populace of the world«. (Kennedy, 303)

From the perspective of a century later, it appears that the immigrant producers such as Adolph Zukor, William Fox, Carl Laemmle, Louis Mayer, the Warner Brothers and others were not inhibited by a strong distinction between high and low culture. They did not doubt that the movies of various levels could pull every member of the public into the theater – high/low/middle class, male, female, educated, illiterate, young, and old. Some of this daring had to come from their own position moving from the class-ridden societies of »Mitteleuropa« to the more fluid mobility of the United States. They looked around without the blinkers of the Protestant skepticism about entertainment or aristocratic notions of the autonomy of cultural expression (see Gabler). Business and art were not separate categories to this cohort. They were willing to spend a lot of money to make a lot of money. Feature length movies were gaining in popularity after 1912. When the very expensive, two hour film, *Birth of a Nation*, earned record profits in 1915, the immigrants were ready to build an industry around such projects.[3]

Adolph Zukor took the lead in creating the vertically integrated Hollywood studio. Vertical integration refers to a company that owns production, distribution and exhibition divisions. Zukor wanted to hedge his bets by controlling all three levels of the film business. The money was in distribution and that was the original business of his company – Paramount. However, distribution had constantly to have new products in the pipeline and so Zukor turned the company's resources towards large and multiple productions. Then he worried what if there were not enough theaters willing to show his movies? Zukor lowered this risk by buying his own theaters. (Hampton, 239–242)

Fox, Laemmle, Loew and the Warner Brothers followed Zukor's lead in adopting the business model of vertical integration. They located their production divisions in Southern California. Here was a relatively newly developed part of the country with just the right population and industry base to support film production without crowding it as it had been in New York City. Here was a new industry for a new region, without the accumulated baggage of old culture. Here was a region that could become whatever the movie moguls wanted it to be.

International borrowings

Some of the staff surrounding the new movie moguls, in particular, Zukor and Carl Laemmle, the owner of Universal Studios, remembered the stories and myths of the old world and thought to re-package them for American audiences. This was natural since they were building European distribution arms after World War One. Universal recruited Erich von Stroheim and Paul Leni. (Schatz, 1988, 23, 88) Paramount imported Ernst Lubitsch, Josef von Sternberg, and Rouben Mamoulian (p. 75). These are only some of the more memorable European film directors that rose to prominence in Hollywood. The California film colony had actors, stars and craftspeople who had come directly from Europe and less often from other continents such as Latin America.

The golden age of 1920s filmmaking made Hollywood an international center. However, this early Hollywood was still very much the American film industry. Those who came here had to learn how to please the American audience. America was the largest and the most profitable single national audience in the world. The foreign audience was secondary. The standard business model was that an American film should reach profits through domestic showings, export was merely additional »gravy«. At one point Carl Laemmle proposed to abandon this business plan and to plan budgets based on global profits. He did not follow through on his proposal. (Wasser, 1995, 427)

The business model was also the aesthetic model. Hollywood formulated the cinematic styles it thought appropriate for Americans and made films accordingly. It borrowed elements from foreign film styles, which it would then modify for American viewers. For example, there was the Soviet montage that derived meaning from the juxtaposition of shots and generally avoided camera movements. Its subject matter generally derived from the ideological needs of the new Communist state. Its settings tended to be natural locations. Sergey Eisenstein scored an international hit with this style when his film *The Battleship Potemkin* was released in 1926. He subsequently came to Hollywood and was courted by the movie moguls to develop American movie projects. Yet, David O. Selznick, working for Paramount at this time, rejected Eisenstein's script for *An American Tragedy* in 1930, despite Paramount's substantial investment in its development. He wrote that it was »not the business of this organization [to offer] a most miserable two hours to millions of happy-minded young *Americans*«. (Schatz, 1988, 77–78) The Soviet approach could not be imported without adaptation and so Eisenstein went back to the USSR with a notable Mexican detour. Consequently, montage became a decorative item in Hollywood, not the heart of a film narrative style. Slavko Vorkapich became the resident Hollywood montage artist adding transitions and other second unit montage sequences to various American films. (Bordwell, 74)

German film Expressionism used bold camera movements and heavily designed sets, and had affinities with romantic painting and dramatic tragedies. Paramount, Universal and subsequently Warner Brothers hired many central European film directors and actors from this tradition. Yet, here again this continental style was re-shaped to fit the escapist formulas that the movie moguls assumed the American audience wanted. Conventional realism supplanted the theatricality of Expressionism. The film studios imposed »happy endings« in place of German grim plot resolutions. Evildoers were always punished in the US. Moral ambiguity was downplayed or eliminated.

The escapist formulas not only pleased the American audience, it pleased international audiences. Hollywood started to assume that what the US wanted, the world wanted. In this manner, the first phase of the relationship between Hollywood and the American film industry stabilized. Hollywood would make films for the American audience. Hollywood would export to the world. Hollywood would recruit foreign talent; particularly people who could work within a style that catered to the American viewers.

The international appeal of Hollywood led to some counter pressures by foreign countries. Many governments stipulated that local theaters had to reserve a large percentage of screen time to locally made films. In Great Britain, Hollywood financed local films in order to circumvent this kind of quota. Governments also tried to control Hollywood's content by objecting to heavy-handed stereotyping of different nationalities, such as Mexico's official protests of representations of Mexicans as bandits. The Americans often accommodated these protests particularly from countries that showed many American films. However, the American film industry was unmistakably American in corporate structure and creativity from the beginnings until the advent of the New Hollywood in the 1970s.

Why did American film achieve international success?

The historic durability of American film dominance in the international film trade has received several explanations. One is the ability of the American film industry to make big budget movies with high-»production« values. Kristin Thompson emphasizes the rapid improvement of American standards during the 1910s due to the imposition of an organized mode of production (88–89). The size of the domestic audience motivated this organization. On a more general level, Wildman and Siwek argue that in addition to the large domestic audience, the global familiarity of the English language gave the economic edge to American films. The affluence of the English-speaking audience justified large-scale American productions.

Hoskins and Mirus' model of cultural discount adds to Wildman and Siwek's language model. They write that »›cultural discount‹ means that a particular program is rooted in one culture, and thusly attractive in that environment, will have a diminished appeal elsewhere as viewers find it difficult to identify with the style, values and behavior patterns of the material in question«. (1990, 86) Foreign audiences do not apply much cultural discounting to American films and shows. Hoskins and Mirus explain that this is because producers have learned to avoid undue cultural specificity in their shows in order to attract a large and very diverse American audience (85). The lessons they learn with a multicultural American audience work with a global audience as well.

Audiences generally favor their own national media products (there are exceptions to this). However, American films benefit because they are always the preferred second choice for viewers in Europe, Latin America, Asia, Australia and Africa, because of their low cultural discounting. Thus, no other national film industry can hope for much of an export market. Even worse, the American audience applies heavy cultural discounting to foreign films and so most international films cannot earn much money in the US, which continues to be the largest national market.

Why are American films so free of cultural discounts? Olson tries to answer these questions by borrowing from current literary theories of polysemy and reader-response. These theories stress that there is no single meaning that is correct for any given text or movie. Meaning-making is strictly the activity of the reader or audience member. Olson applies this to movies albeit with the twist that some movies are more open than others to multiple audiences constructing multiple meanings. He labels these films as transparent (17–19). Transparency is important for export because audiences will be able to assimilate transparent movies into their own way of looking at the world and therefore will enjoy these films better. He goes on to argue that Hollywood films are more transparent than any national cinema. While there are American movies that are decidedly not transparent (Olson cites the obscure *Ulysses* [1967] as one example), these significantly are not Hollywood films.

The former explanations emphasize the content and look of American films. The political economic school of communications shifts the explanation to industrial monopoly power and government policy. Guback's study (1969) is still the most exhaustive one of US film trade practices, which shows how political power combines with economic and cultural dominance. He notes that the US government has lobbied extensively, throughout the century, on behalf of the US film industry in its various disputes with foreign governments over quotas and other restrictions. The US has also exempted film studios from anti-trust regulations in their oversea activities. This facilitated the creation of the MPEA export cartel distributors (cartels are illegal in domestic distribution). In foreign markets the combined power of the studios force exhibitors to lease weak films in order to get popular films (block booking). The US film studios have also been accused of using their economic clout to dump films into foreign markets at prices deliberately set lower than other competitors. This practice is more visible in leasing films for television showings.

From international to transnational

The political and economic analysis does tend to be tied more specifically to historical events than the cultural explanations. Therefore, political-economic analysts were the first to recognize the transnationalization of Hollywood in the 1980s. Transnationalization's first visible sign was a change in financing of Hollywood films. This began tangentially when Slavenberg Bank of the Netherlands (which was taken over by Crédit Lyonnais of France) started to guarantee pre-production loans to the Italian producer Dino DeLaurentiis who had relocated and was now working in the United States. The first film was *Serpico* (1973) which was released in the US by Paramount. Although DeLaurentiis had a partnership with Paramount, he retained his own global distribution network. (Wasser, 1995, 430–431)

This relationship expanded when Crédit Lyonnais helped to finance several foreign takeovers of small American companies, notably, Cannon Films which was bought by two Israeli cousins in 1979.[4] This was below anyone's radar screen until the advent of the video market became apparent. By 1984, video revenues were dramatically increasing Hollywood earnings and within another four years became the largest revenue contributor by surpassing the theatrical market. (Wasser, 2001) At the same time, under a combination of political and economic pressure, European television started to deregulate and expand the number of programming hours. The easiest way to fill those expanded hours was to buy American films and television shows that were already on the shelf. The big step forward in transnational ownership occurred in 1985, when The News Corporation (of Australia) bought Twentieth Century Fox. Sony (the Japanese electronic manufacturer) acquired Columbia Pictures in 1989. MCA/Universal was bought by Matsushita (Japan) in 1991, which sold it to Seagram (Canada) in 1995 and Vivendi (France) acquired it in 2001.

These takeovers, in addition to mergers within the US between Time-Life and Warner, Viacom and Paramount and Disney's purchase of ABC, were motivated by new market opportunities. These opportunities are often described as the new technologies of video, satellite and cable delivery systems but this misses the bigger point. New technologies in combination with television expansion and the growing affluence of a global audience inspired companies to pursue what Thomas Schatz (1997) calls »tight diversification«. This is a more descriptive term than the similar Wall Street neologism »synergy«. Tight diversification describes the strategy of marketing blockbuster films into several different media and formats in order to maximize profits. For example, *Jurassic Park* came out as a theatrical movie in 1993. It was sold heavily as a video cassette and for television showings. It earned huge sums from merchandising toys and as a video game and theme park ride. It has become more than a movie, it is a franchise. Schatz postulates that it is the »blockbuster« movie that serves as the »essential *ur* text within these media franchises«. (1997, 75) Only the economic power of huge transnational corporation can produce the blockbuster and effectively market it in so many markets.

The importance of the global audience for the tight diversification of the movie franchise cannot be overstated. The stakes have grown every higher since this strategy is premised on movies that routinely cost over fifty million dollars to produce. These budget levels started to appear in the aftermath of the mergers described above, and can only be supported by the global audience. Only the deep pockets of the transnational corporation can finance these blockbusters.

In the 1990s, various estimates held that foreign revenues contributed from 40 to 50 percent of Hollywood's film earnings. *Variety* colorfully used the headline: »Earth to H'wood: You Win« for an article estimating that US films earned 90 percent of the 1994 global box office.[5] *Variety* was probably overestimating US dominance but no one in the film industry was underestimating new Hollywood's dependence on global earnings. Global earnings had the effect of increasing volume to offset declining margins. Starting in 1988 and continuing through the 1990s, movies' profit margins decreased by 50 percent. (Vogel, 1994, 45) The high cost of making blockbusters and of marketing them dictated a new business plan. The movie had to earn well in all markets throughout the world in order to justify production. The old Hollywood formula had been overturned; budgets are now based on a transnational audience.

Foreign reaction

European policymakers, in particular the French, did not view Hollywood films as benign cultural gifts made by transnational companies. They still viewed them as a cultural invasion by the American film industry. (Miller, 75–76) Jack Lang, French Minister of Culture in the Mitterrand government of the 1980s, argued that quotas were needed to preserve Europe culture from Hollywood. He proposed that the European Union reserve 50 percent of its television time for European shows, in an attempt to limit the sale of American film and television shows. Although the European Union adapted Lang's proposal as part of his »Television sans Frontières« policy, 50 percent never really limited Hollywood sales which continued to expand. The United States Government took up Hollywood's anti-quota fight in the last round of GATT talks but ultimately agreed to disagree with its trading partners. Both the GATT and NAFTA agreements allow some modification of open trade for the sake of cultural protection. Canada and the European Union continue to have reservation policies that restrict Hollywood imports to a limited extent (see Grantham).

The victims of the transnational blockbuster hurricane were foreign film industries, which struggled with many challenges through the 1980s and 1990s. In 1994, *Screen Digest* reported that »Quite simply, indigenous film production in the EU is suffering some rather severe belt tightening. ... investment per production is tumbling in the film industries of many major film-producing EU countries-including Italy, France, UK and Spain (between 1991 and 1992) even without taking into account the effects of inflation.« (July 1994, 154) *Screen Digest* also reported that Latin America and Far East Asia film productions were declining in the early 1990s. (July 1994, 155–156) The situation has improved in the European Union since the early 1990s with film investments increasing by 133 percent from the low of 1993 to 2000. (*Screen Digest*, December 2001, 380) The situation is murkier in the rest of the world with Japan and Far East Asia reviving while India is stagnant and Latin America is still slipping. (December 2001, 377–380)

In Europe, discussions in the 1990s focused on emulating the global success of American films. The European Union launched several audio-visual initiatives to strengthen development, market research and distribution in addition to traditional support of production. Angus Finney comments that Hollywood only produces one out of every ten scripts it develops while Europeans typically produce one out of every five. This was quantitative evidence of the power a European film director has in contrast to Hollywood where the producer and distributor are all powerful. (Finney, 21)[6] Across the Atlantic, the editor of *Variety* lectured the Europeans on their declining clout through the 1980s, complaining that they were »retreating into a sort of medieval guild system«. (Bart, 5) It is the Hollywood producer who will discipline the writer and director to make the project more commercial in a variety of manners. Certainly one way to prepare a script for the international audience is to eliminate long bits of dialogue. A Belgian subtitler claimed that European films need 60% more subtitles to convey the meaning of the dialogue than Hollywood films (22). One German distributor conceded that »there is no understanding of script or narrative structure in Europe«. (5)

One answer has been to try to match the scale of Hollywood production and distribution. Since the English speaking audience is the richest global language group, there has been a concerted effort to shoot films, even with multinational casts and crews, in English. However, this was not a guarantee of success. *Meeting Venus* was one such conspicuous failure. (Ilott, 15) A further irony is that some European successes have led to increased profits for the American film industry. This occurs when Hollywood remakes European films such as *La Cage Aux Folles*, *La Femme Nikita* (1990), *Tres Hommes et un Couffin* (1986), *Insomnia* (1997) and many others.[7] Quite often, Hollywood earns far more with the remake than the original release.

This phenomenon points to the idea that a film can only reach a global audience if it is launched from a Hollywood division of a transnational conglomerate. In 1987, Disney took the very successful *Tres Hommes et un Couffin* and remade it as *Three Men and a Baby*. It transformed it into a blockbuster which grossed over a $250 million with at least $80 million coming from non-US markets. (Williams and Mørk, 8) This was a graphic illustration of sheer market power. Plot lines were merely tinkered with, not substantially changed. Shot for shot, the American remake *Point of No Return* (1993) barely differed from its French original, *La Femme Nikita*.

Martine Danan has documented how the marketing techniques the transnational film companies perfected in the US have now been imported to France and the rest of Europe, threatening to devastate national cinemas. Another immediate and enduring effect is the monopolization of the American market. The import of foreign films into America, dropped from a high point of 9.1 percent in 1973 to about one percent of the box office by the late 1980s. (*Daily Variety*, October 21, 1991, page unknown)

A new type of film?

Hollywood does not translate these film plots into an American idiom so much as it reformats them as transnational films. This involves a tremendous investment in the production values (in the case of *Three Men* using stars such as Tom Selleck and Ted Danson) and marketing across national and media borders. Thus we have transnational companies distributing movie »franchises« across media to transnational audiences.

Can we move from this industrial analysis of transnational films to theorize about actual content of the movies? We have already touched on Hoskins and Mirus' conclusion that Hollywood films have low-culture discounts and Olson's working through the notion of transparency. Their theorizing becomes a basis for thinking about transnational film, although they do not distinguish between films of the old American film industry and the new blockbusters. To a large degree, the new transnational film merely took elements of the older formulas that exported well (such as the glamour of the American material life-style) and emphasized them. However, these changes of emphasis have resulted in changes of film aesthetic values.

The old Hollywood had a hierarchy of genres that matched audiences with production budgets and marketing expenses. Action films such as westerns and science fictions generally received low budgets and were marketed on a smaller scale to secondary movie houses. These genres developed their own standards and one would not judge the visual pleasures of a western by the standards of a musical. These genres also had their own cycle of birth and death. Some such as westerns and musicals actually ran their course and are no longer viable, except for very deliberate revivals. This system started breaking up in the 1950s.

Through the 1950s and 1960s, the import of foreign films into the US rose, peaking in the early 1970s. A generation of American filmmakers was exposed to the more fluid notion of genre blending prevalent in the European films. Thrillers were crossed with social commentary, romance with road movies, period pieces with serious philosophical meditations. Personal filmmaking attracted mainstream audiences.

In this atmosphere, Steven Spielberg and George Lucas decided to set their ambitions and more significantly their budgets higher for the thriller *Jaws* (1975) and the science fiction *Star Wars* (1977) respectively (Biskind). They gave what was considered »B« level material, »A« level budgets. The resulting visual feast and higher production values worked. These two films earned unprecedented sums of money, not only in the theater but also in subsequent franchise markets of merchandising, video et alia. They were also globally popular. They became the prototype for the transnational blockbuster. But, they lost the original impulse behind the more personal filmmaking of the foreign films. Their techniques produced visceral reactions in the global audience and shortly changed the ability of any specific audience to engage in emotional reflection (see chapter one in Geuens for a discussion of this switch). Their influence has been held responsible for a shift towards action films, a corresponding diminution of women roles, and a reliance on high-concept[8] stories that can translate into foreign sales. The hierarchy of genre has largely disappeared in the era of the transnational film.

Genre blending and high budgets for low genre worked well for bringing in the audience but has it worked as well for the cultural function of film? Transnationalization is a drawback for American filmmaking. Up to now, criticism of Hollywood's dominance has centered on charges of cultural imperialism. This criticism from both leftist populists and cultural elitists bemoans the loss of local and national cinemas and a resulting »imposition« of American values. However, the imperialism critique assumes a certain functionalism, that these films are part of a coherent culture.

The critique tends to ignore the impact that Hollywood is having on its own so-called home – American culture. American popular culture under the weight of the transnational film has largely turned its back on portraying or engaging national dilemmas.

After all, films help us make sense of ourselves by presenting an audio/visual structure shaped by the human imagination. In order to do this film has to address individual viewers as members of a community and of a culture. The narrative ought to refer to the concrete historical situation of the community. This situationalism gives the narrative a connection with the human experience that makes it rich even to those outside the specific situation. The unsituated narrative is more of a pastime; a diversion than an expression. Blockbuster films have low context, little sense of actual communities. In other words, if the community/culture that the film addresses is literally global, then the film has precious little to offer us to make sense of ourselves. A truly egregious example of this kind of filmmaking is *Independence Day* (1996), actually directed by a German for Twentieth Century Fox, an American studio owned by The News Corporation, which is essentially an Australian media conglomerate. The directors had so little sense of context that they absent-mindedly portrayed an outer space attack on the world as strictly a problem with only an American solution. Given this lack of realistic context, we can only imagine audiences enjoying the film because it was a familiar pastiche of special effects rather than a narrative engagement. *Independence Day* is just one of the vast majority of current blockbusters that operate on this transnational level.

In trying to summarize a trend that was apparent even in the 1980s, Timothy Corrigan describes the impossibility of maintaining aesthetic coherency when designing films for all. The blockbuster becomes »an advertisement of promises it usually cannot possibly keep; it must create an audience that does not in fact exist«. (12) Naturally, the film that becomes an »advertisement« for a diverting pastiche of familiarity is easily translated into other media markets such as television, video, merchandising, music and more. There are other suggestions that support Corrigan's characterization. For instance, the movie is treated increasingly as a commodity in mainstream newspapers and magazines. This may be contrasted with a previous principle of treating the movie as entertainment either on the level of pastime or art form. But now the box office returns as gathered by Entertainment Data, a division of ACNielsen, are reported in the *New York Times*. (Wasser, 2001, 168) The box office figures and expectations are often speculated on in the movie review columns. The media coverage has bought into the premise that movies are an advertisement by using these figures to validate the status of the movie. *Entertainment Weekly* is a magazine that gained popularity during the 1990s and owned by the transnational media conglomerate AOL-Time Warner. It has reduced movie reviews to a series of product reports complete with grades and has influenced similar reduction of movie reviews in other outlets.

Transnational Hollywood has created the transnational film that permeates every national site of filmmaking. Perhaps the operative part of the story related above about Sergey Eisenstein is that after Selznick's rejection, he eventually went back home and worked again within the Soviet film industry, evolving a Soviet film style.[9] Now the international filmmaker goes home only to find the same demands for the transnational style that are prevalent in Hollywood. Many filmmakers go back and forth from Los Angeles to their own countries making films in both places. Their work back home often fits the transnational style as well as their Hollywood work. This is the charge leveled against the currently popular young Mexican filmmakers, Alfonso Cuaron (*Y Tu Mama Tambien,* 2001) and Alejandro Gonzalez Inarritu (*Amores Perros*, 2000). Their films are made with private money in a manner to appeal to a younger international audience. It is reported that Mexican critics feel that the content and style of the films owe more to Hollywood than to the rich legacy of Mexican film culture. They cite the American-styled adolescent leeringly approach to sexuality and the political indifference of the two man-boys characters, who appeared to be modeled after American slackers. Cuaron counters that this is just the outraged reaction of an over-the-hill generation of leftist filmmakers (Brooks).

Even if we accept the part of the critique that is generational, the remaining indisputable conclusion is that the transnationalization of Hollywood contributes to a global monoculture. This is part of a general shift in world life-styles and to an extent is unavoidable. However, the power of film is such that it can resist a monoculture. Clever producers and skillful directors make movies that are for specific audiences and exist within specific cultures. The transnational film may fade, if not from the marketplace, at least, from the position of influence over filmmaking styles. It is up to audiences to embrace the culturally specific film. It is up to filmmakers to resist being measured by a global box office. It is up to Hollywood to rediscover the American audience.

Claudia Liebrand
Negotiations of genre and gender in contemporary Hollywood film

Whenever the beautiful, seductive and mysterious heroine first appears in classic film noir (or in the 1980s and 1990s neo noir), the male protagonist – most of the time working as a »private eye«, and frequently on behalf of that very same beauty – experiences the constellation of an enigmatic configuration, the solution to which he will try to find for the rest of the film. As is typical of the genre, a film noir's closing figure demands the disclosure of the secret surrounding the femme fatale, a woman who is both fascinating and dangerous for the detective hero: the protagonist becomes Oedipus solving the riddle of the Sphinx. Thus, the film noir genre reverts to cultural gender narratives and gender stagings – and these, in turn, are employed as central codes and conventions which allow the genre classification as a film noir.[1] In this respect, one can but agree with the findings of Susan Hayward: »Generally speaking, in the film noir the woman is central to the intrigue and it is therefore she who becomes the object of the male's investigation. But ... it is less her role in the intrigue that is under investigation, much more her sexuality because it is that which threatens the male quest for resolution. The ideological contradiction she opens up by being a strong, active, sexually expressive female must be closed off, contained. That is the diegetic trajectory and visual strategy of film noir.«[2]

The gender-related topics concerning the mysterious and dangerous (even sexually dangerous) woman who has to be domesticated and whose secret has to be fathomed, permit the genre classification of these movies in a much more precise manner than, say, the stylistic device of *chiaroscuro* (a characteristic of many expressionistic German silent films as well) does. This claim made with regard to film noir can be extended to all genres: gender configurations are modeled by genres; and gender configurations constitute genres. These gender configurations determine costumes, props, shots, montage procedures, and filmic spaces; another example for this is the western genre. Whenever the hero rides off into the prairie in a conventional western, this action is charged with gender-specific connotations. This active and mobile, traditionally male hero performs an action that may be conceptualized as penetration – he invades a space semanticized as female that is perilous, mysterious, uncanny, and thus represents that dark, unexplored continent which Freud, among others, equated with femininity. The landscape acts as a substitute for a woman's body. This narrative model works without having to depend on the sex of the heroic character – nevertheless, the hero (a generically masculine term) is male more often than female. Teresa de Lauretis has hinted at such gender-topographical connections in an even more precise manner than other theorists (who have shed light upon the interface between narrative structures and gender-specific attributions – Sigrid Weigel, Annette Pelz, Barbara Schaff, to name but a few). Every narrative model, she claims, quotes the difference between the sexes and negotiates it, continues it. These continuations are complex, in no way simple, but characterized by metonymies, chiasmi, which repeatedly stage gender oppositions and negotiate, re-import, assert and/or thwart them. Thus, the western – or the film noir – and other genres may be described as negotiations of gender configurations. As a result, theories of genre and of gender must be connected and brought into productive correlations.

A look at the etymology of the words »genre« and »gender« shows that these concepts are strongly interlinked. Both »genre« and »gender« derive from the Latin term »genus« (species, sex). The shared word root already shows that the concepts of genre and gender cannot be understood as static, unrelated »natural forms« as which they were described by researchers until the 1990s – particularly by film researchers. A methodical desideratum follows from this: ways of research into genre and gender that do not ahistorically freeze their subject matters but that comprehend them as dynamic and unstable must complement each other on a theoretical level and, in this way, profit from one another. After all, the cultural concepts of genre and gender meet in a variety of places, but also thwart and undermine each other – and they must be described in all their complexity. Genres are not »archetypes«, they never materialize in »pure« form: instead, we must take into account the constitutive historicity of genres on the one hand, and their constitutive hybridity on the other. Genres change within and along with time and do not appear as transhistorical dimensions.

Time and again, exponents of different branches of film studies have stated this: that genres change within time and along with it (and that they can »vanish« as well). Christian Metz, for example, has developed a model which assumes a first, »classic« stage. According to Metz, this first, »classic« stage is followed by a stage, in which these classics parody themselves – the game with genre conventions. The last stage is determined by the genre's self-reflectiveness (or, more

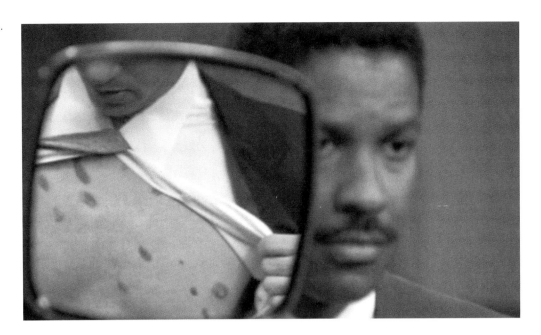

1. *Philadelphia*, directed by Jonathan Demme, 1993.

precisely, first by »contestation« [straining the conventions], then by »deconstruction« [self-cri-
tiquing the conventions])[3]. Metz's views can be transferred to the western cum grano salis[4], but
not all genres can be viewed in this manner without difficulty. One counter-example may suffice:
even around the time of a change in medium, from short to long »silent film«, from the »cinema of
attractions«[5] to comedies with narrative structure, American comedies utilized genre parody as a
means of dealing with the longer format without having to sacrifice the tried and tested methods
of generating comic effects used by slapstick comedies (cf. Buster Keaton's genre parodies). It
should be noted, therefore, that the historical processes of change within genres cannot be described with the help of a terminology infected with »organological« and »teleological« concepts:
genres, after all, are not »naturally grown« forms.

As a result of the constitutive historicity inherent to genres, they cannot be talked about in
general; the specific historic place and the specific composition of a genre film must always be
considered. Consequently, genre conventions are much more fluid than critics of genre films
would generally have it. As Steve Neale has stated: »The repertoire of generic conventions ... is
always *in* play rather than simply being *re*-played.«[6] Every film refers to genre conventions that
have formed throughout a prolonged cultural process – but at the same time, it rewrites, modifies
and constructs them. A genre (often assumed to antecede the film) is therefore always a result of
the films in which it is depicted. This paradox – that films are produced to serve the allegedly antecedent conventions of a genre, which they, in fact, keep reproducing / reconstructing through
their specific contributions – remains a constituting prerequisite for the following thoughts concerning the reciprocity in the relationship between gender and genre.

Genres are concretized in films, and the films shape and modify these genres – stage them.
This is why the relationship between a single film and a genre is a complicated one. Another reason for this complexity is that genre films which stage genres never just operate with the conventions of a single genre (of the action film, the melodrama etc.) – they always employ a (smaller or
larger) bundle of patterns from several genres. This shows that it is not genres that precede the
hybridization of genres; it is rather the genre hybrid that is »antecedent«, and the fixation of single
genres takes for granted a simplifying reading of a constellation that transgresses single genres
whenever it occurs. These findings already apply to early cinema, as Steve Neale has convincingly shown.[7] The constitutive hybridity of genres does not only apply to »Postmodern« films from
the 1980s onwards – however, contemporary mainstream films, especially Hollywood's big budget productions, permit a close look at genre negotiations and genre hybridizations. To describe
these hybridizations, one must speak of genre films and genres; however, these are not conceptualized as being antecedent to the films (which always process genre hybridization).

I will demonstrate the extent to which the gender negotiations of films can be put into a productive relationship with their genre negotiations using two examples: Jonathan Demme's *Philadelphia*, released in 1993[8], and Alejandro Amenábar's *The Others*[9], released in 2001. *Philadelphia*,
the first mainstream film to touch upon the difficult topic of Aids (which contributed to its protagonist, »all-American darling« Tom Hanks, taking home his first Academy Award),[10] tells the story of

successful (homosexual) lawyer Andrew Beckett, who is laid off by his law firm under a pretext after his bosses receive word of his infection with HIV. Supported by homophobic lawyer Joe Miller (Denzel Washington), he sues his former employers for discrimination (a »wrongful dismissal suit«). *Philadelphia* – this brief plot summary already points to that – attempts to blend the genres of melodrama and courtroom drama. In this context, the following points are of particular interest: firstly, which narrative effects are released by the adoption of specific genre traditions and their simultaneous re-writing; and secondly, which kinds of gender and genre negotiations turn a woman's film – as which melodrama is often conceived – into a gay's film. My thesis is that *Philadelphia* negotiates the courtroom drama/melodrama hybrid as a confrontation of different melodramatic forms: as a crossover of the »melodrama of passion« and the »melodrama of action«. I refer to these concepts as discussed by Michael Walker and Steve Neale. As early as 1982, Walker suggested – and Neale refers back to this suggestion – a move away from the exclusive conception of melodramas as »weepies« and the differentiation between the »masculine semantics« of action melodramas (swashbuckling films, war stories, westerns, crime thrillers, adventure stories) and the primarily »female semantics« of »melodramas of passion, in which the concern is not with the external dynamic of action but with the internal traumas of passion«.[11]

As a melodrama, it could be claimed in continuation of Walker's arguments, *Philadelphia* rewrites the »female« melodrama to create a male, or rather gay, »melodrama of passion«. From this perspective, the »gay's film« – named thus for lack of a better term – succeeds the »woman's film«. One has to concede, however, that the term »gay's film« is at least as problematic as the label »woman's film«. Does the term entail a film by gays for gays, a film about gays, a film dealing with topics relevant for gays? The woman's film theorists, too, have their problems deciding on precisely what that label *denotes*: a film for women, a film with »women's topics«, etc. In any case, the woman's film is centered – as Jeanine Basinger attempts to define it – by a woman: »A woman's film is a film that places at the center of its universe a female who is trying to deal with emotional, social, and psychological problems that are specially connected to the fact that she is a woman.«[12] In contrast to this, Jonathan Demme places at the center of its (the film's) universe a homosexual who is trying to deal with emotional, social, and psychological problems that are specially connected to the fact that he is a homosexual.

This substitution of »homosexual« for »woman« follows a cultural dictate in so far as gay men – as the cliché would have it – are seen as effeminate anyway. To position a homosexual protagonist at the »heart of the melodrama« is nevertheless remarkable, since in Hollywood cinema, gay men are negotiated as the most problematic type of men; in this respect, he makes for an »ideal« melodramatic hero: »The standard account ... has not just associated melodrama with women and femininity, it has also seen melodrama as one of the few generic areas in Hollywood in which masculinity in general, and ›virile‹ masculinity in particular, has been consistently qualified, questioned, impaired or castrated – unable to realize or express itself in action.«[13]

Still, the genre negotiations undertaken by *Philadelphia* cannot yet be sufficiently described by the argumentative figure that the displacement of the homosexual protagonist Beckett from a position of active and sovereign masculinity to one of passive, suffering victimhood transposes the melodrama as woman's film into a gay male melo. After all, the film's story, giving an account of Beckett's suffering and dying, is completed by the story of his lawyer, who, on behalf of the severely ill and increasingly devastated Beckett, does battle with the »system«, the societal and legal order (something that is reflected in the film's tag line: »No one would take on his case ... until one man was willing to take on the system«). Beckett's suffering is »balanced out« by Joe Miller's actions as a lawyer, his calculated, suspenseful, gimmicky and surprise-laden performances in court. The courtroom drama – and *Philadelphia* undoubtedly stands within this tradition (as well as within the tradition of melodrama) – can be grouped among action melodramas and their »masculine semantics«, as Walker defines them[14] (although it might not be one of the genre's most eminent representatives). In Demme's film, we witness Beckett's physical decay, his disappearance; we experience his »melodrama of passion«, which is completed *and* foiled by a »melodrama of action« (one that, in this case, relies on thrill and suspense), the protagonist of which is Joe Miller: as avenger of the degraded it is he who demonstrates the capacity to act and who confidently manages to attain more and more leeway as the film progresses. In this respect, *Philadelphia* stages an almost uncanny hybridization of genres that are encoded as »male« and »female«; the film superimposes a »melodrama of action« onto a »melodrama of passion«. Additionally, it transforms the »melodrama of passion«, which traditionally tends to be a »melodrama of women«, into a »melodrama of males« – or, to be more precise, a »melodrama of queer, of homosexual males«. *Philadelphia* thus negotiates the melodrama problem from two different perspectives. One the one hand, the film establishes a constellation in which we witness a »melodrama of action« (at least if we focus on Joe Miller as protagonist who enters into agonal altercations with both opposing lawyers and the prejudices of society) *or* in which we are dealing with a »melodrama of passion« (which stages the ordeal of Andrew Beckett):[15] the melodrama is presented to us as a complicated and hybrid twin configuration. On the other hand, *Philadelphia* rewrites the »melodrama of passion« to the extent that it transforms its heroine into a gay hero.

During the course of the movie, Andrew Beckett is transformed from a smart lawyer to a mute and (half) blind creature. This »melodrama's« gay protagonist thus experiences what Mary Ann Doane has outlined in her conceptualization of the woman's film: Doane describes how the danger posed by the seductive female protagonist is defused by the medical (or judicial) gaze of a male character. In the woman's film, the erotic gaze (of the woman) becomes the medical gaze (of the man): »In the films which mobilize a medical discourse, where blindness and muteness are habitually attributed to the woman, she can only passively give witness as the signs of her own body are transformed by the purportedly desexualized medical gaze, the ›speaking eye‹, into elements of discourse. The dominance of the bed in the mise-en-scène of these films is the explicit mark of the displacement / replacement of sexuality by illness.[16]

Again, the following applies: once »woman« is replaced by »homosexual«, Doane's analysis describes precisely the mechanisms that constitute *Philadelphia*. The suffering creature Beckett is subjected to the camera's and the viewer's look; the extent to which this happens is demonstrated by a key scene during the trial, in which Miller asks his client to expose the upper part of his body, so that the jury might get a look at Beckett's lesions. Beckett undresses in an excruciatingly slow manner (while the entire courtroom stares at him) and displays his upper body, stained and disfigured by Kaposi's sarcomas. One interesting aspect of this scene is the way it quotes a cultural configuration that is highly gender-specific: the striptease – that performance in which a woman undresses while men watch her do so.[17] The stripper takes off her clothes slowly in order to induce suspense and desire, and likewise, Beckett opens his shirt agonizingly slowly: His illness has weakened him so greatly that every movement, to him, is tantamount to martyrdom. When he finally manages to expose his upper body, his lawyer Miller, holding up a mirror in front of him, enables Beckett to look at his own disease-ridden body; in this, he is joined by the mortified courtroom. The cultural configuration quoted here – the striptease and its celebration and staging of eroticism – has been re-written as an autopsy of the moribund. And, of course, this gruesome, literal striptease in court drastically stages the mechanisms of a process the whole film deals with: »defoliation«, the exposure and disclosure of truth – a truth that is related to the »marked« body of Andrew Beckett (superficially marked by lesions, but actually marked by his homosexuality). A mirror is held up to the terminally ill protagonist, he is forced to perceive himself as »stained«. Beckett looks into the mirror, we watch him while he does so (and the camera records that which Beckett sees – the image reflected in the mirror). Additionally, we watch Joe Miller and the courtroom audience observing Beckett's look into the mirror, witnessing a classic formation of subject constitution: the person searching for reflection in this context will not experience the jubilatory moment of fusion with the mirror image as Lacan described it,[18] but must comprehend himself as damaged, as marked by stigmata: here, the film serves the topos of the mirror as medium of truth.

The film makes it extremely obvious that this »truth« has something to do with sexuality, that Beckett's deviant sexuality is both, the topic centering the trial *and* its obscene reverse[19]. This deviant sexuality is presented as dangerous because it is »infectious«. It appears that not just Aids, but homosexuality, too (which the film fantasizes to be a synonym for the lethal disease) is something that infects and infiltrates: homosexuals are invaders. They invade – as Wheeler, Beckett's boss at the law firm, puts it – the »men's rooms«.[20] The dangerous thing about homosexuals is that one cannot *tell* that they are homosexual. If they do not indicate their deviancy themselves, they remain unrecognized, they can mask their sexual orientation. The indignation displayed by the Wyant, Wheeler, Hellerman, Tetlow and Brown law office is based at least as much on the fact that one of their own lawyers is a homosexual and has contracted Aids as it is on Beckett's successful »cover-up«. Again and again, the pleadings of the female lawyer[21] representing the law office aim at the deception, the masquerade, the pretence of which Beckett is allegedly guilty.[22] The central accusation brought forward against him is this: »It was Andrew Beckett who lied, going to great efforts to conceal his disease from his employers. ... He was successful in his duplicity.« Beckett is accused of his successful »passing« – this, in fact, seems to infuriate his former colleagues and incite their aggression more than anything else.[23] He is accused of successfully pretending to be heterosexual and healthy, while actually being homosexual and suffering from Aids.

This motif of »passing« for something else, a topic which, in recent years, has been discussed within cultural studies primarily with regard to gender, but also with regard to race,[24] establishes a connection between the melodrama *Philadelphia* and one of the »model melos« of the 1950s – one that has been discussed at length in academic and theoretical debates concerning the cinematic melodrama: Douglas Sirk's *Imitation of Life*.[25] One of the stories told, amongst others, in Sirk's 1959 film is that of the young girl Mary Jane, who, despite being an African-American, is so light-skinned that she »passes« for white. In an interview with Jon Halliday, Sirk made the following comments on the novel his film is based on: »The only interesting thing is that strand of the action which touches upon the Negro angle: The young black woman who tries to get away from her real circumstances, who is prepared to sacrifice the relationships with her friends and with her family for acceptance in society, and who tries to disappear in the world of Vaudeville, where everything is geared towards imitation. The imitation of life is not real life. ... The young woman (Susan Kohner) chooses an imitation of life instead of her own black identity. The film is a piece of social criticism. You can't run away from what you are. … From that, I wanted to make a movie about consciousness for society – not just about white consciousness, but also about black consciousness. Both the whites and the blacks live imitated lives.«[26]

As is often the case, the director is not the best interpreter of his own work: Sirk's *Imitation of Life* amply demonstrates that which he denies – namely that »racial identities« are based on performance; that one *can*, in fact, run away from that which one allegedly »is«; that the line between life and its »imitation« is one that *cannot* be drawn. Important in this context, however, is the fact that Sirk perceives the »passing« configuration to be the energetic center of the film. *Imitation of Life* does not applaud the female protagonist's masquerade as a confident game with societal requirements, but as breaching the rules of societal borders – an act that has to be avenged and punished. It is no coincidence that *Imitation of Life*, a film centered around the topic of »passing«, is today considered a *paradigmatic* melodrama – a genre which is constituted by the very moment of transgression, the breach of the societal order and the symbolic systems of representation. *Philadelphia* follows classic melodrama by incorporating this notion of transgression, but relocates the »passing« motif from the field of race to the field of homosexuality. However, Demme's film, too, connects the question of sexual orientation – both subtly and less subtly – to problems concerning race. After all, it is a black lawyer who turns out to be the only one willing to fight the »manichaean« (and therefore melodramatic)[27] fight for »good« Andrew Beckett (who is being discriminated against by the »evil« law office).

On the historical level, *Philadelphia* presents Beckett's trial as the continuation of the African-American Civil Rights Movement. Miller decides to take over Beckett's case after witnessing a certain incident in the library: An employee wants to move Beckett – by now heavily marked by his illness – to a separate room. Together, both lawyers read out a passage from a legal text:

Miller: »The Federal Vocational Rehabilitation Act of 1973 prohibits discrimination against otherwise qualified handicapped persons who are able to perform the duties required by their employment. Although the ruling did not address the specific issue of HIV and AIDS discrimination ... «

Beckett: »... subsequent decisions have held that AIDS is protected as a handicap under law, not only because of the physical limitations it imposes, but because the prejudice surrounding AIDS exacts a social death which precedes ... which precedes the actual, physical one.«

Miller: »This is the essence of discrimination: formulating opinions about others not based on their individual merits but, rather, on their membership in a group with assumed characteristics.«

Andrew's mother, too, establishes a link between her son's fight and that of the black Civil Rights Movement: »I didn't raise my kids to sit in the back of the bus«, she says, and thus constructs an analogy between her son's battle against discrimination and the Montgomery Bus Boycott of 1955.[28] Andrew himself appears to become increasingly »ethnically« marked as a result of his illness. To hide his sarcomas, he takes refuge in dark foundation make-up: »You don't think this color is just a little too orange for me?«, Andrew asks the friend who helps him with the application of the make-up. She merely comments: »It's Tahitian Bronze and it works best on these lesions.«[29] This instance of cosmetic expertise is interesting, because it establishes a connection between race and homosexuality; the homosexual is presented as »racially marked«. The film provides numerous other instances of this, but I shall cut short my reading of *Philadelphia* at this point by offering the following roundup: It can be claimed that the film *re-writes* the conventions of the »melodrama of passion« by exchanging the genre's female protagonist for a gay protagonist – nevertheless delivering a precise, albeit gender-reversed, imitation of the mechanisms of the woman's film. Furthermore, *Philadelphia* »contaminates« the passion melo with a »melodrama of action« – another playing field for configurations of race and gender.

In order to demonstrate that negotiations of genre and gender – described here with regard to *Philadelphia* – are not constitutive of melodramatic genres only, I shall now take a brief, concluding look at a horror movie – namely *The Others*. In Amenábar's film, Grace (Nicole Kidman) and her children live in a house on a Channel Island shortly after the end of the Second World War; ghosts appear, and Grace has to defend her home and her children against them. In her influential 1992 monograph *Men, Women and Chain Saws. Gender in the Modern Horror Film*,[30] Carol J. Clover has argued that male and female viewers of horror films (and *The Others* is a horror film, albeit a quiet one) tend to identify with the victim rather than with the perpetrator. Clover (as Linda Ruth Williams has summed up in *Sight and Sound*) »argues that most horror films are obsessed with feminism, playing out plots which climax with an image of (masculinized) female power and offering visual pleasures which are organized not around a mastering gaze, but around a more radical ›victim-identified‹ look«.[31] The horror film viewer, Clover claims, is not a sadist, but identifies with the victim, who, at the end of the film, aggressively confronts her (or his) monstrous »enemy«. Since »victims« in a horror movie are predominantly female, the viewer, at the end of the film and as its climax, witnesses a story of female self-empowerment: The »Final Girl« successfully resists the threat – usually one with masculine connotations. Clover, it seems, reads the horror film genre as one that dismantles gender stereotypes by delegating the position and the attributes of the hero to a – mostly young – woman. Clover's readings decidedly focus on low-culture or splatter movies, in which blood and brains are squirted about. Therefore, the question arises whether her findings may be transferred to a film like *The Others*, which does entirely without gory effects, and which decidedly refers back to patterns of »high culture« (such as James' *Turn of the Screw*).[32] Differences between Clover's Final Girl and Grace can certainly be made out: The Final Girl is, indeed, usually a very young woman (not a young mother), and the threat this Final Girl (who, if one were to look for genre-historical antecedents, can be traced back to the late 18th-century's Gothic novel heroine) is exposed to usually emanates from a psychopathic human monster (as such, it is less »diffuse« than the threat looming over Grace). And yet: the showdown in *The Others* presents Grace as a woman who successfully and energetically holds her own against the dead servants and the invaders of the house threatening her. However, those who have seen the movie know that Grace is not just a helpless, defenseless victim who finally confronts her enemies – she is also a perpetrator. The murderer, the murderers are not after her; she herself is the murderer. Compared to the horror films that Clover argues with, we are faced here with a complication of structure that necessitates the reference to another gender-based theory of the horror film, namely Barbara Creed's *The Monstrous Feminine. Film, Feminism, Psychoanalysis* from 1993.[33] Creed argues that horror films toy with male fears of women as »the monstrous«. Men, she claims, perceive the female capacity to »reproduce«, to be mothers, as »monstrous«. Creed then identifies seven »varieties« of female monstrosity: the archaic mother, the monstrous womb, the vampire, the witch, the possessed monster, the deadly femme fatale, and the castrating mother. Women threaten men, Creed claims, not because, as Freud stated, they are perceived by them as castrated beings; rather, male anxieties are dominated by the *castrating* woman. Creed's conception of the horror genre is of interest with regard to *The Others*, because it features a dimension that is not conceptualized in Clover's Final-Girl model: Grace, after all, is not just an unfortunate victim; she, as a (castrating) mother (who does not merely castrate her children, but kills them), also embodies the horror she believes she is fighting. As a murdering mother, Grace recalls Creed's »archaic« mother. Her red hair prove her to be a witch, her dread of light marks her – and her children – as vampiric. Grace not only feels threatened, she poses a threat. The intricate game the film plays with its audience pivots around the fact that this audience, along with Grace, becomes frightened of the »others«– without recognizing that Grace herself (and not just her somewhat weird educational methods) is frightening. In his film, Amenábar has superimposed two filmic models. As in Clover's concept of the Final Girl, the female protagonist fights against a threat. Different to Clover's model this threat has no »male connotations« – the threat is Grace herself. In this regard*, The Others* can be related to Creed's alliance of monstrosity and femininity as staged by horror films. The staging of gender in *The Others* forces the superimposure and the hybridization of two genre theories. Grace's specific gender performance produces a re-writing of the horror genre – and vice versa. Genres may be described as negotiations of gender configurations, and gender as negotiations of genre configurations.

It should have become clear that with every film (*Philadelphia* and *The Others* are examples meant to illustrate this) both gender and genre are submitted to a process that creates them anew. Semantic connotations of gender go hand in hand with genre conventions; the re-writing of genre conventions adds movement to gender constellations.

Robert Blanchet
Deep impact. Emotion and performativity in contemporary blockbuster cinema

Some cinemagoers probably felt a little cheated when they found out that the most spectacular scene from the trailer to *Twister* (Jan de Bont, 1996) was actually not included in the film. Until then of course the surprising shot with the blown-off tire hurtling directly towards the camera had already achieved its devastating impact. In the screening where I saw the trailer for the first time seven years ago, it hit the audience almost literally like a bomb.

In its original sense the term blockbuster meant precisely this: in the Second World War it was a slang term used by the Royal Air Force to describe a large bomb powerful enough to destroy an entire city block. In the 1950s, it was picked up surprisingly quickly by Hollywood and the advertising industry to promote movies that were particularly successful at the box office.

Strictly speaking this definition still applies today. However, since box-office success is rarely achieved these days without an equally large investment for production and advertising costs, the term has become almost synonymous with the big budget Hollywood film per se. Thus, large scale Hollywood movies are called »blockbusters« even if in reality the financial expectations are not met and the would-be mega-hit actually turns out to be a dud.

As early as the 1950s and 1960s, blockbuster movies tried to lure audiences to the cinema with particularly spectacular images: gigantic set constructions, breathtaking panoramas, elaborate crowd scenes and dance choreographies. Yet, at the same time the historical epics and mega-musicals of the so called »wide-screen era« still presented themselves as a rather sophisticated form of entertainment, emphasizing both their visual grandeur and the narrative qualities of their stories – typical examples are *The Ten Commandments* (1956), *Cleopatra* (1963), *Lawrence of Arabia* (1962), *The Sound of Music* (1965) or *Hello Dolly!* (1969).

With the renaissance of the blockbuster concept in the 1970s, triggered by the huge success of films like *The Towering Inferno* (Irvin Allen, John Guillermin, 1974), Francis Ford Coppola's *The Godfather* (1972), Steven Spielberg's *Jaws* (1975), William Friedkin's *The Exorcist* (1973), and, of course, George Lucas' *Star Wars* (1977), this configuration began to change somewhat.

The blockbusters of the »new« or »post-classical« Hollywood cinema were still A-movies as far as their technical and financial standards were concerned. On the stylistic and textual level, however, these films were more indebted to the traditional B-genres. If in the classical studio era the medium was dominated by »mature« genres like the drama and melodrama, the romantic comedy, and the musical, the big budgets and box office hits of the post-classical era have clearly been reaped by a rather juvenile cinema dwelling in the fantastic, action, spectacle, and suspense (e. g. disaster movies, action/adventure, horror films, thrillers, science fiction and fantasy).

As the critics remind us, the stories these genres tell often tend to be shallow and exploitative. Perhaps we might even say that the plot plays a somewhat subordinate role for the entertainment these kinds of movies provide in general. At least I think their appeal is bolstered by an additional element which, for now, we could describe as the attempt to engage spectators on a direct and often literally physical level. It is precisely these aspects I will deal with in the remainder of this text.[1] In doing so, I will first point out some of the formal strategies filmmakers use to achieve these kind of effects. Editing, camera work, sound and of course the actual content of the images themselves all seem to be important to me in this respect.

A prominent device of the horror genre is the startle effect – scenes in which the spectator is startled, typically by a visual event, but in most cases also by an acoustic event which gives the visual event its full impact.

A similar device is what we could call the »gross out« or »gore effect«. That is, images of things we feel to be repulsive, not in a moral sense, but – as with the startle response – in the shape of an immediate and physical reaction which can hardly be controlled by will.

My next step will be to point out what I mean when I talk about how all these effects and devices serve to address the spectator in a »direct« manner. So much for now: I will be using the term »directly« mainly to describe instances of spectator engagement that do not arrive by the displaced process of any kind of identification with the story material, but by targeting the spectator immediately in his role as a recipient.

This does not mean that these effects do not work in tandem with the more common patterns of identification, and that these two modes do not interact with one another. To understand this sort of interaction, however, we must start by differentiating the two basic modes from one another as clearly as possible.

1–4. A frontal attack on the senses of the viewer. The blown-off tire form the trailer to *Twister,* directed by Jan de Bont, 1996.

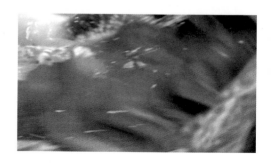

To perform this differentiation, it should, of course, initially be made clear what we mean by a term like »identification«. No other word is probably used as frequently to describe our emotional engagement in the process of film reception, and yet, it remains pretty much unclear what exactly we mean by that.

Does identification mean that I literally step in the shoes of a character and make a one-to-one experience of what that character is currently going through onscreen? Or does it denote a rather loose attachment to that character based on my sympathies for him? Is it true that we »identify« with a character when, for instance, we fear for him in a dangerous situation, or should that kind of emotional engagement not be referred to in a different manner?

These and similar questions have been asked a few years ago by the British film scholar Murray Smith in order to develop a theoretical model for the various aspects of the emotional engagement of cinema spectators. Since I will use that model as a backdrop against which the non-identificatory effects described above stand out, I will outline it roughly and point out two of Smith's most relevant concepts. My aim in doing so, by the way, is not so much a critique of Smith's model, but rather the opposite: an attempt to integrate my thesis into that model and to extend it.

Last but not least, I will try to develop a concept that allows me to describe the non-identificatory spectator address in a positive way. My point of reference here will be the speech act theory by John Austin, and what he has called the »performative«. Again I will give a brief outline of Austin's theory for those not familiar with the term and then show how this theory can be used to describe the structure of the effects mentioned above.

Editing and sound

It has become common place that the editing speed of movies has increased significantly in recent years. As research shows that increase is not quite as dramatic as some would have it.[2] Nevertheless, it is fair to say that since the mid-1990s the action/adventure genre has seen a relatively sustained trend towards fast and extremely fast cuts.

Just to give a brief indication of that: while an average shot length of less than three seconds was virtually unheard of in the last couple of decades, that barrier – as Table 1 shows – is nowadays broken trough almost on a regular basis.

Action/Adventure 1990–2003	ASL
Armageddon (98)	2,2 sec.
Enemy of the State (98)	2,4 sec.
Volcano (97)	2,4 sec.
Face/Off (97)	2,5 sec.
The Rock (96)	2,7 sec.
The Matrix Reloaded (03)	2,8 sec.
Terminator 2 (91)	3,2 sec.
Independence Day (96)	3,2 sec.
Starship Troopers (97)	3,5 sec.
Twister (96)	3,6 sec.
Die Hard With a Vengeance (95)	4,0 sec.
Jurassic Park (93)	5,2 sec.
Saving Private Ryan (98)	8,8 sec.

Action/Adventure 1975–1990	
Rambo: First Blood, Part II (85)	3,2 sec.
Star Wars (77)	3,3 sec.
Indiana Jones and the Temple of Doom (84)	3,9 sec.
Die Hard (88)	4,7 sec.

Table 1: Average shot lengths of action/adventure films.

One of the main reasons for the fast paced and fragmentary editing style of contemporary blockbusters is probably the increased media literacy of cinema audiences, who have learned to follow the narrative conventions of Hollywood cinema with relative ease. According to French film sound theorist Michel Chion, however, there are also some additional factors to take into account.

The introduction of Dolby Stereo in the 1970s and the transition to even more highly differentiated digital multi-channel sound systems in the 1990s not only brought cinema one step closer to the configuration of a spatially enveloping medium in which sound events may be transported dynamically from one place to another – on a more basic level, the additional channels, their exact separation, and the high definition of digital sound simply allowed for film soundtracks to be composed much more densely than it was possible before.[3]

On the one hand – as Tomlinson Holman has pointed out – this increase in acoustic information has led to the fact that films tend to be perceived much faster than they actually are on a purely visual level.[4] On the other hand, though – as Chion argues – the improvements in sound quality have also added directly to the acceleration of the images themselves.

According to Chion, acoustic information can be processed much quicker than images. As a result, short and fast movements – such as a punch, or the flight and the impact of a projectile – gain their full force or even intelligibility only through the additional information of a synchronous sound effect. Chion calls this the »added value«: »what we hear is what we haven't had time to see.«[5]

Chion claims, the better-defined film sound becomes – especially in the high-frequency range – the shorter and faster the depicted actions can be; the more narrative information can be delegated to the soundtrack in general, the smaller the importance of guiding the spectator through filmic space by visual means.[6]

Two other important aspects of sound effects are what Chion calls »reproduction« vs. »rendering«.[7] Reproduction relates to the naturalistic playback of sounds as one might actually hear them in a similar situation taking place within physical reality. One of the key functions of sound effects in that respect is to deliver information about the material conditions of objects and actions in the cinematic space. (Chion's term for this function is »materializing sound indices«.) Is that object made of wood, cloth, paper or metal? Is that sound caused by friction or collision, etc.?[8]

In fact though, film sound rarely limits itself to this more or less realistic representation of events. In most cases, sound effects are not only produced by different means as those we see onscreen, but they also sound much more drastic or merely different as they would in a comparable situation in reality. These differences, however, are not just exaggerations or distortions; rather filmmakers and sound designers aim at creating a sonic substitute for a collection of sensory impressions a given situation might incorporate. »What is rendered«, Chion writes, »is a clump of sensations.«[9]

In the cinema the sound of a punch, the bursting of an explosion, the sound of a body or object falling and hitting the ground not only convey the acoustic properties of their sources, but also an impression of the weight, the force, the velocity and surprise, the pain, the threat and the violence these situations might involve. And probably this is the reason why in the cinema spaceships scream or hum as they fly through the normally soundless vacuum of space; why tires in a car chase squeak no matter what kind of surface they are really on; why gunshots are routinely accompanied by the lashing sounds of ricochets; and why laser shots are almost always rendered with the pulsating or beaming sound of an energetic discharge.

Moreover, when they are emitted by a powerful subwoofer and a well-calibrated surround system, sound effects have come to adopt a literally physical quality these days. In today's cinemas, the pressure of an explosion or the impact of a kung-fu kick can not only be heard, but also be felt in the true sense of the word – with the restriction, of course, that the cinematic sensation can always only be an approximation of the real thing.

Cinematography

Another device filmmakers use to increase the dynamics of the cinema experience is the camera. John McTiernan's action classic *Die Hard* (1988) is a case in point.

With an average shot length of almost five seconds *Die Hard* seems to be edited quite slowly for the genre. One of the reasons for this is the fact that McTiernan and his cinematographer Jan de Bont like to shoot the action so that it can be presented without a lot of cuts. The most important devices used for this strategy are: the very flexible movements of the steadycam; the staging of the action in continuous segments; swift pans which, instead of cutting, glide fluently from one object to another; and the use of rack focus, which again allows the camera to point out the relevant details for the viewer without having to resort to the cut.[10]

It is not so much the editing, but this »long take-like« style that gives us the impression of speed, dynamics and claustrophobia we intuitively associate with that film. Moreover, I believe

5–8. A physical experience. The opening sequence of *Saving Private Ryan*, directed by Steven Spielberg, 1998.

that this notably fluid style – which in similar form also appears in music videos, TV shows like *E.R.*, commercials, and even in art house movies like Lars von Trier's Dogme films – is indeed one of the most prominent stylistic changes we have seen in the 1990s.

Another director who likes to keep his camera moving is critics enfant terrible Michael Bay who has landed his biggest hit to date with 1998s' *Armageddon*.

Similar to *Die Hard* – but in contrast to the style of earlier action/adventure films like for example *Star Wars* or *Rambo: First Blood, Part II* (George P. Cosmatos, 1985) – Bay's camera movements do not remain attached to the movement of the film's objects. On the contrary: Bay likes to use camera movement in precisely those situations in which the characters themselves remain immobile. A very typical example for this artificial »mobilization« are the scenes in the NASA control center: circling crane shots, swift zooms and dolly shots up to and away from the worried faces of the characters, jerky swish pans, and slow drifting dolly shots in close-ups and medium shots constantly signal dramatic tension and keep the films visuals in a steady flow.

Contrary to McTiernan's style, however, Bays camera movements do not serve as a substitute, but as a supplement to a relentless cutting frenzy which runs through *Armageddon* from the film's first minute to its last.

With an average shot length of merely 2.2 seconds and over 1650 shot changes per hour *Armageddon*'s editing speed is twice as fast as that of *Die Hard*, and more than three times the speed of an average Hollywood production from between 1930 and 1950.[11] In addition, *Armageddon*'s rhythm gets even more fragmented by a plethora of explosions, camera percussions, flashing strobe lights, and objects that fly into the camera or appear to just miss it by an inch.

Although *Armageddon*'s uncompromising and at times near unintelligible style makes it clearly an extreme example, the formal devices and tactics used in that film are certainly symptomatic for the condition of contemporary blockbuster cinema.

Just as the sound bombardment of contemporary blockbuster films, Bay's aggressive editing style and camera work are part of an aesthetic strategy that aims to engage the viewer not only by narrative means, but also through an excessive use of devices that are aimed directly at the nervous system, causing sensations of shock, speed, chaos, confusion, etc. As Michael Bay puts it himself: »In terms of the action scenes, I want the audience to feel like they're inside of it. That they are living it, and not just watching it from afar. I like putting the audience at privileged angles, where they're feeling it, rather than just watching it unfold in front of them. So I do try to create chaos with the action. When we have the whole shuttle sequence on the asteroid, I kept trying to think, what would it be like to be in a plane crash? I think it would be the most horrific thing in the world, and it's got to be chaotic to look at, just trying to stylize that.«[12]

Almost the same words are used by Steven Spielberg, when he says that he designed the much talked about »Omaha Beach sequence« from *Saving Private Ryan* with the intent »to give audiences a physical experience, not a laid back voyeuristic one«.[13]

More importantly, the devices used by Spielberg for the opening of his film are almost the same as Bay's: strobe effects; shaky and narrow hand-held camera shots; images of chaotic action and jerky movements; explosions that hit the audience with their visual and acoustic force just as unexpected as the characters; nauseating images of shot wounds and mutilations; and a kinetic and highly defined soundscape filled with the startling noise of squirting sand, buzzing projectiles and a constant staccato of jingling pieces of ammunition hitting the landing barriers, water, and the soldier's helmets.

As I have indicated, I believe that all these effects have one thing in common: they are aimed directly at the reflexes and the sensory apparatus of the spectator. This might sound trivial, but, I think, is still relevant from a research perspective. Firstly, because this aesthetic seems to play such an important role for the consumption of contemporary cinema and secondly, because it hints at a dimension of the film experience that so far has been often neglected by cinema studies.

Murray Smith's model of »identification«

The concept of identification has remained the dominant paradigm to describe our emotional engagement in film. I don't want to claim that identification has lost its importance for contemporary blockbuster cinema, as some critics imply, when they allege that contemporary Hollywood cinema has degenerated into a pure special effects extravaganza. It is more likely that the effects de-

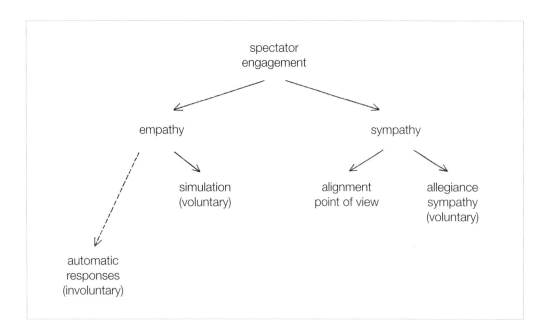

9. Murray Smith's model of spectator engagement (simplified version). Murray Smith, *Engaging Characters. Fiction, Emotion, and the Cinema*, Oxford, 1995.

```
                    spectator
                    engagement

            empathy                    sympathy

                  simulation      alignment      allegiance
                  (voluntary)     point of view  sympathy
                                                 (voluntary)

   automatic
   responses
   (involuntary)
```

scribed above present an additional element which may at times come at the cost of the narrative structure of a film, but will hardly ever lead to a complete collapse of that structure. Even self declared spectacles like *Twister* or *Armageddon* still adhere to the principles of classical Hollywood narration, and one of the primary functions of that system is precisely to invite the spectator to perform identificatory actions.

We are still pretty far away from fully understanding how these kinds of processes work. Nevertheless, theoretical research into the emotional response to film has made considerable progress in recent years. One of the most important contributions to that field has come from Murray Smith and his seminal work *Engaging Characters*.

One of the common assumptions within our everyday understanding of the concept of identification is that we as spectators in some form participate in the emotional states of the characters onscreen. This gives rise to a very basic question: does this participation mean that we undergo the same experience as the characters – or are our own emotional states actually quite different ones?

To illustrate that difference, Smith's model for spectator engagement introduces the distinction between »empathic« and »sympathetic« patterns of identification (due to it's misleading notion, Smith himself prefers not to use the term »identification« but to speak of »spectator engagement« instead). Empathic patterns of identification are those in which the spectator tries to put himself in the situation of the character feeling more or less the same as the person does onscreen. We could also say that in a moment like this we feel **with** the character, whereas a spectator's sympathetic reactions have more to do with what we feel **for** a character in a given situation.

A typical example often mentioned in this context is that of scenes in a horror film in which a character is unknowingly maneuvering herself into the hands of the monster. At this particular moment the character herself may feel something like curiosity, because she's wondering what's causing that strange noise coming from the basement, or she might even feel exuberant cheerfulness because she is on her way to get the party re-supplied with alcoholic beverages. However, what the character does not feel in this case (of course there are other cases as well) is fear. Fear is only experienced by us, because we suspect that there is something evil lurking in the basement and that something dreadful is going to happen to the character. We do not fear with the character, but for the character.

Another difference marked by Smith is the fact that for us to feel empathy towards a character, we do not have to actually like that character or share the same goals or values as she does. This means that I am able to put myself in the emotional state of the villain, although I do detest him from a moral point of view.[14]

In order for us to feel sympathetic towards a character, however, we need a basic cognitive understanding of the situation the character is currently in, and a cognitive understanding of what the character herself is feeling in that situation. Based on these pieces of information and our personal disposition, we then pass our own emotional judgment in another cognitive and – as Smith emphasizes – voluntary process.[15]

10–13. »They sucked his brain out!« Our stomach is churning. Lieutenant Rascak, however, remains cool, because he has seen this kind of things a million times before, *Starship Troopers*, directed by Paul Verhoeven, 1997.

14–17. »Watch out, Burk!« Subtle, but efficient. A classic startle effect from *Aliens*, directed by James Cameron, 1986.

Another useful concept introduced by Smith is that of »alignment« and »allegiance«. I will not go into further detail here though, since my goal is only to show that apart from these »identificatory« patterns, filmmakers also use other devices to rouse our emotions.

As a matter of fact, Smith does so himself, pointing out what he calls »automatic reactions«.[16] As an example for this category Smiths draws on another staple feature of the horror film, namely the so-called »startle effect«: moments in which the spectator jumps at a surprising movement, a sudden noise or both – often to find out that it was merely the runaway cat or some other harmless figure that was causing the stir.

As Smith shows these kind of effects have a different structure than the ones we have discussed so far (Table 2).

Contrary to sympathetic reactions – according to Smith – automatic reactions induce an identical experience as that of the character, and in this sense, the response is emphatic. Unlike empathic and sympathetic responses, however, automatic reactions are a) involuntary and b) do not proceed via the character; neither by way of passing an emotional judgment on the actions of the character, nor by trying to put myself in the emotional state of the character. The spectators emotional reaction arises »directly from the represented visual or aural environment in which the character moves«.[17]

	Type of reaction	Path of reaction	Relation to character's emotion
Empathy	voluntary	via character	synchronous
Sympathy	voluntary	via character	asynchronous
Automatic Reactions	involuntary	direct	synchronous or asynchronous

Table 2: The three modes of spectator engagement.

A question open to disagreement is whether the spectator's emotional reaction is in fact always identical to that of the character in this moment. Firstly, because the acoustic signal that startles us is often not the same as the one the character hears onscreen. In many cases we hear more or less the same noise as the character – for example the meow of a scared-up cat. Often, however, it is only a loud note from a violin or a bass sound that is causing the startle, and this sound, of course, is strictly speaking not a part of the films fictional universe (the diegesis).

The second and more important reason is the fact that the startle effect, in my opinion, may also be used in a way that is asynchronous to the character's emotional behavior. One typical example for this are scenes in which we see and hear a shocking event, but in which the character does not (or not yet) react to the event because it takes place behind her back. Another example would be a scene in which the characters have already left the visible space but the narration stays on to alert us to a shocking detail (e.g. a dead body which suddenly opens its eyes).

The main reason why I would like to discard the »synchrony clause«, however, is because I suspect that if we leave it away, all the effects we have discussed in the first part will fit in this category (which Smith himself mentions only in passim). Just as the startle effect is an involuntary reaction of the spectator that springs directly from the audiovisual representation of the action, the editing frenzy, the strobe effects, the sound bombardment, the camera percussions, and »phantom ride sequences«[18] of a film like *Armageddon* or *Saving Private Ryan* produce an emotional or even physical stress that does not run via any of the identificatory patterns of Smith's model.

As with the startle effect, filmmakers like Michael Bay or Steven Spielberg often use these effects to give the audience an experience that at least tries to approach what the characters onscreen are going through. This is precisely what Bay and Spielberg mean when they say that they want the audience to »feel« the chaos and not just »watch it from afar«. But it does not always have to be that way.

Take for example the gross-out effect which also seems to fit the category quite well. Quite frequently this effect is played out against the grain of the emotional state of the character. Our stomach is churning, the character, however, remains cool because she has seen this kind of things a million times before.

Of course moments like this will also affect our sympathetic stance towards the character. Perhaps I admire her for keeping her nerve while faced with such a gruesome sight. Or perhaps

I feel contempt towards her; or I become scared because I find people of such rudimentary sensitivity rather dubious.

To illustrate my point I will now give a few concrete examples. First a »gross-out effect« from Paul Verhoeven's war satire *Starship Troopers* (1997) that has at least one of the characters remaining fairly cool: Lieutenant Rasczak sticks his arm prosthesis into the slimy hole the bugs have left in the head of one of the soldiers, after they have sucked his brains out. Depending on how well we are able to cope with such images, our reactions to this shot might vary. I suspect however that only few of us will remain as tough as the war veteran Rasczak does.

The next example is a startle effect from James Cameron's *Aliens* (1986). In the laboratory of the colony Ripley (Sigourney Weaver) and her companions discover an array of test tubes holding Aliens: As Burk (Paul Reiser) approaches one of the tubes to take a closer look, the Alien suddenly jerks against the glass.

First of all this is a startle effect that relies solely on diegetic sound. We can also say that we are dealing with one of those »false alarm startles« I have mentioned earlier. We are startled, but as is it turns out nothing bad has happened (at least for now). Most importantly however, this scene is an example for a synchronous startle effect: That is, we as spectators are being startled and at the same time also at least one of the characters. In this case they are Ripley and, though apparently to a slightly lesser degree, Burk.

The third example is from Wes Craven's *Scream 3* (2000) and shows that the startle effect may also be used asynchronous to the emotional state of the characte: Sidney (Neve Campbell) has fled to a room upstairs and is starring anxiously at the door, because she suspects that the slasher might be following her. Actually though, Ghostface then unexpectedly appears in the window behind her. The spectator is startled, the character however does not react to the event because she cannot see it.

Also, in this case the startle event is enforced by an extradiegetic sound effect as contemporary slasher movies mostly do. Thus, we are dealing with a very vivid piece of evidence for the claim that the startle effect per se has nothing to do with empathic engagement. Simply because in this case empathic engagement can be ruled out as the source for the emotional reaction of the spectator.

The fact that there are cases in which we are startled, but the character is not, brings up the question whether there are cases in which the situation is inverted: the character is startled, but the audience is not..

An example for this can be found in the well-known scene from *Jurassic Park* (Steven Spielberg, 1993) in which Dr. Grant (Sam Neill) pretends to be shocked by an electric fence in front of the children. The scene is probably not an ideal example because even for the spectator there is a certain amount of ambiguity. I believe though that most viewers will realize just in time that the apparent threat is only faked and will thus, contrary to the characters, fail to be startled

Table 3 shows a schematic overview of these examples. There are four possible ways in which a startle scene may be played out in a film. Case 1: both the spectator and the character are being startled, was illustrated with the example from *Aliens*. Case 2: the spectator is being startled, but the character is not, was illustrated with the scene from *Scream 3*, and Case 3: the characters are being startled, but the audience is not, was the example from *Jurassic Park*. Case 4 has only been added for the sake of completeness. Since in this case neither the characters nor the audience is startled, it is obviously not very interesting to our case.

	Character	Spectator	Example
Synchronous 1	startled	startled	*Aliens*
Asynchronous 1	not startled	startled	*Scream 3*
Asynchronous 2	startled	not startled	*Jurassic Park*
Synchronous 2	not startled	not startled	

Table 3: Startle scene variants.

The performative axis of film reception

For the remainder of this text, I will now try to develop a concept that allows us to describe the peculiar structure of the non-identificatory spectator address also in a positive way. This concept will take clues from John Austin's speech act theory, in particular his concept of the performative.

18–21. »Behind you!« To the shock of the viewer, Ghostface unexpectedly appears in the window behind Sidney, *Scream 3*, directed by Wes Craven, 2000.

22–25. »I guess that means the power is off.« Dr. Grant plays a macabre trick on the children, *Jurassic Park*, directed by Steven Spielberg, 1993.

John Austin's most important contribution to language philosophy has been to show that language is not just a descriptive instrument that is used to make statements about the world, but that we use language to perform acts which actually change the world. Austin first expressed this idea in his distinction between »constative« utterances and so-called »performative« utterances.[19]

Constative utterances are the descriptive and assertive utterances which until then were thought to be paradigmatic for language per se: utterances like »the ball is red«, or »John goes to the basement«. Statements about the world that can be judged as being true or false, depending on whether the facts they talk about are indeed the case or not.

Apart from these kinds of utterances there are however, as Austin has shown, other utterances which may grammatically appear similar, but which are used in a completely different manner. Standard examples are utterances incorporating the phrase »I promise«. When I say »I promise to come to the conference in Las Vegas« it makes no sense to ask whether that utterance is true or false. The only thing one can ask is whether the person making that utterance is serious about what she says.

By uttering the promise I make a commitment which binds me and that may be called on by my counterpart. Through my promise, I have created a new situation and changed the world to a small degree. We are thus dealing with an action or as Austin refers to it in the first version of his theory: we have made a performative speech act.

Other typical examples – and this brings us closer to our initial topic – are utterances like »Happy birthday!«, »You moron!« or a scaring »Boo!«. In all these cases, by making the utterance, I perform an act that has an immediate effect on my surroundings.

In the case of »Happy birthday!« that act-like aspect – that what I'm doing **by** making the utterance – is congratulating; in the case of »You moron!« I try to insult my counterpart; and in the case of »Boo!« I intend to perform the act of startling someone. One could also say that performative utterances do what they say.

In a later revision of this theory, Austin made a further distinction between the conventional effect that is produced by such an utterance (e. g. the effect of having been congratulated) and the non-conventional effect that might be following from that (e. g. the effect of being delighted). I do not wish to go into further detail at this point though, because, at least for now, I just want to focus on the basic quality of performative utterances that they do what they say rather than just saying something or referring to something.

Of course I don't want to claim that movies actually do perform speech acts in the strict Austinian sense. On close inspection there are quite a few differences between what we may call the »performative« dimension in film and the performative dimension of language. Nevertheless, I believe that the structure of the non-identificatory effects discussed above has also something in common with the linguistic performative utterances that Austin talks about.

Similar to the structure of a performative speech act, the response to a startle effect (for example) is not produced through the description of a situation I can then put myself into on an emotional and intellectual level, or not, but by presenting the situation in such way that it has an immediate effect on me as a spectator. And the same thing can be said about the chaotic depictions of the chaotic content in Spielberg's and Bay's films.

The hectic pace, the confusion, the physical and mental tension of the fictional events is transported to the viewer not just by descriptive means, but by turning the receptive process into an experience for the viewer that at least in its tendency is almost as strenuous. Or to put it differently: by showing us how Ripley is attacked and startled by an Alien the film not only refers to a fictional event, but it produces an aspect of that event immediately within ourselves.

Typically this emotional aspect is one that is also felt by one of the characters onscreen. And it is probably because of this at least partial congruence that we tend to commit the fallacy of thinking of this process as an identificatory phenomenon. Strictly speaking, however, it is in not our ability to put ourselves into the situation of a character that brings about the emotional effect, but the fact that I as a viewer was actually startled myself.

This is not to say that empathic or sympathetic processes of identification do not play a role in this context or that the different modes may not also overlap in such a moment. Per se, as I have tried to show, the startle effect, however, is not a »representative-empathic« phenomenon. Moreover, I suspect that there are many more »performative« or at least non-identificatory effects in the cinema.

What about a surprising plot twist? When the Bruce Willis character in *The Sixth Sense* (1999) finds out that he is actually already dead, he experiences this as a shocking surprise. And since we, too, are surprised in that moment we are again led to believe that we are dealing with an identificatory reaction.

In fact, however, our surprise has nothing to do with that of the Bruce Willis character – at least not in the sense of an internal simulation of that character's emotional state. Our surprise is genuine because also we as a »reader of the text« did not see the event coming. And neither should we confuse this emotion with the sympathetic pity we may feel for the character at that moment.

As with the startle response, we can support this thesis by pointing to an example in which the shock effect is used in an asynchronous way. Unlike in *The Sixth Sense* the narration in *Vertigo* (Alfred Hitchcock, 1958) informs the viewer about the truth about Madeleine Elster's (Kim Novak) death long before Scottie (James Stewart) makes that discovery. A flashback attributed to Judy – Madeleine Elster's alter ego – shows us that it was really not she who fell off the tower, but the body of the already murdered real Mrs. Elster.

The revelation we experience during the flashback certainly helps us to understand how Scottie is feeling when he realizes the truth, and it may also help us to anticipate that moment and modify our sympathetic feelings for him accordingly. But again the original surprise has nothing to do with the two identificatory modes. The only one who is surprised during the flashback is us.

And what about comedy? A genre which, in contrast to, say, the western, is almost exclusively defined through the emotional response it causes in the spectator.

The dominant feeling produced by a comedy is that of comic amusement. And yet, it is a common place that the comedians themselves do not laugh at their own jokes. As a result, empathy (at least as far as amusement is concerned) can once again largely be ruled out. Just as sympathetic engagements can probably only be partially made responsible for the emotional reactions of the spectator.

In this sense, the comedy is probably the emotionally asynchronous genre par excellence. Still, I suggest that filmmakers also employ comedy to bring us closer to the emotions of the characters. Think about a romantic comedy like *Love Actually* (Richard Curtis, 2003) or *When Harry Met Sally* (Rob Reiner, 1989).

As I have indicated, large part of the amusement and laughter in these films is probably caused by processes that do not fall in the empathic or sympathetic category. Nevertheless, our own laughter puts us into a mood that has quite a bit in common with the light-hearted feeling of being in love or having a hot flirt.

With Chion we could thus speak of a »rendering« strategy even in this context. What we feel may not have been produced by the same means that are working on the characters. Nevertheless, these means serve to give us an impression of the emotions of the characters or at least »tune« us into a mood that points in the same direction. Readers familiar with the work of Roger Odin might be reminded of his concept of the »mise en phase«.[20]

Similar processes can probably also be found in suspense-oriented genres like the thriller, the whodunit or the suspense-melodrama. Typically these genres are centered around the revelation of a crime or some other mysterious event: a) for the characters and b) for the spectator.

Thus, also in these genres we are dealing with a double structure. On the one hand the emotions of the characters onscreen and on the other hand the frustration, curiosity, and satisfaction that actually arises out of the play between the spectator and the narration of the film.

Or think about the rarely discussed emotional landscape of cinematic eroticism, or the way film music influences our emotions.

As you can see there are many doors opening here leading to interesting questions. For now, however, I would like to keep these doors shut. Firstly, because they lead us away somewhat from our initial topic, and secondly, because I myself have only just started to explore the way John Austin's theory can be made fruitful for the study of emotion and cinema.

Volker Pietsch
Body Snatchers. Recycling in Hollywood

A déjà-vu experience is a sign of a change in the matrix – a claim made in *The Matrix* (USA, Larry and Andy Wachowski, 1999), a remix of action, science fiction, and horror genre elements that makes use of the John Woo and Quentin Tarantino aesthetic, refers as much to *Alice in Wonderland* as it does to *Superman*, and has its roots in something as ancient as Plato's »Allegory of the Cave«. These days, cinematic déjà-vus have become persistently occurring byproducts of the mass-producing US film industry – but also signs of changes in the matrix. Paradoxically, Hollywood remakes are always the product of technical or societal change, or at least of an assimilation of foreign cultural assets.

From a creative standpoint, remakes of foreign language films are convenient affairs, which is also the reason why often little time elapses between the original's release date and the remake's: Gérard Depardieu, leading man in *Mon Père, Ce Héros* (France, Gérard Lauzier, 1991), got the chance to act in the same role two years later in *My Father the Hero* (USA, Steve Miner, 1993). Only four years were needed to turn *Ringu* (Japan, Hideo Nakata, 1998) into an American box-office hit (USA, *The Ring*, Gore Verbinski, 2002). The United States' film industry is well protected against foreign competitors, as dubbing is usually passed on, and mass audiences are generally not prepared to have a go at watching subtitled film versions. The bulk of European audiences, too, prefers unchallenging Hollywood fare to the often cumbersome movies produced by their respective home nations. Here, awareness of imports from third countries is limited, and conveyed usually by word of mouth. As a result, many viewers get to see a European or Asian story for the first time in the shape of a Hollywood remake. As for the adaptation of the screenplay, most of the time nothing more is necessary than the adjustment of certain cultural specifics. Through film and TV, even non-American recipients have grown as accustomed to US settings as to their own. In a change from Asian film, for instance, gender role attributions are corrected: The Japanese original of *The Ring* saw the female lead character constantly on the verge of tears, and her partner slapping her in the face time and again to pull her back from the brink of hysteria. In contrast to this, the remake's American heroine takes initiative throughout the entire movie. Pessimistic European plots are fitted with a family-friendly happy ending, as happened in the case of *The Vanishing* (USA, George Sluizer, 1992), the remake of the thriller *Spoorloos* (Netherlands / France, George Sluizer, 1988). *The Seven Samurai* (*Shichinin No Samurai*, Japan, Akira Kurosawa, 1953) ride across the prairie as *The Magnificent Seven* (USA, John Sturges, 1960) and are thus transported from archaic Japan to an archaic period of US history.

Remakes of English language films are a different matter. In these cases, the original's cinematic run needs to have ended appropriately long ago for it to come into question as remake material. This circumstance engenders two further problems: Modernizing material may turn out to be more difficult than Americanizing it, since changes in society's mood are less tangible than a foreign society's customs in all their apparent dissimilarity. Additionally, the audience may have got to know the original in the meantime via video and TV. For the remake of an English language film to prosper, its makers must manage the feat of translating an old story for a new generation. In this respect, *Psycho* (USA, Gus Van Sant, 1998) fails specifically because of the awestruck reverence with which it treats Hitchcock's work *Psycho* (USA, Alfred Hitchcock, 1960). The only variation from the original worth mentioning is the remake's use of color; the two films' camera angles, dialogue and even music are only minimally different. Therefore, connoisseurs of the towering original refrained from purchasing tickets. Younger viewers, on the other hand, experience the 1960 pace of the film as much too leisurely. At the time, the uncovering of shy Norman Bates' secrets delivered an effective shock, as his harmless appearance seemed to go hand in hand with 1950's conservative values. Until that point, cinematic menace had mostly emanated from furry monsters or representatives of organized crime. Nowadays, the psychopath concealed behind an everyman façade is an established stereotype, serial killing phenomena have been assimilated by popular culture, and Norman's old-fashioned affectations immediately arouse suspicion. Viewers watching this story unfold at the turn of the century can only shake their heads at Marion's failure to run screaming from the motel when Norman, sitting amongst stuffed birds, parts with wisdom such as »A boy's best friend is his mother.«

In the context of the original version, the film's famous shock sequences – the murder under the shower, the mummified face, Bates in women's clothing – still do work even today, as such drastic scenes just are not expected of a black-and-white film. Compared to the elaborate sadisms presented in *Seven* (USA, David Fincher, 1995) or *Hannibal* (USA, Ridley Scott, 2001), they seem almost harmless when incorporated into a current theatrical release. The family as a hotbed of perversion, the pressure exerted on young people by restrictive sexual morals – these focal points of the film were not altered in the new version, making it hard for viewers living in an age of dissolving family ties and liberal attitudes towards sexuality to relate to the story.

Meanwhile, *Independence Day* (USA, Roland Emmerich, 1995), a new version of the science fiction movie *The War of the Worlds* (USA, Byron Haskin, 1954), may serve as an example of an extremely successful remake. Here, too, the variations are part of the recipe for success. The plot basics have remained the same: Space ships from Mars (from somewhere further away in the case of *Independence Day*) annihilate almost all of mankind, and no conventional weapon can stop them. Both films, however, fill this mould in their very own way. The most conspicuous difference: *The War of the Worlds* has the aliens perish from something as mundane as a 'flu infection. In *Independence Day,* a virus is the agent of their demise as well – but here it is a computer virus. The Second World War had left its mark on the audiences for *The War of the Worlds*, and it is that war which is commemorated at the start of the film with the help of archive footage. The cold war had begun, and an escalation could have meant nuclear apocalypse. Against this background, the use of nuclear bombs in the film proves to be completely futile. The last survivors, who have gathered in a church for prayer, are awarded deliverance through a miraculous twist of fate. The film's lesson can be construed as: »not the military or science can prevent catastrophe, but humility and acceptance of Christian virtues can«.

When *Independence Day* was released to cinemas, the arms race had bankrupted the Soviet opponent. Computer technology was already being sold to private households and appeared increasingly unthreatening, even controllable. The film strengthened the thriving faith in technology (and the sponsors' technology in particular). The bomb still was no solution, but not because weapon technology in itself seemed useless, but merely because it was not up to the standards of the hackers' ingenious artistry.

Although some aspects may have to be revised, the production of a remake is of course motivated primarily by the absorption of attractive elements. The element shared by *The War of the Worlds* and *Independence Day* is the idea of solidarity as a means of mastering changes that are perceived as threatening. In the older movie, it is godlessness in the face of the horrors of war that needs to be overcome; in the more recent film, it is both the disintegration of the family and the prejudice that prevents symbiosis within a pluralistic society.

The death of the clergyman who tries to evangelize the aliens in *The War of the Worlds* typifies the threat to Christian values; their validity is restored all the stronger at the end of the film. In *Independence Day*, it is significant that the invaders intrude on the wedding proposal a fighter pilot (played by Will Smith) is making to his wife-to-be. Accordingly, the audience feels triumphant when Smith vengefully plants a punch on the chin of the first alien he encounters (if »chin« is indeed the correct term in this context). At the end, all family ties are re-established, the wedding ceremony is performed, another endangered relationship is saved, and two children have reason to be very proud of their dipsomaniac father (Randy Quaid). Emmerich's film presents a Jewish East Coast intellectual and an ordinary West Coast African-American as its heroes – under the guidance of a Christian, white president. National pathos is of greater importance in *Independence Day* than in *The War of the Worlds* – that much becomes clear just from the title: even in a world made complex by the disappearance of the blocks, the USA will continue to have the means to protect the human race.

Alongside the renaissance of a societal atmosphere under modified conditions, technical innovations were always major motivating factors whenever it came to producing remakes. After all, the success of *Independence Day* was at least in part based on its impressive array of special effects. The transitions from silent films to »talkies«, from black-and-white to color, or from stop motion to virtual animation – as well as the abolition of the puritanical Hays Code – posed many opportunities to present old stories in a new framework. In the case of *Independence Day*, this enterprise was successful; *The War of the Worlds* had similarly profited from Oscar-honoured special effects which had swallowed up 70% of the film's budget. In other cases, however, such formal attractions are not enough to guarantee high-box office returns – this happens whenever they are deeply alien to the core idea of the original. In this context, *The Haunting* (USA, Jan de Bont, 1999) deserves an exemplary mention. This firework display of digital effect trickery was a commercial failure, since the story of *The Haunting* (Great Britain, Robert Wise, 1963) is effective precisely because of insinuation and ambivalence. While the original leaves the construction of reasons for the film's events to the imagination of the viewer, the remake is an insipid talent showcase featuring visual artistry that has no emotional effects on audiences. In this respect, *The War of the Worlds* and *Independence Day* are markedly different; these films' battle scenes are exquisite catalysts for the compensation of anxieties and destructive energies.

Thus, it becomes apparent that a remake of a tried and tested product does not come with an automatic guarantee for commercial success. As far as the creative process is concerned, remaking material facilitates the finding of ideas – but it also demands the customization of the material to the demands of an ever-changing market. Films that possess a particularly adaptable and yet distinctive plot can be subjected to such overhauls time and again. The stage play *The Front Page*, for instance, was filmed four times: As *The Front Page* (USA, Lewis Milestone, 1931), as *His Girl Friday* (USA, Howard Hawks, 1940), again as *The Front Page* (USA, Billy Wilder, 1974) and as *Switching Channels* (USA, Ted Kotcheff, 1988). The film version of Jack Finney's eponymous novel *Invasion of the Body Snatchers* (*Invasion of the Body Snatchers*, USA, Don Siegel, 1956) has thus far been remade three times; just as unfeeling extraterrestrials occupy the physical shells of American citizens in *Invasion of the Body Snatchers*, new actors keep occupying the original's old roles and filling them with the experience gained from living in a different era. The essence of the plot always remains the same: the ominous dissolution of the individual into totalitarian mass movements. The *Body Snatchers* of 1956 were interpreted as personifying the fear of communist infiltration. In reverse, liberal critics presumed that the film contained criticism of the McCarthy committee's semi-fascist persecution of alleged anti-American activities. Two decades later, the remake *Invasion of the Body Snatchers* (USA, Phillip Kaufman, 1977) was released to cinemas. This film also excels at focussing the fears of its heterogeneous audience.

When, in the 1970s, psychoanalysis became a lifestyle and was touted, along with antiauthoritarian education, New Age philosophy and self-discovery, as a tool for ushering in all-embracing interpersonal harmony, this film detected the threat of a new kind of equalization. Here, a psychologist (played by classily callous Leonard »Mr Spock« Nimoy) plays down all warnings of an invasion as a mass psychosis and finally turns out to be an alien himself. At the same time, the alternative scene's conspiracy paranoia is satisfied as well: it is not a coincidence that Veronica Cartwright likens the spread of alien pollen to industrial pollution, while the cover-up on the part of the police and the city administration is reminiscent of Watergate. In one scene, Donald Sutherland reassures Brooke Adams: »Do you want to see my friend, he's a psychiatrist. He'd eliminate a lot of things – whether Geoffrey was having an affair, whether he had become gay, whether he had a social disease, whether he had become a Republican [!], all the alternatives that could have happened to him.«

The second remake, *Body Snatchers* (USA, Abel Ferrara, 1993), transfers the story to the uniformed system of a military base; here, extraterrestrials can hardly be distinguished from soldiers, because the recruits have already been forced to give up their individual personalities anyway. Finally, *The Faculty* (USA, Robert Rodriguez, 1998), while more of a loose homage than a direct remake, adapts the familiar model to the Darwinist surroundings of a school: A group of outsiders become the victims of an extraterrestrial kind of mobbing which emanates in particular from the sports teacher and his crew (the nightmare of any misfit pupil who is forever the last to be chosen into a team).

In this manner, the same accumulator is charged with new meaning again and again. However, the remake is not the sole form of »recycling« known to Hollywood studios. Box-office hit *The Matrix* hardly contained an original element, but cannot be classified as a remake. The *Matrix* trilogy (*The Matrix,* USA, 1999; *The Matrix Reloaded*, USA, 2003; *The Matrix Revolutions,* USA, 2003; all parts directed by Larry Wachowski and Andy Wachowski) does not copy any complete plot sequence, but rather presents a patchwork of countless films and other works of popular and »high« culture. A similar claim can be made for the *Star Wars* movies (*A New Hope,* USA, George Lucas, 1977; *The Empire Strikes Back,* USA, Irvin Kershner, 1980; *Return of the Jedi,* USA, Richard Marquand, 1983; *The Phantom Menace*, USA, George Lucas, 1999; *Attack of the Clones,* USA, George Lucas, 2002), which, alongside *The Matrix*, are a high watermark for efficient rental and marketing policies. The same principles for success as in the case of remakes apply; here, however, the commercial potential is multiplied – perhaps because these films intensively draw inspiration from contents of the collective memory. From old components, they create a new microcosm in which any member of the respective fan community can feel at home. In one fell swoop, they update pop culture and separate obsolete aspects from enduring ones. Goethe's claim that »He who brings abundance will bring something to many« is as accurate here as it is in the case of parodies. Like remakes, parodies bow to the principle of distorted recognition. However, while remakes adapt an old story to new viewing customs, parodies deliberately over-emphasize the disruption of expectations. Ideally, a remake can be enjoyed without dependence on the original, while a parody cannot. For instance, the comedies starring Leslie Nielsen, or the *Scary Movie* films (*Scary Movie*, USA, Keenen Ivory Wayans, 2000; *Scary Movie 2*, USA, Keenen Ivory Wayans, 2001; *Scary Movie 3,* USA, David Zucker, 2003) presuppose knowledge of a broad range of films.

A parody sending up in detail last season's movies is unlikely to gain an appeal as long-term as that of parodies satirizing the overall conventions of an entire genre. Although John Ford or Sam Peckinpah can certainly not be accused of making the same film over and over again, everyone knows what a typical western movie is supposed to look like. Whole sub-genres are based on the constant duplication of basic constellations – the conflict-laden friendship between two fundamentally different characters (buddy movie) or their would-be amorous relationship (romantic comedy).

In addition to the remakes, other films should be taken into account, too – those that are based on the same event but that derive from it completely unique plots. The O.K. Corral, for example, became the setting for several western films, and none of the scripts are noticeably similar. In a parallel to the principles behind remakes, the motives unique to the archetype are picked up and adapted to the changing expectations of producers and consumers. With regard to the duel at O.K. Corral in 1881, these motives would be loyalty in the face of danger, and the enforcement of law and order in a space that exists outside the law. Admittedly, the expectations of Hollywood and those held by the rest of the world with respect to this topic appeared to be no longer congruent in recent times: *Wyatt Earp* (USA, Lawrence Kasdan, 1994) bombed spectacularly, for which Kevin Costner's much too ancient-looking moustache may in part be to blame. The claim that film cowboys have simply shot their last bullet and that moviegoers are tired of the endlessly repeated western stereotypes, however, cannot hold. Hollywood's inflationary flooding of the market with endless copies of the same template cannot be the sole reason for audiences no longer accepting that genre. The same could be said about swashbuckling or monumental history epics – both genres are currently experiencing something of a renaissance, in spite of their being more than familiar to audiences. Rather, the established, specific content of western stories has, thus far, not been adjusted convincingly to the new generation of customers. In this case, that feat is a particularly difficult one to accomplish, since the patriarchal masculine ideal once embodied by John Wayne or, in a more detached manner, Clint Eastwood becomes less and less relevant, and the dusty herdsmen simply lack the elegance of a lushly dressed sword fighter. In this respect, Costner's walrus moustache is indeed symbolic for an antiquated depiction of masculinity.

Significantly, the famous exception from the rule, namely *Dances With Wolves* (USA, Kevin Costner, 1990) – the trailer for which showed Kevin Costner running his hands through blades of wheat – is an ethno-movie romanticizing the return to a archaic, close-to-nature way of living; as such, it should be seen as, if anything, a predecessor to *Gladiator* (USA, Ridley Scott, 2001) – in which the director has Russell Crowe repeat precisely that gesture – or the *Lord of the Rings* films (*The Fellowship of the Ring,* USA/New Zealand, 2001; *The Two Towers,* USA/New Zealand, 2002; *The Return of the King,* USA, 2003; all parts directed by Peter Jackson), and as a successor to classical western movies, in which cattle herds, Indian tribes and gangs of desperadoes must be civilized.

The ignorant cavalry in *Dances With Wolves*, decadent Rome in *Gladiator*, and Saruman's hellish underground tunnel in *The Lord of the Rings* – the latter half factory, half genetic laboratory – *are* civilization. Contrastingly, in *Wyatt Earp*, civilization is affirmed; here, it connotes the civil liberties that the Clanton gang of outlaws in the O.K Corral must yield to. At present, the negative associations contained within the concept of civilization appear to be closer to people's minds. Humanist values are assigned to the Indians and the Elves respectively. By characterizing the Elves as a spiritual, nature-loving people at ease with itself and equipped with bow and arrow, the films have managed to transplant a romantic archetype from a languishing genre to a flourishing one.

In spite of being based on the same legend, *Wyatt Earp* is not the remake of an earlier adaptation of the Tombstone shootout (*My Darling Clementine*, USA, directed by John Ford, 1946, comes to mind). A remake generally adopts not only the core of the action, but also the structure of its development. To return briefly to *Psycho*: both versions of the film are based on the authentic case of pathological murderer Ed Gein. This case is picked up again in the thriller *The Silence of the Lambs* (USA, Jonathan Demme, 1990); here, however, it becomes the starting point for both a constellation of characters and an action structure completely different to those of the *Psycho* films.

Naturally, the boundaries between types of »recycling« are much more blurred than their makeshift classification as remakes, myth blends, parodies or multiple adaptations of the same historical or literary template can reveal. Endowing a new film with an old subject matter is no longer the only way to re-use a classic. Often, it will suffice to restore old film footage, and to re-insert sequences that were cut at the time: The »Director's Cut« – a concept originally created to save the artistic integrity of the director, and made popular by commercially viable American big screen comebacks such as that of *The Exorcist* (USA, William Friedkin, 1973) in the year 2000 – has been absorbed by the industry. In recent years, the scheme of firstly refreshing the memory of the first movie with the help of a »Director's Cut«, and then releasing sequels, has become popular. It is employed particularly frequently in the cases of films that were last shown in cinemas quite some time ago, and the unbroken attractiveness of which has to be proven to audiences all over again. As a result, a prequel to *The Exorcist* is currently in production, as is another American continuation of *Alien* (Great Britain, Ridley Scott,1979) – the Director's Cut of which could be seen in cinemas in 2003.

Sequels, particularly those to horror movies, often turn out to be less continuations of the original story than actual remakes. The latest recycling tendency within the film production line churning out sequels is the so-called »crossover«. The heroes from several hit films are sent on a joint adventure; exponents of this trend are *The League of Extraordinary Gentlemen* (USA, Stephen Norrington, 2003), *Freddy vs. Jason* (USA, Ronny Yu, 2003) and *Alien vs. Predator* (USA, Paul W. S. Anderson, 2004). That idea is in no way new, and it is basically the same as the one behind video and computer games in a *Pokemon* mould; in those games, pawns can be set on one another in new combinations again and again. In their turn, the producers of these games – such as the Japanese company Nintendo – stand in the tradition of trashy Japanese monster joust films from the 1960s and 1970s that saw mutant dinosaur Godzilla pitting his strength against opponents like the giant moth Mothra, the three-headed dragon King Gidrah or the Smog Monster. Likewise, the earlier days of Hollywood saw popular characters like Dracula, the Wolf Man, Laurel and Hardy, the Little Rascals or Abbott and Costello paying each other visits (as in *Abbott and Costello meet Frankenstein,* USA, Charles T. Barton, 1948). It seems that in the meantime, Hollywood has established a new pandemonium of distinctive characters – meaning brands – that make it possible to hark back to that strategy.

Films with less commercial and more intellectual leanings have always enjoyed quoting Hollywood productions, or rather presenting foils to them – as the influence of Film Noir on the Nouvelle Vague has shown. But to what extent does Hollywood, in its turn, put to use elements of »specialist« movies? Both sides mostly like to incorporate single motifs; entire action complexes are lifted less frequently. The reasons for this are obvious: a remake of *Made in USA* (France / Italy, Jean-Luc Godard, 1966) is, at present, hardly a possibility. The breaches in linear storytelling attempted by Godard in that film are simply too radical. Instead, Hollywood has taken to making use of old B or C films of late – films which were made with a commercial end in mind, but which nevertheless were aimed at a smaller audience. Horror or action flicks with formerly minuscule budgets – for example, *The Texas Chainsaw Massacre* (USA, Tobe Hooper, 1974) or *Dawn of the Dead* (USA, George A. Romero, 1977) – are recreated employing the aesthetics of an A production; the results are *Michael Bay's Texas Chainsaw Massacre* (USA, Marcus Nispel, 2003) or *Dawn of the Dead* (USA, Zack Snyder, 2004). The main reason for such undertakings is the audiences' higher tolerance for violent scenes, which entails that splatter movies only genre fans used to enjoy can now reach a mainstream audience.

The systematic self-referencing of the US film business facilitates not only the creative process of shooting a film, but also its advertising and merchandising. Many poster designers rely on the recognition factor for their work; this is best demonstrated by the almost identical motives on the posters for films such as *Jaws* (USA, Steven Spielberg, 1977) and *Tremors* (USA, Ron Underwood, 1990). Even remainders of old toys are marketed anew – the Mattel company recently sold the Slime Pit playset from *Masters of the Universe* (USA, Gary Goddard, 1987) with a tag referencing the *Harry Potter* films (*Harry Potter and the Philosopher's Stone,* USA, Chris Columbus, 2001; *Harry Potter and the Chamber of Secrets,* USA, Chris Columbus, 2002; *Harry Potter and the Prisoner of Azkaban,* USA, Alfonso Cuarón, 2004), even though none of these feature a snake tower like it.

Essentially, the overview above can be summed up by stating that one of the cardinal principles of Hollywood success is that of self-mimicking reproduction. In this respect, the film industry acts in a similar manner to other fields of business, such as fast food chains or car manufacturers. Products are composed of a more or less stable core element »a« and a mobile element »b«;

the latter is modified cyclically. When taking into account that cinematic movies are, for the most part, narrating works of art (especially as Hollywood production firms exclude experimental films from their product palette), a conflict between »negative« and »positive« forces lies at the core of every movie story line. Adopting Robin Wood's terminology,[1] it can be inferred that it is element that contains the aspect of basic repression. According to this, all drives that fundamentally render impossible the social coexistence of humans are negative unless they are compensated for by positive forces. Element b, however, is exposed to the adjustments of a dynamic kind of surplus repression. Once society becomes more and more heterogeneous and, resulting from this, the criteria for negative and positive forces are multiplied, it is beneficial to the distribution of the product to have that product meet the diverging expectations of the customers (as can be observed in the case of the white, dark-skinned and Asian protagonists in the *Matrix* movies, and those films' blending together of different world religions, myths and philosophies to a point of arbitrariness). The American studio system may also use its prominent position on the world-wide market to homogenize its customers. Yet this idea, a widespread one in times of globalization, is tainted with the stench of paranoia, as self-mimicking reproduction remains evolutionary and reliant on exchanges.

Now that TVs, VCRs and finally DVD players have entered most homes, consumption of films has risen dramatically. An above average number of people have gained impressive amounts of knowledge concerning cinematic works, at least when compared to those familiar with the theater or the fine arts, of which only rudimentary knowledge is common, or with literature and music, fields that produce disproportionately larger amounts of material and thus only allow for sectional knowledge. This potentiated awareness, however, has no restricting influence on the Hollywood recycling system. No remake may be advertised for with a slogan like »The remake of the worldwide success …«, since the impression of monotony is not to be aroused; that of something having been modified, however, is welcome, as a common advertising phrase like »By the makers of …« shows. While children appreciate being told a fairy tale in the same manner again and again, adults, who have seen a certain film, may reject its remake, but will watch it nevertheless, so that they might hold forth about it in front of friends or in chat rooms. The rejection of the remake is turned into an appraisal of the original and one's own originality. Likewise, newer films casually reminiscing their older »role models« offer to their audience the pleasurable opportunity to refresh their own level of knowledge. It can be assumed that the industry's self-referentiality increases in a manner symmetrical to the increase of the audience's cinematic knowledge – especially, as the movie makers are part of the audience, too. A former video store clerk, Quentin Tarantino is *the* prototype for film directors of today and tomorrow.

It is often claimed that every work of narrative art can be traced back to merely a handful of stories. Hollywood has turned this handful into more profitable projects than any other industry.

Christian W. Thomsen

Mixed realities. From HAL 9000 to *The Matrix* – computer and androids in contemporary science-fiction movies

The annual conference of Northrhine-Westphalia's Science Center in Düsseldorf, in early December 2003, was called: »Neuro-Visions: Brain Research in the 21st Century«. Two of its main sessions dealt with the topics »Building Plan of the Human Brain: What Forms our Consciousness?« and »Between Man and Machine. Are we on the Way to an Artificial Consciousness?« Neurosciences, in their interdisciplinarity between medicine, biology, computer sciences and humanities, have become a lead-discipline of the early 21st century. Their visions are widely discussed. Controversies deal with the question whether our behavior is solely explainable by electro-chemical processes in our brain and whether freedom of will is a mere illusion.

Another key point of interest is that of mind and intellect in a machine. A growing number of neuroscientists and computer specialists believe in the creation of states similar to human consciousness in machines. One of the basic questions asks whether an artificial, man-made system, structurally built like a brain, is possible at all and if so, can have consciousness.

Therefore the exact description of all the processes in our brain, how we see, feel, touch, hear, how we think, how we learn, how we create emotions, how we remember, how we forget, are of prime importance. The simulation of information networking in the human brain could allow to connect the human nervous system with an artificial neural net. Thus we would achieve a direct interface between man and machine.

Such questions occupy mind and imagination of science-fiction authors in literature and film since almost the beginning of the genre. Fascination and fear, attraction and repulsion are mutual impulses which stimulate writers, directors and scientists alike. Science-fiction movies, at least in the majority of their manifestations, are visualizations of major scientific and political problems, anxieties, obsessions, dystopia which haunt our societies since the early 20th century. Hollywood, once again, acts as a provider of images, concepts, possible solutions for crisis management as can be seen in the cooperation of script writers, the Pentagon and other officials of the Bush administration after 11th September, 2001.[1]

The interrelation between neurosciences, neurosurgery and science fiction is close but one-sided. Science-fiction writers and filmmakers are extremely interested in popularized versions of actual research programs and theories. Brain researchers rarely, if ever, read science fiction, mainly because they feel it is not »scientific« enough and beyond their dignity to deal with fiction. And Hollywood with its predilection for fights, violence, special effects, shootouts instead of rational solutions is not exactly what serious scientists are looking for.

Once they do they are amazed on the scope of innovative discussions about brain research related problems carried out in science-fiction literature and to a lesser degree in movies. It is, of course, easier for literature to put forward bold theories and daring solutions than for filmmakers, especially in a time where science-fiction blockbusters each devour several hundred million dollars in production costs.

Computers and androids play a decisive role in contemporary science-fiction movies. And we are all aware of venerable traditions of simulated worlds reaching back to Plato's »Allegory of the Cave« and Renaissance conceptions of the »World as a Dream« on the one hand, the desire to decode the core and the innermost construction of life and world and of the creation of artificial men since Faustus and Frankenstein's monster and their continued influence on the film industry on the other hand.

Unaware for most people, apart from Heiner Müller's play *Hamlet-Machine* (1977), yet, it seems to be Shakespeare's Danish prince who starts a particular tradition when ending his ambiguous love letter to Ophelia with the sentence »Thine evermore, most dear lady – whilst this machine is to him, Hamlet.« (II. ii. 122) The heart is meant here, the heart as the central life-sustaining organ, the pump which also was thought the seat of emotions.

Sensualist epistemology, which emphasizes the senses and our body-organs as the sole source and basis of cognition finds entrance into materialistic world views as published in La Mettrie's L'homme machine (1747), in Helvetius' De l'esprit (1758) and Baron Holbach's *Système de la nature* (1770).

Their materialistic image of nature traces all emotions of the human soul or psyche back to mere nerve and brain activities. This is a position that, with necessary modern refinements, is still held by many natural scientists. We all know about the man-machine metaphor kept alive throughout the 19th century until it was gradually replaced by the image of the computer as a

1–8. *2001: A Space Odyssey*, directed by Stanley Kubrick, 1968.

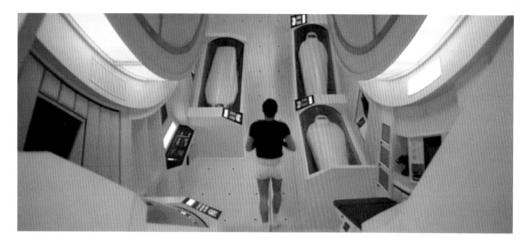

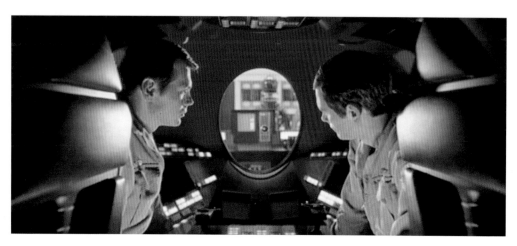

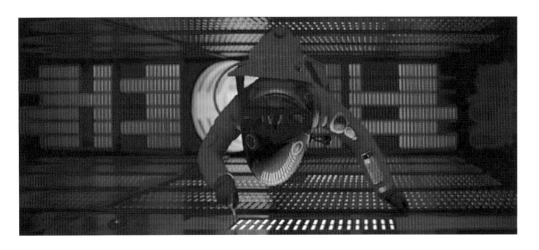

model for the human brain in the middle of the 20th century. That was more and more refined by half-organic computers and neural networks. But as a model it is still current, even if everybody knows that this cannot be an absolute truth and will be substituted by modified theories with the increase of knowledge gained by experiments in many interrelated sciences. Yet the machine image in a way is still valid when e. g. the brain is regarded as a kind of universal interpretation machine translating physical signals into electro-chemical currents of nerve language which the brain localizes and fills with meaning in its respective storage centers. Recent research has found out that the neural network of our brain as well as single cells are capable of learning and that our consciousness is not a static condition of self-awareness and self-reflectivity but a flexible fluid process of information interchanging between different parts and both hemispheres of our brain which makes it the more difficult to artificially imitate the human brain with its 100 billion of nerve cells tightly packed into a head box with a volume of approx. 10 x 10 x 15 cm, weighing 1,35 kg.

As far as science-fiction movies are concerned Fritz Lang's *Metropolis* (1927) still serves as one of the most fertile initiators and stimulators of ideas and images, and Maria, his machine-woman, as the mother of film-androids.

With Stanley Kubrick's *2001: A Space Odyssey* (1968) we reach a completely new level of lasting imagery combined with philosophical reflection. It is used as a quarry for techno-aesthetics, visual ideas as well as for the construction of conflicts between man and computer, cyborg and android ever since without having been surpassed yet.

What makes this conflict such a challenging one in *2001* is the fact that Kubrick has not dressed his central computer, which controls all functions of his spaceship Aries, into the appearance of a robot or into a humanlike android, but HAL 9000 clearly visible remains a modern machine, although endowed with a soft voice, as Georg Seeßlen and Fernand Jung put it in their excellent interpretation »somewhat in between psychologist, child and father confessor«[2] and one-eyed like Polyphem, the man-eating giant in Homer's *Odyssee*. That makes it more abstract and detached at first glance, but upon deeper consideration it makes it more urgent and inextricable as we realize that this machine has human emotions and fights for its survival, disregarding Asimov's three laws of robotics, namely that a robot has, above all, to protect human beings, second to protect himself and third that number one under all conditions has priority over number two.

In *2001* we meet a world of clean and beautiful Bauhaus design carried to the extreme of soulless functionality. The astronauts, by necessity, are trained and equipped to become as machinelike as possible to overcome the disadvantages of the human condition as compared to perfectly built and functioning machines. It becomes evident that a machine world controlled by a perfect computer system makes man superfluous. And up to the present day nobody would deny that astronauts look, walk, behave, and act more like machines than ordinary human beings. The crucial point in *2001* yet is that simultaneously HAL, the computer, is constructed as an over-reacher, who, learning by doing, is capable of crossing the borderline between man and machine, which consists in developing emotions and a feeling of mortality. If the balanced unity between man and technology breaks the outcome is deadly for both of them.

In a world of carefully designed sterility where in accordance with their environment, the dialogues between the astronauts are of the same triviality and banality as the actual radio communication between astronauts and their ground stations, the super-computer HAL develops the entire scale of human psychology from love via suspicion, distrust to hatred and cunning deceit. The two models of world explanation in our culture clash: metaphysics (god) and knowledge (science), but the traditional roles are reversed. The machine argues emotionally and is countered by a survival strategy of mere functionalism. Two thought patterns fight each other. Both withdraw, evade from logical solution the nearer one comes and the end, consequently, is mysticism. In HAL we face the soul in the age of its technical reproducibility, as Seeßlen / Jung have remarked. The machine is described as the – possibly – last human being capable of genuine emotions. 30 years later we meet Ripley in *Alien 4* who recognizes machines because they are more human than humans.

Dave Bowman kills HAL by switching off one of his functions after the other and finally taking away his memory. Watching a computer losing its mind and memory is touching and tragic. What does a machine feel when it dies? HAL regresses into a child, regaining lost innocence, singing the famous Music Hall song »Daisy, Daisy, give me your answer, too, I'm half crazy just for the love of you ...« as his death song.

Early in *2001* we realize that there is no common code of perception in space. There is no right, left, above, below, center or periphery and in the end the difference between life and death is blurred. Time is condensed to a point where death and birth merge and, as in quantum physics, observation creates its own object. Man is finally thrown out of his positivist technical utopia and what remains is enigmatic mysticism, an eternal journey without return. The astronauts in 2001 are no cyborgs, neither is HAL an android, but the direction is clear and the consequences are filled with complexity and complications.

On our time trip into the 21st century we take our next short stop in the year 1982 with two landmarks in the range of science-fiction movies with regard to computers, androids and new concepts of reality consciousness: *Tron* and *Blade Runner*.

Tron has been much underrated, most likely because it turns into a classical fairy tale, after a visionary start of breathtaking images as one of the first computer-generated movies. The aesthetics of *Tron* are outstanding for the time, but the recycling of myths is rather trivial.

A hacker is split by a laser-scanner into molecules and transported into a world inside the computer where he is forced to participate in gladiatorial games. The usual fight between good and bad is that between a dictatorial program called »Master Control« and »Tron« as an honest safety program. User, hard- and software melt into one, man becomes part of the computer and as such he is a better being than the real »fleshers« outside.

At the time computers could generate static images, but could not automatically put them into action. Thus, the coordinates for each image, such as a light cycle, had to be entered for each individual frame. It took 600 coordinates to get 4 seconds of film. Each of these coordinates was entered into the computer by hand by the filmmakers.[3]

It may have been a very small step for the history of mankind, but it definitely was a great step in the history of animations. And the idea that a human brain and finally a human body, bit by bit, slice by slice, could be transmitted into – the matrix – so to say, of a computer, was ingenious. If ever you wonder where Hans Moravec got his ideas for the fifth generation of robots, due in the middle of the 21st century, from, you find possible origins here.[4]

To literally and not virtually transmit the entire body into the interior of the computer is, of course, ludicrous and leads nowhere. It probably can only be understood on the basis of these huge super-computers of a time, when they were still called »Electronic Brains« and where people like Harry Harrison in his *Mechanismo* (1978) designed entire cities as computer structures with skyscrapers in humanoid forms as gigantic electronic brains.[5] That miniaturization was to be the solution for immensely increasing storage capacity of computers had not entered the general public's mind yet. The idea of a virtual alongside a »real« existence inherent in *Tron* confers a place of honor in the history of modern film to this movie, written and directed by Steven Lisberger.

Tron was very successful as a computer game but rather a flop at the box office. In the meantime it may have become cult for a very small elite.

Blade Runner took ten years to be recognized by larger strata of critical and general public awareness as a first rate movie with a firm place in film history.

Do Androids Dream of Electric Sheep? Or do they rather dream of men and women in flesh and blood? Philip K. Dick's ingenious novel dates back to 1968, the year when *2001* was released, and it proves that evolution and history do not continue in straight lines but make sudden jumps and that literature usually is far ahead of film. Dick's *Minority Report* is another proof of that and the most complex of his stories have not found their film versions, yet.

The novel and the director's cut make it perfectly clear what the originally released film version omits, namely that Blade Runner Rick Deckard is a replicant himself. Unaware of it first, uncertain later, and finally he knows. As such he is a fully developed artificial human being, a biotic creation of man like Goethe's Prometheus, only stronger and more intelligent than average humans, but equipped with a life expectancy of only four years: »Here I will sit, forming men / After my own image. / It will be a race like me, / To suffer, to weep, / To enjoy and to rejoice, / And to pay not attention to you, / As I do!« (Translation by Emily Ezust)

And that throws up the whole bunch of ethic, moral, juridical questions and problems. We have to widen our definition of what is reality and of what is man. The final threshold has been transgressed once again.

The basic problems of HAL reappear but now in human personification. The replicants, originally not equipped with emotions, develop genuine feelings, learning by doing. They question implanted memories and ask for real ones. Authenticity, one of the crucial points in Postmodern discourse. Replicants are not clones. They are serial but also unique, like ourselves. The perversion lies in the fact that man creates perfect artificial human beings in order to use them as slaves and killer machines. Reality is a fiction that pretends not to be one. But, when watching the evening

13–16. *Tron*, directed by Steven Lisberger, 1982.

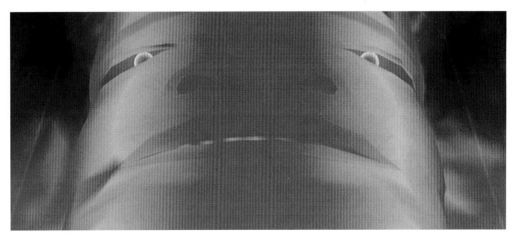

news and seeing those American marines in Afghanistan and Iraq with all their electronic equipment, former nice guys from around the corner, turned into killer machines by their training, remote-controlled by headquarters in Bahrain, Quatar and Washington, one-man fighting units, crawling around in the heat in their heavy armor like clumsy beetles and, in spite of all their electronics helpless against landmines which once their government sold to the tyrants and to guerrilla fighters lying in ambush, one could say with Wagner in Goethe's *Faust*: »Excuse me! But it is a great delight / To enter in the spirit of the ages and to see / How once a sage before us thought and then how we / Have brought things on at last to such a splendid height.« (*Faust*, I, 570–573)

And I ask myself, how in ten or twenty years from now the Geneva Convention will treat the fighter robots which then will be used in American warfare? At that point the image of the »Flesh Fair« in Steven Spielberg's and Stanley Kubrick's *A. I. – Artificial Intelligence*, rises before my inner eye.

For me the cruelest scene in Ridley Scott's *Blade Runner* is the one where Deckart, who already dimly suspects that he is a replicant himself, chases one of those beautiful femme fatale-replicants across the streets and shoots her in the back when she, in utter despair like an animal in a hopeless situation, jumps through a large shop window. All ethical and cultural values I was brought up with are reversed here and justified by the legal authorities: »Hail America, my new found land.« How to treat androids? Ethical, philosophical and juridical questions become the more urgent the further robotics and man-machine interaction proceed.

In the later 1990s Sony published ads in progressive design oriented high-tech magazines for media information like *Wired* showing a beautiful young lady wearing a chip implanted in her left ear like a diamond, while a small disc is slipping right into the back of her head.

Well, some of my friends among neurosurgeons do really implant chips. Chips for paralyzed people which enable them to start walking again. And soon there will be chips for blind people, allowing them to envision at least shapes of things and humans. The Sony campaign was clearly reminiscent of the company's computer game *Johnny Mnemonic* (1995) and Roberto Longo and William Gibson's movie of the same title. In spite of William Gibson writing the screenplay using his cult, cyberpunk short story published in 1981, the movie turned out a complete flop with Keanu Reeves winning the Razzie Award for the worst actor of the year.

The plot runs as follows: In 2021 the whole world is connected by the gigantic Internet, and almost half of the population is suffering from the Nerve Attenuation Syndrome (NAS). Johnny, with an implanted memory chip in his brain, was ordered to transport the overloaded information from Beijing to Newark. While Pharmakon Industries supported by Yakuza tries to capture him to get the information back, the low-tech group led by J-Bone tries to break the missing code to download the cure of NAS which Johnny carries.

My students hated the story, yet I somewhat liked it, because it is so extravagant, or in the word of film critic Roger Ebert: »Johnny Mnemonic is one of the great goofy gestures of recent cinema, a movie that doesn't deserve one nanosecond of serious analysis but it has a kind of idiotic grandeur that makes you almost forgive it. Based on a story by William Gibson, the father of cyberpunk fiction, it has the nerve to pose as a futuristic fable when in fact all of its parts were bought off the shelf at the Used Movie Store.«[6]

Data transfer within Johnny's head at a time when you could send it encrypted via the net is in fact sheer nonsense. But I appreciate the movie because of a number of grandiose, bizarre scenes and because of its grotesque, punky shootout finale furioso, compared with which the great battle scene in *The Matrix Revolutions* is just a gigantic waste of material.

Gibson tried to justify it by saying: »We want to see him get the information for himself, escape, turn the tables on the bad guys. But in the end he does something else, and manages to become a human being in the process. I see it as a fable of the information age.«[7]

Flop or not flop, what that movie proves is that by the mid 1990s the actual development of information technology had overtaken and outdated science fiction of the early 1980s, an acceleration which in fact caused Gibson to stop writing science fiction in 2002, when he claimed, while publishing his latest novel *Pattern Recognition* (2002), that the present development of technology is increasing so fast and widely that science-fiction authors could no longer cope with it.

It needs an extremely educated, philosophical and visionary science-fiction author like mathematician and computer scientist Vernor Vinge who published some of the very best science-fiction stories and novels of our time to explain in simple terms what is at the core of our present interest and the movies talked about in this paper: »All sorts of apocalyptic visions are floating around, but mine is very narrow. It just says that if we ever succeed in making machines as smart as humans, then it's only a small leap to imagine that we would soon thereafter make – or cause to be made – machines that are even smarter than any human. And that's it. That's the end of the human era – the closest analogy would be the rise of the human race within the animal kingdom.«[8]

This, after all, is what Alex Proyas' *I Robot* (2004) with heavy borrowings from *Metropolis* and various Isaac Asimov stories (screenplay by Jeff Vintor) begins to explore. Science-fiction films approach such somber visions which deal with a yet distant future from different angles. In a fantastic soap universe like *Star Trek* with its beginnings in 1978, and ever new sidelines which can be developed into semi-independent plots in each new episode the filmmakers experiment with a great variety of innovative ideas.

It is a classical collection of fantastic stories, in its structure somewhat looking like a modern version of *Arabian Nights*, with fairy tale ingredients, myths, legends, crime-, travel- and adventure-subplots, humorous arabesques immersed into a general science-fiction atmosphere, baked with a tasty space-crust into a kind of science-fiction pizza where the same basic ingredients remain but are varied and spiced with numerous appetizers.

In a universe like *Star Trek* everything is allowed. Strict rules of logic are not applied and human laws of probability count little in realms of outer space where warp engines and time vortices eliminate the laws of nature. Yet even the most bizarre and seemingly most eccentric theories and their visualization are based on scientific, medical or philosophical articles and theories, without, of course, ever having been tested and proved.

A nice and fairly recent example for our topic is *Star Trek. The First Contact* (1998) where with Data we meet a particularly kind and friendly android, the only one of his kind, built after his human creator's own image. His essential desire is to become more human. He paints, sings, is a lover of music, owns a cat, likes to imitate artists and can recombine the creative power of composers, thereby achieving something new and original. That is enabled by his emotion chip which simultaneously makes him more human and less than human, because he can switch it off. This may sound farfetched, but if you look at those American jet fighter pilots who are regularly given drugs with very similar effects before and after their long action, frequently taking 7–10 hours on duty under highest concentration in narrow aircraft cockpits, even a figure like Data comes pretty close to contemporary reality.

The Borgs as counterparts personify a humanoid, semi-biotic cyber-race with collective consciousness, organized like an ant colony which can assimilate the characteristics of every race in the universe. Their motto: »Resistance is futile. You will be assimilated.« Like Gigeresque cyberpunks from a techno scrap yard Borg design celebrates aesthetics of the ugly which in itself embodies everything horrible and repellent like the queen's Gorgo head, via medieval representations of demons and devils and the Frankensteinian monster tradition up to present day high-tech wearables.

Whereas *Star Trek* entertains and amuses on a partly neuroscientific basis as a pastiche of science-, media-, technology- and sociology-fantasies *Ghost in the Shell* summarizes in manga dress the brain-research related science-fiction philosophy as published up to the late 1990s.

Ghost in the Shell (1998) is not a Hollywood movie, but as a British film critic remarked, »just the kind of movie James Cameron would have liked to do if Disney had let him«. Together with *Akira* it undoubtedly helped considerably to start the tidal wave of manga and anime which in the last couple of years has swept Europe and the United States. More and more manga are recognized not only as cheap entertainment but as a highly creative genuine form of art.

Many German kids now even prefer manga to Mickey Mouse and even the ZDF-Mainzelmännchen now look like manga characters in their new make-up. *Ghost in the Shell* also served as one of the major inspirations for *The Matrix*. Without including the manga elements criticism of *The Matrix* cannot do justice to that trilogy. From our present point of view *Ghost in the Shell* is particularly interesting as a climax in the realization of science-fiction philosophy which deals with the further development of mankind in the 21st century, with speculations about mixed realities, cyber-bodies, cyber-ethics, blends, of real, artificial and virtual bodies, hard- and software implementations into the human brain etc.

By that time brain-hacking, the artificial enlargement of the brain's storage capacity, simulated experiences were common ground for science-fiction fans (cf. *Blade Runner* and *Total Recall*). *Ghost in the Shell* interconnects many of these speculations into a story which is more than just a Japanese fairy tale. It is a compendium of philosophical borderline fantasies around neuro-computers, neurosurgery, interfaces between brain and machines. Cyborgs with personal history demand individuation. Questions of identity, self-consciousness in cyber-bodies with computer controlled metabolisms are treated as self-evident and taken for granted for the near future.

That almost necessarily breeds new forms of crime and the Puppet Master, an artificial intelligence without identifiable form, has managed to control the souls of his victims, so that he may continuously be present in cyber-bodies. To generate your own identity becomes a basic paranoia of cyborgs.

Ghost in the Shell depicts a society of total surveillance where the acceptance of cyborgs and other varieties of mixed man/machine beings is the most natural thing. Only memory, reproduction and mortality makes humans human. Therefore new forms of memory are developed, living, thinking unities in an ocean of information looking for physical representation.

The philosophical contents of the millennium debate between Bill Joy and Ray Kurzweil about the future of mankind in the later 21st century, about a transformation and a continuation of the human species into cyber-bodies, have found their aesthetic realization in exactly the same year as the publication of Kurzweil's *The Age of Spiritual Machines*. And with all its Japanese exuberance of choreographed violence *Ghost in the Shell* is a uniquely poetic aesthetic experience.

»We are such stuff / As dreams are made of, and our little life / Is rounded with a sleep.« (*The Tempest*, IV.i 156–158) Prospero's famous quote taken literally emphasizes that our real existence is an immaterial one. That does not mean that it is virtual, but it comes close to that. Have we not all felt a desire, one time or another, to really live in another world, to experience a past or future age? The critic of the first *Matrix* film (1999) in the German weekly *Die Zeit*,[9] talks about this twilight state between sleep and being awake which everybody knows from his own experience. It moulds the atmosphere of the entire movie. Telephones are constantly ringing like alarm bells, the camera plunges headlong down the façades of skyscrapers.

It is as if a drowning person wants to reach the surface all the time, as if a dreamer desperately fights for his awakening in order to find his own self. But in *The Matrix* you never know whether you don't wake up in the next dream. »Do you ever have that feeling whether you are awake or still dreaming?« is one of the first questions Morpheus asks Neo and that is a good characterization of the general atmosphere in the first part of the *Matrix* trilogy which was greeted unanimously positive by international film criticism.

Yet the Wachowski brothers aimed higher. They added a second film which presented a lot of secretiveness and mysterious apocalyptic threats concerning the fate of the world instead of real substance. And the beautiful martial art scenes of the first part, which took the audience by surprise made everybody wonder, were over-choreographed and stretched out too long in the second part *The Matrix Reloaded* (2003), as was the longest, most breathtaking and spectacular car chase in film history. But special effects, once overdone, soon become boring. Technical brilliance, which undoubtedly there is, needs substantial contents in story and acting.

Yet the substance faded away, most of all in the third part of *The Matrix Revolutions* (2003). Why on earth the plural when there is only one final uprise and showdown in the enduring fight between humans and machines?

And the actors? They are challenged with the task of performing their parts in a »real« and a virtual reality. Keanu Reeves, Neo, the chosen One, the Messiah and Savior, fulfils it with a kind of detached aloofness. Almost wordless he appears to move around in a state of trance between sleep and being awake. His few facial expressions slow down the longer the trilogy drags on. Laurence Fishburne, alias Morpheus, god of sleep and dreams, deteriorates from an energetic leader and fighter in the first part to a stereotypical general with the pathos of Henry V and Julius Caesar gone stale in *The Matrix Reloaded* to a leaden guy who grows fat and almost motionless in *The Matrix Revolutions*. Carrie Ann Moss, Trinity, fighting, loving, suffering, grows thinner and thinner from scene to scene until in the third film she looks so careworn that her eventual death becomes a dramaturgical necessity.

Matrix, like *Men in Black*, is the kind of movie that is in absolute need of dark sunglasses to be worn on all occasions, all times of the day, in light and dark, and especially underground. They substitute skilful acting and symbolize »cult« like the slick long leather coats which formerly used to be reserved for Gestapo and SS-officers. But here they are Cult, design, façade, behind which the art of acting hides and finally evaporates. But in their stylish elegance they are also an element from the world of manga and computer games.

Matrix and Jonathan Mostow's *Terminator 3* fall into the same trap of a misconceived future where the machines have won and did not annihilate mankind but enslaved them. In *Terminator 3* it is the computer network Sky Net which is ready to take over world domination, in *Matrix* the machines have succeeded in doing so and their ominous god-figure, stolen out of *Tron*, forwarded to *I Robot*, surrogate for transcendence and divinity in all religions, a kind of essence of collective machine consciousness, has created a program, the architect, which in return created

17–20. *The Matrix*, directed by Larry and Andy Wachowski, 1999.

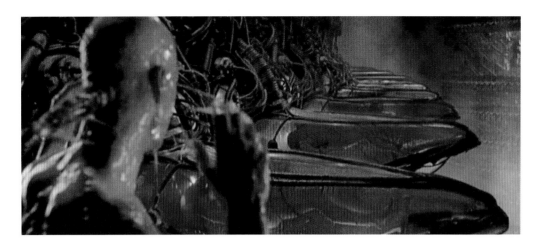

21–24. *The Matrix Reloaded*, directed by Larry and Andy Wachowski, 2003.

25–28. *The Matrix Revolutions*, directed by Larry and Andy Wachowski, 2003.

the Matrix, a network, able to simulate a whole reality, a whole world. Only the Spartan community of Zion, the last human city, survives underground in a Gigeresque- and Piranesi-like hierarchical soldier community of techno-hippies with race segregation and old-fashioned gender roles. An incredible mixture if ever you reflect on the original meaning of Zion, the pre-Israelite fortress of Jerusalem conquered by David, later on the temple area and symbolizing Jerusalem as the city of David. In the psalms of the Old Testament Zion is praised as god's domicile, the nodal point between the worlds of heaven and earth, from whence the blessings of god emanate into the world. Zion as motif for the hope of salvation for Israel and all the world. But who would like to return to a cavernous Zion underground filled with old submarine scrap tech and new information technology? What kind of hope emanates from there? Details and story don't fit together. *Matrix* is an unheard of mix of theological, philosophical, mythological, apocalyptic allusions, a genre mix of thriller, science fiction, love story, western, Kung-Fu eastern.[10] But above all it represents the genre Hollywood is most fond of: the fairy tale. Alice, a. k. a. innocent hacker Neo in Wonderland, short-circuited with *Neuromancer*. If you look upon the trilogy from a manga point of view the philosophical inconsistencies and the sudden breaks and shifts in its narrative disappear, because that is just the way manga are told, where you take situations for granted without asking for strict logic or analyzing them.

Yet there is irony. Not as much irony as in *Terminator 3*, but one could be tempted to interpret the trilogy as an ironical feast of genre-self-referentiality. They are all quoted extensively: *Metropolis*, *2001: A Space Odyssey*, *Tron*, the *Alien* films, *Star Trek*, *City of the Dark* etc. Or is it downright plagiarism?

Matrix balances on a tightrope between a comprehensive ironic treatment of the history of the science-fiction movie and pseudo-religious philosophy which tries to combine eastern and western influences. And while *2001* inevitably ends in mysticism, because the last questions of mankind cannot be answered otherwise, *Matrix* eventually falls down from the tightrope into the heat of that boiling philosophical stew from whence blind seer Tiresias – Neo – Jesus is elevated in a pathetic triumphal ascension into the realm of mystic indefiniteness where all questions are extinguished. Nothing is answered but everything is purged and transfigured into pure light.

What is the Matrix? The control panel of the world computer or the simulated world itself? The metaphor is not unambiguous. It is a program creating programs. You can read every program as a text. You could read the Matrix as the text of the cinema itself. A text that continuously produces visions, pictures, moving images, animations, dreams, myths, the text of the cinema itself as technically hallucinated escapes from reality:[11] »Well, that's one thing you can depend on. Film is not real«,[12] George Lucas once said, and that's for sure.

But the question remains how far it influences our understanding and our intellectual construction of the world? The people in *Matrix* are not cyborgs or androids, they are programs. They ask each other: »Are you a program?« Even Neo is a program. When he is cloned by Australian actor Hugo Weaving alias Agent Smith, the only really excellent actor in *Matrix*, his program is so powerful that he can even assimilate devil incarnate Satan Agent Smith into his own program structure and finally overcome him.

We are all programs, genetic programs turned into biotic individuals, but the android programs in *Matrix* are just electronic simulations and that is inconsequent and trivial.

In the third part such inconsistencies do not really matter, because the borderlines between Matrix and Zion reality have become porous. Less and less of the action takes place in the Matrix. On the other hand the film in an awkward way is trimming its contents upon the chauvinistic ideology of the present American administration and Bible Belt religious fundamentalism. The obsessive belief in the power of guns and firearms may be interpreted either as irony or as infantile surrogate fantasies of suppressed aggressive sexuality which makes old Sigmund rotate in his grave or as »gunfire, the sound of freedom« as one of the technical assistants in the »Making of«-film of *The Matrix Reloaded* claims. Neither ingenious pixel battles nor the overwhelming use of hardware and ammunition solve any of the genuine questions realized in the trilogy. It is made clear that a military super-power can destroy any country. But there is no convincing program for the after-battle-problems: post-war reconstruction of infra-structure, economy, culture, education, health system, schools, etc. etc. On the contrary: the light figure of a redeemer shall solve all problems. Yet there is no Savior around and back on the ground we experience how low-tech missiles, fired from donkey carts, beat high-tech. What remains is a religiously tinted fairy tale.

We have come a long way from *2001: A Space Odyssey* to *The Matrix*. Scientific complexity has multiplied since then, but not that of science fiction. There are steadily spiraling production costs, also special effects, sound worlds, improvements in camera techniques and computer animations.[13] But the basic questions concerning artificial life, artificial intelligence, cyborgs, androids are still the same. And they never found deeper philosophical answers than in Kubrick's *2001*.

There are interesting ideas and experiments tried in films like *Tron* and serial episodes or the discussion of deep human problems in *Blade Runner*. But the techno-euphoria and optimism of the 1960s has given way to high-tech exaggeration but also to technophobia and utterly pessimistic world views of a future in ruins. Not to look for interrelations with political developments like globalization, the loss of a balance of power, the rise of Islamic religious fundamentalism, problems of race and ethnicity, short-sighted entrepreneurial capitalism on the side of the one remaining super-power would be downright silly. And to lead mass audiences to believe in the solution of complex problems through firearm shootouts and martial arts or putting all the hope on messianic figures with super-natural powers is mere stultification and pure escapism.

The present-day Hollywood science-fiction blockbuster does not fulfill the expectations expressed at the beginning of this paper. It relies on special effects, actionism, old societal clichés and the exploitation of people's collective fears. Relationships between men and women are still out of balance. Women are either treated hierarchical as eye-catching ornaments, or sexless careerists, or as over-emancipated artistic killers like in Quentin Tarantino's *Kill Bill: Volume 1*. Trinity in the *Matrix* is just another Kung-Fu, manga and gunfire virtuoso and when the Wachowski brothers realized they had not done enough for women emancipation they let the colored girls in *Revolutions* fire with heavy bazookas. And whooom!!! It is again serial episodes like in *Star Trek* where we find more interesting experiments in human interrelationships.

Film scripts are usually adaptations of literary models. There are plenty of science-fiction authors whose work would be worth filming. To mention but an exemplary few I name Americans Vernor Vinge and Neal Stephenson, Australian Greg Egan and British Stephen Baxter.

According to Donna Haraway and other feminist writers and philosophers like Paul Virilio as well as computer scientists like Hans Moravec or Ray Kurzweil we are in the middle of a development process towards a society of hybrid machines and organisms. Most of the neuroscientists tell us not to believe them. Handling a computer, carrying a hip implant and even occasional cyber-sex don't make you a cyborg. But if you look into a book like Julius Wiedemann's *Digital Beauties: 2D & 3D Computer Generated Digital Models, Virtual Idols and Characters* you see how the beauty idols of young women in Asia, especially Japan, and to a lesser degree in the US. comes closer and closer to computer generated models like Lara Croft.[14] And if you watch international pop festivals and awards you will see how aggressively sexy protagonists of the scene like Kristina Aguilera imitate manga and anime models thereby setting standards for the teenage generation.

There are, without any doubt, developments under way, which could decisively change the human species like cloning, the implementation of brain chips, dubious experiments with our genetic structure, a »big brother is watching you«-society of constant surveillance, the diminution of democratic liberties. And public awareness as well as legislature in every democratic country has to be on the lookout for dangerous consequences, while the greatest danger may lie in developments which gradually sneak into our life. And, of course, the military like the terrorists are equally dangerous. Fundamentalist brain washing on the one side vs. possible brain implants on the other.

Our definition of reality has to be widened by the fact that now everybody accepts computer generated virtual realities as part of our everyday reality. Virtual, mediated and »real« realities gradually merge, creating »mixed« realities which cause that feeling of uncertainty so characteristic for the beginning of *The Matrix*.

It is still a long way to scientifically decipher the secrets of the human brain, not to speak of the human psyche. And to build artificial brains or quantum computers with the same capacity and complexity may – hopefully – be out of reach altogether. Meanwhile let us hope for critics and audiences who demand science-fiction entertainment and humor combined with the visualization of those fantastic experiments and dangers modern sciences are really concerned with. And let them be embedded in genuinely moving human relationships. Science fiction as testing ground for futurological considerations seems to be more necessary than ever before. But not the kind of films Hollywood produced in the first years of the 21st century.

Nevertheless they offer plenty of stimulating ideas. And what we should and could do is to initiate an interdisciplinary research program with workshops where science-fiction authors, filmmakers, media artists, philosophers, neuroscientists, psychologists, medical engineers, robotic engineers, sociologists, media and literary scholars should discuss and exchange their ideas concerning fiction that deals with science and science that may overtake fiction.

Christian W. Thomsen

The recycling of myths in Hollywood science-fiction films, exemplified by Roland Emmerich's *Stargate* (1994), Luc Besson's *The Fifth Element* (1997) and Andrew Niccol's *S1m0ne* (2002)

Myths are stories. Apparently, people living in organized societies – cultures that is – cannot make do without mythical stories. These narratives contribute to the finding and founding of a culture's identity. One of their essential components is a narrative core with dynamic, variable, fluctuating edges. This means that these stories are being updated throughout the course of history, and change along with it. But in spite of all changes, the narrative at their core must remain visible. In this context, Jan Assmann talks of a »culture of remembrance«.[1] According to this concept, myths examine the ways in which societies remember, and in which societies imagine themselves by remembering.[2] Thus, they provide patterns of interpretation for societies' respective present times and patterns of orientation for their future actions that are both based on the past. In this regard, the question of veracity is immaterial, it is sufficient that they exist, are continuously updated and regenerated.

Mythical stories have in common a high quota of fictitious content, as well as certain rituals and aesthetics. Hence, they can be associated with literature, religion and artistic creation alike. Consequently, historical myths tell of the sacred, the supernatural invading the world. One central component of their rituals is the dimension of the sacrifice.[3] As societies become ever more secularized, myths become ever more profane – without this development, »urban myths« would not have arisen. However, these myths retain their imagery and their collective significance and, therefrom, some semblance of ritual and religious content. There is a tendency, particularly in Hollywood films, to only ever hint at the dimension of the sacrificial rite and to let that dimension dissolve in happy endings. In its original form, it can still be witnessed in exponents of the epic film genre such as *Rob Roy*, *Braveheart* and *Gladiator*.

As the internationally most important and most influential system of feature film creation, Hollywood is particularly susceptible to mythical stories, their variations and updates, and the reason for this is that its products firstly and foremostly bow to the iron rules of capitalist commerce, which means that they have to tell topical, memorable stories with mass appeal and some »human touch«; these, in turn, must be capable of evoking collective feelings. Here, being memorable – within the framework of the mixed, essentially multi-medial feature film system – implies the coaction of images, sound, music, lighting, interiors, architectures and further components, always combined with accomplished acting, facial expression, gestures, and human bodies, meaning stars. Hollywood cinema, after all, is tantamount to star cinema. Once all other generalizations have been split up into many sub-genres and groups by the dissecting gaze of the scientist, Hollywood can still be reduced to the common denominator »star cinema«. And that is just why people go to the cinema: to see and to experience outstanding human beings – stars, as it were – descriptively narrating exciting, enthralling stories, not to reconstruct scientists' theories.

Apart from that, any genre theory must be couched in highly abstract terms. This also goes for science fiction – the one category that, through cinematic means, constantly updates and varies the ancient novelistic form of the »Staatsroman«, the utopian novel, literature's dystopias, literary journeys to distant worlds and futures and scientific experiments, and presents excursions into the close-by, yet far-off worlds of the human body, its molecular and genetic structures and their manipulability. Precisely because science-fiction films keep visualising those collective societal demands, keep translating into images the anxieties, obsessions, utopias of their respective age, they demonstrate a particular affinity towards myths.

Myths have, at all times, been staged with the aid of »special effects«. These have included battles between chthonian elemental forces or between gods and heroes, haruspicy and ornithomancy as performed by priests, thunder and lightning being seen as summoners of divine will, or of the spirits the like that of Hamlet's father. Special effects are myths' favourite offspring. And where else could such effects be staged more convincingly than in science-fiction films, where they may culminate in the eschatological near-disintegration of all matter (as could recently be witnessed in the *Matrix* trilogy)?[4] But enough of theoretical preliminary remarks – let us, now, demonstrate and analyze some actual examples.

I shall begin with Roland Emmerich's *Stargate* (1994), a film directed, co-written (with Dean Devlin), but not produced by Sindelfingen, Baden-Wuerttemberg's own »Little Spielberg«.[5] Like star cinematographer Michael Ballhaus, directors Roland Emmerich and Wolfgang Petersen are two of the very few Germans who have managed to attain renown and success in Hollywood.

Science-fiction movies, war epics like *The Patriot* (2000), disaster and monster films such as *Independence Day* (1996) or *Godzilla* (1998), traditional big-budget Hollywood cinema are his specialty. In *Stargate*, the myths surrounding the world of ancient Egyptian gods are merged with modern technology – a topic challenging to the imagination which, at the time, could rest assured to attract the interest of a mass audience still familiar with the pseudo-scientific phantasm of someone like Erich von Däniken. At a cost of 55 million dollars – a medium amount when compared to today's budgets for similar films – *Stargate* was, at the time, one of the most expensive productions in cinema history. Most of the work effort was put into special effects, buildings and scenery, and legions of extras. Ten years later, that effort has deflagrated, having nevertheless ignited the creation of a soap universe of ever increasing sophistication (*Stargate SG-1*), and thus having been worthwhile.

The culture of ancient Egypt, especially in combination with biblical themes, has always been a topic of interest to Hollywood – historical epics of the 1950s such as Michael Curtiz's *The Egyptian* (1954), Howard Hawks' *Land of the Pharaohs* (1955), Cecil B. DeMille's *The Ten Commandments* (1957) spring to mind. Their influence can be felt even in films like Anthony Minghella's film of Michael Ondaatje's novel *The English Patient* (1996).

Emmerich and Devlin, however, hark back to a time before the first pharaohs appeared. They begin their tale at a point 10 000 years ago, when Ra, sun-god and beneficial creator, presided over Egypt. He had come to earth from somewhere in the universe in a pyramid spaceship. When his reign ends for unspecified reasons, Ra flees through a star gate of non-terrestrial material to a planet millions of light years away, taking thousand of fellahs with him as slaves and vowing to continue his existence as pharaonic oppressor. He seals up the stargate (for all time, as he believes) so no-one might follow him. While this story may not sound very likely, it nevertheless conforms to myth, as Egyptian myths know no chronology, but merely sequences.[6] That is why in their plot, Emmerich and Devlin make use of old set pieces from popular pulp magazines such as *Amazing Stories*, *Wonder Stories* and Rider Haggard's *Lost World* romances from the 1930s. This is revealed later in the movie – it begins with the discovery of the Stargate during an excavation in 1928. For decades, its strange inscriptions remain undeciphered, until in the present age, the US army attends to the matter with its trademark confidence, energy and problem-solving competence while employing the help of brilliant, youthful Egyptologist Dr. Daniel Jackson, the latter a lovable, brash-but-goofy variant of the tried-and-tested »mad scientist« motif. With the support of highly efficient computer programs, the Stargate is once again rendered fully functional, and a decision is made to have Marine Colonel Jonathan »Jack« O'Neill lead an expedition to the star expected, as it were, at the other end of the tunnel, and to explore that »new frontier«. As is apparently common army practice, the Colonel's hand luggage contains a neat little nuclear explosive device meant to shield the USA from any harm a far-off civilization might want to do it. After all, you never know. Beside some representatives of military grades, O'Neill is accompanied by Daniel Jackson who, in his capacity as Stargate and Egyptology expert, is supposed to guarantee a safe return to Earth. They enter the Stargate's time travel and molecularizing mechanism, and hey presto! – don't ask me how – they switch to superluminar velocity in the twinkling of an eye, ending up in a remote galaxy and on sun-god Ra's planet. The expedition group's journey ends in a kind of space depot-pyramid-temple hybrid as abandoned as some train station in a godforsaken Arizonan desert dump, but much larger and templeesque. Apart from that, desert – just like in Egypt. Stupidly enough, the travellers fail to find a way of re-opening the Stargate for immediate return. And so the story takes its course. The area is scouted, a huge desert city is discovered, the inhabitants of which – as is later revealed – have been damned to prospect for the ore from which the as yet unknown divine king Ra generates his main engines and, in general, the source codes for his system of power. No further details are related to the viewer.

It is a well established fact that American chocolate bars not only glue up one's teeth – they also establish nation-linking friendships, and thus, the Americans are received by the fellahs in a manner just about as friendly as Americans would have Afghans and Iraqis receive them these days. Divine ruler Ra senses mischief and sends some of his miniature stealth bomber drones to deliver a retributive barrage. Next, we witness not only inevitable romances between Colonel O'Neill and a desert lad – a plot thread meant to grant the Colonel compensation for the death of his own son – as well as the fellah chief's daughter and junior scientist Jackson (who are such a nice couple, after all), but also and especially the power struggle between the fellah-supported Americans and the divine ruler Ra's tyrannical regime.

Finally, the film's myth inventory comes into full effect. It appears that, by all means, Emmerich had some competent advisors. Ra rules the land from an architectural complex that is space-

ship, palace and temple all at once. Similar to Jonathan Swift's airborne island Laputa from *Gulliver's Travels* (1726), it is a city structure with the ability to fly, and a construction modeled on (or imitated by) the Great Pyramid of Gizeh. When they appear, Ra, the leaders of his royal household, and his warriors are all clad in Egyptian gods' costumes, with Ra, larger than life as he is, wearing the mask of the sun-god and that of dog-headed god Anubis, the warriors wearing masks of hawk-headed god Horus as well as smaller Anubis masks. Here, the film conforms to myth in that Horus, falcon-shaped, remote god of heaven and eldest of the all-Egyptian gods, supplies the first part of all pharaohs' sovereign's names. Anubis, ruler over the realm of the dead, is a sentinel and a companion, a friend and an aide to the burdened and downtrodden, and a fair-minded judge in Aminse, the netherworld of the dead. In ancient Egyptian myths, even the gods are, in fact, mortal. The sun-god and the luminaries are swallowed every day by Nu, Queen of the Skies, and reborn after passing through the realm of the dead. Primordial and sun-god Re (Ra in the movie) embodies the »Not Yet«. He was around when nothing had yet been created, meaning before all time, and he will be around until the end of the world, when everything retreats into chaos. Being a god is equal to having and exerting power. »I am Re, Lord of the Heavens, who is on Earth«, he speaks in ancient inscriptions. »I shall bring to you splendid things, as a father does.«[7] Egyptian kings were gods and humans at the same time, and acted as mediators between humans and gods. But once the king began to embody merely the incarnation of the deity he was no longer a god in the fullest sense of that term. As a result, he represents god's omnipresence in the world of mankind. By his death, he is, in turn, deified. This belief's proximity to notions behind Christian faith is evident.

The plot outline sheds some light onto the material's dramatic potential. And what does Emmerich turn it into? When they first appear, the half-animal, half-human figures give rise to premonitions of dread, of the sublime, the awe-inspiring qualities of the gods. But their positive properties are turned on their heads. After taking off their masks, Ra and his followers are quickly reduced to mediocre human villains, mere rogue representatives of rogue states. Ra turns out to be a wholly egotistical, power-hungry tyrant. To us, all this appears strangely familiar, and the ambiguity contained within the film's mythical dimension loses all of its potential impact.

Jaye Davidson, who previously appeared in Neil Jordan's *The Crying Game* (1992) and, in that film, appeared to fully savour the tragic dimension to the existence of a person of indeterminate gender, here plays the Egyptian divine king's hermaphroditism with the soft brutality of a beautiful ladyboy, without ever being capable of the megalomaniac satanism of, say, Beckford's Vathek.

Time and again, the clash of modern myths of technology and ancient myths of gods is reduced to banalities. The archaic battle between good and evil is decided by the power of the bomb. The »weapon of mass destruction«, which Ra had wanted to hurl back through the Stargate to earth with its might increased hundredfold, finally destroys the rogue ruler and his pyramid-spaceship-palace in a gigantic flash of light. The scene does conjure up unwitting thoughts of alleged evil incarnate Saddam Hussein in his hole in the ground, reduced to dwarfish dimensions.

The film leaves behind images of American weaponry fetishism, and the stale aftertaste of American neo-colonialism. Emmerich has been known to attempt compensation for his German origins through particularly chauvinistic patriotism in his other movies, too. Even while entering the time travel and molecularizing gate, the soldiers cling to their assault rifles and wave them about as if, in doing so, they might gun down an enemy. The infantile sexual fantasies acted out in such scenes of relentless shelling! Fittingly, Colonel Jackson, upon arrival at the temple-pyramid-space depot, exhorts his men to »zap 'em all«. But the Anubis-and-Horus-mask-warriors, only equipped with primitive lances featuring bulb-shaped, mightily booming, fire-spewing lumps at the tip, just shoot the Americans down (after which they get up again unharmed, nonsequentially).

The fellah slaves the Americans had spurred on to revolution behave in a manner any American administration of recent decades really wished Arabic and other Third World populaces to behave. They beg for American weapons, rise up, and overthrow every aspect of the system they knew thus far only to replace that with a simulation of parliamentary democracy based on the American model.

In the end, at least they have learned how to properly salute the American military way. In the film's final image, the actors' facial expressions – harmless, ignorant and naïve, or false, depending on view – deliver its political message, one that has already degenerated into ideologies of freedom. And once again, parallels can be drawn, an American Foreign Secretary can be envisioned bringing forward alleged pictorial evidence for Iraqi weapons of mass destruction as justification for starting the Iraq war, images that had been published in many European magazines

. Weapons, moreover, about which the former UN Chief Weapons Inspector,
has, in the meantime, stated that their non-existence has been known for ten
onscious phantom hunt had been instigated in Iraq. Meanwhile, the extent to
government's disastrous Iraq policies are founded on quasi-Hollywood-
rges bit by bit. The ensuing devastation of values held by the Christian occi-
le effect.

te – one that may serve as an example for countless other American films
nce fiction, war or disaster genres – epitomizes the large extent to which
ally exploited for a mass audience. In that respect, myths contribute to the
wareness – a function always attributed to them.

said about 1950s biblical epics that »Moses' Egypt was really America«,[8]
ilar level can be made for the 1990s and *Stargate*. The realities of the cinema
p until they become nearly indistinguishable. While President Clinton could
f the Special Command troupe that, in a daring mission, rescued two
ts from Bosnian forests by saying that they had shown conduct worthy of
war movies, President Bush, dressed as a Top Gun wearing the very same
, marches along the deck of an aircraft carrier and, in a victory pose, an-
complished«. The long-term parallels and continuities between cinematic
e astonishing.

form of fiction that affects the pretence of being anything but. Yet that kind
lity can end badly. If it had been Emmerich's intention to present the
lemonic false front for suppression, then his modern myths of technology,
y are in no way less diabolic false fronts for self-deception and the stupefy-
lic. Every day, American soldier's bodies become testaments to these tac-
sel said about Assmann: »Myths examine the ways in which societies re-
they imagine themselves by remembering.«[9]

erich's *Stargate* may serve up some grandiose images developed further
ly, other writers and directors in the numerous episodes of the *Stargate*
the film nevertheless embodies almost every negative cliché associated
pean and, increasingly, American critics: superficiality, black-and-white
phasizing of action scenes, militarism, chauvinism, thoughtless handling of
historic facts, »special effects« instead of substance, and suchlike.

In my second example, a French-American co-production, »old Europe« does not merely strike
back – in union with Hollywood, it proves that the science-fiction genre is capable of producing
parody and self-parody in close proximity to depth.

Luc Besson, »enfant terrible« of French filmmaking, became acquainted with Hollywood during
his years as a moviemaking apprentice, and a number of American stars (Bruce Willis, Gary Oldman
or Ian Holm, to name but a few) are favourites of the director that keep reappearing in his films.

The Fifth Element, made in 1996 and first screened in 1997, is more than a brilliantly
sparkling science-fiction parody. In spite of some faults (which may be due to the fact that
Luc Besson created a basic draft of the film as a comic in 1975 while still a bored 16-year-old
pupil), the film offers a self-contained and consequent plot which deals with topics such as the
implementation and the updating of ancient myths in new media in an exceedingly creative
manner.

In an obvious reference to *Stargate*, the film takes as its starting point an excavation site at the
pyramid complex of Gizeh. Every five thousand years, dog-headed, armour-wearing god-aliens
descend to earth in a fantastic spaceship in order to prevent primal, elementary evil from annihi-
lating the world. This time around, however, the mission fails and can only be repeated once a
further five thousand years have passed. A leap in time. Two hundred and fifty years from now,
primal evil in the shape of a gigantic fireball resistant to any and all attacks with nuclear weapons
or other arms threatens to wipe out all life on earth. Life can only be saved by the fifth element
in the guise of Milla Jovovich who is travelling in her spaceship on her way to save earth. Said
spaceship, however, is shot down by alien supporting troops of evil, the repulsive Mangalores,
and crash-lands on the moon. From there, left-over genetic material is brought to a Franken-
stein-style laboratory, and reactivated. And behold, what doth emerge from the lump of matter,
equipped with all necessary memories? 'Tis a miraculously fair maiden endowed with superhuman strength and intelligence, but o so weak, fragile, and in need of help!

She takes as her accomplice the former space hunter and present-day aerial taxi driver
Corben Dallas, played by Bruce Willis. Confederate of evil on earth is Jean-Baptiste Emanuel

9–16. *The Fifth Element*, directed by Luc Besson, 1997.

Zorg a.k.a Gary Oldman, who, with all his might, strives for ownership of the remaining four elementary tables that, in combination with the fifth element, can prevent humankind's demise. Before that happens, just as time is about to run out, numerous tumultuous complications and near-catastrophes take place.

It sounds chaotic, which is what it is, and the story itself is hard to re-tell – but there is a structure to it. Thanks to some outstanding performances – with Chris Tucker as DJ Ruby Rod the freakiest of them all – being combined with excellent camera work as well as brilliant ideas and images, the story leads to a film that was a huge box-office success in old Europe, while occasionally asking too much of American audiences with its countless parodies, allusions and cross references to various film genres. *Stargate*, *Brazil*, *Blade Runner*, the *Alien* movies, but also the Bond films are courageously pushed over the top and, thus, reduced to absurdity.

As far as our particular topic, namely myths, is concerned, it is primarily the myth of the immaculate, innocent child coming to save the world and mankind that is ingeniously varied here. To be precise, the divine child is not a boy, but a young woman. And what the cradle was to Baby Jesus, the genetic reactor – a machine the appearance of which also entails an update of the myth of Frankenstein's monster – is to Leeloo (for that is her name), who mythically embodies the invasion of the world by the sacred and its readiness for sacrifice.

No sooner than she awakes, she is wrapped in Jean Paul Gaultier's thermo-bandages which, shortly after the film's release, became another provocative outsider's idea turned fashion article. Gaultier, who, in his designs, has always let his prankster's attitude run riot through traditions, styles and gender boundaries, has designed all of the film's costumes. Beside the appearance of many well-proportioned models, this leads to a refreshing wealth of ideas becoming apparent in all character's garments, as well as the most different theatrical body stagings imaginable being played out and then being treated ironically and, with relish, appearing as constructs within society's cabinet of role playing. Thus, *The Fifth Element* becomes a festival of body stagings almost unrivalled in cinematic history.

The Fifth Element reflects remarks made by Jean-Jacques Wunnenburger in 1994 in his text on »Mytho-phoria. Forms and Transformations of myths«,[10] namely that nowadays, myths must be understood as endless, open texts with a capability for infinite further development: »New mythic texts are created through controlled procedures of overlapping, of intercultural blending, and of intertextual crossovers that are not without elements of humour and irony.«[11]

Beside the aforementioned sacred and technological myths, it is the myths of the modern metropolis (New York, aliens, space travel, Bond movies) the film's satiric ammunition is aimed at. The myth of the metropolis – dealt with, in recent times, by *Minority Report*, but also by Japanese and Korean manga and anime cartoons such as *Akira*, *Ghost in the Shell* and *Wonderful Days* – reveals the extent to which Besson's film is rooted in comic culture.

Japanese and American hotel chains have already got their plans for spaceship hotels all but wrapped up. In the case of space cruiser »Flosden Paradise«, the spaceship image is taken literally; a gigantic paddle steamer, this luxury hotel liner ploughs through the vastness of outer space. Those who make certain demands when it comes to holidays can be found spending New Year's Eve or their honeymoon weekend there, welcomed by floral wreaths and Hawaiian dancers and surrounded by corny American hotel luxury.

That ship, however, also becomes the site for the film's fierce James Bond-style shoot-out, as a result of which it is dismantled into its constituent parts. But before this can happen, a glorious metamorphosis of myths takes place. The divine »Plavalunga«, a bird-beetle-man-alien-diva, sings a poignant aria from Léon Delibes' Indian-set fantastical opera *Lakmé* (1883). The Plavalunga is Gaultier's and Besson's ultimate bizarre creation, made as if to prove Ivanceanu/Schweikhardts theses about the zero-body – according to which nowadays traditional bodies belong in an historical archive for melancholy relics.[12] The Plavalunga can certainly be interpreted as a modern variant of the myth of the siren. »Come here, renowned Ulysses, honour to the Achaean name! / Steer your ship ashore and listen to our two voices; / For no one ever sailed past us in a black ship, / Without staying to hear the enchanting sweetness of our song.« (Homer, *The Odyssey*, Book XII, 184–187)

Thus the sirens lure Ulysses as he approaches them – and they promise to him their omniscience. But Circe had alerted her lover to the fact that he who travels to them will not return home: »For they sit in a green field and warble him to death / With the sweetness of their song / And there is a great heap of dead men's bones lying all around / With the flesh still rotting off them.« (Book XII, 44–46)

Allegedly, this passage is the literary version of an ancient faith governed by the dead, according to which a man's dead soul, envious of the living, will feast on their blood and thus tear them away to the hereafter.[13]

The four elementary tables with the ability to save mankind are discovered inside the body of the dying Plavalunga, of all places; after that, hell breaks lose. Zorg – if anything, a chaplinesque would-be Hitler – can rage as much as he likes. He and his smelly Mangalores are doomed to perish in the shoot-out. Primal evil may threaten the world, but the world is saved by the female shining light in the shape of the perfect woman, the fifth element, which, at its core, is an embodiment of the myth of romantic love, divine light, life in death, remnant of a fictitious chronology of salvation. With *The Fifth Element*, Luc Besson has created a cult film with which a fantastical, bizarre, highly artistic element has been added to the history of cinematography.

On to my third example, Andrew Niccol's film *S1m0ne*. It was first shown in the USA on August 23rd, 2002, and while a fully dubbed German version is available, the film will most probably never be seen on German cinema screens, as it failed abysmally at the American box office. Since it seems like this country's distributors fear the risk of the film suffering a similar fate here, I should like to introduce my thoughts on *S1m0ne* with a brief prehistory.

In October of 2000, I was flying back from Toronto to Frankfurt. On the plane, I read one of those well-known magazines that combine entertainment with airlines' house advertising. The image of an extraordinarily beautiful model captured my attention, and I read the accompanying article. In spite of the fact that up-and-coming models face great difficulties in trying to be booked by agencies and receiving jobs, this blonde beauty had been hired on the spot by 200 agencies (among them some of the world's most famous ones) simply because of her photographs – even though no one had yet seen her in the flesh. It was only then that her alleged agency disclosed the secret. What I was seeing was an artificial figure created at the computer by five UCLA students. In that figure, these students had accumulated all the ideal measurements and notions of flawless female beauty currently dominant in the United States. Thus, proof had been delivered of how even professionals could no longer tell a »digital beauty« from a real one. The case gave a boost to the infectious discussions of recent times concerning virtual bodies and digital actors.

IMDb's sparse data give no account of whether Andrew Niccol was familiar with this successful example of a digital model, or whether the general discussion led to him writing a script about a digitally created star. Additionally, neither online documents nor the DVD's inevitable »Making of« film contain only the smallest mention of the fact that *S1m0ne* – apart from being the movie variant of a current discussion concerning bodies – is also the latest version of one of the most popular ancient myths, namely *Pygmalion*.

It should be mentioned that the five students, probably without knowing, are working on tried-and-tested territory and following a classic recipe: »For a long time, it went without saying that beauty had little to do with nature. The ideal body as created by art was always an artificial body. One recipe for the creation of ideal beauty was that thought up by Zeuxis, a concept that caused a sensation during the Renaissance as a result of being put into practice by Alberti. Beauty does not imitate nature – it exceeds it. An immaculately beautiful woman can therefore not be created from *one* model; ideally beautiful parts must be collected from many female bodies and then be assembled. The artistry lies in synthetically bringing to life the ›assemblage‹ as an organic entity.«[14]

And so, without further ado, we arrive at *S1m0ne*. Since it is likely that hardly any reader has seen the film, here is a brief synopsis of its plot: Viktor Taransky, once a successful Hollywood director, finds himself in a creative and existential crisis. His most recent films were flops, his wife, a leading Hollywood studio executive prone to nagging, has left him, and the leading actress in his latest movie displays unbearable affectations. All of a sudden, an anonymous computer freak contacts Viktor – note the »telling« name and its similarity to »Roman Polanski« – and offers him software that will enable him to create a totally realistic human being with the help of a computer, and to then integrate that being into a film.

Even before any tests can be carried out, that computer freak perishes from a terminal eye tumour. Viktor experiments with his program and generates an actress to whom he gives the tongue-in-cheek name S1m0ne (simulation one); surprisingly, the film she stars in becomes a huge success. As a result, the press, Viktor's colleagues and producers all wish to meet S1m0ne, and Viktor must take a lot of trouble to repeatedly find new ways of keeping his star's identity a secret.

Success creates hunger, even obsession. Viktor continues to write and direct more films with S1m0ne, who always acts alone in front of a blue screen and is then combined with other actors

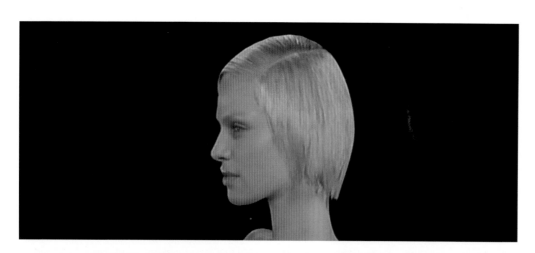

and scenery. S1m0ne's performances achieve ever greater successes, and naturally, the press and audiences become ever more curious as to what this publicity-shy star is all about. Finally, S1m0ne – in her capacity as the alter ego of Viktor – wins two Oscars, one for »Best Direction« and one for »Best Leading Actress««, but even at the ceremony, she is only present as an image. As public pressure and the fuss made by the press become increasingly demanding, Viktor, by now pretty desperate, initially sees no other way out but to ruin S1m0ne's reputation by letting her direct and act in the film *I am Pig*. However, even that sorry effort's absolute tastelessness is received rapturously by audiences. Viktor sees his last resort in destroying, killing S1m0ne by drowning all relevant footage and software in the sea. But nobody believes him; feminists, re- porters, fans and colleagues all accuse him of having murdered S1m0ne out of envy, resentment, jealousy. Viktor goes to prison, is charged with murder, and becomes a candidate for the death penalty. That is when he discloses the truth. But again, nobody believes him – the illusory star is too powerful. His lawyer advises him to plead manslaughter or mental derangement, when Viktor's daughter Lainy, who had smelled a rat and written a *Pygmalion* story on her computer some time ago, accidentally manages to recreate S1m0ne on the studio computer. S1m0ne is back. She is alive. She had only taken some time out. Viktor is released, his ex-wife takes him back in, and with her, his daughter and S1m0ne, he moves to a big new house on Venice or Malibu Beach. And they live happily ever after.

This idea is not a new one and yet of current interest for both Hollywood and the entire inter- national movie business. When will someone manage to create the first convincing digital movie star? How does one secure the digital rights to one's own body? How does one defend oneself against digital stars? These are topics that are definitely on the minds of producers, actors, agents and unions, and that are discussed academically by legions of gender researchers. Granted, *Final Fantasy* flopped big time in 2001, but does that affect the future in any way?

S1m0ne is definitely a comedy of many facets. Its commercial failure in the US must be blamed on the film's high intellectual standard, its comparative lack of plot and its slowness. Andrew Niccol has a habit of eschewing mainstream success for aesthetic and thematic experi- ments, as his previous films – his debut *Gattaca* (1997), and *The Truman Show* (1998) – have demonstrated. *Gattaca* in particular is a film that truly keeps splitting audiences down the middle. Some believe it to be one of the best science-fiction films of all time, founding that opinion on its camera work, its direction, its colors and scenery as well as its treatment of the highly topical problems concerning genetic engineering, others think it is old hat, and epigonal old hat at that.

Al Pacino, *S1m0ne*'s leading man, delivers a Hollywood-satirizing acting showpiece that is a masterstroke, even when measured by Hollywood's standards. Rachel Roberts, young Vancouver debutante, is not only beautiful in her role as S1m0ne, but also artistically convincing.

For us, *S1m0ne* counts for a real find precisely because no-one has as yet dealt with, or at- tempted to analyze, the film's mythical dimension.

Amongst all the stories from ancient mythology, the *Pygmalion* tale is lent particular erotic radiance by tradition through Ovid's *Metamorphoses*; its inclusion in the latter opened the gates to manifold fantasies of dramatic and musical treatments. In Ovid, the story of *Pygmalion* – along with a host of other examples – is attributed to the singer Orpheus: According to the myth, Cypriot sculptor Pygmalion, disgusted with shameless women, wants to remain unbound by mar- riage, but falls in love with his own creation, a woman's statue made of ivory. Aphrodite, goddess of love, comes to the sculptor's rescue and breathes life into his artificial character. She arranges the marriage of the two, and blesses that marriage with the birth of daughter Paphos, after whom a Greek island is named.

Skipping the entire list of ways in which that material was received throughout the Middle Ages, early modern times and the Modern Age (times that saw an emphasis being put on the story's comical, satirical and spicily erotic aspects, and during which that story was retold in countless variations in both opera houses and theaters), I should like to focus on its most re- nowned and most successful 20th century version, namely George Bernard Shaw's *Pygmalion*. Shaw's concept of the »new woman« contributed a great deal to the modern woman's emanci- pation towards development of a self-assured, independent, active personality. Even after the Second World War, the British class system guaranteed that someone's speech and ways of ex- pression could make or break a professional career. That is why phonetics professor Higgins keeps remodelling poor flower girl Eliza Doolittle's pronunciation, until she – just like future prime minister Margaret Thatcher, in her youth shop assistant in her parents' small grocery store – has learned to perfectly imitate the nasally arrogant pronunciation of the British »upper class«. Older readers may well harbour memories of Alan Jay Lerner's and Frederick Loewe's musical version of Shaw's *Pygmalion* – *My Fair Lady* – similar to mine; forty years after my time as a student, I still find myself being haunted by that musical's songs, as did hundreds of thousands of other Germans at the time: »The rain in Spain stays mainly in the plain«, we would warble.

Shaw ends his educational experiment with neither a fairytale wedding of professor and Cinderella, nor a pessimist re-establishing of social barriers; instead, the story finishes with an act of self-liberation into an economically independent and self-governed life on the part of Eliza.

To that »turning of the screw«, Niccol adds further fresh and original twists; he basically harks back to the origins of the myth. But where the ancient sculptor treated marble and ivory with hammer and chisel as well as imaginative precision, the digital media artist sculpts with the aid of zeroes and ones, and those ominous simulation programs. In doing so, he not only creates curves of the body and facial expressions, but also a voice, a way of speaking, a walk, a form of behaviour.

According to Barbara Vinken, oscillating between that which has a soul and that which is soulless creates the fascination with which the advertising body is regarded in prêt-à-porter fashion, and swaying between that which is animate and that which is inanimate determines the structure of the fetish.[15] Niccol's Viktor Taransky, being a »victor«, a wannabe-macho-man-creator, toys with all of these possibilities by ascribing to S1m0ne – and into her artificial body – properties of various stars from cinema history. In return, he, too, is toyed with and manipulated by his artificial creature.

I shall pass on the possibility of a historical digression on the development of modern sculpture, from Rodin until today, for instance, but the evocation of the massive physicalness of Rodin's works in the reader's memory may suffice to measure the distance that has been crossed in that field in a space of 100 years – up until today's video sculptures, the infinite variety inherent in digital sculptures, the possibilities for development visible in holograms. In that, virtual body stagings have surpassed the possibilities of all conventional sculptures, while still being incapable – even in the guise of three-dimensional animation – of stimulating the senses of touch, taste and smell so essential for truly sensual erotic experiences. The fact that daydreams can be visualized with the help of algorithms is an achievement of the computer age. The body becomes a construct – even more so than in traditional film: here, it can be manipulated, varied, made to fluctuate, to be imaginary and yet so real. However, the virtual sculptor's yearnings and desires turn into a constant conflict between himself and his creation – just like in real life; in a split-consciousness scenario on the part of its creator, that creature develops a will of its own and a publicly observed personality, and is therefore no longer infinitely changeable, as Taransky had initially believed. As Goethe put it so magnificently: »Spirits that I've cited / My commands ignore!«

If one were to think of Futurism's myth of the machine, according to which man only truly becomes soul-gifted man through the machine, »anima qua machina«, it might become clear to which extent the digital age provides that phrase with a completely new set of ambivalences. For the digital creations, too, can tyrannize their sculptor, make him depend on them, drive him into dependence and desperation. Just imagine the further fate of Viktor Taransky in the house he shared with his ex, played by Winona Ryder, his daughter and S1m0ne, the latter obliged to keep filling the family's coffers! In the end, even comedy becomes burlesque. Viktor and S1m0ne sit next to each other on the couch as S1m0ne cradles her digitally sculpted baby in her arms, all aglow with the happiness of a young mother announcing that she has ambitions to embark on another career – in politics. This time, it is Taransky's daughter Lainy who is responsible for the virtual sculpture, and who has consciously updated *Pygmalion*. In the film's final image, it remains unclear whether she has also simulated her biological father so he and S1m0ne might act as a virtual couple from now on. That, indeed, would be a representation of the winding Moebius strip of self-generating myth production in the shape of adaptive software. Not that Niccol could be suspected of taking it quite as far as that, but, as is generally known, images just cannot be trusted these days. If not characters, then at least images are infinitely variable. All that can be imagined can also be turned into an image which, in turn, can be manipulated.

Thus, the simulation of myths opens the gates to an endless continuation or metamorphosis of the ancient text.

»I am the death of the real«, S1m0ne says at one point in the film. Who can say what is real, the likes of us retort, used to intellectual creations as we are. Yet, in another one of the film's trademark ironic twists, the myth is inverted, as Niccol not only animates the sculpture, but has a live actress play a virtual sculpture. Lara Croft, at the very latest, has demonstrated that it is not just the robots, the film androids, the »digital beauties« who aim at looking ever more real, ever more realistic; there is also a growing trend among real humans – women in particular – to try and resemble digital creations. In Japan and some other Asian countries, this trend has become a genuine movement, and it is beginning to contaminate the USA. It is only a question of time until it arrives in Europe. Looking at the international music scene, one cannot help but notice the way that pop singers such as Christina Aguilera who aggressively flaunt their own sexuality have been styled to resemble a »digital beauty«. And their influence on the current generation of teenagers is immense.

Rachel Roberts, the actress playing S1m0ne, has accurately described the way she first had to learn how to move like a digital character, not to blink, to avoid quick arm movements, etc. So take a closer look at who it is coming down the road, today in film, tomorrow, perhaps, in real life. But one thing is for sure – myths are alive, even though Aphrodite may long since have signed over her services to Bill Gates, and new, secularized myths have been added to the ancient ones.

My brief overview of ancient myths in modern Hollywood movies may only have dented the surface of the topic, and it can in no way be described as exhaustive. Still, I hope it has demonstrated one thing – that Hollywood, too, is not what it used to be. It is a far cry from being homogenous. It has become more layered, more transnational, more experimental (at least to a certain degree) – and it is as alive as it used to be. As is »old Europe« with its myths! Myths, that – even in Hollywood film – are not merely recycled, but also display an astounding amount of tenacity and mutability.

Gudula Simone Moritz
Pentagon pictures. How Hollywood has its scripts censored by Washington

»9/11«

Ever since September 11, 2001, the world seems to be not only more strongly divided than ever, but segregated: into friends and foes, into America's opponents and its allies. In the USA itself alliances have also been forged on a national scale since »9/11«, bringing one particularly illustrious union to public attention: that between Hollywood and Washington.

Immediately after the terrorist attacks of September 11, at the beginning of October 2001, scientists, military personnel and producers, directors and special effects engineers from Hollywood met at the Institute for Creative Technologies in California. Their intention: to draw up possible scenarios for retaliation. Two months after the attacks, Bush's adviser Karl Rove invited a crew of hand-picked directors and producers to exchange ideas. The topic: possible Hollywood contributions to the war against terrorists.

A short while later, the news broke that Hollywood's No. 1 producer, Jerry Bruckheimer, was shooting a reality TV series for Disney's TV channel ABC about the American troops' lives in Afghanistan together with Bertram van Munster, a friend of Donald Rumsfeld – courtesy of the Pentagon. The scenes were shot last summer. While scarcely any independent journalists were allowed access to the US troops in Afghanistan, Jerry Bruckheimer shot his military soap on location – a tribute to the army, as he calls it.[1]

From that point on a new catchword was finding its way into media talk: militainment – a new genre in the art of entertainment.

History

And yet, the close connections between Hollywood and the Pentagon are not new at all. On the contrary: Hollywood and the American army are a well-established team. Their alliance has survived several American governments. Since the 1920s Hollywood has been rendering services to US military propaganda and in return has profited from its generous support.

In fact the first ever joint film project on which Hollywood and the US military collaborated was an immediate success. As early as 1927 the former War Department supported the production of the silent movie *Wings*, directed by little known William Wellmann. The American Air Force offered considerable support during the production, which enabled the filmmakers to make an almost exact reconstruction of military operations carried out in the First World War and also gave the film crew access to planes and military bases in Texas. The cooperation worked well for both sides: William Wellman was able to reproduce First World War air battles with a new perfection. This even earned him the first Oscar ever awarded for Best Film of the Year in 1928 (which at the time was just known as *Academy Award*).

With this commercially very successful film the army had found a new advertising medium: for the first time in history soldiers were recruited in cinemas. In his book *Guts and Glory* historian Lawrence Suid wrote this about the new Washington-Hollywood dream team: »As a result of this cooperation, ›Wings‹ stands out as the standard against which all future combat films and all military assistance to Hollywood must be measured.«[2]

Apart from the gaining of prestige, the most important reason for the American army to recommend itself as a sponsor of Hollywood films is the recruiting of soldiers. Sixty years after *Wings* the film *Top Gun* (Ridley Scott, 1986) was to set new standards for recruiting soldiers through a Hollywood film: with Tom Cruise starring as a young recruit on his way to becoming a fighter pilot in *Top Gun,* the US Navy put up information stands in the cinemas where motivated young men could pick up application forms to take home with them. With success: the Navy reported a run on recruitment offices after *Top Gun* was launched in the cinemas.

After a minor correction to the script, the film was strongly promoted by the Navy: the subplot, a love affair between Navy pilot Maverick (Tom Cruise) and Charlotte Blackwood (Kelly McGillis), was only accepted by the Navy after the character was changed from a female officer to a civil expert. The changes were made because personal relationships within the Navy were a delicate issue.[3]

The Navy generously rewarded this, with technical consultants, approx. 20 Air Force pilots, access to Miramar Naval Air Station and a small fleet of F-14 jets worth $ 37 million each. A charge was made only for fuel. (All in all Paramount paid $ 1.1 million to the Navy, $ 886 000 of which were for the use of five different aircraft types.)[4]

The producer of this 97-minute publicity film for the army was Jerry Bruckheimer – together with his business partner Don Simpson.

Black Hawk Down

Jerry Bruckheimer also produced a movie that was a big blockbuster in the US: *Black Hawk Down* directed by Ridley Scott (with a profit of $ 108 million in the States alone by mid-July last year), a lavish epic about a controversial army operation. Somalia in 1993: 19 dead Americans and an unsuccessful army retreat.

But the movie retells the humiliating story differently – in a patriotic version: soldiers demonstrating heroism and individual courage in the hell of Mogadishu. A dirty, but legitimate war. Horrible, but necessary – just like the one Bush and Rumsfeld have been invoking ever since September 11. (cf. *Spiegel*, 15. 7 .2002). *Black Hawk Down* was shot before September 11, 2001, and yet it became the film of the day: in summer 2002 the war in Afghanistan showed a striking similarity and in winter 2003 parallels to the war on Iraq became apparent.

The protagonist in *Black Hawk Down* is the combat itself – the audience is caught up in the fray, among very authentic scenery which only became affordable as a result of the Pentagon's grants towards the making of the film: the US Army lent 35 Black Hawk helicopters for as little as $ 2 million and more than 100 soldiers to the filmmakers for shooting the movie in Morocco, a perk in production aid worth millions. Defense Secretary Donald Rumsfeld even appeared at the movie's premiere.

Before starting the movie, Jerry Bruckheimer visited the Pentagon several times to seek support, which was easy to obtain for this film because the book by the journalist Mark Bowden, on which the script was based, is on the army's reading list for its recruits. In an interview, which he gave in February 2002 in Berlin, Jerry Bruckheimer said: »The army wanted the story to be told. And: The army is very proud of this movie.«

Last year, I also had the opportunity to interview Ridley Scott during his promotion tour for *Black Hawk Down*: here is an excerpt from the interview:

»... The film ends up as being anti-war and pro-military. Because I think militia now under the present circumstances today – this is not cynical – under the auspices say of the US because they are so watched so scrutinized so criticized by every community that it becomes pro the idea that someone must go in and intervene and it happens to be the US.«

»This film was also made with the collaboration of the Pentagon. To what extent did the Pentagon support the film?«

»Well, this is a long negotiation, goes on for like three months and there is a department in the Pentagon, I dealt with them before, Jerry Bruckheimer dealt with them four times. Very simply, if you want to have and use some of their facilities, they want to see what the script is, because they want to see how they are being represented in the material and also how it is being interpreted because material can be written one way and interpreted in another.

They are quite sophisticated in terms of that, you can't pull the wool over their eyes, it's a long negotiation which goes on through the whole process of planning to the extent I've been filming already seven days and I didn't have the Black Hawks, I didn't have the helicopters, so I had to think of other things to film.

There were lots of other prep things I had to do so I started that. I had on stand-by eight Hueys in Germany ready to be sprayed black to be made to look military. Because I could rent civilian Hueys but I can't rent Black Hawks and I wanted the Black Hawks because that's what they were and that's what happened, that was accurate. So I really needed their help. So after a lot of negotiation and clarification of exactly how I was gonna do it they gave me full help. They asked me if I wanted two advisors who had actually been on the ground in Mogadishu throughout the whole process and I said ›yeah, absolutely‹.«

»And did you have to make some changes to the script?«

»Weird, peculiar things like saying ›We are embarrassed about seeing a Black Hawk with Delta shooting a wild pig from the air for barbecue, we don't do that.‹ I said ›but you do‹. He said ›I know we do but it's embarrassing, so can you take it out.‹ So silly, funny little things which are to do with, I think if you really wanna take it right down, American tax payer is saying why is the gasoline I am paying for and that Black Hawk being used to bring down the pig so that the guys can eat. I said because you've been eating fish for six weeks and the guys want meat!«

»You also tried to collaborate with the Pentagon in another project called *GI Jane*. However, it didn't work out ...«

»Yeah, yeah, they didn't want to shave her head. They said that was faddish or trendy. The guy that was interviewing me had a short hair cut and I said: ›Then your haircut is faddish. You are trendy.‹ He said: ›What are you talking about?‹ I said: ›You got the same hair cut then.‹ And he said: ›Yeah, but women wouldn't do that.‹ I said ›How do you know? You haven't got one in this department.‹ So that argument went on. So their requirements would have essentially kind of dismantled the reasons for making the film. ...«

»Coming back to *Black Hawk Down*, what would you say were the big advantages of involving the Pentagon in this production?«

»Oh, I got Black Hawks, I got little birds, I got the best flying team in the American Army. Those guys that brought in those machines were probably one of the best, the very best of helicopters in the army, in the air force. They came right down that street, did exactly what you saw. There were no tricks, that's all real. Even the crashing helicopter, that's no CGI, that's real. He's reversing an eight-ton chopper into spiral motion for me.«

Ridley Scott was rather reticent in the interview and not very communicative regarding the changes the Pentagon wanted made to *Black Hawk Down,* to a script which generally speaking very much toed the line. We will hear more about this later on from the American Ministry of Defense's movie liaison officer.

But what became clear in this interview was how important an authentic, realistic setting is for filmmakers.

As a means to success, being true to life is seen as a question of principle in Hollywood. But transporting authenticity and a meticulous attention to detail in a movie costs a lot of time, effort and money. Here the Pentagon's sponsoring is very much in demand because it reduces the costs for the film production immensely.

But the Pentagon expects something in return: the right to censorship. Film producers have to be prepared to accept the script changes dictated to them.

But even famous film producers can be brought round to the government's point of view thanks to the Pentagon's generous sponsorship. According to the *Spiegel*, after making a few changes to his script Wolfgang Petersen paid less than $ 8 000 for the jet fighters featured in *Air Force One*.[5]

John Woo's film *Windtalkers* (2002) about the Pacific War in 1944 also had to go through some changes.

For example: according to the screenplay a US marine – codename: the Dentist – was supposed to crawl across a battlefield scattered with victims of the battle between the USA and Japan. The directions in the screenplay originally read: »The Dentist bends over a dead Japanese soldier: he does what he always does: he looks for gold in the mouths of the dead. The Dentist pokes around with his bayonet, turns it and has great difficulties getting the gold out of the corpse's teeth. He says: ›Come to Daddy‹.«

The Pentagon's verdict: cut it. The producers argued there was proof that scenes like this actually occurred. But to no avail. And since they did not want to forego the collaboration of the marines, they didn't shoot the scene.

Mister Hollywood in the Pentagon: Philip Strub

What the symbiosis between Tinseltown and Washington looks like I have already alluded to. But one cannot help thinking that there has to be a liaison agent between Hollywood and the Pentagon; someone who is pulling the strings behind the scene. And there is: Philip Strub, Vietnam veteran, graduate from a filmmaking academy and movie liaison officer in the Pentagon since 1989. Internal nickname: Mister Hollywood. Strub is a powerful man; he reads scripts and decides on behalf of Donald Rumsfeld who is allowed to play with the military's expensive implements of war and who isn't. The condition: the military has to shine in a positive light.

I interviewed Philip Strub in the Pentagon in March 2002. The following is an edited excerpt from the interview:

»How did the army get involved in the production of *Black Hawk Down*?

»I should tell you first of all that in my office we deal with all the military services not just the army and each military service at the department approaches in exactly the same way. That is, we ask to look at the script, we read the script, we determine whether or not it meets our criteria for support and whether or not the support which is being requested is something we can provide. It doesn't make any sense for us to fall in love with the script and discover that the filmmakers want to use three aircraft carriers for four weeks. It's just not logistically feasible so at the same time we are looking at the script we are also looking what's being asked and trying to determine whether it's something we can provide. If we do at the end of this review process determine that the script is something we can work on in terms of content, in terms of the military portrayal and what is being requested is something we can provide, then we enter a phase of negotiations where we look again both at the logistics and the script. Maybe there are some things in the script that we don't think are very realistic. We might ask the filmmakers whether they are willing to change those things, negotiate those things and if we come together at the end of all that then we authorize production assistance and can go about getting the assistance underway.«

»You just mentioned that the script has to meet certain criteria, such as realism, before you will get involved. What other criteria have to be met?«

»Well, the criterion is very simple. It's whether or not the production in question gives us the opportunity to tell the American public something significant about the US military, increase the public's awareness of the US military and be of some benefit to recruiting and retention at the same time. You don't have both of those. I think it arguable whether or not *Black Hawk Down* is a great recruiting vehicle but it's an important film from our perspective in communicating what really happened in Somalia in 1993 and also the capabilities of the soldiers who were involved in that type of operation.«

»So how did you get involved with this specific project? Did Jerry Bruckheimer approach you?«

»Oh yes. Typically, filmmakers approach us. We are not out in Hollywood knocking on doors and pitching ideas and trying to generate interest among filmmakers. It's almost invariable that they will come to us with an idea and sometimes with a fully written screen-play and often we had nothing whatsoever to do with it. We had no input, we had no technical advice during the whole creative process that led to a first-draft script. That's not at all unusual. There are times when they come to us with an idea and we help filmmakers by granting access for script-writers and producers to installations. They can observe military training operations, they can talk to military men and women, we do that quite often too but most of the time filmmakers approach us with a fully written script and such was the case with *Black Hawk Down*. Mister Bruckheimer had told us while he was in pre-production on *Pearl Harbour* that long before – they hadn't even begun production to *Pearl Harbour* – he already acquired the book rights to *Black Hawk Down* and told us about it. So we knew he had that picture in the back of his mind.«

»When you were approached with this project, did they have to make some changes to the script as a prerequisite for collaboration?«

»The first draft was just that – it was a first draft script and neither the creative people nor we were entirely satisfied with it. It was a little simplistic, in their attempt to avoid the politics of the book and the details of the book they had gone a little in the other direction and it was a little simplistic. They recognized that, they wanted to change it. The script matured considerably through successive rewrites and we were as happy as they were that it did so. And then there were some aspects of the book that we felt didn't entirely reflect military realism, relationship between the special forces and the rangers, some things like that and there were some changes made in that regard as well as time went on.«

»Could you give some examples of that?«

»Well, let me think ... (short pause) – I think we felt that there was an impression, there was rivalry or maybe even some aggressiveness in the relationship between special forces, soldiers and the rangers which was not realistic at all and we just said that it was too much, there could be some competitive spirit that was certainly realistic, an appreciation of what one force can do and the other force can't do, naturally, there is a certain legendary status that attaches itself to special forces, soldiers or sailors, they train for a longer period of time, they have skills that the other forces don't have but we thought that it was a bit exaggerated and we were interested in that toned down or in some cases eliminated and the film-makers felt the same way. It didn't do for them anything dramatically either, so they were already heading into the direction of making most of the changes themselves.«

»Jerry Bruckheimer said in the interview that the army wanted this film to be done, that it was very important for the army that the book *Black Hawk Down* would be made into a film ...«

»Yes, I wouldn't focus on the army, although this is an army picture, of course, it's from beginning till the end an army picture, he's right, just it wasn't only the army that was interested in having the picture made. There was broad interest within the military hierarchy to have this film made, uniformed and civilian, it was quite wide-spread, people were very aware of the book, they were certainly aware of the operation in Mogadishu, they were very aware that the public's concept of that operation had over time characterized as a failed mission to capture Moham-med Aidid which was arguably an inaccurate version or at least a one-sided version of it and this was an opportunity to tell the real story or at least to tell a story about valor and capability and endurance that people were unaware of from just the slivers of the horrific news film mater-ial from that period. ...

The army didn't cooperate on *Apocalypse Now* or *Platoon*, they did work on *Hamburger Hill*, marines didn't work on *Full Metal Jacket*, so most of these pictures of that era, either they didn't come to the Pentagon asking for help or they didn't get any help.«

»I believe that the filmmakers from *Apocalypse Now* asked for help ...«

»Yes.«

»Why didn't they get any help?«

»Well, occasionally you have a screen-play that has a fundamental show-stopping problem and in the case of *Apocalypse Now* the show-stopping problem was an army soldier, army officer who was sent on a mission to kill another army soldier, army officer and it's just one of those show-stopping problems. Much like in the movie *Crimson Tide*. In the movie *Crimson Tide* the fundamental show-stopping problem was an armed mutiny aboard a nuclear submarine and the navy just found that unacceptably unrealistic. And once you have a problem like that there is not much point in saying ›Oh, by the way, you don't wear the dolphins on the white shirt or the rib-bons are in the wrong order.‹ It's sort of pointless to go looking at things like that when you got some really big problems.«

»There was actually also a film by Ridley Scott the Pentagon didn't work on, which was *GI Jane*. Why was that, I wonder?«

»There was no single show-stopping problem with *GI Jane*. Just a whole host of big and small inaccuracies that taken altogether just proved to be too much.«

...

»One of the most topical films that obtained collaboration by the Pentagon is the movie *We were Soldiers* which is actually about the Vietnam War. Isn't this quite difficult for the military to tackle a topic like this?«

»No, I think the Vietnam War is a topic that many people from the military would like to see treated in the way that *We Were Soldiers* is treated. It's the first picture that we were aware of that does justice to many of the veterans who fought in that war. The image of the Vietnam veteran in the movies of the past is not a very accurate one and certainly as such not very flattering. It tended to focus on all the bad things that happened and none of the positive attributes that our military forces displayed in that sad war. So *We Were Soldiers* is a major corrective or redemptive effort in that regard. To tell people, well, this is the way things were for many people. It was horrific combat, but there was bravery, and heroism and self-sacrifice, the enemy was not demonized – this is a good thing for us.«

We Were Soldiers (Randall Wallace, 2002), finally, is the movie on the Vietnam War the army had been waiting for for decades: the true story of the Americans' first battle against the Vietcong in October 1965, where 450 GIs were surrounded by 2000 soldiers of the North Vietnamese forces. The Pentagon generously supported this war movie starring Mel Gibson and got everything they wanted in return: a professionally produced patriotic movie with a real star.

And it brought relief to the troubled US military soul after all those critical Vietnam movies like *Apocalypse Now, Platoon* and *Full Metal Jacket*, a confrontation with America's past that the Pentagon could not, of course, endorse. The Vietnam War shown in nightmare-like scenes did not fit into the Pentagon's film sponsoring concept.

The alliance between Hollywood and the Pentagon is a partnership in which one side dictates the conditions: the Pentagon. So another film that had no chance was *GI Jane*. Director Ridley Scott changed the script several times – but all in vain. For the Pentagon principles were at stake: this movie stars Demi Moore as the first woman to be admitted to the training program of an elite American army corps. From the Pentagon's (and also Ridley Scott's) point of view a woman in such a position is simply not realistic.

For Philip Strub, movies are undoubtedly a powerful means of direct influence. And so it is es-pecially in movies that the American military should be portrayed in a favorable light, which means that subsidized films have to present a politically correct image of the US military (cf. *GI Jane*), an image which is also exclusively positive – Philip Strub would call this form of representation realistic. Criticism of any kind is undesirable.

The Pentagon also refused to support *Forrest Gump* (Robert Zemeckis, 1994). An internal memo from an army spokesman to Philip Strub declared that the Army did not after all admit morons: »The generalized impression that the Army of the 1960s was staffed by the guileless, or soldiers of minimal intelligence, is neither accurate nor beneficial to the Army. I cannot substantiate the notion that the army ever attempted ›an experiment to put together a group of dumbos and halfwits who wouldn't question orders‹.«[7]

Outlook

In Hollywood, profit and patriotism seem to be marching forward harmoniously in step. According to Philip Strub, the terror of September 11 did not have any considerable effect on Hollywood's demands for Pentagon grants – business as usual: scripts have kept piling up on his desk just like before.

This is no wonder since costs of $ 100 million per film have become commonplace in Hollywood. In view of such dizzying sums, the studios' willingness to serve the Pentagon is not likely to decline. After all, alternatives on the open market are extremely expensive: filmmakers can also hire military equipment from the Israeli army, for example, and that without censorship. Yet, there is a snag: the Israeli army charges approx. $ 20,000 per hour for using an F-15 fighter.

Angela Krewani
Hollywood's new brand. Independent film production

The first wave of independent film production entered Hollywood in the wake of the studios' crisis in the late 1960s, when Hollywood had to compete for audiences. Since the main competitor was television, the studios started to produce for the rivaling medium. This enhanced the need for visual material and thus the 1960s saw a bunch of young, socially engaged film directors experimenting with filmic languages. The 1970s returned to a more conservative agenda. Steven Spielberg's first blockbuster *Jaws* appeared in 1975 being followed by *E. T.* in 1982. Both confirmed the movement towards audience oriented cinema, while at the same time the 1960s directors were driven out of Hollywood. (Biskind, 2004, 9–11)

Having been produced outside the established film industry and therefore being autonomous in their making, independent films have always been understood as a mode of filmmaking outside and against the Hollywood system, thereby challenging notions of linear narrative and traditional visual aesthetics. Hollywood has always been confronted by independent filmmakers, but most of them displayed a radical practice as can be seen in films by John Cassavetes, Andy Warhol and Paul Morrissey. Another generation of truly independent filmmakers paving their way into Hollywood were John Sayles, Susan Seidelman, Jim Jarmusch and Spike Lee in the 1980s.

Nevertheless, over the years the term »independent« shied away from the idea of a radical film practice towards a more conventional film routine. Thus independent film production became a viable part of contemporary Hollywood. The integration of the new wave of independent film is due to a variety of factors that have to be examined. In this sense »independent« does not denote a radical film practice any longer, but it »has become a label that makes it easy for people to analyze things that are a lot more complicated«, as director Alan Rudolph remarks. And Tom Safford, who programmed at Sundance in the 1980s, notes that »there's an enormous confusion as to what the term independent means. It's a word used to describe everyone from Gregg Araki, who makes features on a budget of $5000 a piece, to Sydney Pollack.« (Levy, 1999, 2)

In this sense »independent« is understood as a label for film production at the margins of the Hollywood system, feeding on Hollywood and eagerly partaking at the mainstream film culture. The new protagonists of independent film are more or less well known directors such as Steven Soderbergh with *Sex, Lies and Videotape* (1989), David Lynch with *Wild at Heart* (1990) or Joel Coen with *Barton Fink* (1991).

Academy Awards are another indicator for a film's success as well – and the flowering of independent film manifested itself in the nominations and the Awards. In 1987 all five nominees for the »Best Picture« award came from outside the Hollywood establishment: Oliver Stone's *Platoon* (1986), James Ivory's *A Room With A View* (1985), Roland Joffe's *The Mission* (1986), Woody Allen's *Hannah and Her Sisters* (1986), and Randa Haines' *Children of a Lesser God* (1986). *Howard's End* (1992), *The Crying Game* (1992) and *The Player* (1992) were not only successful at the box office in 1992, but they collected more Oscar nominations than the big-studio releases. Subsequently Hollywood tried to gain control over independent film production. (Levy, 1999, 14–15) The 1990s nearly saw an oversupply of independently produced American films: roughly 300 films were produced in 1994 and more than 700 in 1997. (Garvin, 1998)

The rise of the independent film over the last two decades – especially the 1990s have been termed as its decade – and its affiliation with Hollywood is closely linked to a variety of economic, organizational and cultural factors, voicing the structural change of the Hollywood system. The main agents of this change are:
– increased opportunities and capital in financing indies;
– greater demand for visual media driven by an increase in the number of theaters and the impact of the home video market;
– supportive audiences;
– decline of foreign-language films in the American market;
– the proliferation of film schools across the country;
– the emergence of Sundance;
– the development of new organizational networks (Levy, 1999, 20–21.);
– aggressive distribution.

A reason for the growth of independent film production was the strong support in film financing outside the classical full studio support. Although there are a number of new financing models for independent films brought about by the decentralization and transnationalization of Hollywood, films are usually financed through two alternative models. Either through providing the production costs by one or more companies or through an arrangement, where the distribution agreements guarantee or advance film production. This practice is usually based on a completion bond. Special completion bond companies such as Film Finances organize a deal in which they give financial assurances to banks or other lenders ensuring that the producer will deliver the film at a certain date. Upon delivery, the distributor will pay its advance minimum guarantee to the lender, thereby repaying the loan.

A lot of independent films deal with split rights, meaning that the financial success on one market will not be offset against a lack of success on another market, thereby eliminating moneys that should be paid to the filmmaker or the investors. Another important factor in the consolidation of film production has emerged from the opening of the overseas markets and the increase in home video and DVD: Since the American market was especially tentative towards foreign film production, independent film finance went into the international markets and started to co-produce. In this context some European television stations – having started to engage in film – came into the deal. Moreover, a lot of well-financed European companies such as Polygram, Bertelsmann and CLT-UFA proved that they could compete with the major studios. In addition, European film production provided various subsidies, grants, and governmental films. (Garvin, 1998)

Another reason for the increase in independent film production was the impact of the Sundance Institute, which should not be underrated: the Sundance Institute was founded by Robert Redford in Utah in 1981, where he gathered colleagues and friends in order to discuss how to vitalize and preserve the creativity of the American film – as separated from Hollywood. Sundance consists of a variety of programs administering film production such as the Writers Fellowship Program, which includes working retreats and grants, providing writers and filmmakers with an opportunity to get into contact with other creative artists working here. (LoBrutto, 2002, 409)

The associated film festival was added in 1985 when Robert Redford »wanted to create a place where people could go and develop stories outside the pressure of commercial demands«, voices the festival co-director Geoffry Gilmore. By the end of the 1980s the Sundance Festival had turned into the most important festival for independent film: 100 films – either fiction or documentary are screened from over 3000 submissions. (Germain, 2001) Apart from the Institute and the festival Sundance started to enter the market through diversification by exploiting a variety of horizontal markets. In 1998 it signed contracts with denim fashion designers like Ralph Lauren, Tommy Hilfinger and Levi Strauss letting them place their wares in independent films: Fashion companies were happy to support independent films since they hoped to underwrite their advertised image as »youthful« and »unconventional«. (Roman, 1998) In this regard independent film production entered – not as film, but as a kind of lifestyle product the mass consumers' market.

Sundance's branching out into film distribution as well as into the television and home video market also accounted for the rise of independent film. In 1997 Sundance signed a contract with General Cinema Theaters (CRT), which is the US' seventh largest theater circuit. Both companies merged and decided to construct additional 300 screens in different locations in order to distribute and screen independent film. Thus, mainstream cinema was blended with independent cinema, as the chairman happily announced: »We've been impressed with opportunities in the independent film market and have tried to find a way to bring it into our mainstream movie theater product.« (Kramer, 1997)

Besides the cinema market, Sundance entered the home video and television market as well: this step is due to a more general development in film production, in which the gross from the home video market started to equal those from the box office. At the same time Sundance entered the broadcasting business in 1996 with the Sundance Channel, a commercial-free cable outlet for contemporary independent feature film and documentaries (unsigned, 1998). By the end of 2000 Sundance Channel was intended to reach 40 million homes. One of the reasons for the success of Sundance channel is – in the sense of tight diversification[1] (Schatz, 1997) – the affiliation with companies such as Amazon.com, with the rental companies Blockbuster Video and Joe Boxer. Sundance has offered fully integrated marketing campaigns, designed to help affiliates to increase subscribers and digital sales without raising brand awareness of Sundance Channel market by market basis (unsigned, 2000). In this regard Sundance market policy represents a typical example of the new independent film and its distribution. As will be demonstrated later on, the impact of independent film production within Hollywood's production structure swapped from film production itself to the distribution of film. Thus independent films could easily be produced, but failed to enter the cinemas because of the closed distribution practice. The economic concentration on distribution has changed Hollywood's business practices since the late 1980s, film was not only produced but also distributed for a horizontal market consisting of cinema chains, television stations and video rentals. Even the traditional Hollywood establishment had to acknowledge the success in film production, screening, distribution and marketing Sundance had achieved.[2] Thus Robert Redford was awarded with an honorary Oscar in 2002, a definitive sign that Hollywood »views Redford less as a rebel than a savior«, since Sundance films played an increasing role in the Oscar competitions. (Chagollan, 2002)

The enlarged market for film production and the growing acceptance of traditional Hollywood for outsiders corresponded to the emergence of new film schools and film students. In 1996 *US News and World Report* listed the top five film schools: the University of Southern California ranked with New York University as the top school, closely followed by the American Film Institute and the University of California at Los Angeles and the California Institute of the Arts. The film schools tried to pave the path for their students into Hollywood as well as the alumni try to be worthwhile in providing students with a useful entrance into the business. According to Levy's figures about 75% of USC graduates are equipped with Hollywood jobs. (Levy, 1999, 34–39)

Another important catalyst was the founding of Miramax by Harvey and Robert Weinstein in 1979. This year the brothers from Queens, New York, moved their tiny production company to Manhattan: Miramax was named after their parents Miriam and Max. Although they started as a minor production company, Miramax grew steadily and meanwhile it dominates the independent scene along with the Sundance Institute. Harvey and Robert Weinstein started out running rock concerts and organizing college film shows during the 1970s. (Biskind, 2004, 9–26) Their experience in film distribution began with the acquisition of distribution rights of films they hoped would provide them at least with some profit. Miramax became quite successful with Billie August's *Twist and Shout* (1986), where it acquired the North American rights for $50 000 and made revenues at the box office of about $1.5 million well known films such as *I've Heard the Mermaids Singing* (1987), *Working Girls* (1987) and *Pelle the Conqueror* (1988) were all successes for Miramax. (Wyatt, 1998, 79)

The breakthrough came with acquisition of the distribution rights of Steven Soderbergh's *Sex, Lies and Videotape* in 1989. The film was produced by selling the video rights to RCA-Columbia Home Video in advance. Winning the Audience Awards at the Sundance Festival and the Palm d'Or at Cannes, *Sex, Lies and Videotape* was sold by Miramax as a sexy comedy on relationships, supported by an erotically aggressive advertising. It grossed $26 million at the domestic box office. (Wyatt, 1998, 79) *Sex, Lies and Videotape* has opened the market for unusual, usually sexually more explicit films. The year 1989 usually counts as the starting point for the independent success in the 1990s. After the success of *Sex, Lies and Videotape* Miramax prevailed with its aggressive marketing politics, favorably attacking the MPPA ratings system. Miramax films such as *Scandal* (1989), *The Cook, the Thief, his Wife and her Lover* (1989), *Tie Me Up! Tie Me Down* (1990) and *You So Crazy* (1994) all received X ratings from the ratings board.[3] (Wyatt, 1998, 80) Miramax integrated the unfavorable ratings into its advertising and consecutively released Peter Greenaway's *The Cook, the Thief, his Wife and her Lover* unrated – although underlining the number X in the advertisement. Following on this Greenaway's *Drowning by Numbers* (1987) was placated with the silhouette of a naked man and woman embracing, matched with a critique's commentary that went: »Enormously entertaining. No, one gets eaten in this one.« The MPPA believed this to be too suggestive and the film received an X rating.

In some ways Miramax' ratings strategy gives insight into the social politics of independent film production: whereas in the wake of traditional Hollywood film production films aimed at family values, independent film – especially Miramax productions – picked up issues of social criticism and engaged its audiences in current and timely issues. With the release of Neil Jordan's *The Crying Game* (1992) Miramax painstakingly stepped into the discussion about gender and homosexual rights. *The Crying Game* revolves around an ex-IRA activist having a love affair with a homosexual transvestite. Central to the plot is the protagonist's belief in the gender of his girl friend, who in the middle of the film turns out to be a transvestite. The film was released in November 1992, a month after President-elect Bill Clinton had promised to reverse the bans on homosexuals in the military (Tucker, 1993) and it spurned the discussion about homosexuality and military values. Thus an – otherwise art-house film – grossed with $62.5 million at the box office. The success was mainly due to Miramax marketing politics, which was commented upon by *Variety* as the following: »Miramax sold the film as an action thriller with a big ›secret‹. If it had been realistically pegged as a relationship film with gay connotations, it might never have broken beyond the major cities.« (Wyatt, 1998, 81) In a similar fashion Miramax marketed Antonia Bird's film *Priest* (1994) – about a conservatist gay priest – through releasing it on Good Friday. Having caused widespread media trouble through this release, one headline read »Protest Delays Wide Release of Priest;

1. *Out of Sight*, directed by Steven Soderbergh, 1998.
2. *Full Frontal*, directed by Steven Soderbergh, 2002.
3. *Solaris*, directed by Steven Soderbergh, 2002.

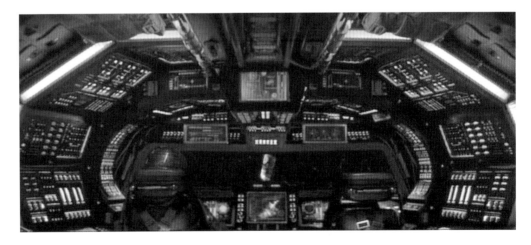

Miramax Bows to Catholic Group and Reschedules Controversial Film's General Distribution Till After Easter«, Miramax rescheduled the film. (Wyatt, 1998, 85; Rosenbaum, 1995)

Given the topics of Miramax' films and its marketing strategies, Miramax belongs to the hybrid / complex companies of the globalized Hollywood. Contrary to the »truly independent« film of the 1960s and 1970s, which shed away from all forms of commerce, the Weinstein brothers eagerly embraced big money. In 1993 Disney acquired the Miramax film library of nearly 200 films for about $ 70 million which gave the Weinsteins better opportunities on the home video market and pay television. Figuring the deal with Disney Miramax was allowed to spend $ 750 million on film. (Wyatt, 1998, 84) On the Disney side the deal gave their products a new diversity which had been lacking in the Disney, Touchstone and Hollywood Pictures output. (Lyons, 2003) The Disney deal enabled Miramax to spend more money on film distribution and advertising, which furthered the fast launching of film as well as the promotion for Miramax films on the Disney owned ABC programming. »Nearly all of the central cast of Quentin Tarantino's *Kill Bill, vol. 1*, for example, appeared on ABC's *Good Morning America* prior to the film's release on Oct. 10.« (Lyons, 2003)

With enough financial backing independent films could be brought into the big European and American film festivals and artists could land studio contracts. Additionally the Sundance Institute and Miramax stepped substituted the eviscerated NEA funding. (Rosenbaum, 1995)

The Disney contract, which at first ran of five years, was renewed and is now to be renegotiated in 2005. Disney allots Miramax with a $700 million annual marketing and production budget thereby giving Miramax an allowance up to $30 million for a film, which Miramax sometimes could exceed as it was the case with *Kill Bill*, which cost Miramax an estimated $55 million. (Lyons, 2003)

In a recent article in *Variety* Charles Lyons sums up the achievements of this 11-years union, which – initially – was labeled as a »culture-clash«. (Lyons, 2003) Since the union Miramax saw its profits rise each year. In 2003 it was worth an estimated $3 billion. The profits of 2002 are assumed to be the highest profits in its history, due to the nearly $300 million at the box office for *Chicago* (2002). (Lyons, 2003)

Over the years Miramax' films have gained an impressive list of Oscar nominations, due to the Weinstein brothers' taste for projects attracting top talents to movies impressing Oscar voters. In his time with Disney the company had at least one best picture nomination each year. In 2003 its films received 40 Oscar nominations, including 13 for *Chicago*, 10 for *Gangs of New York* (2002) and 9 for *The Hours* (2002) (a Paramount co-production). (Lyons, 2003) As one source close to the Weinstein's mentions, »they're interested in making these large tent pole films, but the important thing for Disney and Miramax is that they haven't lost sight of the smaller- and mid-budgeted films that have consistently made them successful, both artistically and financially«. (Lyons, 2003)

Miramax's top 10 pics

Domestic box office*

1.	*Chicago* (02)	171
2.	*Scary Movie* (00)	157
3.	*Good Will Hunting* (97)	138
4.	*Spy Kids* (01)	113
5.	*Spy Kids 3D: Game Over* (03)	111
6.	*Pulp Fiction* (94)	108
7.	*Scream* (96)	103
8.	*Scream 2* (97)	101
9.	*Shakespeare in Love* (98)	100
10.	*The Others* (01)	97

* in million $ through Oct. 16, 2003 (Lyons, 2003)

Market share (Jan. 6 to March 30, 2003)

Distributor	B.O.*	% share
Disney	304	17
Miramax	216	12
Paramount	203	11
Fox	180	10
New Line	180	10
Warner Bros.	174	10
DreamWorks	174	10
Sony	154	9
MGM	73	4
Focus	45	3
Universal	24	1
Other	49	3
Total	$1.77 Billion	100

* In millions of $ (DiOrio, 2003)

As mentioned above, the new independents of the 1990s and beyond differ from the »real« independents of the 1960s and 1970s, not only through theit organizational structure, but through their aesthetics as well. They function as art film and are commercially successful at the same time, as the films of Steven Soderbergh document.

Soderbergh started his career with the film *Sex, Lies and Videotape* for which he received the Palm d'Or at the film festival in Cannes for the best film in 1989. This prize denotes the beginning of the new independent wave of the 1980s. Following on this Soderbergh released *Kafka* (1990), *King of the Hill* (1992), *Fallen Angels* (1993), *The Underneath* (1994), *Schizopolis* (1995), *Gray's Anatomy* (1996), *Out of Sight* (1997/98), *The Limey* (1998/99), *Erin Brockovich* (1999), *Traffic* (2000), *Ocean's Eleven* (2001), *Full Frontal* (2002) and *Solaris* (2002). Interestingly enough, Soderbergh has not progressed from an independent auteur into a mainstream filmmaker, he instead has managed to move along the line between mainstream and independent. Two years after his Academy Award winning film *Erin Brockovich* Soderbergh produced – once again with Julia Roberts – the experimental film *Full Frontal,* shot only with a digital camera. Solicited after his position within film production, Soderbergh claims to move on both sides:

DV: »A lot of people split the film making community into Hollywood and independents, but you fit into both. Why do you think that is?«

SS: »Well, probably because I don't make those sorts of distinctions. I never have. You can read interviews that were done during the period of *Sex, Lies and Videotape*, in which I was very clear about the fact that I don't really care who's paying for films, and I don't think it's really relevant. But you can make general distinctions between what those types of film do. I guess I agree, for the most part, with William Goldman's assessment that studio movies reinforce things that we want to believe, and independent films challenge those ideas. And I think that's generally true, although I've also seen the opposite. It just depends on what story you're trying to tell. If you're making *Ocean's Eleven*, you're not there to challenge anybody's idea of anything. It's just there to have fun. *Full Frontal* is opposite. It's absolutely there to challenge you and provoke you. And I like both of those. I don't want to do either type of film all the time. So I guess I've just been lucky.« (Reed, 2002)

The succession of Soderbergh's films proves his manifold filmic intentions due to which films such as *Sex, Lies and Videotape*, *Full Frontal, Schizopolis* and *The Limey* figure on the experimental side and *Erin Brockovich, Ocean's Eleven* or *Traffic* are more deeply located in the classical Hollywood tradition.

Summing up I want to discuss the range of aesthetic possibilities within Soderbergh's films. The most impressive aspect of Soderbergh's career up to now is his affiliation with independent film and its experimental aesthetics. Given that he started his career with *Sex, Lies and Videotape* in 1989. His *Full Frontal* hooks up on the topics developed in *Sex, Lies and Videotape* and gives them a further turn. As mentioned above*, Sex, Lies and Videotape* counts as first entry of new independent film production into Hollywood. It explores the relationship of four different people and mainly their attitude towards sex: Graham, being impotent and somewhat shy breaks into the marriage of Ann and John: Ann is outweighing her frustration about her marriage in a therapy and John is compensating by an affair with Ann's sister Cynthia, who herself feels inferior to the more beautiful and socially successful Ann. Openly admitting his impotence Graham makes up for his lack of sexuality through taping women discussing their sex lives with him.

The film is usually understood as allegory on AIDS, preventing people having corporeal contact and transgressing their desires to »safer« (sexual) practices. This may be one important aspect of the film, but in the context of Hollywood's enormous structural and economic upheavals the film underlines the changes in film production and filming technology. The low-key lighting and the documentary approach towards editing defy the high-key Hollywood aesthetic, the integration of video material provides the impression of low-budget amateur production. But Soderbergh's mastery is not the experimental integration of low-key material into film, but firmly planting it into the center of the film, thereby shaping the film's meaning.

Sex, Lies and Videotape revolves around character and its appearance, introducing a set of characters who are primarily cheating on each other. The only attempt at finding some »truth« about themselves is Ann's middle-class participation in a psychotherapy and Graham's radically intimate questions such as: »What is the most unusual location you ever masturbated at?« Through his intensive investigation into other people's private affairs the films positions itself not only into a tradition of filmic voyeurism but comments upon the introduction of the video camera and the VCR recorder into the market. Especially the pornographic industry was changed through video, since the »live« peep show and the small pornographic cinema vanished in favor of private home consumption. Throughout the 1980s the video camera and video production had the flavor

4– 6. *Ocean's Eleven*, directed by Steven Soderbergh, 2001.

of pornography or at least voyeurism. (Bernstorff, 2003, 145–154) Soderbergh plays with these images through letting Graham tape the intimate conversations and watch them while masturbating himself. Video denotes a search for truth, which cannot be fulfilled: in the end Ann's yuppie husband John watches her confessing to Graham, and when she finally bows down to kiss him, Graham turns the camera off in order not to reveal what is going to happen between Ann and himself.

If filmic pornography is understood as a radical attempt to document the orgasm as ultimate truth, documentary film – in its attempt to catch »life itself« – falls not very far from these intentions. In a broader context Soderbergh's experimental aesthetics can be considered as reflection on filmic truth and the introduction of a more documentary-orientated style into film-making. Soderbergh returns to this idea in *Full Frontal* and develops it further: the film starts with fake credits and the introduction to a completely different film, shot on 35 mm. A film in film is established before it turns to the actual film, shot with a digital camera. *Full Frontal* has turned away from the depiction of sexuality and it explores the lives of six people being involved in the film industry. Similarly to *Sex, Lies and Videotape* Soderbergh focuses on the actors, letting them improvise action and dialogue. This formula endows the film with a documentary quality, which is underlined by the low-key, more or less »natural« lighting. Soderbergh himself justifies the use of a digital camera as following: »Well, it seemed like the one way to do it, at least the portions of the film that are supposed to be »real«. The sections of *Full Frontal* that are supposed to be part of a film (within a film), we shot on 35 mm. And, at the same time, I was sort of playing around with perceived notions of aesthetics. Why does chasing somebody around with a DV camera and adopting a documentary style of shooting feel more real than other sections of film that are shot in 35 mm, in which the camera doesn't move around a lot and the cutting is very traditional? Even though they're both fake, why does one feel more real? I was playing around with that question and making the audience ask that question, especially as the film goes on and the relation between the two becomes clear.« (Reed, 2002)

Soderbergh goes on to explain his use of video, the different cameras and most important, the different cultural spaces video and film inhabit. Interestingly enough he aligns his use of video to the development of television and »real-life« television formats: »Mostly because in the intervening years, reality television of all sorts has become more prevalent. I'm very curious to see the response to *Full Frontal*. I have a feeling if I'd made this exact film 13 years ago, it would've been more difficult for people to accept the aesthetics of it. But I think today they won't have any problem with it because they've seen much video and film together.« (Reed, 2002)

Following this ideas on the impact of television and digital imagery in contemporary culture, Soderbergh provides us with a profound reflection on the meaning of the visual media and the construction of reality. Whereas mainstream Hollywood cinema tends to offer us a more or less unquestioned visual representation of the world, Soderbergh deeply explores our understanding of reality as well as the lack of stable »truths«.

Although *Sex, Lies and Videotape* (1989) and *Full Frontal* (2002), along with *Schizopolis* (1995) and *Kafka* (1990) express the experimental »independent« range of Soderbergh's work, his more conventional productions manage to employ this aspects as well.

Even the traditional *Erin Brockovich* (1999) for which Julia Roberts has been bestowed with an Academy Award, partly drifts away from sheer conventionality. Contrary to the usually more glossy productions Julia Roberts is so well known for, *Erin Brockovich* stars the actress in an understated manner. The action is less important compared to the dialogues, which are the real zest of the film. And *Erin Brockovich* provides the audience with an idea of a film engaging in a genre and leaving it at the same time.

Soderbergh's other quite successful films manage to stoop down to Hollywood's mainstream aesthetics while similarly subverting it. *Traffic* (2000), which won four Academy Awards, deals with drug trafficking between the US and Mexico. The film – shot by Soderbergh himself with a digital camera (Distelmeyer, 2003, 229) – employs a threefold plot: the story of the cops Javier Rodriguez and Manolo Sanchez, chasing drug traffickers in Tijuana (Mexico), of the judge Robert Wakefield, whose daughter is an addict herself in Ohio and of the undercover-cop team Montel Gordon and Ray Castro who take the big fish Carlos Alaya into custody. Consecutively his wife Helena begins to understand where their riches have come from and she enters his vacant position.

Shot with a hand camera, *Traffic*'s visual style is often compared to the Danish Dogma movement, which in its manifests and films explicitly spoke out against »Hollywood« style. Additionally Soderbergh equips his three different plots with three different colors: yellow for the Mexican parts, white for the Californian and blue for the Ohio portions, once again obstructing narrative and visual continuity. The film's production story documents the difficulties of locating such a product within the Hollywood system. Originally the film was planned to be produced by 20th Century Fox, being promoted by the chairman Bill Mechanic, when Soderbergh fell out with the company. Against usual business habits Bill Mechanic dissolved the contracts and supported Soderbergh in founding a new production company, USA Films, in order to produce the film. Against all expectation the $50 million film was extremely successful. It gained over $120 million at the domestic box offices and received four Academy Awards and international prizes. (Distelmeyer, 2003, 226)

While films such as *Sex, Lies and Videotape* or *Full Frontal* definitely underline »independent«, experimental style, *Ocean's Eleven* and *Out of Sight* aim at a Hollywood audience and Hollywood visual, high-impact style – but at the same time redefining some elements of Hollywood style. Both movies feature George Clooney as »gentleman gangster«, especially *Ocean's Eleven* is a remake of a *Rat Pack* classic from 1960, (starring Frank Sinatra, Dean Martin and Sammy Davis jr.)

one of the icon's of coolness at that time. (Kuschnerus, 2003, 237) Steven Soderbergh was fully aware of the difficulties of the remake: »The problem is with these names you have to bust your ass not to get beaten up. Everybody's thinking ›it just better be good‹. People are basically waiting to see if you screw it up. Nobody is going ›wow, congratulations‹.« (Soderbergh, 2002)

In order to set himself apart from the original, Soderbergh invests in his actors, their performance and especially their dialogue. Short lines such as the conversation between Tess and Danny such as:

Tess: »Didn't you get the divorce papers?«

Danny: »On my last day inside.«

Tess: »Told you I'd write.«

recall the elegant, witty dialogues of Howard Hawks' films or the erotic interplay between Humphrey Bogart and Lauren Bacall. (Kuschnerus, 2003, 239) While the film explores Hollywood's classical tradition, the visual style branches out into a completely different direction. Although there is high-key lighting, the film once again employs video as a central metaphor. Central to the robbery are surveillance systems, without which the plan could not have been realized. Consequently the head-quarter of the group employs large video screens and a set of cameras, screening the action in the casino and in the safe rooms. Less obvious than in *Sex, Lies and Videotape* but still quite explicit, Soderbergh once again ironically comments upon the concept of low-key, video imagery and documentary truth. Terry, the casino's owner, is deluded into thinking that his safe has been robbed through a video, showing fake surveillance pictures of a robbery. Believing in the authenticity of these images, he sides up with the gangsters in order to cheat on the insurance company. While this is taking place – and the staff being convinced that the casino really has been robbed – the original, »real« robbery takes place, without someone shooting pictures of the event.

Apart from the central video scenes, *Ocean's Eleven* employs a highly sophisticated visual style: there are static and dynamic split screens, jump cuts, crossing the lines, associative montage, slow motion, time lapse, freeze frames, flash backs and unmotivated close ups. (Kuschnerus, 2003, 241). All these devices provide *Ocean's Eleven* with a highly aesthetic complexity, quite unusual for a mainstream Hollywood gangster movie.

Summing all this up, Steven Soderbergh's work can be regarded as paramount for the new independent film-making. Relying on a completely changed institutional and economic structure, the independent film-makers have understood not to oppose mainstream cinema, but to accept and subvert it at the same time.

Randi Gunzenhäuser
Hyperkinetic images: Hollywood and computer games

This essay suggests that analogue and digital forms of entertainment[1] have far more to do with each other than is commonly acknowledged and that film no longer clearly occupies the dominating role within this relationship. Steven Poole, for example, describes the economic relationship between Hollywood films and computer games as one of increasingly intense competition: »Videogames today are monstrously big business. Their present status is [sic] largely to do with the shift in demographics ... In the 1980s, videogames were indeed mainly a children's pursuit, but now games ... are targeted at the disposable income of adults.«[2]

In the 40 years of their existence, computer games have managed to increase not only their economic, but also their aesthetic and technical influence on films. Today, the complex relationship between these media has to be examined from diverse angles. I want to introduce some analytical aspects which I consider important when describing the love-hate relationship between the moving images of film on the one hand and those of computer games on the other. I'll concentrate on action-centered examples, not only because the action genre is successful on both markets, but also because it provides me with a narrative starting point, a center and a dynamic plot device.

I want to propose the thesis that within this genre, speed and flexibility are becoming increasingly more important – not only in respect to objects and bodies but also in regard to the interaction between the different media. Pictures are currently developing a new hyperkinetic quality within and between the media.

The essay is divided into two parts. I'll start by roughly sketching the past of the relationship between movies, as a narrative medium, and computer games, as an interactive one. Two examples will illustrate my argument: *Tron* and *Max Payne*. In 1982, the Disney movie *Tron* was the first film dealing with the then incomprehensible world of video games by spectacularly using computer graphics. *Tron* was important in helping to shape the filmic idea of a gaming cyberspace and has recently been made into a game which, as it turns out, is more successful than its filmic predecessor.

Part two of the essay will introduce the game *Max Payne* which set new aesthetic standards in 2001, to be followed by an even more spectacular part two which came on the market in late 2003. *Max Payne* keeps pushing the rules of visual physicality to new limits. It both extends traditional filmic action practices to games and further probes the possibilities of accelerating moving images until they reach hyperkinetic dimensions captivating the user in hitherto unknown ways.

At the outset it is important to acknowledge that computer games, just like movies, don't follow a static set of rules, but rather have developed generically specific characteristics. Genres like strategy, action, adventure, or sports games fascinate different kinds of players and help in establishing communities centered around their respective qualities and the particular talents they tend to sustain. Accordingly, I compare movies and games on the basis of genre. The action genre which is my main interest here is a profitable field of study for two main reasons: First, it is a hybrid genre to begin with[3] and secondly, it is an extremely popular one, since it has established a tradition of exhibiting a peculiar visionary power.[4] Similar to early silent film which Tom Gunning calls »the cinema of attractions«,[5] it celebrates the medium and the sheer spectacularity of a technically enhanced fictional world. Therefore, both action movies and action games tend to attract audiences interested in media technology.

In regard to questions of transmediality, I am not dealing with objective features or static sets of rules for either films or computer games. Rather, the myth of Hollywood's visionary power is being recreated in computer games, thus empowering the digital media which in turn are being co-constructed in films, an enhancement of their own impact in the battle for market shares.

Seen in this context, the most obvious relationship between films and computer games would seem to be the least interesting one: from the start, film titles cite games and games take up film titles, plots, and characters. Hollywood, hoping to cash in on the economic success computer games have had since the early 1990s, modelled film projects after computer games, for example *Super Mario Bros.* (USA, 1993), *Street Fighter* (USA, 1994), *Mortal Combat* (USA, 1996), or *Wing Commander* (USA, 1999).

Fighting games have repeatedly been criticized for their violence; they traditionally allow players to fight each other with exaggerated martial arts moves. *Street Fighter* (1987) and *Street Fighter II* (1991/92)[6] introduced a new visual excess to fighting games, relying on a »comic-book style with characteristically jerky animation«, as Steven Poole writes.[7] *Mortal Combat* became

1. *Max Payne*, Rockstar Games, 2001.
2, 3. *Max Payne 2. The Fall of Max Payne. A Film Noir Love Story*, Rockstar Games, 2003.

4–6. *Tron 2.0*, Buena Vista, 2003.

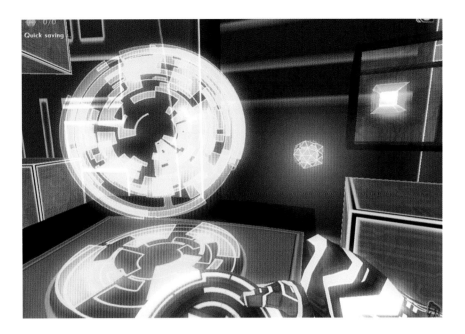

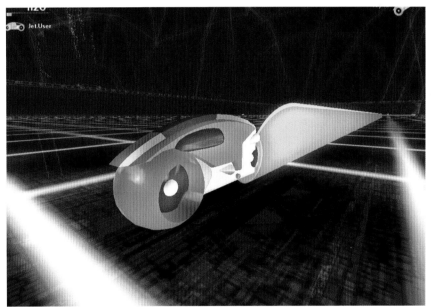

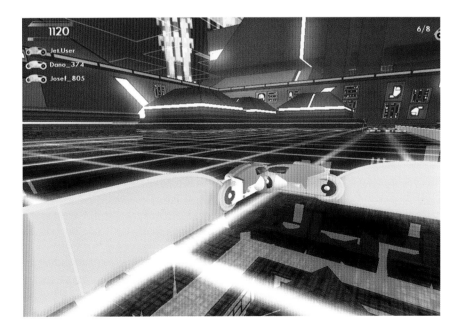

famous for its excessive depiction of violence, especially its so-called death moves which include the ripping open of the loser's body after a fight. These features were hardly ever literally translated into Hollywood's feature films[8] until Quentin Tarantino's *Kill Bill* (2003); they nevertheless helped to establish martial arts even more firmly within the action genre of both media as well as to strengthen the intermedial relationship not only between games and films or between eastern and western visual traditions, but also in regard to comic strips and animation movies or manga and anime, respectively.

Several Japanese directors, for example, adapted *Street Fighter II* to animated movies, TV series, and videos, thus creating a specific national game-to-film tradition which has since also been exported to the West. Although the quality of these Animés is dubious, Jonathan Clements and Helen McCarthy state: »[Gisaburo] Sugii's theatrical release [*Street Fighter II* from 1994] sets the standard for the entire game-adaptation subgenre and has been much imitated … Unlike the live-action version … starring Kylie Minogue and Jean-Claude Van Damme, the anime didn't have to try for a younger audience by cutting out the fights, nor was it limited by some cast members without any martial arts experience … *SFII* … adds two elements that would become staples of fighting-game adaptations – a mind-control subplot to orchestrate fights between supposed allies, and a shower scene to showcase a female character in the nude.«[9]

All these games and their movie translations present gender differences which seem much too clear-cut – not just by introducing tough male fighter characters, but also funny jump-and-run types like Nintendo's *Donkey Kong* (1981) or its plumber mascot Super Mario, both designed by Shigeru Miyamoto.[10]

Steven Poole writes about the relationship between the sexes in so-called platform games such as the two-dimensional *Mario Brothers* (1983) and *Super Mario Brothers* (1985) in which the hero's aim is to physically jump from one spatial level to another, always trying to evade or overcome obstacles, to finally reach the uppermost level where his prize is awaiting him: »… women are literally on pedestals, with men constantly striving to attain their level. It is an interesting example of plinth ideology …«[11] Obviously, male characters dominate these games and the movies modelled after them. In his monograph *Docuverse: Zur Medientheorie der Computer*, Hartmut Winkler, along with other contemporary critics, stresses the correlation between certain types of digital media, for example computer games, and the gender of computer users. He deduces that computers tend to reinforce macho media cultures which seemed to have almost disappeared in other, more traditional media.[12] Accordingly, the influence of male-centered computer games on films and on an ever younger film audience should not be taken lightly or even disregarded.

At the same time, this influence is not altogether one-sided and it shouldn't be inferred that genders are constructed as being stable. An increasing number of female players underscores this aspect. In contrast to the cliché that men actively play computer games, whereas women only play a role as decorative, passive addenda to the games' scenery, many women now actually play games. Women make up 30 per cent of the players in Europe today, and up to 50 per cent in the US.[13]

Following this trend, games have started to feature some heroines who also appear on the film screen. The British game *Tomb Raider* has been staging Lara Croft since 1996 and has made her the most famous heroine of a third-person shooter. Due to its third-person perspective, the attractive and oversexed Lara of the game is mostly seen from behind. Apart from exposing her expressive shape, Lara is an efficient killer – at least in the hands of a skillful player. The amazing possibilities of moving her – Lara cannot only run but also jump, climb, swim, and crawl – make her an avatar over which it is extremely difficult to exercise power. However, the feeling of power over her increases parallel to these complications until one has acquired enough gaming experience to successfully handle her.

Along with many other computer game heroines[14], Lara is the product of long-standing intermedial relationships. She was created in the tradition of comic strips such as *Wonder Woman* (1941) and *Tank Girl* (1988), and in the tradition of film robots and cyborgs like Maria in *Metropolis* (1926) or Eve in *Eve of Destruction* (1991). In view of the spectacle of the female body in these texts in which breasts, thighs, and hair figure so prominently, Scott Bukatman writes about the popular comic-book superwomen of the 1990s: »Overall, the trend has been toward masculinized, even phallic, women – armed to the teeth and just one of the boys.« (114) Movies, sharing this past of making a spectacle of women's bodies with comics and computer games, are most efficient in reproducing the fetishist spectacularity of the female body typical for action computer games. Nevertheless and depending on the respective audience/players, various, even contradictory assessments of these characters are prevalent today.[15]

Whereas the movie *Tomb Raider* (USA, 2001) did its best to superimpose Lara's looks onto Angelina Jolie's body, a live actress can hardly be expected to replicate Lara's acrobatic moves or evoke the specifically interactive, hands-on relationship a player cultivates in regard to his or her avatar. The film's post-production computer manipulation had problems in trying to recreate the never-tiring, altogether artificial, technically perfected bodily presence which makes Lara an omnipotent gaming heroine. It certainly couldn't recreate the bonds which bind a gamer to his or her avatar who in turn relies on the player as her helpmate if not, at times, as her master.

In computer games, there often exists a similar discrepancy between openly superhuman, clearly artificial bodies which definitely belong to a comic book tradition on the one hand and photorealist, illusionist graphic and auditive effects on the other[16]. Players are enveloped in 3D-spaces in which 3D-characters throw dynamic shadows, sound moves along with bodies, and surfaces constantly change along with the light, the direction of the wind, or any touch, but also with an explosion. Both these tendencies – one excessively foregrounding special effects as special, the other potentially erasing their spectacularity and creating detailed verisimilitude, a reference to the player's experience of objects in the world – are well known from animated movies such as *Toy Story* (1995), *A Bug's Life* (1998), *Antz* (1998), *Small Soldiers* (1998), or *Shrek* (2001).

In animated films, one can refer to this mixed strategy of realist conventions and their excess as »hyperrealism«, well known from Disney movies.[17] As Donna Coco points out, many animation specialists worked in both fields as early as in 1997,[18] software and filmic animation increasingly complementing each other. The obsessive thematization of intermedial relationships as exemplified in the converting of computer games or comic books into movies in the 1990s not only testifies to the film industry's new interest in and advancement of digital technologies, but also demonstrates the fear of an increasing competition between »old« and »new« media.

This competition is further incited by games like *Blade Runner* (1997), *Deus Ex* (2000) or *Deus Ex – The Invisible War* (2003/04) which introduce flexible game-plays. Their digital worlds are open to different kinds of morals and thus to different ways of being in the fictional universe. They compel the player to act as a »*Deus ex Machina*«, forcing her to come up with individual strategies and decisions by which to overcome obstacles and conflicts.[19] For one specific problem, the programmers didn't script and therefore prescribe merely one solution, but rather many. The players are expected to forge creatively their own paths through a relatively complex universe. By groping one's individual way through the maze of possible decisions, one shapes the personality of one's character and actively influences the way other characters react toward one's avatar. Character growth, known from narrative media like print texts or movies, becomes possible and increasingly important not just in role-playing games but also within the action genre.

At the same time as the complex interplay of classical, illusionary visual, auditive and narrative effects makes the ambience of digital games look more filmic than ever before, films integrate more and more digital effects, both visibly and invisibly. Steven Poole points to George Lucas's practice of digitally modifying his actors' performances[20] and writes: »In this purely cosmetic respect, it is true that videogames are converging with films.«[21] This technique was perfected in *Final Fantasy*, a feature film released in 2001 and based on the Japanese action-adventure series of the same name which dates back to 1987. *Final Fantasy* is exclusively a digital movie which replaces live actors entirely with animated characters that are supposed to be read as »human« and in that sense as »authentic«. Despite its lack of success, this film heralds a formal coinciding of film and computer games in the future.

The fear of an even harder competition between film and computer games and of a possible replacement of traditional film by digital media overlooks the fact that these media function according to different rules. A film achieves continuity in respect to narration and character formation by means of editing. Within a computer game, only video sequences are cut; the actual playing sequences are characterized by loops and thus by the possibility and necessity of saving and repeating scenes.[22] Therefore, players of computer games actively have to bridge the gap between gaming and narration. On the one hand, they have to train their playing skills and often repeat difficult scenes until they can be played smoothly – a necessity constantly interrupting the narrative flow of the game. On the other hand, increasing playing skills propel not only the action forward but also the plot. As one fights, answers questions, and solves problems or puzzles, one gets ahead, shapes the character of one's avatar, and the narrative moves on.

The loop adds important characteristics to digital games. It interrupts any preplanned continuity, introducing chance, the necessity of practicing, and potentially endless repetitions of not quite the same scene as a means to evade »death« and destruction. The loop gives the player a chance to prove herself as an active mediator between the virtual world and her own by means of her capabilities of closure; it strategically connects the player to her inhuman, omnipotent, otherwise unapproachable avatar.[23]

The fact that narrative is organized differently in computer games and films precludes easy translation, not just from game to film, but also vice versa. Although there are many examples of computer games which bear the names of films, such as *Star Wars*, *Blade Runner*, *The Matrix*, or *Lord of the Rings*, not many are successful. These clones are often evaluated by degrees of »authenticity«: The more closely they resemble their »original« in tone and atmosphere – not in respect to narrative –, the more authentic they are considered to be. This claim to authenticity is not only paradoxical, but also obsolete in times of Postmodernism and digital reproduction. The effectivity of a computer game or a film must be established within the respective medium and its rules.

The influence of films on computer games and vice versa is not restricted to such methods of translation. In 1982, *Tron*, for example, presented an aesthetics of cyberspace, relying on the idea of the arcade game. »It was the first film actively engaged in an aesthetic dialogue with videogames ...«[24] Following Ellen Strain, Routledge's introduction to the new media has a chapter on »Virtual V[irtual] R[eality]«, »the representation of speculative forms of VR and cyberspace in science-fiction films«[25], ironically creating, as Philip Hayward writes, »a simulacrum of the medium in advance«. Hayward explains that »these discourses are significant because they have shaped both consumer desire and the perceptions and agenda of the medium's developers«.[26] The movie *Tron*, showing off its flashy computer graphics, is an example of this strategy involving human actors in a graphic environment.

As can already be seen on the cover of the storybook and the poster for the movie, the aesthetics of *Tron* rely on a play of color and light. Electronic space here is presented as grids of light standing for pure data. *Tron* creates the space inside an arcade game, a public gaming computer. This digital space is permeable by, but at the same time dangerous to, matter, based on the tradition of the matter vs. anti-matter dichotomy known from older science-fiction texts, for example, by Philip K. Dick: the hero, Kevin Flynn, is being absorbed by an alternative electronic universe, becoming a character in an action computer game. As a self-conscious avatar, he is forced to engage in fights and ultimately beats his real-life enemy who has entered the electronic realm as well.

Tron's hallucinatory cyberspace is characterized by danger, fights, and speed – in every sense of the word. The intensely illuminated outlines of spaces as well as of objects and characters allude to comic strips and drug-induced dreamworlds. Characters speed through this world, a space exempt of real-life obstacles, faster than light. Similar to the figures in many cyberpunk novels published in its wake, the men leave their bodies behind without having to relinquish the illusion of their immortality.

Despite its financial failure, the movie initiated a series of products in the gaming world. For example, a game of exchange cards which stresses the resisting core of the human hero caught in a digital world – a body that matters because it is constructed as a heroic subject. Another product was an arcade game, *Discs of Tron*, developed by Bally and Midway, which medially turned the story into a »real«, not a »virtual« virtual environment in 1983.

Whereas an early game version of *Tron* for the personal computer was not successful, the recent action game *Tron 2.0* (2003), developed by Monolith, sells well;[27] and the soon to be released game *Tron 2.0: Discs of Tron* by Lavastrom is already celebrated as being the most »authentic« translation not only of the film story into cyberspace, but also of the arcade version onto the platform of the personal computer.

Monolith's *Tron 2.0* can be played in single- or multiplayer mode. The perspectives can be changed according to the player's whim, establishing either a third- or first-person point of view. Speed is not only the most important feature of this gaming cyberspace but also the precondition for successful movement. Bodies made up of pure energy speed through this space and fight each other. The end of a life cycle signifies the chance for a new beginning, another training session on the way to perfection.

Physicality is an important component of the action genre and physical systems of computer games don't automatically follow cinematic rules. This is partly due to the gaming principle of interactivity. The game, being an interactive set-up, doesn't just have its own world-building philosophy, it has its own physics and its own biology. »There is a direct link between convincing videogame dynamics and gameplay pleasure«, as Steven Poole points out. (63) And gameplay pleasure doesn't coincide with viewing pleasure. Accordingly, the rules of realist illusionism known from Hollywood films are not the same as those established in games. The properties of objects and bodies in a movie are restricted to their visual and auditive characteristics whereas in a computer game they follow the additional imperative of having to be pleasurably and successfully handled.

So far, films and computer games have mostly been compared in respect to subject matter and narrative structures – areas in which most computer games turn out to be deficient being oriented toward models of action and reaction, interactivity between users and machines or between players. Furthermore, the repetitive loop is a typical element of computer games. Thus, in addition to giving illusionist pleasures, to creating the illusion of re-creating a non-fictional reality, computer games please us by offering the opportunity to dodge defeat. This effect of the repetitive loop which characterizes the structure of games has already entered movies and introduced the principle of repetition with slight differences leading to different plots and endings, as can be seen, for example, in *Nirvana* (1997), *Lola rennt* (1998) or *eXistenZ* (1999).

Transmedial relationships are being complicated by the contemporary abundance of contextualizations stated, for example, by producer Lorne Michaels in regard to film, television, and rock intertexts in *Wayne's World*: »We live in a time when nothing will ever go away again. [Everything is] on a channel somewhere. All cultural references are, to a ten-year-old, perfectly familiar.«[28] Jim Collins deems »semiotic excess« a characteristic of contemporary Hollywood film, and this excess includes endless references between different media like film, television, music videos, comic books, and other media.[29] This holds true not just on a national scale, but also on an international one, as the influence of manga, anime, and Hong Kong action movies on today's computer games as well as Hollywood movies is plainly evident.

One important effect of these developments is the speeding up of movements and editing, making speed an ever more important ingredient of action scenarios. At the same time, formalized bodily movements become foregrounded: aesthetic perfection and ritualized exactitude which have always played an important role in Asian fighting traditions have by now entered both computer games and movies. Hilary Radner argues that it becomes increasingly difficult to decide in which direction influences move.[30]

The movie *The Matrix* is in fact already the product of many influences from both Western and Eastern action film and philosophical traditions. Routledge's *New Media: An Introduction* uses the film as a »case study« for supplementary marketing and calls the related chapter »What is Bullet Time?«, coined after the title of a short documentary on the making of this CGI special-effects-driven film.[31] The authors write: »If in *The Matrix*, as in other special-effects-led films, the pleasures of viewing lie in the tension between immediacy and hypermediacy, then *What is Bullet Time?* (a short documentary included on *The Matrix* VHS and DVD [1999]) is positively orgiastic. It explains how the effects were achieved, and presents the stages of the construction of the illusion: from wireframe computer simulations of the positioning of cameras and actors, to actors suspended from wires against green screens bounded by a sweeping arc of still cameras, and so on through digital compositing and layering of backgrounds and the effects of bullets in flight.«[32]

Effects like bullet time, catching bullets in flight, are being explained and celebrated *as effects* in this making-of film. Martin Lister and his co-authors make a point of the explicit hybridity created by the mixture of the digital and analogue media and celebrated by this short documentary.[33] This hybridity helps to speed pictures up and to involve viewers in a new way.

These effects are important not only for today's action movies, but also for computer games, especially for action games like *Max Payne*. The kinetic aesthetics of computer games have influenced Hollywood movies, further foregrounding the spectacularity of graphic effects, building computer-generated worlds which are far from illusionist. The main raison d'être of such digital universes is to motivate the viewers and involve them in a technically perfect matrix emulated not just by other films, but also by computer games like *Max Payne*.

When *Max Payne* came out in 2001 it quickly became famous (not to mention infamous and, therefore, banned in Germany) for its »bullet time«, a slow-motion technique already known to action fans from *The Matrix*. In *Max Payne*, two kinds of slow motion or sniper modes exist: one of them slows down every character's movements, so the aiming of a gun becomes easier. At the same time, ducking and diving – »shootdodging« – are of major importance for the Max Payne character. The second bullet time is very costly – you can only use it if you have enough energy left and it only lasts for a short time. It does offer a pay-off, though: now only Payne and the player experience an even more drastic slowing down of time and can gun down an otherwise overpowering number of enemies.

This technique was perfected by adding aural precision in *Max Payne 2. The Fall of Max Payne,* a film noir love story. In part one Max Payne is given a traumatic past: He lost his wife and daughter to an assassin, goes undercover and investigates the murder along with a case the government is involved in. In part two, the hard-core action plot is supplemented with a love motive, a strategy which is quite unusual for any action game. Just as in *Blade Runner*, the love plot adds immersive aspects known from genres like hardboiled detective fiction or the film noir, but at the same time *Max Payne* excessively outstrips the gender characteristics typical for these older genres. It makes Max Payne's lover not only a femme fatale but also a hired killer.

In addition to video sequences, both parts of *Max Payne* include comic strip sequences by way of which the different pieces of the puzzle fall into place and the plot is being put together scene by scene. Also typical are the constant cross references to TV series and movies. As the two protagonists, Max Payne and Mona, who is after the same man as Max, detect the clues leading them to a sobering end: Mona is killed, Max survives, »waking up from the American Dream«, as the final part III of Max Payne 2 is called.

Although *Max Payne* uses many filmic techniques and refers to other media, it combines them in a way which is typical for computer games. As opposed to a movie, a game shouldn't merely be enjoyed as a spectacle, but must be played, and involves the player in different forms of interactions. The game's main objective is the repetitiveness of the act of playing as well as the amount of time consumed which is considerably longer than it takes to watch a movie.

Jay D. Bolter and Richard Grusin stress that the »new« media employ digital technologies in order to refashion older media, the »old« media »refashion themselves to answer to the challenges of the new media«.[34] Hollywood films traditionally presented instances of identification by offering changing perspectives, emphasizing subjectified points of view, a probing camera eye, dialogical cuts, voice-over and dramatic music. Narrative continuity was the ordering imperative of editing. The aim of the game has always been to make the player feel herself to be part of cyberspace computer games complete with enveloping 3D-technologies and the possibility of choosing different perspectives at the cost of narrative unity, of a tight construction of the plot, and of edited point-of-view shots.

As Lev Manovich points out in *The Language of New Media*, computer games at times want to involve the player in the action and want her to forget the inherently mediated structure of the game. At other times, they show passages which foreground the structural and formal aspects of the game and the process of gaming: they reveal pull-down menus which have to be used or – as in the case of multiplayer games – make it necessary for players to chat in order to coordinate their actions.

The immersive parts of a game serve to make the players merge into the ludic space and action, whereas the often self-reflexive passages help to structure one's actions and to communicate strategies with other players and thus influence the development of the game. Lev Manovich describes this changing character: »The screen keeps shifting from transparent to opaque – from a window to fictional 3-D universe to a solid surface, full of menus, controls, texts, and icons. Three-dimensional space becomes surface; ... a character becomes an icon. ... We can say that the screen keeps alternating between the dimensions of representation and control. What at one moment was a fictional universe becomes a set of buttons that demand action.« (207 f)

This tension between stasis and action, between stalling and speed is also being constantly enforced by the media which surround computer games. Both strategies are directed toward opposing objectives of computer games, yet each is aimed at immersing players into the world of the game: trailers announcing a new game, intros establishing the main narrative contexts, strategies, and aims. The making-of genre points in the same direction. All these aspects are true for films as well and point in the direction of an increasing and at the same time dispersed immersion of audiences and players.

To sum up: Today, the relationship between Hollywood movies and digital games is neither restricted to economic aspects nor dominated by film any longer. When looking at action-dominated films and games, it becomes apparent that both have traditionally celebrated their own visionary, technically created power, making them contemporary media of attraction. Accordingly, they tell a story which runs parallel to their narrative plot, a technical metanarrative.

The increasing foregrounding of technical mastery is accompanied and pushed still further by the use of martial arts and the abundance of stylized, perfectly timed movements which become more and more important in many different media both in the East and the West. Not only have the bodies which are shown on screens become more and more flexible, but also subjectivities and genders, respectively. Character growth is becoming an important factor in today's digital action games.

Digital games and movies alike make a point of creating »mixed« characters which are endowed not only with a spectacular, oversexed, and seemingly obvious bodily form but also with the possibility of growing in unexpected directions like in the *Matrix* trilogy or in *Deus Ex*. They tend toward ever elusive and fluid subjectivities which make use not only of developments in poststructural philosophy but also in the field of artificial intelligence.

Apart from subject matter, fighting techniques, and character formation, the strategies of visualization are presently changing: techniques known from animation movies and comic books have entered digital games as well as films with live actors. Illusionary and realist effects compete not only with spectacular visual ones, but also with auditive, and musical ones, creating the impression of »hyperrealism«, an effect traditionally confined to animated movies. The mixed effects of the hyperreal concern every aspect of the making of movies and games.

The mixed character of the hyperreal is enforced on the international market where the different media interact and influence each other ever more strongly. Every medium has to compete with the others for market shares.

Accordingly, games as well as movies direct an increasingly forceful grasp toward their audiences or users respectively, both try to immerse us ever more strongly into the action. »Immersion«, a term usually only used within the discourse of the new media, can now be applied to movies after their fall into the digital as well. Immersion requires a specific hyperkinetic dynamics – the dynamics of speed, movement, and tempo or control typical for both computer games and movies of the action genre today.

Images of digitally improved bodies with perfectly timed and synchronized movements abound, bodies which become ever more changeable, flexible, and unpredictable. They don't rely on traditional gender characteristics and can adapt more quickly and more effectively to adverse circumstances than ever before. In the face of ever stronger enemies, both male and female characters can increase their psychological as well as their physical powers – an aspect not only a game like *Max Payne* but also Quentin Tarantino's movie *Kill Bill* (2003, 2004) clearly demonstrates.

The future of computer games and films definitely lies in more thoroughly immersive technologies for groups of users and film-goers who hitherto felt excluded from these media and / or specific genres. I suggest that in order to achieve this effect, these technologies will develop in different directions: games will probably show more networked multiplayer action, movies will include ever more digital special effects and might offer individual perspectives and different choices of plots. Both games and films might move toward a stronger synchronization of ever faster body movements with images and more intensifying sound. As I have argued, neither the directions nor the dominance of influences can be predicted in advance or even clearly deciphered after the fact.

Dietmar E. Fröhlich
Architecture and film. The reality play

Introduction

Architecture and film have had a close relationship since film first appeared on the world stage at the end of 1895, when the train shot into the station at La Ciotat, the city where Auguste and Louis Lumière played midwife to Cinema. There is no film that does not contain architectural images and environments. Film exists in real space as much as in virtual space. Architecture, as an »ordering device« occupies those spaces. Buildings and cities have played a great part in all the attempts to conquer the temporal dimension inherent to film. In passing through an environment, literally moving past a fixed point in the Cartesian system, we decode the narrative, the temporal aspect of film manifests itself.

Natasha Higham in her essay »Cinem(a)rchitecture: signifying the imaginary city in film« states that »architecture gives film its believability; setting the mood, character and time and place for the action while inextricably providing sequential cues – the temporal unity of a scene shot at different times, in different locations and from different camera angles«.[1]

This essay will investigate the roles that architecture plays in film, and see how film influences the production of architecture. From the beginning, the city has been the place where film found its first »set« and plenty of stories to recount.

The arrival of virtual reality gave new tools to the visionary eye of the film director: new film architecture is suddenly within easy reach. Utopias on celluloid tell us about the inner longings of society, it is film as a mirror of society in the guise of architecture.

We will also look at architecture in »disguise«, real buildings that make a cinematic Utopia possible, and how buildings can change their »personality« and give a film its distinct memorability. We will see how architecture stands in as a metaphorical double for the protagonist, when the hero lives in a certain type of house and the villain in another type.

Film directors oftentimes act as architects when choosing the frames to be shot, and some architects build cinematic architecture that lends itself to a starring role.

This investigation is conducted from an architect's point of view, one who »... in the cinema ... watches a narrative which is beyond one's own control, in dreamlike darkness, in the company of strangers and typically also with a close friend or two, having paid for the privilege.«[2]

Trailer: architecture and film

Dietrich Neumann in *Film Architecture: Set Design from Metropolis to Blade Runner* speaks about »three roles that architecture plays in film«:[3]

As a »reflection and commentary on contemporary developments«, as explored in *Minority Report*,[4] where a gadget-driven traditional »period« architecture is counter-pointed with high-tech buildings accessed by skyways reminiscent of Fritz Lang's *Metropolis*[5] in a Washington, D.C. of a few decades from now. *The Truman Show*[6], the actual town of Seaside in Florida, show this prime example of the New Urbanism[7] of the 1980s as the place of alienation and plastic reality shows.

As »a testing ground for innovative visions«, as seen in *The Fifth Element's*[8] vertical city; its pod rooms for living; the smart houses and the automated, traffic solutions; in the future cities, the densely packed agglomerations, that are featured in George Lucas' *Star Wars*[9] series; and in the possible binary architecture, the virtual architecture of the *Matrix*[10].

And as »a realm in which a different approach to art and practice of architecture can be realized.« One recalls the ever-changing *Dark City*[11] with its architecture adapting to necessities just discovered when »plugging« the humans' thoughts and emotions, an architecture driven by external data similar to the approach that, for example, the Dutch architecture collaborative of MVRDV[12] takes when letting »objective« data streams guide the design process. One thinks of the virtual constructs of *The Thirteenth Floor*,[13] where realities are blurred, and again, *The Matrix* with its virtual spaces indistinguishable from reality.

Architecture helps to establish relationships between the actor, the environment and the spectator. Assisting in visualizing the temporal aspect of the narrative, it is also a major component of the psychological space of a scene, the creation of a certain mood through the set. It is difficult to imagine film without any kind of architectural space. Architectural terminology has infiltrated our everyday language in the same way it did with the language of film.

1. *Minority Report*, directed by Steven Spielberg, 2002.
2. *The Fifth Element*, directed by Luc Besson, 1997.
3. *The Matrix*, directed by Larry and Andy Wachowski, 1999.
4. *Dark City*, directed by Alex Proyas, 1998.

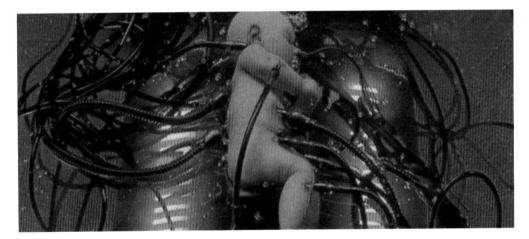

5. Antoine Predock, classroom / laboratory / administrative building, Cal Polytech, Pomona, California, 1987–92.
6. Frank Gehry, Guggenheim Museum, Bilbao, 1991–97.
7. Coop Himmelb(l)au, Gasometer housing estate, Vienna, 1995–2001.

The effect of cinematographic work on real life illustrates the power of cinema – we learn how to read visual clues and how to see through cinema, we are introduced to the effect of architecture through the sets. At the same time, the importance of real life architecture for film reaffirms architecture's primacy over the virtual construction of film.

Buildings and cities, are just as much a part of film as are the actors. Documentaries and fiction films alike oftentimes feature architecture as the protagonist of the film. Architecture appeared in the first film ever made. The Lumière brothers used a train entering the station as a device to show spatial depth, movement and sequencing necessary to evoke the passage of time. Georges Méliès also used architecture, mostly fantastic set architecture as the main ingredient of his stories that astonished his audience. Film needs real and set architecture to locate, pinpoint and advance the story told.

Filmic space is shaped by the focal length of the lens. Architecture, as a big portion of the production design of the film, can set the tone and the overall mood of the film. Architecture defines the visual depth of a scene.

Architectural space and filmic space have many things in common. Architecture is often dubbed cinematic referring to these certain commonalties of the two meaning that architecture unfolds over time creating a narrative conversely. It is oftentimes the architecture that makes a movie a memorable.

In the wake of the virtual reality revolution in film, mainstream Hollywood productions rely more and more on the capacity to produce special effects to achieve success at the box office. Hyperreality allows us to see bullets fly in slow motion (*The Matrix*), gives us the chance to view scenes in 360 degree angles at the same time (*The Matrix*), reconstructs the Colosseum (*Gladiator*),[14] or lets a whole city morph into a new one every 24 hours (*Dark City*). This cinematic reality is made and conveyed so convincingly that one could almost believe the world shown is real.

Even the environment the actors perform in is becoming a virtual one. The idea of a totally invisible space (to the actors) as the staging ground for the story seems to become increasingly common. Film is becoming a spatially multi-layered product mixing live acting with computer-generated images. One might want to ask the actor, how it feels to perform in a spatial »vacuum«.

With the content of the majority of movies shifting ever more towards action, the opportunity to employ these new digital techniques of creating spaces and environments has increased dramatically. Sometimes the quality of these new virtual spaces is more convincing and exciting than that of real spaces. These new space-creating techniques even can drive the narrative of the film like in *The Matrix* or *The Thirteenth Floor*.

On the other side of the relationship, architecture has learned to apply film techniques to design, to represent and advertise its creations: spaces are thought of as being measured in sequences, editing has become a technique of design, zooming in and zooming out defines architectural elements and assemblies, viewpoints and angles of perception help to invigorate designs. The architecture of Coop Himmelb(l)au, Antoine Predock, and Frank Gehry, just to name a few, owes to the visual language of cinema. In this architecture that language is »heard« and »read« in its three-dimensional version.

Despite all the inventions and technological improvements in cinema, the British filmmaker Peter Greenaway in an interview with Ania Krenz thinks that »... architecture is the ultimate multimedia and it creates the situation which exists for everyday living ... you can forget cinema, painting, ... but you cannot avoid architecture. We need it, it is one of the essential elements.«[15]

Speaking from an architect's point of view, architecture will always remain an impressive and memorable component of life and of the movie. It is also safe to assume that, at least not in the foreseeable future, film will not be able to replace a real world experience of space and time as offered through architecture.

Architectural space in film is the most tangible manifestation of distance and dimension, of scale and even of time.

Typologies of space

Space vs. speed

What is the significance of space to our perceptions? Philosophers and theoreticians have pointed out lately, that space has been replaced by speed. It is not the variation of space that captures our attention, but it is the phenomenon of speed that has changed our way of experiencing the environment. Speed afforded by the computer and the Internet, and the possibility of being in different locations at virtually the same moment, and the film-like spooling of images presages the presence of virtual spaces and the expansion and contraction of time that determines our perception.

The advent of the Internet, and the seemingly infinite possibilities of computer cyber-space, has left architects somehow sitting in the back rows of the theater.

Lagging behind the technological revolution, remaining more or less in a kind of stasis, architects seem to have become obsolete. If the drama of space has given way to a drama of speed, architects have outlived their existence.

Despite all the focus on speed and cybernetics in theoretical discussions, space still remains as the defining criterion when looking at the built environment, as does space even in film. Space has not surrendered yet, nor has lost its validity for a discussion of architecture and urban design. Architecture, our environment, is experienced through movement in, around, and through spaces.

Temporal-spatial experiences drive the narrative of a film as well. Passing markers or location points helps us to read a film. Likewise, moving from point A to point B helps us experience a building from different angles, thus allowing its multi-layering to become evident. Even with the emergence of »speed« as a major factor in our perception, architecture, and its being there, positions us in our environment and helps us orient ourselves. We can measure temporal development against fixed points in space.

Spatial experience in film

When Orson Welles used a wide-angle shot to keep all the objects focused in the picture plane in *Citizen Kane*,[16] it heralded in a new way of treating cinematic space. Here the spatial treatment was directly applied to serve the purpose of the film and to transmit the cinematic ideas. Welles used the camera, and the choice of focal length of the lens, to evoke the desired spatial effect, an effect that was corresponding to the story and the personae of the protagonists. A wide-angle shot not only would give a certain distance and objectivity to the scene, but would also incorporate actors and objects into the frame. With this innovation Welles achieved a »broadening« of the story and at the same time a more objective, documentary-like form that would not have been possible with a shorter focus length.

With the film *Citizen Kane* Welles had introduced a new spatial dimension to film. »Film captures movement and change in time, and contrary to the other arts, it is able to project movement onto a two-dimensional screen, collapsing space and time inside the frame … In film, images translate into spatial experience through the interplay of camera movements, such as dollying, tracking, and zooming. At the same time, film is based on a plot, a narrative which suggests a beginning (of a process) and an ending (a resolution). But contrary to common belief, this is not a linear process, because film can be disoriented with respect to time and space.«[17]

8. *Berlin: Symphony of a Great City*, directed by Walter Ruttmann, 1927.
9. *The Man with the Movie Camera*, directed by Dziga Vertov, 1929.
10. *A Zed & Two Noughts*, directed by Peter Greenaway, 1985.
11. *A Beautiful Mind,* directed by Ron Howard, 2001.

Architecture and film

Architecture is immobile, but an architectural experience is based on movement, such as standing in a space and looking around, or walking along a corridor.

»From the 1920's and after, film and architecture were, in a fundamental sense, entirely different media utilizing their respective technologies, the one to simulate space, the other to build it, now, by contrast, the increasing digitalization of our world has rendered them if not the same, at least coterminus.«[18]

Sergey Eisenstein, a pioneer in architecturally stimulated films, developed a comprehensive theory of what he called »space constructions« that found new meaning in the romantic formulation of architecture as »frozen music«: »At the basis of composition of [architectural] ensemble, at the basis of the harmony of its conglomerating masses, in the establishment of the melody of the future overflow of its forms, and in the execution of its rhythmic parts, giving harmony to the relief of its ensemble, lies that same ›dance‹ that is also at the basis of the creation of music, painting, and cinematic montage.«[19]

Walter Ruttmann's *Berlin, Symphony of a Great City* (1927)[20] and Dziga Vertov's *The Man with the Movie Camera* (1929)[21] are coming close to Eisenstein's »space conctructions« – both films are extremely rhythmically structured, and both employ architecture to transport the narrative as well as the formal aspects of the film.

Cinematic space

The French philosopher Gilles Deleuze in an interview speaks of an »open classification« of cinematic space that can manifest itself in many ways.[22] Deleuze names the organic or encompassing space such as in westerns, or such as in Kurosawa's films, who adds immense amplitude to the encompassing space. It is the functional lines of the universe like in the neowesterns, and Mizoguchi.

Cinematic space is depicted in the flat spaces of Joseph Losey, it reappears as disconnected spaces with undetermined junctions, such as in the style of Bresson, to morph into the empty spaces, as encountered in Ozu and Antonioni. The stratigraphic cinematic spaces are defined by what they cover up, to the point that we »read« the space, as shown in Jean-Marie Straub's work, whereas Alain Resnais' work investigates topological spaces. But in the end, there are as many spaces as there are inventors.

Deleuze further states that »light and space combine in very different ways … in all these instances, one sees that these classifications of light and space belong to cinema yet nonetheless refer to other domains, such as science or art, Isaac Newton or Robert Delaunay – domains that will take them in another order, in other contexts and relations, and in other divisions«.

For Deleuze, »a work of art always entails the creation of new spaces and times (it is not a question of recounting a story in a well-determined space and time, rather, it is the rhythms, the lighting and the space-times themselves that must become true characters). A work should bring forth the problems and questions that concern us rather than provide answers. A work of art is a new syntax, one that is much more important than vocabulary and that excavates a foreign language in language … in creative works there is a multiplication of emotion, a liberation of emotion, and even the invention of new emotions.«

A typology of space

When investigating space the categorization into four main types of space – physical space, virtual space, temporal space and mental space – is helpful to understand the ideas behind spatial concepts in film and in architecture. Overlaps of these four main types occur.

Physical spaces

Cinematic spaces as discussed in architecture, are characterized by their disclosure over time; a development in movement, a change in angles of perception, and epic and dramatic unraveling of the narrative. They are physical spaces with qualities derived from cinema.

Peter Greenaway in an interview about architecture and film asks, » ... how can you relate to space in film? – through movement...the camera is an ideal way of looking at architecture. It is also distance too ... you can participate in architecture, but you are not involved in it ...«[23]

Greenaway's films are shot in symmetrical frames, and in architectural »elevation«, using color to drive the narrative. Here »elevation«, an artificial view of complete frontal features, combined with symmetry within the framing create artificiality. This method aids the metaphorical character of the narrative and gives the film its »distance« in general. Architecture shown in elevation emphasizes monumentality and abstraction, thus the distant and clinical mood of his films.

Alfred Hitchcock in his film Vertigo[24] uses »floor plan« shots to create dynamic space. His famous reverse tracking shot creates a three dimensional spatial distortion that hints at the mental incapacity of James Stewart's character, detective John »Scottie« Ferguson, similarly to the portrayed mental space of John Nash (Russell Crowe) in A Beautiful Mind[25].

Horizontal spaces in film transport the idea of tranquility and movement, they can show the epic vastness of space and the landscape as in classic westerns. Vertical spaces imply drama of ascension and the fear of falling expressed through vertigo, swaying above the ground that are so appropriately engendered in The Fifth Element, Spider-Man[26], The Matrix and Batman[27], but also in the crucial final scenes of Blade Runner[28].

12. *Spider-Man*, directed by Sami Raimi, 2002.
13. *Batman*, directed by Tim Burton, 1989.
14. *Blade Runner*, directed by Ridley Scott, 1982.
15. *Lara Croft: Tomb Raider*, directed by Simon West, 2001.

Urban spaces are the stage for speed and change, for fast-paced life and stories, for reality, but also for visions of the future (*Metropolis, Minority Report*, *Blade Runner*).

Open spaces evoke limitlessness and freedom. They play on agoraphobic connotations and isolation such as in Wim Wenders' *Paris, Texas*[29] opening scene.

Enclosed spaces can play on fear and isolation, on claustrophobic fears rampant such as in the *Panic Room*[30] where the nature of the architecture is an integral part of the strategy employed to the »game« by the protagonists.

Virtual spaces

Film space is of course virtual space. It can depict a real environment (by photographing the reality) that becomes virtual once on screen, but it can also be constructed in a virtual space, cyberspace – by a computer. The virtual spaces possess a temporal quality, are essentially ephemeral. The virtual spaces such as those created with the help of a computer are the perfect ground for spatial experiments – be it the simple recreation of long-gone architecture like the Colosseum in *Gladiator*, or the creation of a new spatial experience such as Zion in *The Matrix* or the cities of science-fiction movies such as those in George Lucas' *Star Wars* films or in *The Fifth Element*. The computer-generated image (CGI) allows for creating spatial experiences far beyond the possibilities of reality.

Virtual spaces have captured our imagination so much that the idea of them becomes the narrative (see *The Matrix*).

The idea of virtuality (see *The Matrix*) enters the realm of filmic reality. A layering of realities occurs that allows for an immersion into another world, at least for a short time.

Many times films, especially the ones set in a futuristic world, would be the starting point for the development of a complete secondary world of TV shows and games and toys. And they would spin off a series of sequels and even prequels to the original.

The increasing popularity of computer games lately created a reverse development. In the case of *Tomb Raider*[31] the production of a successful computer game: Here the film recreates a virtual world that before only existed in cyberspace. Virtual becomes real as a set, to become a virtual world again when on the screen.

Before that move became popular we had the realization of the virtual worlds of the comic strips in *Batman, Superman*[32], and *Spider-Man*, worlds drawn on paper. Now we encounter the visualization of worlds and spaces that existed as electronic streams of energy in cyberspace.

Temporal spaces

The medium-inherent temporality of film renders its spatial creations ephemeral as well. A sound space, for example the claustrophobic audio space in the beach-landing scene of *Saving Private Ryan*[33], builds up to a »physical « experience of concussions through volume, and is gone the next moment. No physical evidence remains that proves the existence of this temporal space. Technically speaking, all space in film is temporal and exists only for the fraction of the frame's illumination.

Musical spaces are another example of a temporal construct. Music exists only for a moment, with the aid of memory. Composers such as Edgar Varèse and Yannis Xenakis, the long-time partner of Le Corbusier, tried to create musical spaces, sometimes in connection with a built piece of architecture collaboration such as Varèse with his *Poème Eléctronique* for Le Corbusier's Philips Pavilion at the 1958 World Expo in Brussels.

The renowned cellist Yo-Yo Ma builds audio spaces with his interpretations of J. S. Bach's music making Piranesi's abstract *Carceri*[34] come alive. These choreographed spaces become harmonic and dissonant spaces, vibrating structures of the moment attended by visual imagery that hitherto had no connection.

Nevertheless, architecture is not »frozen music«, but is made up of spaces and buildings, the complement of solid and void, and the arrangement of these two opposites can fall into a choreographed dance. A symphony of shapes and forms can erupt when experiencing the city and its architecture, one of the many components that constitute the urban fabric. The shapes and masses, the material and the play of light on the textures, the look of glass and steel, the street noise reflected off the walls, they all play the tune of the metropolis.

The building in the landscape can vibrate and create sound. Buildings in an assemblage may follow the rules of counterpoint or they improvise freely like the musicians in a jazz formation.

Buildings and cities can be orchestrated and disjointed, but they always remind us of music (*Berlin: Symphony of a Great City; Man with the Movie Camera*). And sometimes there is the building that hovers in silence (see Celeste M. Williams, »The Architecture of Silence«[35]).

Mental spaces

Mental spaces not only tell us about the state of mind of the protagonist in the film, but they may disclose the psyche of the script writer, and director as well.

Mental spaces are ephemeral constructs, realized through the cinematographer's choice of lighting, the director's choice of framing. The production designer, and the set help to create these mental spaces.

A witty and hilarious comment on architecture and space, on life in general, can be found in *Being John Malkovich* by Spike Jonze (1999).[36] What does it mean to live and work on a »1/2 floor«? It may be a picture of our repressed longing for adventure, when we have to go down a tunnel leading right into the brain of John Malkovich. It feels like sliding through the birth canal to see the light of life. We later also experience the space that is being occupied by the people living inside John Malkovich's head – a metaphor for our desire to dream. We inhabit that mental space, the electrically charged virtual space of someone else's brain by proxy, our imagination is on full throttle.

The architecture of the mind was also explored in cinematic terms in *A Beautiful Mind*, directed by Ron Howard (2001), production design by Wynn Thomas, art direction by Robert Guerra. An attempt was made to visualize the tormented mind of John Nash played by Russell Crowe, his excursions into his own mental landscape of a »secret service« he was never without. When dangerous plots were depicted as real, the set hinted at the possibility of another reality, such as the war room.

16. *Being John Malkovich*, directed by Spike Jonze, 1999.
17. *Stalker*, directed by Andrey Tarkovsky, 1979.
18. *La Notte*, directed by Michelangelo Antonioni, 1961.

Ron Howard portrays the mental state of his protagonist through the means of »real« looking experience (»war-room« scenes). A parallel life, a parallel mental state runs as a convincing picture of reality alongside the actual life. Only small improbabilities (the »implanted code«) alert the viewer to the difference.

Andrey Tarkovsky uses the camera and the single shot to portray the inner state of his protagonist, thus exploring the mental, psychological condition of man. His visual space is a direct reflection of the »soul« of the character. He creates haunting spaces of desire and longing in *Nostalghia*[37] and *The Sacrifice*[38], and his spaces of supreme loneliness are manifest in the *Stalker*[39]. The often times claustrophobic spaces, the enclosed environment, the occurrence of the temporal (water) reflect the longing of his protagonists. The ethereal, metaphysical of Tarkovsky's films are mirrors of his »heroes« who always move within a virtual, mental world. All the buildings and landscapes the characters have to navigate are a direct reflection of their inner life. Time and space become the means to reveal the story of their struggles. This results in a dreamlike experience when watching Tarkovsky's films. Everything happens in a different sphere, like floating above the ground in suspended time.

Whereas Tarkovsky uses raw nature and decaying buildings to portray loneliness and entrapment, George Lucas's in *THX 1138*[40] shows Robert Duvall (THX 1138) attempting to leave the prison composed of »white«. The means applied to achieve the impression of this space being very simple, yet the effect of the design of this non-space nevertheless succeeds in directly reflecting the state of mind of the prisoners. It is a vast unidentifiable realm without limits or boundaries where for only a few moments the hope of a limit – thus freedom – flickers.

The empty spaces of Michelangelo Antonioni's films, such as *La Notte*[41], *Professione: Reporter*[42] or *Il Deserto Rosso*[43], their wide and horizontal spaces are alienating, just like their characters are alienated. He preferably uses the existing architecture of Milan, Ravenna or Rome in his films to depict the state of mind of his characters, and sometimes as the setting and playground to develop and then end the conflict between them. The architecture Antonioni chooses to star in his films reflects on the psychological status of his protagonists. For him, architecture plays an active role in the narrative of the film.

The city in film

When cinema was new, in the early 1920s of the last century, it was almost synonymous with big city life. It was a form of entertainment, a medium that was suited perfectly to the metropolis. It was a reflection of life in the hustle and bustle of the city, it mirrored the metropolis, and the metropolis surged with impulses from actions and images seen on film.

»The city is not perceived by cinema as it is seen by its inhabitants, but because the dwellers go to the movies, they can therefore cast a renewed glance on the city and their way of inhabiting it.«[44]

In its early years cinema was distraction for the masses according to writers like Georg Simmel and Walter Benjamin, and the new phenomenon was well described and analyzed by sociologists and philosophers like them.

For Walter Benjamin, the dominant experience of modern life is that of shock: »In street crowds and erotic encounters, in amusement parks and gambling casinos, the technologically

altered environment of the industrial city exposes the human sensorium to physical shocks that have their correspondence in psychic shock« – And that shock was found in the city and the cinema.[45]

»Richard Sennett argues that from the 19 century on the city becomes a series of ›sequential displays of linear differences‹…. and that the city expresses itself through apparati of visibility that direct the spatial practices.«[46] This disclosing itself in a linear fashion can be interpreted as a mode of the cinematographic qualities of a city, the close relationship between city and film. »The city appears as a cinematographic space in its own right; it is a starting point in that cinema emanates from the city only to return within.«[47]

»Any urban site illustrates, in an elementary way, how the patchwork spatial network of the city can be interpreted as cinematically intense. Amid the dense fabric of a city, several small streets and alleys feed into a large avenue; a particularly narrow alley leads from the avenue to an open space – a walk: three different spatial experiences in rapid succession. Although continuous, the city is more blunt than seamless, more startling than predictable. The disconcerted continuity of this urban moment recalls the disparity between adjoining yet dissimilar images in narrative cinema – alien spatial fragments somehow unite into a cohesive (albeit abrupt) web. The turn of a corner, like the flick of a film frame, can redefine the nature of a disjunctive, heterogeneous spatial continuum.«[48]

City spaces

According to Elizabeth Mahoney,[49] Night on Earth[50] by Jim Jarmusch (Aris Kaurismaeki section) is concerned with the homogeneity and simultaneity of urban experience, which it celebrates. It has connections among others to Wim Wenders, Until the End of the World[51]. Joel Schumacher's Falling Down[52] (1992) represents according to Mahoney the dislocation between the subject and the city – the city encodes absolute alienation and fragmentation and focuses particularly on a crisis of masculinity through and in the urban.[53]

The spatial juxtaposition public vs. domestic space is structuring the narrative of the film, according to Mahoney, and in Night on Earth, she sees the scenes in the taxi point towards the transitory nature of urban experience.

Cinematic space can portray an urban environment which is dense and full. It can transmit feelings of alienation as well as evoke the comforts of home. It can believably offer a sense of urban density imbued with speed and adventure, while at the same time being »amoral«. An urban environment tends to lend itself to the portrayal of future visions of the world whereas the rural space oftentimes is used by filmmakers to define family, home, open space and freedom, filled with traditional values and nostalgia.

Urban space stands for the densely solid, rural space for the void. In terms of moral or ethical qualities most of the time it is the urban environment that is portrayed as void of morals due to its perceived anonymity, whereas rural settlements and pastoral lands suggest a life guided by ethics, although this is not always the case as evidenced in Terrence Malick's Badlands[54] and other films of its genre.

Exterior as well as interior spaces make up both urban and rural landscapes, and may be treated quite differently depending on their context.

19. *Minority Report*, directed by Steven Spielberg, 2002.
20. Seaside, Florida.

Exterior spaces in urban settings can suggest civic places but can also be treated as claustrophobic traps where the rule of law is absent. These exterior urban spaces seem to come second to the interior spaces of a city. Interiors of skyscrapers are the ideal settings for a character that is not always living strictly by the law, whereas the protagonist is often seen in relation to the wholesomeness and grandeur of nature.

The exterior spaces of the rural kind are evidenced by the breathtaking landscapes of John Ford's westerns but also of George Lucas. »Tatooine«[55]; they are the idyllic hideaway in *Minority Report* as well as the utopian escape promised at the end of *Blade Runner*.

Exterior spaces are mostly shot on site requiring framing of the existing buildings as needed. Oftentimes the computer will edit in or out structures to perfect the image wanted. Interior spaces are most often still created in the studio thus allowing the traditional set designer to exert a greater degree of control over the end effect.

The blurring of film and life

A different kind of retro can be seen in *The Truman Show* by Peter Weir (1998): The life of a salesman / adjuster is a TV show he is unaware of. It is lived in a place that feels like a movie set – and this place is an actual residential development, Seaside, Florida, courtesy of the New Urbanists, the architects Andres Duany and Elizabeth Plater–Zyberk. The production designers sought a place so »perfect« that it would be the ideal environment for the »artificial« existence of Truman Burbank. They did not have to construct a set, as Seaside already existed. Just like the Disney-run Celebration,[56] Seaside is a community where one's conduct is strictly regulated; where everybody is the »good guy« (see above) that lives in a reconstructed period-style house, neat and clean and proper. These possibly well-intended manifestations of some of the New Urbanists' view on life and city planning seem to herald a more restrictive age than the McCarthy era could have been. It is terrifying to think that movie designers find it possible to construct their »plastic heaven« from real life. Will there be isolation and loneliness in the end after all?

This sort of uneasiness in the American relationship with contemporary modern architecture could be interpreted as a counter-reaction to the overpowering effect of the primary architectural manifestation of the 20th century known as the International Style, or as the need for a »history«, or a »past« to maintain one's place in society. How can one reconcile this disparity between progress and tradition, between contemporary values and conservatism?

When looking at present-day urban development and architecture in the United States, there appears to be a connection between Hollywood's portrayal of contemporary architecture, and on a larger scale the metropolis, as a metaphor for things that are amoral and wrong. On the other side of this spectrum, Hollywood sees the eclecticist and historicist approach to architecture, the denial of the city as the moral and good side of life. A look at the actual development of the American city, especially at the big border towns along the US-Mexican »frontline« tells a different story. There is no nostalgic planning by New Urbanists, rather we face a dynamic and accelerated

growth that does not know any limits or order. If we compare for example El Paso – Ciudad Juárez[57] to Seaside (*The Truman Show*), the contrast could not be starker. The disparity between wishful thinking and harsh reality is striking. The idyllic pastoral suburban settings of Hollywood's heroes homes – from *Minority Report's* detective John Anderton's house outside Washington to even *What Dreams May Come's*[58] paradisical home for Chris and Annie Nielsen (Robin Williams and Annabella Sciorra) – cast against the unhindered life-instilled burgeoning of the megalopolis of the 21st century where planners and architects have very little power and means to influence the direction of its development.

The chameleon effect

When Ridley Scott has Deckard wander through the Los Angeles of 2019, the *Blade Runner* moves through a city composed of the existing architecture of Los Angeles, combined with stage sets designed by Syd Mead to become a reality that is a composite of real and fake. Similar to our wondering whether Deckard is an android or a human, we can't exactly pinpoint what is real and what is set. The blurring of the set with the superimposed real buildings creates a space of intense psychological value that speaks about a not too distant future world, where architecture is a mirror of the people inhabiting it. This chameleon effect can be summed up as a response that allows us to continually reinvent an existing space through its contextual location in a film.

An excellent example of how built architecture can be used to suggest an environment totally different from its actual setting and intention is the Ennis-Brown House by *Frank Lloyd Wright*, built for Mabel and Charles Ennis in 1924. The house is located in Southern California and has become an icon through its rich history. Filled with Mayan imagery, it was the first house Wright built primarily from custom-cast concrete blocks which are reminiscent of carved stones. It is currently listed in the National Register of Historic Places and has been declared a Cultural Heritage Monument by the City of Los Angeles. The last owners, Augustus O. Brown and Marcia Brown donated the house to the Trust for Cultural Heritage Preservation in 1980, and it was renamed the Ennis-Brown House. It is memorable to a larger audience though, from the film *Blade Runner*

21. Frank Lloyd Wright, Ennis-Brown House, Los Angeles, 1924.
22, 23. *The Thirteenth Floor*, directed by Josef Rusnak, 1999.
24. Myron Hunt, Ambassador Hotel, Los Angeles, 1918.

(1982) in which it became Deckard's home. In *Blade Runner* the Ennis-Brown House is taken out of context and divorced from its dramatic hilltop overlook. In the film it is only after taking the elevator upward that we pass through a portal into Deckard's apartment, the mysterious and transformed retro-future Mayan exterior of the Ennis-Brown House now used as an interior. Through the unusual and eclectic furnishings composed of technology that could exist in the foreseeable future, but as yet does not, and of genuine antiques, in this case Art-Deco objects designed in their time with the future in mind, Deckard's apartment becomes personal and real to us through an identification with our own mixtures of objects of different eras. It is a particularly successful camouflaging of the original architecture, transporting it to another time period. What happens with the Ennis-Brown House, the disjointed use of parts of the building to create a new imagery of a home, happens to many other buildings as well when they are used to suggest a vision of another place at another time.

The first films the Ennis-Brown House was featured in were *Female* (1933) by Michael Curtiz[59] followed by *The Black Cat* (1934) a horror movie by Edgar G. Ulmer[60] who for the first time had Bela Lugosi and Boris Karloff star together. Then, Vincent Price appeared in the *House on the Haunted Hill* (1958/59) by William Castle[61] featuring the Ennis-Brown's exterior. In the years since *Blade Runner,* the house formed the backdrop for numerous movies and commercials, among them *Black Rain* (1988) also by Ridley Scott[62], *Grand Canyon* (1991) by Lawrence Kasdan[63], *The Replacement Killers* (1998) by Antoine Fuqua[64], *Rush Hour* (1998) by Brett Ratner[65] and *The Thirteenth Floor* (1999) by Josef Rusnak. In all these films the interior or exterior of the house was used in a context separate from its original location. The »house« was located in Los Angeles at one time (*Blade Runner*) in Hong Kong (*Rush Hour*) another time. Its interior is used as an exterior façade for one set here, then, the exterior façade suddenly turns up as part of the interior of an apartment in another film. The Mayan motif of the walls lends itself to many interpretations. In one instance it is utilized as a decorative element, in another it evokes an intimidating environment. The iconic and enigmatic imagery of the Ennis-Brown House is so pervasive to filmmakers and audiences alike, that it can show up in such different settings as described above.

Another example of an architecture transported is the Ambassador Hotel in Los Angeles, designed by Myron Hunt (1919–21), and former home to LA's longest lasting nightclub, the *Cocoanut*

Grove. It is listed in over 60 films as a filming location. The hotel lobby is featured in *The Thirteenth Floor* in its original function as a lobby, the place where one of the main characters, Hannon Fuller / Grierson, played by Armin Mueller-Stahl, is a regular, albeit under a different name, once transported back in time to the Los Angeles of the 1930s. The Ambassador is the place where Douglas Hall / John Ferguson finds the first clues in his investigation of the strange case of Fuller's death. Yet, in Steven Spielberg's *Minority Report* (2002)] the Ambassador is featured as the home of Lamar Burgess, the character played by Max von Sydow, expressing the ambiguity and power of the character's nature.

The future noir of *Gattaca*[66] also uses built spaces of the 20th century to become sterile voids of the late 21st century. *Frank Lloyd Wright's* Marin County Civic Building, and *Antoine Predock's* classroom / laboratory / administration building for Cal Polytech in Pomona, California are the buildings that frame the narrative. Here the good and the bad (and the distinction is not that easily made) inhabit retro-future spaces. The camera angle, the furnishings or the absence thereof, as well as the lighting, all create a place that convincingly speaks about the future. It is interesting to note that George Lucas also used Wright's Marin County Office in his *THX 1138* in the early 1970s, before he could afford to construct the elaborate cities of the outer rim of the universe for his *Star Wars* trilogy.

Nothing else but real architecture can stand better for the idea of the power of a ruling system on the one side and the helplessness and being-at-will of the citizen on the other side. One might think of Albert Speer's monumental neo-classical buildings for the »Third Reich«, or just simply of many other government buildings or headquarters of divers corporations. Two good examples of cinema to illustrate that aspect of the chameleon effect are Julie Taymor's *Titus*[67] and Terry Gilliam's *Brazil*[68] – two films nearly twenty years apart in their making. These two films deal with the question of power and power play, with the forces of destiny and being powerless against the run of events once started.

Julie Taymor chose the Palazzo della Civiltà Italiana (del Lavoro) of the *E.U.R.* buildings in Rome, Italy as the setting for *Titus*. The buildings of Benito Mussolini's Fascist Rome, designed as if vacillating between the ideas of the young modern architectural movement and an abstract interpretation of historical, namely Roman classical style, reflect the vacillating char-

25. Frank Lloyd Wright, Marin County Civic Center, San Rafael, California,1959–69.
26. Antoine Predock, classroom / laboratory / administrative building, Cal Polytech, Pomona, California, 1987–92.
27. *Brazil*, directed by Terry Gilliam, 1985, showing Ricardo Bofill's Abraxas, Marne-la-Vallée, France, 1982.
28. *Brazil*, directed by Terry Gilliam, 1985.

acters of William Shakespeare's *Titus Andronicus,* as well as they recall the absolute power of a dictatorship.

Finally, in Terry Gilliam's *Brazil*, the architecture of Ricardo Bofill's Abraxas in Marne-la-Vallée near Paris is where Sam Lowry, played by Jonathan Pryce, inhabits his high-tech apartment that becomes the stage for central service's plumbers exploits. This mega apartment block built in the 1970s at the height of short-lived Postmodernism in architecture, in the film stands for what loyal government employees are privileged to live in – a domineering, forbidding monumental structure composed of innumerable small living quarters reached by monorail and elevators. Anonymity is guaranteed – but not for the eye of central services with its dehumanizing machinations.

As can be seen from these examples, built architecture can play a prominent role in movies, either in its original location, or inserted into another world. The power of architecture manifests itself through the fact that one and the same building can fulfill so many diverse requests as imagined by leagues of film directors and production designers.

The villain's domicile

»The house shelters daydreaming, the house protects the dreamer, the house allows one to dream in peace.«[69] (Gaston Bachelard)

Throughout the history of film architectural space and sets have been an integral part of a film, the mise-en-scene is what gives the movie its certain flair. It establishes the relationships between the actors and the objects in space, it creates the space the audience will experience.

Architectural space in film oftentimes was not merely the reproduction or representation of the present-day status of architecture, but instead was trying to suggest a way of life by emphasizing particular aspects of architecture. In many films, the architecture created for the film anticipates the future of the built environment. It is this architecture that transports the audience into the future. Buildings, cities, whole new worlds and even universes have been created to give us the impression of life in the future. This future was white and promising in the early decades of the film, only to become increasingly the picture of a disillusioned society in space.

The retro-future

The future world in *Dark City* by Alex Proyas (1998) is made up of the architecture of a city, in this case a retro-1940s *noir* set, possibly modeled after Chicago or New York during that era. Here an alien species uses architecture as one of the devices to find out about what humans are like. Like one of Italo Calvino's *Invisible Cities*[70], the dark city is rebuilt every night according to the latest findings, and the experiment is conducted in a Kafkaesque manner of the most choking type of nightmare. No sunlight penetrates the dark skies, and the personalities of the inhabitants change as often as the image of the city itself. No one remembers the past as the present is concocted anew by the aliens every twenty-four hours. Only when something goes awry with the experiment on one individual, are we allowed to understand the forces and intentions behind this ever-changing cityscape. One finds out at the end that the blue sky the protagonist is looking for, the *Shell Beach*, is only a painted canvas veiling the truth, that we are alone on a planet – or is it even a planet? – hi-jacked by some greater intelligence than ours, and that we are just a grand experiment.

Is the story of *Dark City* a parable reminding us of our own existence? Are we oblivious to what is happening in the city? When things change rapidly and yet we don't even notice, forgetting the past, having little interest in the fate of the city and its architectural inhabitants are we any different?

A predilection for retro-cities and a retro-future is also present in Tim Burton's *Batman* series:[71] Gotham City is still based on the Marvel comics[72], but here its soaring towers and dark alleys are styled with sexy high-tech touches. Its somber colors suggest a city that is beleaguered by dark forces; but the viewer expects the Dark Knight to deliver the city from these forces.

In Batman the hero ventures forth only at night summoned by a beacon, to combat the evil that is loosed by the fading light. Despite its womblike appearance where his dual nature is sheltered, Batman's cave could be a model for a »bachelor's pad« as elucidated by Joel Sanders »Stud: Architectures of Masculinity«[73], or for a shelter in post-nuclear times. A cave that keeps one's identity safe, it is a secret hideout made to play out one's fantasies.

Whereas the portrayal of architecture as such generally does not seem to be part of the narrative of most films, Hollywood on the other hand continuously turns out fantastic visions of future cities and buildings in its movies. It is the visualization of the interior space of the soul that poses a challenge when comparing these futuristic film sets with the cinematic environments that are used to describe or complement the status quo of a character's interior life. It is not the literal translation of an emotion or mental state into a design of a space, but the subtle hint at the mental and psychological state of a character through the choice of the ambience he moves through that adds depth to the film's layers.

If these films are looking from inside and attempt to link the inhabited spaces to the psychology of the characters, implied a causal relationship between the spaces and the actions taking place in them, science-fiction movies like *The Fifth Element, Strange Days*[74], or the *Batman* and the *Star Wars* series provide a look at spaces from the »outside«. They depict architecture in a traditional sense, as something that conveys power and wealth or intimates poverty. In the *Batman* series one might be tempted to associate the spaces that Batman calls his home with his psyche. The dual persona that lives within Batman's soul, playboy during daytime, dark knight and enforcer during the dangerous night hours is reflected in the looks and make-up of his mansion and the lair below.

The villain's domicile

The use of built environments, often indicates the attitude of the filmmaker, or the society and zeitgeist the film is made in. Mark Lamster, in his essay »Wretched Hives« – George Lucas and the Ambivalent Urbanism of *Star Wars*«[75], shows how George Lucas, one of the Hollywood's foremost directors, displays his disapproval of the city by allowing these dense environments to become seats of »evil«. As seen in his *Star Wars* epics, the evil empire resides in a mega city »Coruscant« and in a super dense starship, the »Death Star«. The hero, Luke Skywalker grew up on »Tatooine«, a rural desert planet, and also thinks of it as a refuge. Lamster points out that Lucas himself built his Skywalker Ranch in a remote rural setting. This strange rejection by many Hollywood filmmakers of the city as an environment that actually allows for diversity and makes stories possible seems to coincide with a traditional undercurrent in the American psyche that espouses the rural self-sufficient man and possibly started even before Thomas Jefferson proclaimed his ideas about America (»I view large cities as pestilential to the morals, the liberties, and the health of man«).

George Lucas and his crew create fantastic architecture and cities, but it seems obvious there is a certain disdain of the »city« and all it harbors. This rejection of the city still seems to live on not only in Hollywood, but even more so in the reality of suburbia. The city in opposition to its suburbs sounds like good vs. evil in Hollywood terms.

Architecture is used to create the mood of the film, the ambience for the story to develop. Does architecture provide hints for the viewer to determine if the actor is a »good« or a »bad« guy? Where do heroes reside, where do villains live in?

Joseph Rosa in his essay »Tearing Down the House«[76], points out how Hollywood usually places the »bad guy« in a modern environment perceived as cold and anonymous, whereas the »hero« usually aspires to or lives in a comfortable, nostalgic period-style house in a pastoral landscape. He traces this trend back to the films of the 1930s and 1940s when modern architecture was seen as something »dangerous« and even lascivious. Joseph Rosa had pointed out that Hollywood places villains into modern or contemporary houses whereas the heroes mostly reside in traditional houses. The heroes, or identification figures generally prefer to live in suburbia or in an idyllic setting, the crooks are the ones that live in the dangerous and soulless modern city with its concrete, glass and steel cubicles.

Very rarely is it that the hero lives in a modern or contemporary apartment or house. The fact that the hero lives in a period-style house might surprise us, but it seems to be in keeping with the widespread acceptance and preference of period-style houses over contemporary houses in the United States. This might point to an underdeveloped understanding of contemporary architecture, to a lack of good and influential modern architecture, or to a feeling of a need for history, even if faked and only superficial like a »contemporary« period house. There are surely many other reasons for that phenomenon, but it remains a fact that the villain is modern (referring back to the subconscious fear of the metropolis and all its temptations during the first decades of the 20th century as investigated by Georg Simmel[77], Walter Benjamin, and others).

The architecture that is populated by these villains of the cinema is actually »real«, mortar-and-brick architecture, and in most cases architecturally valuable. The work of architects like John

Lautner (Malin »Chemosphere« Residence – *Body Double,* Brian de Palma, 1984[78] or Richard Neutra (Lovell Health House – *L. A. Confidential,* Curtis Hanson, 1977[79] oftentimes appears in Hollywood films. Many of these houses, documented by esteemed photographer Julius Shulman as marvels of the Modern Movement, can be detected in numerous movies that needed spectacular settings for their villains. This dangerous precedent may permanently cause architecture of the Modern Movement to be undervalued and be incorrectly portrayed. The average American already identifies much more strongly with »gingerbread« houses than treasures of architectural pioneers coming ever more increasingly under the wrecking ball.

One can detect in this a longing to return to one's »roots«, to the romanticized beginnings of the United States.

The French (national) movie icon Catherine Deneuve in an interview with Charlie Rose believes that cinema is a direct reflection of a country's cultural attitude and understanding.[80] This cultural attitude Deneuve is talking about, this dislike of contemporary architecture and the big city itself as seen in many films can only be partly explained by tying it back to the country's agricultural roots. If that were the case, all other countries would have to have a similar understanding of architecture as agriculture was the base of their existence when they were formed. It is only speculation (by a European trained architect, the author) that there are a number of reasons why contemporary architecture fares so badly in many Hollywood productions. For these speculations one has to assume that Hollywood represents the taste and cultural level of the average moviegoer.

There would be Thomas Jefferson's assessment that cities are pestilential (see above), that agriculture is an «equalizer» for a just society, that being in concordance with nature is »good«. I would also say that there is a big educational gap among Americans. Interest for the arts and architecture is very small compared to Europe. In Europe many governments have understood the value of good architecture, new developments are discussed publicly in the papers and on TV. Generally, the awareness of the population is greater and renewed constantly. It strikes one as peculiar that in a country that prides itself on its technological progress and advancement contemporary architecture would have such a small niche in the public discussion. Many Americans would see the city as the place where numbers of unimaginative and dull office buildings represent modern architecture. And indeed, the majority of these buildings is projecting a sterile, clinical and cold persona. Many contemporary residences, even if published widely, might be associated with that. And then there is the constant longing for history, which seems to be only found in the buildings and objects of the Victorian era. Hand in hand there goes a certain horror vacui, and a need to conserve history by collecting memorabilia. A modern house does not seem to have that potential – one should think of the spare interiors, the decoration and ornamentation-poor spaces as seen in many magazines. And then there might be the idea of »the good old times«, where there were no villains and everything was harmonious – one of the big white lies in every society.

In America, housing is almost exclusively constructed and advertised by builders. These builders come up with a basketful of eclectic designs aiming to evoke »tradition«. And this is what the vast majority of Americans gets to know about architecture. I think that the lack of »respect« of contemporary architecture in movies as expressed through its assignment as the »villain's domicile« could be summed up as the result of the lack of architectural education and awarenes of the general public. It is misunderstood and misinterpreted – if consciously or not remains to be answered.

31. *Star Wars: Episode I – The Phantom Menace,* directed by George Lucas, 1999.
32. John Lautner, Malin »Chemosphere« Residence, 1960.
33. Richard Neutra, Lovell Health House, Los Angeles, 1927–29.

Virtual space and binary architecture

Eighty years after the cinema was born, the introduction of the personal computer revolutionized our life.

Almost immediately the computer and film would begin a symbiotic relationship that would have a dramatic impact on the art of filmmaking. Computer-generated images were starting to replace set design and architecture to enhance the life-like appearance of a production.

This fecund relationship between film and computer would eventually take us out of this world into a virtual universe that cinema always had aimed for.

With an increasingly sophisticated application of computer-generated images (CGI's) to the production of film, especially in the realm of set design and in the special effects department, movies are providing us with never before imagined worlds. The advent of the digital architectural space as used in film has in fact strengthened filmmaker and critic Eric Rohmer's 1940s postulate of an architectural metaphor essential to cinematic imagination as well as filmmaker Peter Greenaway's confirmation that architecture will remain when film has vanished.[81]

Computer animation is used more and more widely and diversely in the production of movies such as *The Matrix, Dark City* or *Minority Report*. Lessons learned in the creation of animated movies – formerly drawn and colored – are applied to live action films, one genre benefits from the other. Spaces are constructed in the virtual realm, in cyberspace, through the movements of actors in front of green screens interacting with imagined spaces or wire-frame virtual actors imbued with the expressions of living actors such as the Gollum in *The Lord of the Rings* trilogy.[82] A reversal of virtual and real takes place continuously, on the screen as well as during the shoot.

Perceiving (virtual) space

34. UN Studio, Carnegie Science Center, Pittsburgh, Pennsylvania, 2000, competition project.
35. UN Studio, Moebius House, Het Gooi, The Netherlands, 1993–98. Model.

According to the *Encyclopedia Britannica* (CD version 2003), a virtual image is »an image (as seen in a plane mirror) formed of points from which divergent rays (as of light) seem to emanate without actually doing so«, and virtual reality is defined as »an artificial environment which is experienced through sensory stimuli (as sights and sounds) provided by a computer and in which one's actions partially determine what happens in the environment«.

According to this definition, virtual reality in film then could not be called such because as of yet there is no way for the audience to determine through their actions what happens in the plot or the environment on screen.

For the moment, virtual reality in film is mostly used as a tool to create realistic and hyper-realistic images (computer-generated images, CGI's) or to have actors move in and out of spaces beyond the physical reality (*Matrix*).

»Perception changes with culture; technology certainly effects culture and vice versa.«[83] (Chicago architect Douglas Garofalo in an interview)

These new ways of perceiving space, the possibilities afforded by the computer to conceive space and time in a totally new way have been appropriated not only by filmmakers but also by architects. Digital imaging and the creation of virtual architectures have expanded the architect's capabilities to create a vision of the future environment, new landscapes of desire, visions of a »binary architecture«.

So far this vision of a future architecture has been explored by architects such as Greg Lynn mainly as a formal exercise that led to »blobs« and warped spaces, new formal expressions made only possible because of the computer. Regarding this development, Neil Kaye thinks that »… the populist conception of digital architecture is centered around fashionable ›blob form-making‹… blob architecture has tried to position itself as a radical re-interpretation of Euclidean geometry and rationalist perspective space. In essence, by refusing to position itself within normative paradigms, it has done nothing but further estrange itself from critical and cultural dialogue that is architecture« He sees the emergence of another, true »digital architecture« in its attempts to understand the idea of 4D-architecture – »what it means to actually build in time«, to model performance of architectural systems and even cities.[84]

This concept of building in time, of a truly dynamic architecture, approaches the nature of the moving images.

Mike Linzey in *Some Binary Architecture – Sites for Possible Thought* lines out the framework for a »true« binary architecture away from the »mere« formal attempts such as blobs and warps. He believes that the field between two binary poles, the region of uncertainty, is ambiguous enough, so full of potential for interpretation and consequently solutions, that it holds the greatest promise for a new architecture where refined differences are explored.[85]

This seems to indicate that hybrid architecture will be the way of the future. A hybrid architecture, between certainty and doubt, a conglomeration of virtual and real spaces seems to be akin to what we can already see in film – the merging of real and virtual images and spaces into one fantastic (hybrid) adventure.

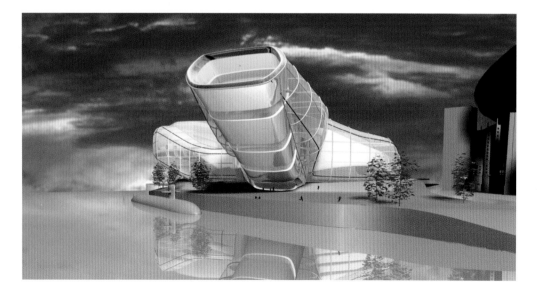

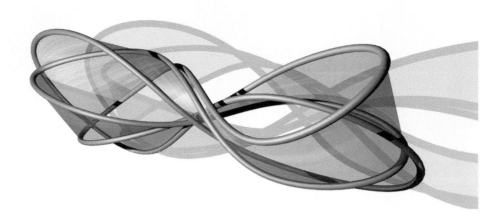

Virtual worlds in architecture and movies

A first effort to inhabit virtual space was executed in *Tron* by Steven Lisberger (1982)[86], further attempts have been made in Kathryn Bigelow's *Strange Days* (1995): one can buy and relive virtual adventures that have been recorded from real incidents. In *Until the End of the World* (1991) Wim Wenders introduced the idea of recording visual memories with a mental device so blind people could experience the outer visual world as seen through the eyes of others.

Thinking of the multi-angled shots in *The Matrix*, of the simultaneity of events and scenes, of the blurring of space and time, the attempt to visualize an interrupted space-time continuum and a fluid concept of space we would be led to believe that the future might have arrived – at least in film production. But is there any architecture in the real world that would attempt to achieve similar goals?

In the architecture of Pritzker Prize (the »Nobel Prize« in the architecture world) winner Frank Gehry with its seemingly impossible fluid building envelopes we see the result of the application of a software program that was created to design Dassault fighter jets. Sophisticated software not originally intended for architectural use helped to create a vision – similar to what is happening in film production. Zaha Hadid, the Pritzker laureate of 2004, has been designing flowing, dynamic spaces that imply space beyond the physical – one thinks of her first big success, the Hong Kong Peak up to her interior spaces in the Monsoon Bar in Tokyo, or the iconic calligraphic ski-jump tower in Innsbruck. Greg Lynn's experimental spaces that mostly still only exist in cyberspace paved the way for many other architects' attempts at a new architecture driven by the computer.

The application of computer programs that allow the creation of these never before seen spaces and environments is one common thread between filmmaking and architecture. Together with the availability of this new software in the 1990s, the concept of speed and time as seen in the writings of Paul Virilio and Vilém Flusser and the idea of communication flow and exchange as the generating force are among the ancestors of these experiments in architecture.

These ideas were introduced in the practice of many of the Dutch architectural offices such as MVRDV and UN Studio to name but a few. MVRDV showed in their exhibit piece for the Venice Architecture Biennale 2002 how they use data flow, or better how they let the data flow dictate the direction of their design. The individual design will of the architect is substituted by a flow of »objective« data that the computer »turns« into design decisions. The architect's task is to interpret and utilize these streams of information. Ben van Berkel and UN Studio show a flowing spatial concept in their Moebius House. The house inspired by the Moebius strip could fit into Linzey's idea of a binary architecture.

All these architects attempt to execute the idea of virtual space in their built work more or less successfully – what they achieve is a hybrid architecture that is promising and exciting for the future of the field.

The idea of simultaneity and synchronicity, the concept of looping time and virtual space, of cyberspace as an inhabitable realm might be the originator of movies like *The Matrix*.

The synchronicity of space and time as seen in films like *The Matrix* seems to be in keeping with the evolution of the cyber age. This raises a myriad of questions and opens itself for just as many speculative investigations.

The Matrix by Andy and Larry Wachowski (1999) led us into totally new realms of virtual reality. The shooting of the movie applied new methods such as the »bullet shot« to take us beyond a perceivable reality. The story itself took us into a world where the virtual applied through a computer would mesh with the real, where time was reversed and warped. The world Neo, the hero lives in is a virtual world, but the architecture is real, the one used for the film as well as the way it is portrayed. Maybe it is this mix, this blurring again, that suggests that there is really another dimension out there, one that could conceivably become noticed.

A blurring of different manifestations of space is well under way – a blurring that has entered the field of »traditional« architecture as well. With the help of the computer, new and never before envisioned spaces have been created, at least on the screen, and are awaiting their birth in the material world. It remains to be seen how far the concept of a binary architecture will push buildings and cities, and if it is the ambiguous realm of the in-between as described by Mike Linzey,[87] or if it is the formal world of blobs and their derivates that fulfills a vision. More likely it will be a hybrid architecture that re-evaluates and remixes all these different approaches and concepts to form a fascinating, dynamic and interactive smart architecture of the future.

With the Kunsthaus Graz, Austria, Peter Cook (formerly of Archigram) and Colin Fournier gave an answer to Lev Manovich's question if new (digital) architecture can be the new architecture of space where a layer of information is overlaid on the physical space, and how to integrate information and form, the new challenge for architecture after new media.[88] In the Kunsthaus (2003) we can see an homage to Archigram's visions of the 1960s, their fantastic and imaginative drawings of buildings and Walking Cities.[89] What has not been possible forty years ago is now with the help of the computer. Beyond that homage to their own beginnings the architects attempted to integrate a media layer into the skin of the nozzled blob that has landed like a »friendly alien« (official nickname of the Kunsthaus) in a city of many historical strata. The site itself is a palimpsest in the best sense of the word, the content of the Kunsthaus fulfills the concept of a changing, dynamic art scene. The building is cinematic and futuristic – maybe retro-futuristic –, but it is definitely one of these hybrids come into existence thanks to the computer.

Virtual reality – narrative and space

Virtual reality is not only the means to construct an imaginary world, but has become a function of the plot concept itself. In films such as The Matrix or The 13th Floor the blurring of boundaries between a real and a virtual world has become the driving idea of the plot line. The protagonists move »in and out« of these two seemingly antipodal universes in search of their goals and to complete their missions. The »human« real world is the one that has to be defended, but this can only be accomplished through action in the virtual world. Humans fight computer programs, humans struggle to escape the binary nightmare they unleashed on themselves. Hand in hand with

36. Peter Cook and Colin Fourier, Kunsthaus Graz, 2001–03.
37. *The Matrix*, directed by Larry and Andy Wachowski, 1999.
38. *Alien*, directed by Ridley Scott, 1979.

these plot lines certain religious overtones in these types of movies have emerged: in the *Matrix* trilogy (or should we call it »Trinity«) Neo is »The One« to save the world from the machines. The concept of virtual reality as a world inhabited by humans produces ideas of a mix of Christian and Far Eastern beliefs and values. This seems to be aimed to appeal directly to a young computer-savvy audience.

Strangely enough, the architecture seen in the films is a mix of early 19th century (pre-) industrial landscape and machinery and high-tech gizmos. The recurring similarity of the imagery of *Metropolis* in *The Matrix Reloaded*[90] or *The Fifth Element* speaks of Fritz Lang's creative genius. The city of *The Fifth Element*, as well as the subterranean city of *The Matrix* is clearly modeled after *Metropolis* – down to the machines that move the gates of Zion seemingly straight out of Lang's classic. The dirty battle ships of *The Matrix* are cousins of the Nostromo (spaceship)[91] of *Alien*[92], and again of Archigram architects' Walking City.

Revisiting the final installment of the *Matrix*, *The Matrix Revolutions*,[93] it only confirms that the film borrows heavily from predecessors: architecture shown is taken or adapted from preceding science-fiction movies such as *Metropolis, Dark City, The Fifth Element, Star Wars, Alien* series[94].

The »man-made city« in the present is an orthogonal construct – wire mesh? – that is straight out of a video game. Modernistic slabs stretch skywards and Neo is »flying« through the »matrix« of the city. Its image recalls memories of Superstudio's ideas of the global grid of the 1960s, married to Mies van der Rohe's dream of functionalist skyscrapers of the 1920s.

Despite evolving in the »matrix« or in cyberspace, the story is intimately tied to the architecture, the film set. No »Zion« would have been possible without Tarkovsky's *Stalker* or Ridley Scott's *Alien* filled with ominous pipes and ducts. There would be no »Zion« without Lang and Besson, Menzies[95] and Lucas.

»Zion« is a mixture of *Things to Come*[96] and *Star Wars*' council chamber. The gritty industrial, sewage-system evoking image of man's city was first produced in *Alien* and also belongs to Tarkovsky's *The Zone*[97]. One can easily imagine the Stalker popping up from one of the numerous manholes that puncture the ducts.

Whereas the scenes concerning the architecture in Zion are rendered almost hyper-realistically, the cities – namely the machine city and the city on earth-level – lack that same quality. They rather become abstract comic-book or computer-game versions of a »generic« metropolis. The »machine city« is an »alienesque« agglomeration of mainly vertical cone and cylinder-like towers, a city that resembles a town built of Lego or Bionicle[98] sets, with little blinking red LED's glued to the structures.

The virtual world that Neo and his friends enter to fight for Zion's survival is actually our present-day world. The virtual city of *The Thirteenth Floor* is a Los Angeles of the 1930s. And *Dark City* is modeled after a 1930's or 1940's New York, it does not matter that it is floating in space. Why is it that the virtual world is modeled after the present or past, whereas the »real« world is a futuristic version of a Hong Kong times a hundred? The appearance of the concept of virtual reality as part of the plot goes hand in hand with the presence of a cult like community the heroes and villains belong to. The »virtual concept« borrows from old Nordic sagas and Classical Greek and Roman mythology. One would wish that there could be a »true« vision of a virtual world, a future universe that is different and unique and not just a snapshot of the past.

Looking at the other side of the coin, the portrayal of the virtual and real world in these movies has been so perfected that it looks believable and real, but that the boundaries between those »realities« blur. Not only the protagonist himself is lost in these dual worlds he finds himself in, but also the audience must now watch out not to become similarly confused.

We wonder if the spaces depicted in these movies are spaces that are inhabitable by a physical body, and if »conventional« architecture now can take a page from the worlds portrayed in films.

But that might have to do with how many architects actually are avid and observant moviegoers.

Will we encounter more and more computer-generated spaces, more virtual environments? Or will we still see movies shot on location, showing us real, physical architecture and cities portrayed in ways we have not seen before? Space for surely will continue to play an important role within the narrative of a movie, adding to the illusion shown on screen.

Space in movies tends to appear more powerful than space in real life. Thinking of the swirling spatial effects in films like *The Matrix* or in *2001: A Space Odyssey*[99] some decades ago might lead us to the conclusion that film space, or virtual space is the ultimate spatial experience we can have nowadays. No actual volumetric environment can compete with the magic effect out of the computer. Does that mean that movies, virtual reality will supplant the architectural experience?

Perhaps the advent of extreme sports and X-Games are an attempt to begin to experience physically what can only be experienced in the imagination through film.

Even if the movie industry is on its way to provide us with a totally satisfactory artificial environment in lieu of the traditional one, if the »feelies« of Aldous Huxley[100] come true, it cannot mean that life is going to be a virtual odyssey as seen in *The Matrix*.

The sensory experience of inhabiting real architecture is not comparable with the sensory impact of virtual structures, to paraphrase Coop Himmelb(l)au: »Architecture must burn, freeze, bleed«, one's body must take the risk to experience physicality.[101]

The architect as film director (and vice versa)

According to Jean Nouvel, who likes to compare his buildings to cinema, cinematic space is about sequences that unfold when experiencing a building:

»Architecture exists, like cinema, in the dimension of time and movement. One conceives and reads a building in terms of sequences. To erect a building is to predict and seek effects of contrast and linkage through which one passes … In the continuous shot/sequence that a building is, the architect works with cuts and edits, framings and openings … I like to work with depth of field, reading space in terms of its thickness. Hence the superimposition of different screens, planes legible from obligatory points of passage which are to be found in all my buildings.«[102]

If Jean Nouvel asserts that his buildings are conceived like a film, that they offer a cinematic experience, than the New Mexican architect Antoine Predock gives us cinematic architectural spectacles. His buildings are so photogenic and so »chameleon-like«, that they are a welcome addition to any film set. They are grandiose, abstract, futuristic, and very sculptural. They provide a perfect three-dimensional, full-scale set. When reviewing *Gattaca* one remembers the architecture that gave it its distinct look and mood. The headquarters of the space agency are located in Frank Lloyd Wright's Marin County Civic Building, and Jerome Morrow and Vincent Freeman, the two protagonists live in Predock's CalTech University Building, Pomona, California. (This building is also featured in *Impostor* [2002][103] and *Crime and Punishment in Suburbia* [2000][104].) In *Gattaca*, Predock's imposing and abstract institutional architecture takes on the guise of an apartment building that adds to the coldness and isolation of *Jerome's* and *Vincent's* lives. Predock succeeds in positioning his architecture in the landscape in such a way that it automatically enhances the drama. That might be sometimes a bit too exaggerated fo rmodern life, but it indeed fits the term »epic and cinematic«.

If Predock is one of the many architects that consciously or not design cinematic architecture, Lebbeus Woods[105] is someone who creates fantastic landscapes and cities on paper; architecture that grows out of destruction and desolation to aspire to a new vision of the world. His work is truly filmic and visionary, a visual and intellectual feast. One of his intriguing and at the same time terrifying creations, the »Neomechanical Tower (Upper) Chamber«, the design of a room with an automated seat that travels up and down the wall, recalling a strange kind of »torture apparatus«, was used almost literally for *Twelve Monkeys*.[106] It is the interrogation chamber where *James Cole* is questioned about his scouting expeditions.

Michelangelo Antonioni states about filmmaking: »Here's an occupation that I never get tired of: *looking*. I like almost all of what I see: landscapes, characters, situations. On the one hand, it is dangerous, but on the other, it is an advantage, because it allows for a complete fusion … between reality (or unreality) and cinema.«[107]

In this he expresses the secret wish of many architects – to be able to realize a vision, to fuse all the dreams into a coherent and readable reality. And so far, this is only possible in film. Antonioni himself does not seek to create a vision of a future architecture, he rather uses the existing urban condition to heighten the drama of his narrative. Seldom has a film director used architecture so consequently and successfully to drive a story. Oftentimes his architecture in film is a direct reflection of the mental state of his protagonists.

Peter Greenaway, painter turned filmmaker, in an interview about architecture and film asks: »How can you relate to space in film? – through movement … the camera is an ideal way of looking at architecture. It is also distance too … you can participate in architecture, but you are not involved in it.«[108]

Greenaway, who not only makes films but also curates and designs exhibits that deal with similar subjects as his films do – taxonomy, artificiality, art history – tends to shoot his films in an architectural way: all his frames are symmetrical, centered and frontal. The actors cross a stage, the set, and the architecture is seen in a way we normally would not see it – in pure elevation with minimal perspective. This gives his films a certain artificiality and distance and may be a didactic

method of someone who wants to cram us with information so we can make out some order in the visual onslaught. One must immediately think of his portrayal of Rome's antique monuments in *The Belly of the Architect*[109], or the staged views of *The Draughtsman's Contract*[110].

Greenaway is also fascinated with architectural themes in his narratives as evidenced by *Inside Rooms: 26 Bathrooms, London & Oxfordshire, 1985*[111], or *H is for House*[112]. Even his installations may carry architectural titles such as *Stairs*[113]. Of all filmmakers he comes close to what one used to think of an architect – »a multi-faceted man for all seasons«, the universal man.

If Greenaway provides us with two-dimensional elevations, Alfred Hitchcock in *Vertigo* introduces the reverse tracking »floor« shot to add a twisted 3-dimensionality perspective. Not only does Hitchcock use several existing architectural sites for his set, but he simultaneously works with the verticality and the horizontal sections through the plan shot of his set to portray the tortured mental state of his phobic detective played by Jimmy Stewart.

In *Blade Runner* the film director Ridley Scott and the »visual futurist« Syd Mead created one of the most memorable architecture in film history, the Los Angeles of 2019, a conglomerate of real buildings, models and neon, »a combination of New York and Hong Kong on a bad rainy day«, as they themselves described it. The film would not have become the iconic experience *par excellence* for architects and film buffs alike without the architectural vision of these two men. Legions of architects and filmmakers have taken clues from this film, and numerous papers have dissected the meaning and impact of its architecture.

The commonalities that architecture and film have, are principles that are critical to both professions – those primarily being point of view, the idea of being the leader of a team effort, the desire to touch their audience both emotionally as well as intellectually. Both are working with visuals and colors, they both design with light. Architecture and film are both sequential and temporal, only in the inhabitation do they differ greatly.

Learning from Hollywood – the Venturi effect

A common language between film and architecture

The architect and theoretician Robert Venturi wrote two seminal books that have significantly influenced the discussion of architecture and consequently the approach to design a great deal. The first one *Complexity and Contradiction in Architecture* (1966)[114] contributed to what would become Postmodernism in architecture, and the second one, *Learning from Las Vegas* (1972)[115] continued to investigate the idea of »ducks« and »sheds« in architecture. A »duck« is a building that expresses what it is through its form, while a »shed« puts up a front that says »I am that«. Most American buildings are sheds. In *Learning from Las Vegas* Venturi shows that the neon façades transport information about what goes on inside the shed, which is basically a box housing different functions. This information becomes the architectural element of memorable quality. And by applying his ideas to their design approach many architects »learned from Venturi«.

Learning from Las Vegas taught designers to transmit information on and with buildings, and how to »sell« the architecture. They learned from advertising specialists and from the entertainment entrepreneurs. The Las Vegas Strip is comparable to a film in three dimensions, it is temporal – dull during the day, yet magically alive at night, it buzzes with emotion and anticipation, it takes one into a world of illusion and make-believe.

Does film produce a »Venturi effect« for architects? Does architecture produce a »Venturi effect« for film? If there is a learning process, there should be a common basic language in both architecture and film.

One of the many common qualities of architecture and film is the relation between the languages of architectural space and cinematic space.

Space plays such an important role in both disciplines, that one is tempted to presume a common language, a common vocabulary and grammar exists. Film could not exist without space, the illusionary volume that surrounds the actors and houses the objects, the mise-en-scene, and it is obvious that we live in space, that we inhabit architecture. Time allows the experience of both film and architecture.

One common thread between filmmaking and architecture that has a bearing on visual language is the application of computer programs that allow the creation of complex new spaces.

Natasha Higham, the film scholar, also pleads for a »Venturi effect«, »to increase our understanding of the relationship between film and architecture«; to learn from each other so we can improve our capabilities to express our visions for architecture and urban design.[116]

A building can only be experienced when walked through, when inhabited. The unfolding of the spaces is comparable to the unreeling of scenes in a film. A narrative usually is a linear development of a story, where one thing leads to the next, it is the piecing together of disparate entities or units. If cinematic means having a narrative, one would be cautioned to not see it in such a one-dimensional way in regards to architecture, because architecture is multi-layered, multi-dimensional, and within these manifold dimensions one can place the fourth dimension, the aspect of time. The idea of a temporal expanse brings us back to the cinematic, the unveiling over time. Whereas a film has a beginning and an end, the reel, and in this case can only be experienced in one dimension or direction; a building can be experienced in many ways. There is no forced (although sometimes prescribed) order of how to experience the architectural space. We can navigate through the building's Cartesian system any way we choose, thus working our way through time. We are always in the present progressing one step towards the future. The cinematic space of architecture surpasses the architectural space of film in quality and variety. But with the advancement of cyberspace, that might change in the »not too distant future« when we can move back and forth in time, albeit in a virtual space.

One could argue that the difference between a film and a piece of architecture is the presence or absence of time. As pointed out before, the temporal aspect exists in both cases making experiencing film and architecture possible. Only the measuring of a building in time, in walking through and by it and by being aware of its ability to generate a »history«, gives an impression of the space created, and the disclosing over time is part of film's nature. The experience of both architecture and film happens in a dynamic way. With the passing of time the space, the story evolves. Without the temporal dimension, we cannot know about space or story. The »experience« of architecture through images is only a weak supplementary measure compared to the consumption of the space in reality. Therefore this problem of space-time makes it so difficult to adequately speak about architecture or present it in a show as described in an essay »Representing Le Corbusier: Film, Exhibition, Multimedia« by Tim Benton.[117] The quality of the multi-sensory experience of architecture is still unsurpassed as of now, as an immersion into virtual space that touches all the senses has not been achieved yet.

Over the relatively short time period that film and architecture have existed side by side, a mutual didactic experience has occurred. Sergey Eisenstein for example was an architect who introduced architectural language and thinking into film. Hans Richter, also originally an architect, used film and its visual power to propagate modern architecture in the 1920s and 1930s.[118] In Hitler's »Third Reich« architecture was conceived and staged like a filmic epos by Albert Speer in order to overwhelm the masses emotionally. In 1939 the documentary film *The City*[119], shown to an estimated 45 million visitors at the 1939/40 New York World Fair, was successful in propagating the suburb, thus initiating the trend towards sprawl in present-day America. Present-day architecture sometimes takes its clues regarding spatial development form the cutting and editing techniques of film. The French architect Jean Nouvel openly admits that he designs with the techniques of a filmmaker. Bernard Tschumi, the former dean of Columbia University's architecture school writes about »event architecture« and filmic qualities in buildings and cities. On the other side, many film

43. *Star Wars: Episode I – The Phantom Menace,* directed by George Lucas, 1999.
44. Luigi Vanvitelli, Royal Palace of Caserta, Italy, mid 18th century.
45. *James Bond – Dr. No,* directed by Terence Young, 1962.

directors use the emotional potential of architecture to transport their films' stories. The starkness of buildings stands in for alienation as seen in Antonioni's films, or in the use of Predock's buildings to evoke another time in *Gattaca.* George Lucas creates new architecture for his *Star Wars* series but at the same time counts on the convincing emotional qualities of real architecture as seen in the Royal Palace of Caserta, Italy, where Amidala and Anakin fall in love.

Many young architects utilize the fast-paced editing techniques of film and video clips to design the spatial sequence of their buildings, more and more they incorporate the »temporal« aspect consciously as seen in ever-present computer-generated image videos used to »sell the building«.

»Most cinematic and urban effects, regardless of their specific formal attributes, can be considered as a function of the edit, another common tool of architecture and film. To edit means to manipulate an existing entity into something new; cinematic and urban experiences arise from a similar condition of transformation. Because the distinction between the original and the transformed entity is not always clear, editing creates ambiguity, that zone where multiple interpretations are possible. The effect of the edit, in both cinema and architecture, is a surreal intensity arising out of the transformation of the perfectly familiar into the perfectly extraordinary. The surreal can arise only from the real, not form the ideal. Both cinema and the city and its architecture capitalize on the fact that manipulation motivates an unconscious sense of ambiguity« that allows us to experience architecture and film anew over and over again.[120]

For Natasha Higham, film as well as architecture have become a subconscious part of our everyday life, memory, shading our impression of places we have never experienced influencing to the point of dictating how we should feel, think and operate in a particular space.

»Architecture aids film in communicating with its audience. Film aids architecture by inspiring the average filmgoer to take an interest in the built environment and to experience within the realms of cinema what they may never experience in real life. Film also returns to architecture a mass medium where both the trained and untrained can become the critique, where architects and wannabe-architects can realize dreams that cannot be constructed in real life.«[121]

A common language and tools to express that visual language certainly exist between architecture and film, but the direct application of grammar and vocabulary is not always possible or wanted as both media are too different in the end – one is two-dimensional and physically uninhabitable yet emotion-driven, the other one is physical in all its aspects and may morph in its perception through time.

Conclusion

Peter Greenaway, the film director, believes that »most people are visually and architecturally illiterate. People's attention has to be drawn to such a phenomenon called space.«[122]

An architectural agenda

It does not seem that Hollywood, and the film industry in general, has any specific »architectural« agenda it wants to disseminate, or that cinema wants to fulfill an educational goal regarding architecture. Architecture in film is usually the means to convey a certain mood of the narrative. Propagation of good architecture for its own sake is not the primary objective of a movie.

Hollywood yields great influential power in propagating a »taste« or »style« from fashion to human behavior. But regarding architecture, we have to ask ourselves if we ever say we would like to live in a house we have seen in a movie. Speaking from the architect's point of view, there is of course built architecture of high quality in many films – one may only think of many of the »villain's domiciles« such as the John Lautner houses of the 1950s and 1960s, or Richard Neutra's Lovell Health House featured in *LA Confidential.* One may also recall Antoine Predock's buildings that gave *Gattaca* its look, and of course, Frank Lloyd Wright's work that is also featured in the same film to realize the depth of this quality.

When we think of »movie architecture«, architecture and interiors built for specific films, Ken Adam (*James Bond* series) and Syd Mead (*Blade Runner*) and their personal visions come to the forefront. But overall, cinema does not advocate architecture, particularly not contemporary architecture, in such a way that the general audience would start developing a better appreciation of quality architecture after having seen a movie.

On the other hand the reverse, architects (and even the general public) being influenced by film and especially its techniques, has happened nevertheless. The mass media film and television dominate our daily life, we see in visual staccatos and hear in sound-bytes. At first glance, it seems the language of film has a stronger hold on our life than architecture. But concurring with Natasha Higham[123] and Peter Greenaway,[124] it is fair to say, »architecture will remain when film is gone (and architecture affords film its temporal structure)«.

Both mass media, architecture and film, keep influencing each other, albeit in an asymmetrical way shifted towards film as the greater source of ideas and spatial innovations although architecture occupies a deeper and more significant place in our memories through true spatiality. The future holds many promises for both film and architecture in terms of exciting spatial innovations and adventures not the least due to the computer's ability to explore complex spatial visions.

For the foreseeable future it will remain the task and privilege of built architecture to provide us with the full range of sensory experience, with film and computer to provide the exploratory construction of space. Meanwhile, the »symbiotic« relationship of film and architecture will continue to open up new frontiers of space and time.

Celeste M. Williams
Cinema architecture in the United States

History of the movie theater in the twentieth century

Spectacles, from the Latin »spectare«: to watch, have been part of human culture since ancient times. The Greek theater, the Roman version of the theater, the Caesarian doctrine of »panem et circenses«, executed to perfection in the Colosseum and the Circus Maximus, have set precedents on how to entertain, educate and placate the populace. Traveling troubadours during the Middle Ages established theatrical groups such as the actors of the Globe Theater and the Teatro Olimpico in Vicenza, passed on the tradition and further developed the art of the play and with it its home, the theater.[1] In the Teatro Olimpico the architects Andrea Palladio and Vincenzo Scamozzi produced an illusionist environment, the first completely closed theater of its kind.

In many respects things changed very little as far as the architecture of entertainment was concerned over the ensuing centuries. Communal entertainment relied on the desire of the populace for societal interaction and evidenced a successful economic strategy. Over centuries the development of the dramatic arts led to the development of the theater as a specialized, separate building type. Increasingly today »spectacle is the rule rather than the exception«.[2]

At the turn of the 20th century, the first films were shown in spaces adapted ad hoc to the occasion, in nickelodeons, in halls, in the open air, or in storefront spaces that were L-shaped in plan. This configuration allowed for the audience to be seated in front and behind the screen, which was installed in an angle at the »knee« of the L-shape. The better seats saw the movie as filmed, the cheaper ones saw it from the back, mirrored.

One could say there was a functional relationship between the screen and the building, but no indication that film was being shown, an activity that could be guessed only after the movie theater had become a specialized typology.

The first buildings designed to screen films were modeled on variety and vaudeville theaters, with a stage in front of the screen that also allowed for live entertainment. These were multi-functional buildings. There was also an orchestra pit for the musicians accompanying silent films and oftentimes an electric organ, which commented musically on what was happening on the screen. In the beginning the new medium did not project a distinct architectural expression. Theater typology provided the guiding design principle. Soon architects began to react to the challenge of making the theater into more than a variation of a traditional stage building or a shelter for a screen, they sought to make it into an environment that would speak to all the senses by designing movie theaters based on the prototype of lyric theater, the opera house. From these so-called »hard-top« or plaster-ceilinged movie theaters the movie palace of the 1920s was developed. By the 1920s there came to be an intimate relationship between the movie theater building and the films shown inside.

Architectural revolutionaries from Germany and Austria, Gropius, Piscator, and Reinhardt, proponents of the »Totaltheater«, were not the only ones who worked on the environment surrounding the production of a play or the screening of a film in the early 20th century. There were architects, in the USA especially, who dedicated their energy towards creating fantastic »houses« for the movies. Not the avant-garde figures known from text books on twentieth century Bauhaus architecture, many of these architects, such as Thomas Lamb, John Eberson, Joseph Urban, and Friedrich Kiesler, started out as opera and live theater architects who turned their expertise toward the new task of designing a movie theater typology.[3]

Films began to change cities and the way of life of their inhabitants. Movie houses became magnets of night-life. They attracted an audience hungry to experience the glamorous lives portrayed on the screen. In this respect they provided respectable entertainment for working class and middle class. Movies were affordable, and they appealed to a broad spectrum of the public, not just to the elite who frequented high-art events such as opera. The movie theater became integrated into established social structures. By the 1920s each town's Main Street emulated the big cities, making their movie theaters centers of urban life. The cinema was starting to shape the city, and the movie palaces, especially the »atmospheric theaters« in the 1920s, a theater type with a domed planetarium ceiling and exotic interior sets, tried not only to provide a sensory experience but to distract from the screen to guarantee that the audience did not become totally lost in the movie.[4]

Walter Benjamin and Georg Simmel attribute the exuberant decoration of the early movie palaces to the idea of distraction. As Walter Benjamin stated in *The Work of Art in the Age of*

Mechanical Reproduction, 1935/36: »Architecture is the prototype for film. Both are received by a collectivity in a mode of distraction«[5] This is a form of experience that occurs incidentally, disjunctively, »absent-mindedly« and refers to Benjamin's and Georg Simmel's ideas about flaneurs and the masses. One problem though, was also projected through film. Film was an art of the metropolis and was also suspect to many, just as the big city raised fears of the unknown in many people at that time. It opened windows to the world that many people were not yet prepared to look into.

The exotic movie palaces rose in the 1920s and the 1930s, in Europe as well as in the United States, where they originated. After World War II theaters became less opulent in accordance with changing demographics and tastes. The theaters became more streamlined and less decorated which also reduced costs. They projected the image of the new machine age with its requisite sleekness and speed. These post-war theaters were to serve a generation of moviegoers.

In the 1950s there was a surge of outdoor drive-in theaters for an increasingly affluent car culture in the US, but these venues were largely dependent on season and weather, yet they provided a backdrop for post-war American culture.

The movie industry lost ground with its customers in the 1960s and early 1970s, with the advent of television in everyone's household. Cinema construction slowed down, and many theaters, especially the downtown movie palaces of the 1920s, were closed.

With the development of the multiplex type during the 1970s, the movie industry sought to lure back their clientele. The promise of being able to choose between more than one movie shown at the same location was the guiding principle for reestablishing customer curiosity and loyalty. These principles are still in effect today, albeit strongly influenced by new technological innovations.

The latest in mainstream cinema strategy is to develop whole entertainment areas around the multiplex that functions as the anchor, as architecture's effect is conjured mainly for the purpose of what Richard Ingersoll terms »scenography«.[6]

As will become evident, the economics of the film industry and modern technology influence the development and the design of the theater architecture.

The multiplex concept

In the 1960s with the competition provided by color television sets, it became clear that existing approaches towards marketing films, as well as the buildings in which they were screened, would have to change. Film companies were able to produce significantly more products and a federal ban on film companies owning theaters provided the impetus for independent corporations to develop the multi-cinema concept for screening a variety of films from different studios simultaneously. These movie theaters were conceived entirely different from previous theater concepts and increasingly along corporate lines.

Suburban multiplexes began as quadroplexes in the 1970s. Such industry pioneers as AMC (American Multi Cinema), under owner Stan Durwood, housed six or eight auditoriums in a long »warehouse« configuration, tied to existing suburban shopping malls. Standard models were entered transversely and were symmetrically balanced into equal numbers of auditoriums flanking the central concession and ticketing area with dual projection booth »bridges« serving two to four auditoriums.[7] Loew's and General Cinema favored twin cinemas, which fit more easily into the existing fabric of denser cities and often had auditoriums on multiple levels accessible by escalator. The Baronet and Coronet movie theaters located in midtown Manhattan appealed to a sophisticated urban audience during the 1960s and 1970s and gently introduced the idea of »twins« to a city beginning to abandon the old movie palaces. In the 1970s other new developments nationwide began to be located within existing shopping malls, where they fit into the new »interior street« environment.

Movie theaters began to be designed based on studies in traffic planning, with space for concession stands replacing the public gathering space at one time accorded for social activities. Instead of greeting friends in the lobby, one immediately lined up following the ticket purchase (still at the exterior ticket booths) to buy drinks and snacks that would be taken into the auditorium. In the American model individual tickets were all alike, except for being coded to different films in different auditoriums.

Since movie theaters returned as much as ninety percent of their opening week's film profits to the studios whose products they were showing, the theaters became largely dependent on the profits from their concession stands. Architectural planning in the 1980s began to shift away from an emphasis on the auditorium to a focus on their primary economic generators.

The concession stand with its chromed popcorn poppers, glass cases of attractive candies, and soda dispensers took precedence in the lobby where it was oftentimes centrally located.

For the first time market surveys of products and psychological studies of responses to color played a large role in the disposition and planning of the lobby. Research into customer preferences showed that color schemes involving red, brown, orange and amber tones elicited the strongest hunger excitation as opposed to cooler bluer tones, which elicited a calming relaxation response. In accordance with accepted American color schemes of the 1970s and 1980s, many movie theaters were outfitted in this appetizing palette, reflecting the colors of the food stuffs sold.

In Europe, by contrast, tickets were priced differently based on the location of seats and vantage points, as in live theaters. This created a difference in the way one was seated. Due to the more relaxed nature of knowing in advance where one's seat was located, as well as a ban on eating in the auditorium, Europeans would partake of refreshments in the lobby, where a café atmosphere was often recreated.

In US cities where downtown and suburban theaters of the 1930s and 1940s were still in operation, the practice of »splitting« began to appear in the 1980s. In this scheme the balcony of an existing movie theater was isolated from the larger auditorium and then »twinned« or tripled, creating two or three smaller auditoriums for films which were longer running or whose audiences had shrunk from the opening, weeks before. In some urban schemes movie theaters were also split longitudinally, producing twins, which was usually less than satisfactory acoustically. In all cases the requirements of projection booths, and adding or relocating rooms, created more complexity in the plan.

Only a few inner city cinemas remain as first run theaters, fighting for their survival. Oftentimes, these houses are run by »independent« companies, since the multiplexes are owned by such big distributors and production companies as Universal, Sony, or MGM.[8]

The megaplex entertainment complex

At the turn of the 21st century multiplexes are no longer merely a series of movie theaters clustered around a shared lobby. They have evolved into entertainment complexes that encompass other facets of consumer-related services such as restaurants and retail sales outlets. Emerging from a twenty-year practice of merchandising tie-ins to films, multiplexes now not only include concession stands but may incorporate cafés based on the European model or even boutiques.

One type acts as a freestanding »anchor« for an adjacent retail complex. Derived from the shopping mall concept pioneered by Gruen Associates in the 1950s, longitudinal elements including pedestrian paths are »anchored« by distinct corporate retail entities at terminal ends. If growth continues to expand other anchors can be »plugged-in« to the apron of parking that usually encircles it. Increasingly these anchors are megaplex entertainment centers.[9]

Multiplexes are now defined in film industry jargon as movie theaters that have up to sixteen screens.[10] Theaters featuring over sixteen screens are now termed megaplexes. The megaplex concept follows the idea of suburban corporate retail developments, which create larger regional super-centers that respond to feeder neighborhoods, as opposed to more numerous local stores. Where formerly four-, six-, or eight-screen multiplexes were located in nearly every suburban neighborhood, patrons must now drive farther away to reach a megaplex of up to thirty screens. The movie industry in the United States seems to be more and more car-oriented in the sense that patrons must drive increasing distances to see movies nowadays.

Modern megaplex design can be most easily explained as a series of responses to specific program criteria. Economic factors as expressed through developmental square footage costs, corporate branding and identity issues, functional traffic diagrams, and the spatial needs of stadium seating, play a role in the process of creating new theater complexes. To this list of requirements may be added the »vision« of the architects for creating an imagery that will be an additional draw for theater patrons.

Most modern multiplexes fall into one of two types, the urban multi-cinema complex located in the interior of existing multistorey buildings, or the suburban freestanding »greenfield« complex. The »greenfield« megaplex, one that literally lands in the center of previously undeveloped real estate, is by far the most frequently developed type in the US and the type most desired by multiplex corporations. Located near other suburban or ex-urban developments, the megaplex features first-run movies, the most profitable film industry product. To appeal to the projected fourteen-to-twenty-four-year-old audience, economic and spatial formulas have been created through corporate research that inform the architectural program.

One thing you cannot expect form a megaplex is to have a wide choice of different genres of movies. Megaplexes tend to run mainstream box-office hits, as they have to recapture profit quickly. The arrival of the multiplexes has created the paradox that although many screens are available, the choice of films has diminished rapidly.

In an interview with the television talk show host Charlie Rose, the actor George Clooney complained that the American film industry is not interested in producing movies that might have lasting impact on viewers: »… something you would talk about even a week later…«,[11] but only in box-office receipts during the first two or three weekends, which is the most defining factor when producing a movie: the immediate return on the investment.

The standard plan layout is based on functional traffic diagrams and work in a manner similar to other public amenities, such as shopping malls and airports. In the greenfield complex, where land is more plentiful and less expensive, theaters are laid out for horizontal efficiency, with vertical massing elements expressed externally proportionate to the interior volume necessary to accommodate larger stadium seating. Special spatial volumes for IMAX theaters, which frequently accompany 30 screen megaplexes, are also usually expressed in the external architecture. Suburban megaplex theaters tend to be planned symmetrically, with larger volumes flanking the central entry lobby, and decreasingly smaller arrays of theaters clustered around secondary gathering spaces near the ends of wings, as in airports. This allows for more efficient movement of personnel and centralization and reduction of concession stands.

Such complexes are usually surrounded by a large parking apron and may have prominent entry plazas to direct patrons from greater distances. This parking apron may occupy acres of land, with an environmental impact that is oftentimes extremely negative. Large heat sinks are generated due to the massive expanses of concrete, and with tree removal to provide maximum parking, the lack of water absorption frequently causes increased run-off in thunderstorms.

In the United States the new megaplexes are mostly constructed of concrete tilt-wall or light steel-frame constructions covered with dry-vit exteriors as in shopping malls. These construction techniques and materials are relatively inexpensive and efficient due to standardization. They predispose the creation of box-like flat-roofed buildings.

Aside from massing elements, such architectural and graphic devices as brilliant color, neon lighting, and vivid signage enhance corporate »branding«, the unmistakable symbols of recognition of each individual multiplex corporation.

Once one enters the realm of the megaplex, the lobby has now taken the place of the theater auditorium in prominence. This is where the architectural magnetism must occur to engage and draw in prospective patrons. Tall interior volumes, dramatic color schemes, catwalk exits, murals, dramatic lighting and advertisements are all employed to provide an invitation, and present diversions while people stand in line for concessions, chat with friends, or wait to enter their respective auditoriums.

In the public spaces beyond the lobby, concession stands serve not only as dispensing stations but also provide stopping points and visual cues to guide filmgoers and their different auditoriums. Each wing features a central stand, banks of toilets, and diminutive secondary lobbies, from which auditoriums radiate. Paths to wings often feature videogame arcades, simulators, or graphics of upcoming films along with video monitors showing film clips and trailers.

In the screening rooms the focus has shifted away from the majesty, exoticism and seductiveness of the movie palace auditorium to the »black box« concept. In these minimalist auditoriums theater distractions are kept to a minimum not only to enhance the high-tech movie viewing experience but emphasize the commercials and advertising screened before the feature. As opposed to earlier audiences who resisted becoming »part« of the film, modern film patrons have come to expect a near virtual experience.

Rising technology costs are offset by a reduction in architectural finish costs. Self-automated 35 mm platter system projection on advanced light reflective screens combined with patented THX or other »sensurround» sound systems are the core of the new realism.[12] Corporate identity in the auditoriums is achieved simply by the use of repetitive color schemes, logos, or carpet patterns. Sometimes it is only the stadium seat with its color and ubiquitous cup holder that provides a clue to differentiate between one company's theater and its competitors. Coming full circle, viewers have returned to the concept of a »total entertainment compound«, a concept that had

2, 3. Gensler and Associates, Sony Theaters Lincoln Square, New York, 1994.

been achieved, in the palaces of the 1920s, although seemingly much more architecturally then.

The urban megaplex provides a different set of design challenges for architects today. Due to the higher costs of urban infill or retrofit sites, urban megaplexes project more selective first-run film products towards a more mature over-twenty-five audience. They share audiences with film arthouses, independent, and foreign film venues. Theater auditoriums are less numerous due to spatial restrictions, and may be vertically stacked leading to less efficient traffic and an increase in required personnel. Escalators and elevators add to the cost of construction, even if these costs are offset by increased volumetric drama through the architecture. In addition adjacent mid-rise parking garages are frequently necessary as an adjunct to mass transportation. Oftentimes the structure of this utilitarian »twin« of the multiplex is architecturally more interesting, or simply larger, than the multiplex itself. Through the structure economically expressing the spatial variations necessary to its function, the garage can exhibit its movement of cars, as opposed to the multiplex, which by its nature must be composed of closed boxes.

To balance their higher ticket prices, the urban metroplexes attempt to appeal to more affluent and sophisticated patrons who count the architectural experience as part of the entertainment.

In the lobby dramatic architecture may prevail, combined with more expensive finishes and exotic lighting to conjure the ambience of luxury. Refreshments at the concessions may be organic or imported specialties, and a café or small restaurant may be an interior node within the lobby. Corridors sport framed art and lighting fixtures are conspicuously »designed« in the promenade to the screening rooms.

In the auditoriums of urban metroplexes, elegant fixtures and seating are the norm. Although the goal of low distraction is still desired, decorative elements may once again make an appearance to enhance the surroundings. Interestingly more aspiring theaters have a lower rate of vandalism, so the initial costs of fixtures are often offset by lower maintenance costs.

Architecture firms may take differing stylistic approaches based on the locale of the cinema. At the turn of the 21st century, the trend is toward sentimentality, in which the past glories of lost movie palaces are yearned for with nostalgia. Theater designers, acutely aware of the history of movie theaters, have become overtly referential. Whereas theater design from the 1930s until the 1980s tended to reflect a forward-directed approach, architects in the 1990s began to play to sentimentality through an iconography drawn from the history of film and the grand movie palaces. In New York City, Sony's Lincoln Square »Avalon« theater (1994) by Gensler Architects draws from the iconography of film history as well. Exotic scenes flow from Moorish and Egyptian motifs to Chinese influences.[13]

Despite this trend a few innovative architects have rejected the yearning for the past by creating multiplexes reflecting the architectural era in which they were built in. Drawing from a palette of industrial materials appropriate to the freeway environment it adjoins, Richard Rauh's Venture 12 cinema in Duluth, Georgia is plastic and dynamic, with its architecture being the main advertisement as commuters whiz by. One of its principal longitudinal façades acts as a giant billboard attracting attention through specialized lighting effects visible blocks away, as looking and reacting stretch distances when time passes at the maximum speed limit, not on pedestrian time.[14]

Whereas in the United States the trend has been the construction of entertainment centers, multiplex malls, mainly in suburban settings, European corporations integrate these structures into the established city fabric. A good example for the European experience is the UFA Palace in Dresden, Germany designed by Coop Himmelb(l)au.[15] Another is the UCI Kinowelt (multiplex) at the former Annenhof Kino in Graz, Austria, designed by Szyskowitz and Kowalski.[16] Both cinema environments date from the mid-1990s. These inner city examples from Europe differ from American multiplexes in the lesser number of screens they feature, their insertion into existing urban sites, and in the case of the UFA Palace, a highly stylized futuristic stacked multiplex where the plastic architecture takes visual precedence over mere functionality. The UFA Palace's dramatic deconstructivist architecture acts as a giant media wall to attract passers by to its environs.

One of the strongest features of the urban megaplex is its synergy with other resonant locales in the city fabric. There seems to be a taste consensus in the type of movies and the retail products particular audiences are drawn to, and restaurants and café's fall into this trend as well. The urban megaplex fits well with other similarly designed establishments that strengthen their mutual nature by attracting the same patrons. They become in effect a larger destination.

Houston and megaplex entertainment complexes

One US specific city can serve as an example of how the cinema landscape presents itself currently: Houston, Texas, the fourth largest city in the United States.

In the early 1990s, Houston was chosen to serve as a test case by major US corporate film distributors in their perennial turf wars. The result is that the city is saturated with over 400 screens, concentrated mostly in suburban multiplexes.

Houston is a prime example of suburban sprawl. The city's appetite for swallowing up land and communities in its path of expansion is legendary. Houston is the quintessential car city, built for and around the car, with its freeways being one of its principal monuments. Houston has no zoning code, and its motto seems to be tear down rather than preserve.

Into this environment, the Edwards theaters chain opened two franchises in 1999 and 2000. One of them, the Edwards Grand Palace Stadium 24 Cinemas with 24 screens is located in the business district of Greenway Plaza in a comparatively urban spatial format. The other is a suburban megaplex located on Interstate 10, a main east-west US crossing.

The urban Edwards 24 is in a new construction with a mid-rise garage adjoining it. It is surrounded by Late-Modern office towers and smaller strip centers, only a block from the US 59 freeway and Richmond Avenue, a suburbanized entertainment thoroughfare. As a big blank box it is quite a contrast to the neighboring steel and glass office towers. Its flashing neon façade identifies it as a movie theater. The lobby faces a small side street paralleling the box, allowing for easier street entry, and features a two-story space that can be entered via multiple levels when coming from the adjoining garage. The concession stand is the central attraction besides the two banks of box offices but here space for seating has been allocated to the upper and lower lobbies. A 600-seat capacity auditorium dubbed the »Grand Palace« asymmetrically balances wings of smaller screening rooms.

The Edwards 24 sister megaplex is called Marq*E 23. It was designed to house an IMAX theater as the 24th screen. The Edwards chain also projects hit movies onto the over-sized IMAX screen. This multiplex was conceived as the anchor building to a shopping mall, the Edwards Marq*E Houston Entertainment Center. The theater shell sits on a vast parking lot with a few trees dispersed sparingly throughout the lot. Its »greenfield« site is a former industrial location demolished for redevelopment. The theater is the terminal building of a double row of other entertainment facilities including a skating park and a live theater. With the creation of the »multiplex mall«, places to dine out, and perhaps even have a conversation in, have been relegated to the cinema's encircling entertainment facilities, which also include pool halls and other various gaming halls. The novelty of this center is that the shops and other attractions form an open-air mall offering dining, gaming and small shops, an anomaly in air-conditioned Houston. A plaza separates the theater from the mall row. The plaza features a band-stand and multiple kiosks for independent vendors. A splashing fountain and benches simulate the comfort of a city square. The sur-

4. Edwards Marq *E 23, Houston, Texas, 2000.
5. AMC Studio 30, Houston, Texas, 1997.

prise is that this plaza is actually used by many movie patrons and is very popular with teenagers who have made it their own.

The theater is composed of a series of monolithic boxes with bright façades. Here the neon tubing reaches around the top corner of the building so it can be seen from the freeway. The entrance lobby features an interstellar space theme with patterned terrazzo flooring and vivid film graphics covering its double-height space, which is only accessible at ground level. The lobby contains a mega concession stand, with satellites in the wings inside the »ueber« box, and the ticket booths here are internal and flank the curvilinear entry zone. Adding to the space image are murals that eclectically depict scenes from movies featuring celebrated film stars. A few of the entrances to the individual theaters are »themed« such as »Cleopatra in Egypt«. But inside the screening room, ornament is reduced to red upholstered stadium seating and a black ceiling. The sound equipment is visibly mounted on the walls. It appeals dually to nostalgic whimsy and Houston's image as »Space City«, since NASA is located here.

Another greenfield megaplex is the AMC 30 Dunvale located off Westheimer, Houston's main east-west thoroughfare, which is over 20 miles in length. Here one finds a drive-up to the outer shell of the theater, the largest in the city. It seems to embrace the »fried-egg-scheme«, a building amidst a sea of concrete paving, and the siting could easily be described as exurban on its enormous tract of land, but for Houston's Westheimer Strip this complex is merely suburban.

The AMC Studio 30 is symmetrically organized externally with a circular entrance plaza, which reflects the AMC paradigm for megaplexes designed by Jon Jerde.[17] The path from the parking lot is arranged in a linear fashion with repetitive outdoor light standards displaying posters of the featured films. The terminus of the approach is an electronic message board with the film names and show times. As patrons disperse to right or left, the »portal« is composed of triple semi-circular curved box offices with entrances between, which lead to the round plaza. Neon and colored lights frame the ramp leading to the theater. The plaza's central feature is a lighted fountain with jets spurting from holes in the stone tiles and glass block lit from below. A central axis leads to the main entry doors, above which the façade presents the full thrust of its activity.

Internally the AMC Studio 30 is symmetrically arranged, with a main concession stand and four flanking theaters (14, 15, CS 16, 17), and two wings containing theaters 1–13 and theaters 18–30 on the ends of the two aisles. Each wing is composed of thirteen auditoriums and a satellite concession. One problem of this type of multiplex in Houston is that it is so removed from urban activities that there is a tendency to leave as soon as the film ends.

Other multiplexes seem to encircle Houston: Cineplex's Tinseltown franchises sport a façade in an up-dated Art Deco style in blue and red neon with four steamship stacks arranged in a line high above the lobby façade to call out to those approaching from the parking lot. Their average number of screens is 24. Other Cineplex theaters have a similar disposition and are most frequently found in extra urban areas.

Art-film houses and independents

6, 7. Gensler Architects, Angelika Film Center at Bayou Place, Houston, Texas, 1997.
8. The Kirkland Partnership, Inc., Famous Players Theater, Festival Hall, Toronto, Canada, 1999.

The development of megaplexes has affected the fate of the downtown movie palaces the city once had. Houston was home to the first atmospheric theater and several other opulently decorated movie houses. These have been razed to make place for either downtown parking or some other type of commercial building. The idea of preservation seems to be suspect for Houston. Only four of the vintage Art Deco theaters remain, with two functioning as other types of businesses. A beautifully preserved one is a book store, another a church, and a third's remaining façade ironically acts as a front for a video store, which demolished the theater interior to erect a warehouse for its products.

The only continuously running cinema since its inception in 1939 is the Art Deco River Oaks Theater. It is owned by a smaller national company, Landmark Theaters, which regularly rescues worn theater gems for current use. It too converted its large auditorium with balcony into a three-screen theater.

The Greenway III Theaters is the sister theater of the River Oaks and is also owned by Landmark Theaters. Its past is a varied and colorful one though, as it was created in 1972 to be AMC's smallest multiplex in Houston. Conceived of as a foreign film showcase that also exhibited independent films in their infancy, the Greenway III was host for many years to the Houston International Film Festival. Departing from AMC's standard film product, such directors as Wim Wenders and John Sayles were regularly featured before they went mainstream, contributing to their crossover appeal. The excitement of premiering top European films, or the latest from Japan, China and »Bollywood« or underestimated sleepers such as the »Elephant Man« was contagious for sophisticated Houston filmgoers. It was an unusual locale for a touch of Hollywood, being located in the underground concourse of the same highrise office park where the quite differently configured Edwards 24 was built twenty years later. It is on the same level as a cavernous parking structure, which serves the towering highrises above. Now working in tandem with the River Oaks, the Greenway III has a combined six screens worth of foreign and independent fare for its audience.[18]

These theaters are two of three corporate theaters that show films that are not exclusively mainstream for a population of almost two million. Other theaters that show independent and arthouse movies are The Museum of Fine Arts Houston, which uses its Mies van der Rohe-designed Brown Auditorium, and the Rice Media Center at Rice University. The River Oaks survives on the loyalty of its urban niche audience, who love its genial atmosphere and its adjoining Art Deco shopping center with popular restaurants and boutiques.

One unique multiplex, with eight screens, with a different approach to cinema and entertainment is Houston's Angelika Film Center.[19] In a similar manner to its New York City sister theater, it was opened in 1999 in a publicly owned building in an effort to revive the downtown business district of Houston, which had become a virtual office monoculture void of street life. It is adjacent to theaters such as the Houston Grand Opera, the Houston Symphony, the Houston Ballet and the Alley Theater in the downtown Theater District. The Angelika shows an eclectic mix of films, and the architecture of the theater itself is more exciting than one might expect for a space incorporated in a revitalization project. It occupies the shell of the former Albert Thomas Convention Center, which had been vacant since 1987. The vacant building was re-programmed as a mixed use entertainment complex containing restaurants, cafés, space for live performances and a specialty multiplex. The liveliness of the Angelika is predicated on the fact that it derives it energy from the city's heart. The drama of the illuminated highrise office buildings glittering above its glazed entry atrium and restaurant and bar lends an air of glamour and sophistication to an evening out at the cinema. The twin obelisks of Philip Johnson's Pennzoil Place and the Niels Esperson Building of the 1920s form its visual backdrop. The Angelika Film Center's entrance lobby faces Jones Plaza, a public square outfitted for outdoor concerts, and beyond it Jones Hall, home to the Houston Symphony. The Angelika offers a restaurant and bar in its lobby as a »hook«, where the purchase of a ticket is not tied to the café, which is operated by an independent lessor. The restaurant has a terrace for outdoor dining. It connects to the other activities around Jones Plaza and there is a street life similar to the one portrayed in the grand days of the lost movie palaces. The interior of the lobby exhibits vintage movie posters and paraphernalia, the concession stand is comparatively small and does not dispense »fast food«. The auditoriums have smaller capacity, from 90 to 400 seats, but are equipped with the latest technology. The programming is similar to an art-house, with independent and mature audience mainstream film bookings. The clientele also differs, with the Angelika projecting itself toward inner city-dwellers.

The architecture of the lobby designed by Gensler Architects represents a modern thematic treatment of the existing rough shell. The materials of the original building are exposed and contrasted with new surface materials for the furniture and floors. The concession stand is of exposed stainless steel, vintage French graphics abound, and there is an atmosphere of contemporary architecture, a rarity in Houston.

Conclusion

A classic experience of the inner city, a trip to the movie theater, has been all but lost with the takeover of the suburban mall multiplex. Neon lights have been replaced by the ubiquitous blaze of orange sodium parking floodlights and the only glitter is provided by the blinking lights on the flat front of the theater box. Often the accompanying facilities do not exude an aura of excitement or welcoming, and the sobering cheap effects of a plastic fast-food mentality applied to the world of cinema is what remains. No one can deny the improvements that have been achieved in the technology of movie production and projection, or the comfort of almost recliner seats in the stadium arrangement. The sound and picture quality is superb, but where is the adventure and excitement of the night on the town? Even the architecture reflects that attitude. The arrival of the IMAX Theater with its elongated vertical screen several stories high, an overwhelming viewing experience, has not affected the architecture. It is merely housed in a bigger box.[20]

This disconnection with architecture, while representing a void to those who came to enjoy movie theaters as a separate passion from the films being shown, could provide the blank slate upon which a new movie theater history might be written. Gensler's Michael Darner believes that architecture can be the defining factor in the success of new multiplexes. With such a large degree of homogeneity, and only branding differentiating corporations, architecture can go a far way in making a success of a theater complex.[21] The Paramount Famous Players Theaters in Toronto makes a conscious effort to use architecture as a »draw« for its patrons. Turning away from the nostalgia of many new multiplexes the Paramount exudes an air of futuristic glee with its space motif ripe with glitzy surface treatments, reflective surfaces, models of spaceships and mod lighting schemes.[22]

Many of us still think »traditionally« when thinking of movies and cinema houses, yet an economic model of profit combined with technological systems and corporate image are the strongest influences on the cinema architecture of today. A similar formula already was in place in the cinema development of the 1920s.

The future of movie theaters may lie though not only in the pure architectural spaces they are composed of with their digital technologies, but more in the type of services that will increasingly be offered to niche markets. Already movie-goers have been offered ticket purchases online to ease physical waiting lines, next there may be an increasing market for luxury cinema in the form of a »golden class« of tickets. Currently being tested in the Asian markets, ornately decorative fine movie theaters are featuring reserved reclining seats with lap blankets where patrons may be served drinks and concessions by wait staff similar to business class airline tickets. These theaters may also offer concierge services with five star restaurants and bars in their larger complex.

In the near future movies will be digital and interactive. What will these cinemas look like when we are viewing giant plasma screens from satellite-accessed digital media, and don't need a projection booth, or when we are wearing a cyber bodysuit in a dark non-sensory space? What will happen to the collective experience of the cinema, an experience that is so much part of the idea of movie? Architects Tom Kovac and Geoff Malone with their design for French Generic Cinema have already begun to address this problem.[23] Their design is still recognizable as an architectural expression of a concept, but will we even need that in the future? Is the cinema as a type and icon doomed once again, or will we always yearn for a darkened space where we can experience emotions together, and an architecture to serve as the backdrop for images of film life?

Pamela C. Scorzin

Authentic replicas, or just like a Hollywood movie. Notes on the cinematised Las Vegas Strip

»Las Vegas is the greatest city in the world. And now that we have Paris, it's even greater!«, newly elected Mayor Oscar B. Goodman proudly told the media at the beginning of the new millennium. And it appears that for the 21st century, the neon-lit city in the faraway Nevada desert[1] is becoming a new attraction as well as a pilgrim's destination, the ultimate fairytale park for adults and earth's most exciting adventure paradise for sensation-seeking tourists. It is all because Las Vegas, this gigantic US-American, (Post-)modern urban sprawl, every night gives birth anew to a seductive mirage arising out of an amazing sea of light, made of millions and millions of pulsating, flashing light bulbs and gaudily colored, dazzling neon tubes. In the 1990s, spectacular street shows involving meticulously planned dramaturgies and huge architectural complexes doubling as scenery began to augment the characteristic, shimmering neon world of legendary old Las Vegas. The early neon signs, oftentimes portrayed and cited by American pop artists (such as the famous old »Stardust Sign«, a visual signal that once jutted out from amongst the dense forest of advertising signs and boards along the Las Vegas main boulevard, the famous Strip) have, in their capacity as »icons«, truly, and presumably indelibly, burned themselves onto our collective retina. New digital billboards, innumerable computer-based LED panels, and especially the would-be cultish »Fremont Street Experience« a 130 meter pedestrian precinct in downtown Las Vegas roofed by two million computer-controlled light bulbs as well as the constant tumultuous rattle of the chrome-covered, shiny slot and game machines in this earthly urbanistic gamblers' paradise, all make passes at their visitors' favor, money and possessions as cheaply effects-laden as ever, non-stop for twenty-four hours.

Las Vegas, the »Capital of Entertainment«, rather immodestly celebrates itself as the »First City of the 21st century«. The tourists that come here are spurred on by the eternal hope for the redemptive first price. They arrive as if by magic, incessantly, from countries all over the world, and descend, in legions of landing planes, onto this hastily expanding El Dorado of mega-casinos and adventurous leisure parks. But in all of this, does Las Vegas, »city of the one-armed bandits«, really play host to that many more (small) losers than (big) winners? Everything in this US-American amusement capital revolves around games, fun and spectacle, the essentials of the modern entertainment industry. Institutionalized entertainment instead of internalized boredom for the masses. Without a doubt, the new »economy of adventure« reigns supreme in this town, and it produces ever more artificial worlds and gigantic, multi-colored images for a society notorious for its insistence on fun and free time. Here, you are readily spellbound and bewitched »by the artificial sky, the artificial hell. You become prisoner of the dice, the cards, levers, buttons and bowls.

1. The Venetian, Las Vegas.

Time coagulates and becomes an eternity of gambling in which lust and addiction unite« (states Wolfgang Bongers in *Unterwegs*).

The forced compression of artificial architectures of adventure thus transforms the real town into a symbolic hyper-reality. Las Vegas has become the new Mecca and the metropolis of American mass entertainment, competing even with Hollywood, the close-by factory of illusions, and showing off its commercial fictionalization of architecture. After all, even the architecture of Hollywood films is primarily the architecture of fiction and of illusory spaces.

In this surreal desert place, cinematic architecture is no longer created according to old Bauhaus guidelines – it is governed by the regime of the new and global leisure and entertainment industry and the mode of media-induced experiences: »Additionally, you can learn from films and filmic images that the architecture of houses, streets and towns is not just a problem of order, function and economic efficiency; here, building incorporates psychology, atmosphere and imagery.«[2]

The brave new world of media and film »made in Hollywood« is another factor that significantly shapes the city's contemporary architecture. The aesthetics and the rhetoric of contemporary cinematic images do have an influence on constructed reality: the latter presents itself in the shape of an artificial collage and montage, of a mixtum compositum of historical attractions with the permanent possibility of arbitrary switching and quick changing. Here, Hollywood's commandment appears to have been internalized particularly deeply: everything seems to be ruled by larger-than-life versions of narrative, illusionist and populist ideas.

Truly, all of this leads to the materialization of the extra-large, cinematized mega city, appearing on the remote, westernmost horizon, glittering promisingly: a new »metropolis« of pure services, of Postmodern tourism, of perfected leisure offers and, last but not least, of ultimate American showbiz. We are experiencing the post-industrial »city of consumption« in which everything exists to serve entertainment and enjoyment.[3] In the candy-colored, brightly-lit atmosphere of this florid, totally commercialized New World which seems to be supported by nothing more than the cult pillar of the tertiary sector, world-famous architectural set pieces and instances of tidy, yet magnificent Old World and old historical scenery miraculously celebrate their joyous resurrection, freed from thoughts of monument preservation, so that John Doe, America's own »Lucky Hans«, might imagine himself as actually ploughing his way through a place »Far, Far Away«, its (holiday/film) dreams now effectively tangible and real, even while traveling through his own country. As is generally known, world architecture, in the media age, is always film architecture, and vice versa.

Thus, the desert witnesses the bloom of illusions as big business and the new experience economy. Besides, in the midst of the Las Vegas Strip's new, magical fittings endowments that concretize a rainbow-colored, visualized world of dreams, buildings in the scenery that are older than five years are marked with the aura of the historic. With their sceneries and their movie architectures, Hollywood's film studios are another area where genuinely constructed edifices are only ever present as reconstructed fragments and copies, mostly created from transient, cheap materials for the moment of production. A brief ramble through this fascinatingly artificial mega city in the Southwest of the USA – still (or once again) the Promised Land to Europeans – suddenly transplants us into completely different spaces and times, an experience perhaps comparable to impatient zapping through private and commercial TV channels. That expedition, as is the standard for the Homo Americaniensis species, is executed in the speed of the fordist age, namely in a fully air-conditioned automobile. In the new money wonderland, the locations have been concentrated, visually condensed and economically simultanized to fit the expectations of all the modern-day Alices: »Visitors to Las Vegas want extraordinary experiences within the shortest possible space of time; they receive a sign that obviously stands for Paris (for instance) – and they're happy with it.«[4] Similarly, classic movie architecture in Hollywood primarily functions as a giver of signs and meanings, plays its own role within the business of illusions. The city itself becomes a purely supportive (filmic) image.

In this place, one experiences first of all the »aesthetic« hallucination of reality, as French simulation theorist Jean Baudrillard once put it. A leisurely drive along the 4-mile Las Vegas Strip – the American variation of old European strolling and promenading, best executed in a Cadillac or a Chevrolet, as that much etiquette is compulsory even in a country as otherwise unconventional and easy-going as America – takes us along the American Viennese Ring road from avenue to avenue, from block to block, as half-recognized sceneries and topographies pass by in a flash. Grand, static sceneries, emotionalising tableaux and overwhelming decorations, built exclusively for our movie-pampered eyes-turned-cameras!

Las Vegas is not far from Hollywood, and it seems that here we have found a place where the fantastical machinery of illusions and dream worlds have become total and real. The city space is

merely a production in front of buildings-as-backdrops based on Old World paragons. The city is the Show! Once again, America lives up to the cliché of being a country that supplies the whole world with visions and dreams. Both successful Hollywood cinema and the Las Vegas Strip cleverly displays a spectacular scenery that is all make-believe and pretence, one that has been rhetorically and aesthetically refurbished – a mise-en-scène based on architectural history. Still, according to ancient ideas harbored by the educated bourgeoisie going to the cinema was always closer to escapism than to a genuine cultural experience from which one could learn and be edified. And yet, everyone held the desire to (co)experience a dramatized and idealized different life. On the other hand, both Las Vegas and Hollywood mostly deliver comfortable fare in the shape of popular standards, stereotyped genres and easily comprehensible, easily recognisable items.

Furthermore, the idea of culture as alienated nature is repeated once again: after all, the shimmering atmosphere of the red-hot Mojave Desert is where the mirror and double images flower. At its center, an unreal paradise of fantastical artificiality: is it not the young clone of the old Canal Grande that flows through this real space of the imaginary, a promising, azure blue-tinted river in the midst of an incredibly prosperous oasis of quick happiness and cheap consumerism shrouded in a near-faceless, far-off no man's land, in immediate vicinity to the famous Death Valley? Delusion and »projection«, craftily enhanced by lots of hidden high-tech – it is only here in the superlative American Venice that the gondolas romantically make the venerable new Canal's waves splash in a way that can still be heard on the first floor. No problemo! Meanwhile, the Piazza San Marco has been fully roofed over, and the actual desert climate has been counteracted by pleasant air-conditioning; additionally, the square is fully and, thus, securely lighted around the clock.

Under the observation of art historians, Italian stucco artists and painters have created full-scale replicas and, at the same time, cunningly recreated Venice according to the specifications of a professional direction of imagery; thus, Venice has shrunk to the film set dimensions of being 240 meters in diameter. The staged city as a protagonist! That is why Norman M. Klein speaks of a »condensed city« with highly Baroque illusory effects: »These condensed cities often hark back to shrunken New York streets built in the 1920s for Hollywood studios.«[5]

Thus, in Las Vegas the Bridge of Sighs connects the marvelous Doge's Palace with the inevitable shopping mall, while the pittoresque Rialto Bridge leads directly to the parking garage. The most famous set pieces and visual landmarks of the Venetian laguna town between sky and sea, the Doge's Palace, the Rialto Bridge, the Campanile, the Ca d'Oro and the Piazza San Marco as bequeathed symbols of architecture and majestic dignity standing for old European splendor and glory, perhaps standing a little closer, as economics demand, but reconstructed in their original scale from genuine, precious materials as well as cheap plaster and Styrofoam – in

2. B. Marino, *New York – New York, Las Vegas*.
3. René Burri, Las Vegas Strip.
4. Fremont Street, Las Vegas.

this remote, cultureless, stony desert, they all mutate into striking architectural ciphers that donate atmosphere, prestige, flair, glamour, luxury, tradition, emotion, identity and historicity. After all, the USA had trained well for such unusual projects, as Malibu's Paul Getty Museum with its reconstructed Roman papyrus villa proves. Moreover, a spectacular Postmodern theater-of-illusion-as-hotel such as the Venetian in Las Vegas may be understood as reality montage, constructed and composed according to the practices and the aesthetics of effect behind the most common methods currently used in Hollywood's digital image productions.

As we rub our (camera) eyes, we gaze in uninterrupted amazement at what we perceive behind the windscreens-turned-visual-screens. In breathtakingly fast (camera) shots, we pass by our cinematized dream destinations on a fictitious (television film) journey without any kind of physical exertion or even bodily movement, and everything is consumable and image-sized, and seen through Hollywood's Technicolor filter of vision: the Carribean, Luxor, Disneyland, Hollywood (MGM), New York – New York!, Monte Carlo, Paris, Bellagio on the Lago di Como, Bally's Las Vegas, Caesar's Rome, Monte Carlo, San Remo, Arabia, finally the Hofbräuhaus in Munich … (Further tourist city highlights such as London and San Francisco are already being planned.) Not to forget, naturally, ancient, near-sunken Venice. »Las Venice«, as it were – the new, architecturally cloned Venice, Venice 2.0, officially christened. »The Venetian Resort, Hotel & Casino«, lies only a few driving minutes from other popular attractions and highlights from the sublime cultural and architectural history of Europe. Completely fit for consumption and nicely cleansed, preciously lined up as if strung on a shimmering chain of imitation pearls, we move on along our swift ride and glance at all the outstanding gems of ancient high culture situated between the countless, gigantic, modernistic hotel complexes, large-scale casinos, fun rides and shopping malls, geared only towards the masses, commerce and popularity. Thus, culture becomes completely consumable.

»The effect on the sensual grasping of the city could not be more dramatic. Previously, the single casinos were self-sufficient places of incident. Between, say, the Egyptian Luxor pyramid and the Caesar's Palace with its Forum Romanum lay a fifteen-minute car ride through a city which, at least by day, appeared to be a relatively regular town of the American West. The fact that it was necessary to negotiate temporal and spatial distances had a neutralising effect. Visiting the different fantasy worlds hidden away on the inside of the hotel casinos did produce a succession of distinctive aesthetic experiences, perhaps comparable to seeing several movies in several cinemas.

Nowadays, the fantastic can be observed in every building, and a dreamlike hullabaloo has ensued in which memorised cultural images blend into one another in a way that suggests a cracked-up cutter sticking together the high points of a dozen very different films. Amused, amazed, irritated, the eyes of passers-by swing from the Treasure Island to the Empire State Building, from lost South Sea empires to the Eiffel Tower, from the Pyramid of Luxor to King Arthur's candy-colored castle«[6]

The current Las Vegas Strip, too, favors fast editing and visual bombardment with excerpts, fragments, jumps and changing perspectives.

And it seems like nothing will work without the attention-begging gates and inviting portals that lead to the insides of the modern temples of enjoyment and the gambling halls, all of them, in a reflection of a studio tour, mock-ups and cheap imitations of easily recognizable architectural celebrities and mass media-compatible landmarks. Furthermore, there are star doubles and doppelgangers on every (street) corner, just as there are a dozen Elvis impersonators on the numberless Las Vegas show stages. Film characters cavort here en masse, too. The Star Trek Hilton, for instance, hosts a Star Trek Convention every year, displaying its imitations of the would-be-cultish Deep Space Nine backdrops. Therefore, you might just meet Captain Kirk or Mr. Spock »in real person«, if not a few genuine extraterrestrials as known from popular Hollywood movies like *Mars Attacks!* (Tim Burton, 1996), *Independence Day* (Roland Emmerich, 1996) or *Men in Black* (Barry Sonnenfeld, 1997) – however, most of them do not live too far off, namely in Los Angeles, Hollywood, as Will Smith a. k. a. James Darell Edwards sarcastically claimed in part one of *Men in Black*. The synthesizing of reality and fiction, real space and virtual space is as much apparent in Las Vegas as it is in Hollywood film, when, for instance, »Tim Burton's retro aliens in *Mars Attacks!* choose the upper section of the strip to launch their invasion of planet earth, their lasers rhyming nicely with the majestic lights of the Stardust pylon.«[7] Meanwhile, the Terminator himself governs neighboring California since 2003.

Even the genuine architectural landmarks that came into being during the brief cultural past of the relatively young United States of America itself, namely Disneyland or the famous Manhattan Skyline, including – in somewhat miniaturised form – replicas of the Chrysler and Empire State

Buildings, the latter once again the highest edifice in New York City following the tragic events of September 11th 2001, are part of this ultimate »City of Entertainment« in the Federal State of Nevada and salute the visitors who flock here, young and old alike. Statistically, though, these visitors never book themselves into the gigantic themed hotels with their thousands of beds for any longer than approximately three days. That is about the length of time the superficial allure of the computer-designed backdrop-like fittings will last, once you allow yourself to be carried by the intoxicating illusion of fiction, narration and simulation, and by the fascination for perfectly staged, cinematized architectural images. For it is they that promise, at least for a short time, to chase away the monotonous boredom of American everyday life with cinematic effects. A world of backdrops, fitted with items from Disney fairytales, cleverly arranged to unfold its full aesthetic impact, colorfully lighted and temporarily consumable, a world that, in the space of a quick holiday, turns one's real life into an exciting film, with the tourist as the hero and protagonist. In Las Vegas, the artificial reality of a movie truly, for once, becomes a concentrated and concrete reality into which one may immerse oneself both physically and mentally. The tourists and visitors, in their turn, are invited to experience a strange, remote or bygone culture for their entertainment and distraction. »Authenticity«, arranged here in the shape of backdrops and scenery, does become much more consequent and Postmodern, meaning artificial to a point where ironic refraction becomes professional standard to a much larger degree than has been achieved in many of the other US cities, with their artificial shopping and / or recreational Shangri-Las. After all, the North American shopping centers in particular »are theatrical spaces, challenging stages on which the drama of consumption is played out. For the construction of these environments, their planners avidly borrow from Hollywood. First of all, the spaces are constructed in such a way that the visitors, once they have arrived, feel encouraged to leave all their doubts behind – just as in a darkened cinema.«[8]

The Grand Tour of the 19th and 20th century across ancient, tradition-laden Europe, once obligatory and now almost legendary, all of a sudden appears to have become obsolete for the followers of this new, real, entertaining, illusory world, all the more so as Las Vegas is by now in a position allowing it to big-headedly demonstrate that it has an almost genuine museum tradition of its own – museums, however, here exist on a meta-level: witness the new museum for neon art or the much-loved »Liberace Museum« at 1775 E Tropicana Avenue, that wonderfully tacky temple to real strass and false tassels, in which the late Mr. Showmanship's old pianos and scurrilous threads are treated like relics of Holy Trash and High Camp. In the newly opened restaurant »Picasso«, nine paintings and some original drawings by the homonymous Spanish painting superstar decorate the walls. Right next door, at the Bellagio Gallery of Fine Art, Las Vegas hotel tycoon Steve Wynn has exhibited his private art collection, estimated to be worth 300 million dollars: from Rembrandt to Cézanne, from Renoir to Jackson Pollock – only the crème de la crème from the sublime history of art is represented. And those who bring along the necessary small change can have those works wrapped up for them and take them home. Thus, the McDonald's of art museums only recently, after Berlin and Bilbao, widely opened the doors of further subsidiaries for a mass audience here (and then, partly out of economic considerations, closed them again). The two new Guggenheim branches in Las Vegas boasted real works of art in the midst of fake scenery and true-to-original replicas. One is reminded of the phenomenon of original commissioned art created by several artists for the sets of American soap operas, as the widely covered example of successful TV series *Melrose Place* has already shown. It would be cynical to claim that here in Las Vegas, the city of »authentic replicas« (as an official statement had it), originals were treated as merely the (better) copies! The term »original« does not appear to be part of the Las Vegas dictionary anyway. And if one were to briefly cast one's mind back to the completely reconstructed »ancient« Venetian opera house La Fenice in real Venice that was re-opened in late 2003 – where is the difference in the cult of reconstruction now?

At any rate, the opening of the Guggenheim Las Vegas and its first exhibition »The Art of the Motorcycle« resembled a grandiose Hollywood production: manager Thomas Krens arrived on the scene accompanied by an impressive entourage of venturesome bikers, part of which, as a matter of course, was the legendary *Easy Rider* (Dennis Hopper, 1969) Dennis Hopper himself. In true style, as if they had just climbed out of an American road movie, wearing real stubble and authentic bikers' gear, they got down from their crackling hot machines parked outside the hotel; meanwhile, the bikers' old cult films flickered steadily over the monitor screens stood between the virtuoso arrangement of exhibits by star architect Frank O. Gehry.

One thing that is most definitely unique about Las Vegas is the multitude of professional, live entertainment shows performed several times a day: There are those created by the uncrowned

5. The Venetian, Las Vegas.

188

true rulers of this ultimate capital of genuine American entertainment, the two German magicians Siegfried and Roy – they work their illusionist magic at the first of Steve Wynn's themed hotels, the classy »Mirage«, a place they have abided by and at which they have been exclusively residing since 1990; these men, dressed up in fancy costumes, always wear professional smiles, and, as is the norm for exclusive, true leaders even in a country governed by mass democracy, they are always accompanied by their exotic life guards – a group of rare white tigers! In this surreal arena, however, we suddenly observe, as Slavoj Zizek put it, a 2003 invasion of the real and the oppressed into this immaculate machinery of illusion. What happened was that one of the trained, noble luxury creatures attacked its tamer Roy in a very real manner, while the audience initially believed that life-threatening attack to be part of the perfect show's illusionist game … After all, the »Mirage« is a downright palladium for the sale of illusions and fantasies: an artificial park for adults with a green rain forest in the hotel lobby, a volcano in the park that sprouts forth hourly, spectacular eruptions and smoke with a pleasant coconut aroma. On neighboring »Treasure Island«, fully choreographed sea battles take place at the top of every hour, featuring pillaging pirates and wild buccaneers just like well-known Hollywood movies used to do, and so on. (And might there not be a Johnny Depp around for us tonight?)

In the dark of the Las Vegas night fever, we vaguely remind ourselves of a book on architectural theory from the 1970s named *Learning from Las Vegas*. That small pamphlet was granted sainthood by followers of Postmodernism, and in the bright and cheerful 1970s, a decade which unbelievably embraced low instead of high culture and indulged in off-key camp, it turned American architect Robert Venturi into an overnight worldwide celebrity and a pop-architectural guru »at its best«. And thus, at the start of the new millennium, that is to say after the fulminant international triumph of Postmodernism, we once again wistfully and expectantly glance westward … but, alas, there was something else we wanted to learn from the cinematized Las Vegas Strip, a place where nowadays you will find more »canards« than »decorated sheds«.

It's a good job that in the meantime, Rem Koolhaas has been there, too, he who recently bestowed upon us a minimalist container of reddish brown corten steel for the precious Old World art treasures right in the middle of the brand new »Venetian«. Koolhaas' steely »jewel case« now offers a lot of space for the sensational guest performances of old European treasures of art from St. Petersburg to Vienna, as planned by Thomas Krens, exceedingly enterprising manager of the Solomon R. Guggenheim Foundation. After all, Las Vegas is where all of the following converge most effortlessly: art and commerce, consumption and cliché. And yet, nobody here ever talks of kitsch! Art and business merge and, in doing so, effectively use their (economic) synergy effects. Learning from Las Vegas once again? But, after all the formal excesses and lapses in taste of Postmodern architecture's inflationary epigones right in front of our own homes, what else is there to learn from this cityscape out West, governed as it is by the unbeatable magic double »big money and big business« – even more so, apparently, than international centers of trade and exchange such as New York, Tokyo, London or Frankfurt, a cityscape witnessing a rapid and merciless acceleration of architecture and urban development, pushed ever forward by repeated constitution and demolition, outrageously expansive and yet – behind the gaudy scenery – bizarrely, uniformly bleak? It seems, though, that today, that one slogan advertising has always favored – »Go West!« – holds true more than ever. Thus, bearing in mind the »former champion of Postmodernism« Robert Venturi and his serene trademark sense of humor and irony, we keep watching the latest spectacular large-scale projects of recent architectural history's new and headstrong form of »architainment«. We watch the new, cinematized Las Vegas, the one that has become a Mecca for incredible sensations, simulations and stimulations, for fantastical suggestions and exciting, three-dimensional, accessible scenery, for Hollywoodesque stagings and near-cinematic images. All in all, a ›scripted space‹ par excellence. And California – and, thus, Hollywood – isn't that far-off, either. Both here and there, all that counts is the game of imitation, illusion and imagination. The allure and the attractiveness behind these spectacular architectures is based on their cobbled-together and daydream-like existence – both here and in Hollywood studios: building parts and dummies stand around as if they had been cut out of reality. For the visitor, city does not always denote a huge whole – sometimes it is little more than that corner of experience and adventure, behind which the forest and the desert begin.[9] In Las Vegas, the architectural settings – both in reality and within the medium of old and new Hollywood movies – allow us to see the world without ever leaving: if the world is a stage, then this place sells the cinematic stage as the real world.

In a way comparable to notorious Hollywood movies, the former dusty highway to Los Angeles, today's dazzlingly colored Las Vegas Strip with its imposing backdrops, its intoxicating neon lights, decorative ads and accessible architectural images presents modern, sensation-seeking men and women with the fascinating experience and the exceptional adventure of unexpectedly being whisked away to another place, of suddenly being transported to another time, of immersing one's senses in an imaginary world, of simply being a direct part of it – just like the astonished kid protagonist in the Schwarzenegger movie *Last Action Hero* (John McTiernan, 1993)!

To completely lose oneself in the staged images, to immerse oneself in different (adventurous) worlds cut off from miserable everyday life and supported by nothing but beautiful illusions, affecting stagings and spectacular fictionalizations: the visitor, hungry for adventure and imagery, »soaks up fictions and realities as conscious images, he does not care to what extent the single image is rooted deeply and preciously in reality. The main thing is that it's there, it's visible, and it's open to experience«.[10] Vegaesthetics meets Hollywood! And there is nothing modern tourists like to experience and consume quite like the city itself. However, Las Vegas itself is no longer a city in the modern sense, as Gundolf S. Freyermuth has already pointed out: »Here, attempts are made on a scale unlike anywhere else to produce today – on an analogue level – that which virtual reality techniques may promise, but which they cannot yet deliver in tolerable quality, considering today's technical possibilities: the experience of distant spaces or imaginary worlds, as well as myths and fictions that can be both accessed and participated in (and interacted with, P.C.S.).«[11]

It can be observed that the themed Las Vegas hotels deliberately construct those artificially imitated, cinematically simulated atmospheres that beg their audiences for attention and fascination. They are the seductive sirens among the daughters of the mother of all arts, namely fine architecture, who devote themselves shamelessly and copiously to excessive amorous dalliances, finding their reflections rather in the stereotyped quoting orgics of popular architectural styles and precious monuments than amusing entertainment and pure enjoyment, and who thus – if not creatively, then at least in the most visibly exhaustive manner – serve the voyeuristic society of spectacle, fun and experiences our constantly, watchfully critical Cassandras of social science have diagnosed here, there and everywhere. We want to be seduced into imaginary worlds with processed and conveyed experiences in a manner similar to that offered by the great American cinema of entertainment, and thus, we slip ever more deeply into the traps (of perception) set by the totally commercialized marketing of adventures and experiences, the kind that used to be available for free in former times. In the copies of reality, we are privy to a purely cultural form of capitalism, a unique and original capitalism of images.

Why not employ the aid of academic scientists to investigate into precisely what it is that this spellbinding architecture of backdrops and the architectural dummies – set up for five years, almost an eternity in fashion, basically just one season – truly have to offer. Taking their cues from the notorious car perspective and the panoramic wide screen aesthetics of the Las Vegas Strip, these artificial image worlds, at first glance and above all, offer fleeting impressions, fragmented splinters and small visual bits of the colorful global media world, easy-to-digest déjà-vus from the international travel businesses' exclusive advertising films and trailers and from the visual compendiums of global travel as well as from the above-average cognitions of old encyclopedic knowledge. Additionally, there is the delight in seeing the perfectly staged architectural spectacle which, in the distant Old World, used to go by the name of King Ludwig II. of Bavaria, or opera and theater in the grandiose style coined by Wagner (or Semper, respectively). These emotionalizing, sumptuous backdrops and translocated populist façade architectures on the new Las Vegas boulevard may appear to us as having been made of substandard materials, as constructions made of papier-mâché, copied for urban stagings and reproduced with the highest of artificial, illusory powers – and yet, many find in them more than just a substitute, more than funny pop surrogates for their faraway, absent originals one has possibly never visited and never, in reality, inspected.

Viewed from the perspective of the Las Vegas Strip, they are a successful collage and montage of striking icons, images, picture codes and stereotypes that work like strategic billboards and atmospheric movie backdrops. The three-dimensional, fictitious world of images is turned into a real, surrogate world. But then again, not a single scene in Michael Curtiz' cult movie *Casablanca* (1942) was filmed in Africa; that entire Hollywood movie was made at Warner Studios on Warner Boulevard No. 400 in Burbank, North Hollywood, between early May and late July 1942, on sound stages Nos. 9 and 21.[12] Did it make a difference for us at all?

The sensational reconstructions and replicas additionally stand for the »obtaining« of exclusive cultural goods and values of the chic and perhaps morbid Old World by the relatively new one – acts that must seem strange to Europeans. According to conventional (European) wisdom, that world is per se a culturally impoverished, untraditional, virtual one which, in spite of itself, does have the uncontested monopoly on the production of entertaining, young movies. As the Romans of the 20th century, the Americans appear to harbor an impressive will to cultural representation, even if that will – in another parallel to Ancient Rome – does sometimes manifest itself in genuine copies. In this, the Americanized copies do not only symbolize the, as yet, most extreme form of commercialization of architecture and its traditional styles, but also the deliberate, hedonistic display of the American »anything goes« ethos, or, in other words, the purchase of even non-material things such as the specific atmospheres, emotions and ecstasies that cling to these openly quoted historical architectures as idiosyncratic breaths and sentiments, made possible only with a sufficient amount of capital. One example is the world-renowned sentimental romanticism of Venice – spread by millions of honeymoons and romantic movies – , as offered in pleasantly democratic style – not least via the World Wide Web – by the newly-constructed Resort Hotel Venetian in Las Vegas as an instance of inexpensive, exceedingly romantic luxury for Mr. and Mrs. Everyman, with that added little extra when compared to the aged, ruined original: »The world's most romantic city is now in the heart of the most exciting destination location.« It seems like the modern advertising philosophy of »get two in one« remains unbeatable! Better and more than the far-off original, one that remains a mere phantom image or a pale memory – that is how the more entertaining (new) reproduction advertises itself as if it were a refabrication, preventing the desire and the longing to see the original (older) model from the outset. Here, remakes and plagiarisms are likely to become the better product, the economized duplication, the even more perfect world of adventure. After all, Hollywood movies, too, always present life as a little more exciting and colorful ... So, »welcome to this pleasure-city«, one with a semblance of an ideal movie world already known for its cheap weddings and quick divorces.

Consumption and entertainment are everything these days, even modern architecture comes across as hypocritical as it fulfils the seemingly harmless function of chatting pleasurably about petrified professional entertainers. The themed hotels of Las Vegas are brilliant, astonishingly hypnotizing architectural constructions that mainly serve the build-up of totally illusory worlds and adventurous architectures spurred on by the search for profit. At the same time, they are perfidious expressions of our well-hidden, secret desires – »to be like Alice or Dorothy just for once«, to briefly dissolve in, willingly and readily play along with the put-up job these illusions are – just like members of a cinema audience. Spectators imagine themselves as parts of what momentarily strongly affects their perception and emotion via the visual experience of looking (on). In Las Vegas, the virtuoso immersion methods of Hollywood screens return to genuine reality. We mirac-

6. The Venetian, Las Vegas.

ulously experience a projection and a feint of that which is not there and which nevertheless surrounds us – just like in a movie. Great Potemkinesque US city? After all, what is of importance here is the power of suggestion and the magic of artificial surface aesthetics only. Always a colorful masquerade, the city is reduced to a mere movie brochure. Apparently such bizarre, artificial towns are no longer conceptualized by national or international architects or urban developers, but by specialized construction managers and scenic artists of Hollywood. From now on, there can be only one rule: »Form follows fiction.« The architect takes on the mantle of stage designer, scenograph and cineast – master of a carefully directed mise-en-scène de monde.

The architecture of films is not just an expressive architecture of images – to a similar degree, it is always a vivid architecture of meaning and declaration. In a parallel to successful stage sets, just a few striking set pieces and significant image codes must suffice to create a correspondingly memorable atmosphere and an exceptional mood. Thus, when Munich's young photographic artist Alexander Timtschenko was planning a new photographic cycle on Hollywood scenery, he got a much more acute sense of the artificialness and the predominant pattern of colorful combination of several partial worlds while in Las Vegas than he could ever have hoped and expected from actual Hollywood backdrops.[13]

The inhabitants of and visitors to this town, too, suddenly find themselves occupying the roles of extras or joyously consuming protagonists amidst a powerful, loquacious urban scene production. Meanwhile, the employees of this gigantic contemporary entertainment and service machinery – over-friendly as ever – obviously get to experience their daily, less than well-paid work underneath the overwhelming ceiling frescos by Venetian Renaissance maestros – copied here in thrilling American pop-art colors – as nothing but fun and games. The only professional qualification you need is to be perfect at acting and professional at pretending. We are seeing, to quote master director Martin Scorsese, the drama of total »disneyfication«.

At least on the American Canal Grande, the gondolas keep swaying rhythmically to the strains of the gondolieri imported from faraway Bel Paese Italia, who may warble slushily, but at least – at times – true to the original, while security personnel of this latest superlative themed hotel – patrolling in the toy uniforms of Italian carabinieri, and always in view – theatrically distracts attention from the omnipresence of the video surveillance systems hidden on every corner. More enthusiastic tourists may almost believe themselves to be secret participants, cameos even, in a new instalment of the extremely successful *Truman Show* (Peter Weir, 1998).

All that is missing are the lovably annoying flocks of pigeons that simply would not be trained to fly in regular formations above Las Vegas; they are something this aseptically glass-covered, never uncomfortably flooded, never smelly, absolutely clean and near-sterile US-Piazza San Marco with its wonderfully sky-like, illusionist, hypaethral space sorely lacks; still, it does have its share of leaking water pipes. After all, construction mistakes can happen anywhere, even in the beautiful gamblers' paradise, because – as always – the devil is in the details. On the otherwise comfortably friendly and cheerful Piazza, we pay the cameriere (!) for the imported, genuinely Italian espresso with hard dollars or, even better, with an international credit card and e-cash, while he thanks us for the tip with a nice, foreign »grazie e ciao!« Las Vegas 2000, a cinematic/opera-like multi-media performance, with the audience as the choir.

Las Vegas is the place where the Disney virus, rampant throughout the entire world, has obviously struck fiercest of all. After the diagnosis, there now follows the description of the symptoms: the simulation is clearly given preference over cruel reality, while the copy still has the ambition to trump the distant, ancient original at the product level, with the help of cinematic stagings and well-directed dramaturgies. In line with the contemporary advertising philosophy behind cult brands, we are constantly told that »It is not simply Venezia, it is the Venetian!« Thus, we experience a Venice upgrade. A new Director's Cut: a second, improved and sensually heightened remake of the Old World! Traveling to Las Vegas is, to quote Umberto Eco and Jean Baudrillard once more, another station on the journey to the magic kingdom of hyper-reality, as it were. Both architecture in films and the edifices from Las Vegas' recent architectural history only serve the great illusions, simulations and fictions. To live in the style of a Hollywood film just once – but only after having gawped at Las Vegas as a real backdrop to movies[14] from the safety of our old-fashioned cinema seats: in Andrew Bergman's *Honeymoon in Vegas* (1992), for instance, Adrian Lyne's *Indecent Proposal* (1993), Martin Scorsese's *Casino* (1995), Mike Figgis' *Leaving Las Vegas* (1995), Terry Gilliam's *Fear and Loathing in Las Vegas* (1998) or Steven Soderbergh's *Ocean's Eleven* (2001). The cityscape architecture built after images is transformed back into cinematic imagery, only to serve as a model image for films. So we, the audience, are constantly captured in virtual realities, trapped into illusions.

In Hollywood films, however, the shimmering, genuine backdrop that is Las Vegas City does not only work as a new, Postmodern place of desires, but also, significantly, as a perfidious and cynical metaphor for all sorts of dark human chasms and errors. Its spectacular architecture does mirror mental states, emotions and romantic desires as well as incurable addictions and hallucinations. For the most part, however, the ancient topos of the city with negative connotations still dominates – Hollywood, the dream factory, suitably likes to interpret Las Vegas as a nightmare. The reason for this is that he/she who has become completely involved in this town founded entirely on games and illusions, will apparently find it extremely hard to get away from it. Addicted and lost behind the glamorous backdrops, with no hope for rescue or a cure – as acted out by Nicolas Cage in *Leaving Las Vegas*. It is precisely the set pieces and fragments of these new, sensational architectural worlds à la Hollywood-Las Vegas that make up the pseudo-historical matrix for a particularly immersive experience, a brief, enjoyable stay in the virtual town of artifice – and all the while, behind the gleaming façades, the new transnational leviathan lies in wait for us, along with the filthy lucre and Hollywood's mystic *Wizard of Oz*. After all, the gamblers of Las Vegas are bribed, temporary underlings that would give their all for just that. Mundus vult decipi…

Meanwhile, the likeably crude, pop-vulgar Las Vegas Strip of the 1960s and 1970s that Robert Venturi described so graphically and extensively (and that he rendered optically palatable as an unusual architectural concept) in his studies has been replaced by a gorgeously representative main boulevard with eccentrically illuminated, enormous fountains and ultimately bizarre light shows that also features further rivaling street attractions and their effective sceneries, elaborate stories and real actors as well as stunt people. Today's motto should be *Learning from Hollywood*, Mr. Venturi! Here, in the American desert, sea battles with pirates à la Hollywood actually happen every hour, on the hour. To make that possible, even the city's last public pavements have been privatized. The old casinos and saloons have recently been mingled with big shopping malls and fancy restaurants. Sweeping golf courses, expensive luxury apartments and countless wellness centers for recreation (after the game) line the town's fringes as they endlessly disperse into the, as yet, desert-like periphery. And all of a sudden, they all promise new test-tube luxury and urban exclusiveness. The first celebrity residences have begun to lure the first fans into town. The city's old image as a notorious paradise for gamblers and modern adventurers – still somewhat objectionable – truly has been worked on a lot. Its former reputation as an infamous American Gomorrah and a tough gangland area has almost been forgotten, so that nowadays, Las Vegas can present itself as emphatically family-friendly, just like all the related, big Disneylands of this world. As in mainstream Hollywood, some sort of secret production codex reigns over everything: to maintain its new, friendly image as an exciting town of leisure, entertainment, universities and congresses, old, historic Las Vegas has put on a fashionable quilted coat made of comically colorful and magical theme parks in the style of Disneyland, Orlando, Florida. But really, certainly another ounce of cinematized backdrop romanticism in the style of flashy postcards is not going to do the city of many wedding chapels any serious harm (even according to its highly ingenious professional developers and powerful investors), all the more so as even our views of everyday tristesse have long since been conditioned by Hollywood, the dream factory. As mentioned above, Hollywood films, too, are always much more colorful and spectacular, and our apperception truly attuned itself to that phenomenon long ago. These days, we refrain from beginning tales of our exceptional experiences and adventures with the phrase »It was just like in a dream…«; rather, we prefer »It was just like in a Hollywood movie …« – words which, last but not least, many Las Vegas tourists are supposed to use time and again.

References and notes

Christian W. Thomsen / Angela Krewani: Preface

Klein, Christina, »Crouching Tiger, Hidden Dragon: A Diasporic Reading«, in: *Cinema Journal*, 4, 2004, pp. 18–42.
McLaren, Angus, *The Trials of Masculinity: Policing Sexual Boundaries, 1870–1930*, Chicago, 1997. Mosse, George L., *The Image of Man: The Creation of Modern Masculinity*, New York, 1996.
Wyllie, Barbara, »Hollywood in Crisis?«, in: *The Cambridge Quarterly*, 32, no. 2, 2003, pp. 181–184.

Christian W. Thomsen: 9/11. Before and after

[1] John Frow, »The Uses of Terror and the Limits of Cultural Studies«, I/I, 2003, www.highbeam.com.
[2] Howard F. Stein, »Days of Awe: September 11, 2001 and its Cultural Psychodynamics«, in: *Journal for the Psychoanalysis of Culture and Society*, September 22, 2003, www.highbeam.com.
[3] Mark Leibovich, »Fear Factoring: Nervous About the Terrorist Threat. People Imagine the Worst«, in: *The Washington Post*, May 1, 2003, Section Style, www.highbeam.com.
[4] Ibid.
[5] Cf. Timo Kozlowski, »Hollywood als Orakel? Drei Jahre vor dem WTC-Anschlag spielten Bruce Willis und Denzel Washington dessen Folgen durch«, www.heise.de/bin/tp/issue/dl-artikel.cgi?Artikelnr 13375.
[6] Cf. Toyo Ito, *Blurring Architecture*, Milan, 1999.
[7] Michael Staiger, »In diesem Spiel gewinnt immer der Entschlossenste. Bilder des Terrors im Hollywood-Kino«, in: *Online-Forum Medienpädagogik*, www.kreidestriche.de; http://home.ph-freiburg.de; staiger/texte/staiger_terror_im_hollywoodkino.htm.
[8] Cf. Mark J. Lacy, »War, Cinema and Moral Anxiety«, in: *Alternatives: Global, Local, Political*, November 1, 2003, www.highbeam.com.
[9] »US-Army sucht Hilfe bei Hollywood-Filmern«, in: *Spiegel Online*, October 19, 2001, www.spiegel.de; »Hollywoods Kreative beraten US-Armee«, October 10, 2001, www.film.de.
[10] »Hollywood zieht in den Kampf«, in: *Spiegel Online,* October 19, 2001, www.spiegel.de.
[11] »The Day After«, October 13, 2001, www.focus.de.
[12] »Das Trade Center wird erneut getilgt«, September 20, 2001, www.diewelt.de.
[13] Ibid.
[14] »Hollywood trauert um Terror-Opfer«, September 12, 2001, www.film.de.
[15] »Hollywood verschiebt Filmstart«, September 14, 2001, www.wundv.de.
[16] Lacy, op. cit. (note 8).
[17] Tom Doherty, »The New War Movies as Moral Rearmament: *Black Hawk Down* and *We Were Soldiers*«, in: *Cineaste*, June 22, 2002, www.highbeam.com.
[18] Ibid.
[19] Lacy, op. cit. (note 8).
[20] Cf. »Hollywood trauert um Terror-Opfer«, September 12, 2001, www.film.de; »Schockreaktionen«, in: *epd Film*, November, 2001, www.filmdienst.de.
[21] Stein, op. cit. (note 2).

[22] Ibid.
[23] Ibid.
[24] Carlo Rotella, »Affliction«, in: *The American Scholar*, 71, 1, 2000, pp. 48–51, quoted in Stein, op. cit.
[25] Stein, op. cit. (note 2).
[26] Ibid.
[27] Ibid.
[28] Cf. Gregory Barsham, »The Religion of *The Matrix* and the Problems of Pluralism«, in: William Irwin (ed.), *The Matrix and Philosophy*, Chicago and La Salle, 2002, pp. 101–110, p. 114.
[29] Ibid., p. 114.
[30] Cf. Andreas Kilb, »Dr. Michael und Mr. Bush. *Fahrenheit 9/11*. Ein Kino-Pamphlet verschenkt die Wahrheit«, in: *Frankfurter Allgemeine Zeitung*, July 28, 2004, p. 29.

Karen A. Ritzenhoff: On the cutting edge. New visual languages in film-editing conventions in Hollywood

[1] Richard Barsam, *Looking at Movies: An Introduction to Film*, New York, 2004, p. 334.
[2] David Bordwell and Kristin Thompson, *Film Art: An Introduction*, New York, 2004, p. 493.
[3] Interview, Ruby Rich, www.aronofsky.tripod.com.
[4] Todd McCarthy, *The Edge of Hollywood*, part of the tape series *American Cinema*, 1995. Distributed by FoxVideo, POB 900, Beverly Hills, CA 90213.
[5] Barsam, op. cit. (note 1), p. 334.
[6] Bordwell and Thompson, op. cit. (note 2), p. 487.
[7] Barsam, op. cit. (note 1), p. 306.
[8] J. Dudley Andrew, *The Major Film Theories: An Introduction*, Oxford/New York, 1976.
[9] Andrew, op. cit. (note 8), p. 56.
[10] Ibid., p. 63.
[11] Herbert Zettl, *Sight, Sound, Motion. Applied Media Aesthetics*, Wadsworth, 1999, p. 299.
[12] Zettl, op. cit. (note 11), p. 297.
[13] David Kehr, »Eerie Shots, à la ›Vertigo‹, But no Sign of Stewart«, *New York Times*, September 9, 2004.
[14] Bordwell and Thompson, op. cit. (note 2), p. 294.
[15] Ibid., p. 295.
[16] Zettl, op. cit. (note 11), p. 265.
[17] Ibid., p. 291.
[18] Ibid., pp. 301–302.
[19] Ibid., p. 304.
[20] James Berardinelli, film review, www.movie-reviews.colossus.net/movies/t/requiem-dream, 2000.

Kay Hoffmann: The digital cinema dilemma. Obstacles to digitalizing the movie screens

[1] John Chittock, »Back to the Future: the Cinema's Lessons of History«, in: Christopher Williams (ed.), *Cinema: the Beginnings and the Future*, London, 1996, p. 224.
[2] Quoted in Richard Sietmann, »Pixel-Palast. Die Studios auf dem Weg zum Digital-Kino«, in: *ct'*, 19, 2003, pp. 35–36.
[3] Patrick von Sychowski, e-mail from July 13, 2004.
[4] Kevin Kelly and Paula Parisi: »Beyond Star Wars, what's next for George Lucas«, in: *Wired*, February 1997, p. 165.

[5] In detail cf. Kay Hoffmann, *Am Ende Video – Video am Ende? Aspekte der Elektronisierung der Spielfilmproduktion*, Berlin, 1989.
[6] Oskar Meester, *Mein Weg mit dem Film*, Berlin, 1936, p. 66.
[7] Hans Vogt, *Die Erfindung des Tonfilms*, private print, Passau, 1954.
[8] Albert Abramson, *Electronic Motion Picture. A History of the Television Camera*, Berkeley/Los Angeles, 1955, p. 1.
[9] James Sterngold, »Digital Studios: It's the Economy, Stupid. George Lucas Sees Technology as a Wondrous Tool and a Cost-Cutter«, in: *The New York Times*, December 25, 1995.
[10] »Mating Film with Video for One from the Heart«, in: *American Cinematographer*, 1, 1982, p. 22.
[11] Kay Hoffmann, »Electronic Cinema – On the Way to the Digital«, in: Thomas Elsaesser and Kay Hoffmann (eds.), *Cinema Futures: Cain, Abel or Cable? The Screen Arts in the Digital Age*, Amsterdam, 1998.
[12] Herbert Spaich, *Von Atlantis bis Urania. Filmtheater in Baden-Württemberg*, Gerlingen, 2003, pp. 20, 21.
[13] Ulrich Pätzold and Horst Röper, *Multiplexe. Formen und Folgen eines neuen Kinotyps*, Düsseldorf, 1995, p. 24.
[14] »Die offiziellen Zahlen der FFA«, in: *Filmecho/Filmwoche*, 6, 2004, p. 6.
[15] Gerhard Schulze, *Die Erlebnisgesellschaft*, Frankfurt am Main/New York, 1992.
[16] Knut Hickethier, »Kino in der Erlebnisgesellschaft. Zwischen Videomarkt, Multiplex und Imax«, in: Irmbert Schenk (ed.), *Erlebnisort Kino*, Marburg, 2000, p. 161.
[17] For recent developments of special effects cf. Kay Hoffmann, »Die Digitalisierung und das Kino. Zur populären Geschichte des ›electronic cinema‹ und der Schaffung neuer Bilderwelten«, in: Lorenz Engell and Britta Neitzel (eds.), *Das Gesicht der Welt. Medien in der digitalen Kultur*, Paderborn, 2004, pp. 157–170.
[18] Tom Gunning, »The Cinema of Attraction: Early Film, its Spectator and the Avant-Garde«, in: Thomas Elsaesser (ed.), *Early Cinema: Frame, Space, Narrative*, London, 1990, pp. 56–65.
[19] Sterngold, op. cit. (note 9).
[20] Birgit Heidsieck, »22. IFP: Indies im Digital-Fieber«, in: *Filmecho/Filmwoche*, 39, 2000, p. 36.
[21] »Cannes Line Up«, in: *Scene to Screen*, 12, summer 2003, p. 5.
[22] Chris Dickinson, »Star Wars: Episode III«, in: *Scene to Screen*, 12, summer 2003, p. 6.
[23] Gundolf S. Freyermuth, »The Future of Cinema: Synthetic Realities«, in: Joachim Polzer (ed.), *The Rise and Fall of Talking Movies. The Future of Cinema: 24p*, Potsdam, 2002, pp. 49–50.
[24] Hoffmann, op. cit. (note 5), pp. 113–121.
[25] Homepage »About DCI«, July 10, 2004, www.dcila.com.
[26] Eric A. Taub, »Among Film's Ghosts, Its Future«, in: *The New York Times*, June 19, 2003.
[27] Press release, November 12, 2003, www.dcila.com/press.
[28] Andreas Fuchs, »4K bestimmt die Kino-Zukunft«, in: *Filmecho/Filmwoche*, 25, 2004, p. 39.
[29] Thomas Til Radevagen, »Kino der Zukunft – Zukunft des Kinos«, in: *Filmecho/Filmwoche*, 48, 1996, p. 16.

30 Bernd Jetschin, »Auf die schnellere Spur gewech-selt«, in: Filmecho / Filmwoche, 25, 2004, p. 10.

31 Bernd Jetschin, »Sicherheit und Qualität in der gesamten Kette«, in: Filmecho / Filmwoche, 25, 2004, p. 8.

32 Presentation by Patrick von Sychowski at the IAMHIST conference in Leicester, July 16–19, 2003.

33 Jetschin, op. cit. (note 30), p. 10.

34 Press release, June 25, 2002, www.kodak.com.

35 Birgit Heidsieck, »Die Kinos müssen keinen Cent dazubezahlen«, in: Filmecho / Filmwoche, 16, 2004, pp. 16–17.

36 http://news.bbc.co.uk/go/pr/fr/-/1/hi/entertain-ment/film/3714937.stm, May 18, 2004.

37 Andreas Kramer, »Mehr als Fernsehen auf der Leinwand«, in: Filmecho / Filmwoche, 22, 2004, p. 15.

38 Paula Parisi, »Cameron Angle«, in: Wired, April, 1996, pp. 178–179.

39 Freyermuth, op. cit. (note 23), pp. 52, 53.

Jean-Pierre Geuens: The digital world picture

1 The Sony 24-frame digital camera with its Panavi-sion lens has already been tested by different direc-tors. Digital projection made its debut during the re-lease of The Phantom Menace, while Bounce was »dropped« from orbiting satellites directly into some specially equipped theaters.

2 Cf. past issues of: RES, Film & Video, Millimeter, DV, Videomaker, etc.

3 For more on this, check: »The Future of Film-making«, in: American Cinematographer, vol. 81, no. 9, September 2000, pp. 73–90, and »Reflec-tions on the Future« (a compilation of interviews with directors of photography by An Tran and Tommy Nguyen), www.cinematography-world.com.

4 Ron Magid, »Master of His Universe: George Lucas Discusses The Phantom Menace and the Impact of Digital Filmmaking on the Industry's Fu-ture«, in: American Cinematographer, vol. 80, no. 9, September 1999, pp. 30, 32.

5 The seminal book on this topic remains George P. Landow: Hypertext: The Convergence of Contem-porary Cultural Theory and Technology, Baltimore, MD, 1992. Closer to home, Wide Angle has devoted an entire issue to different aspects of the digital rev-olution in vol. 21, no. 1, January 1999.

6 Martin Heidegger, Basic Writings, David Farrell Krell and William Lovitt (eds.), San Francisco, CA., 1977, p. 294.

7 For more on this, cf. my essay, »Visuality and Power: The Work of the Steadicam«, in: Film Quar-terly, vol. 47, no. 2, winter 1993/94, pp. 8–17.

8 Walter Murch, In the Blink of an Eye: A Perspective on Film Editing, Los Angeles, 1995, pp. 75–76.

9 The dramatic incident was recorded in Michael Leszczylowski's film, Directed by Andrei Tarkovsky, 1988.

10 George Spiro Dibie from the International Cine-matographers Guild has brought attention to a not so cryptic appeal by Sony to movie producers to economize by using video crews as opposed to film crews. George Spiro Dibie, »Shame on the New York Times«, www.cameraguild.com/news/guild/shame_nyt.htm.

11 My argument is based on observations gleaned in student and low-budget filmmaking. On more professional sets, the cost of the project may be enough to keep talent and crew in check.

12 Lev Manovich, »The Logic of Selection«, 2000, http://rhizome.org.

13 With this in mind, let us also recall Karl Mann-heim's insight: »The new impulses, intuitions and fresh approaches to the world, if they have no time to mature in small groups, will be apprehended by the masses as mere stimuli.« Karl Mannheim, in: Man and Society in an Age of Reconstruction, New York, 1941, p. 87.

14 Anne-Marie Willis, »Digitisation and the Living Death of Photography«, in: Philip Hayward (ed.), Culture, Technology and Creativity in the Late Twentieth Century, London, 1990, p. 204.

15 A good analysis of the impact of the digital image on the notion of realism in the cinema can be found in Stephen Prince's essay, »True Lies: Perceptual Realism, Digital Images, and Film Theory«, in: Film Quarterly, vol. 49, no. 3, Spring 1996, pp. 27–37.

16 Jean Baudrillard, Simulations, New York, 1983, p. 4.

17 Magid, op. cit. (note 4), p. 27.

18 Quoted in Philip W. Jackson, John Dewey and the Lessons of Art, New Haven, CT, 1998, p. 22.

19 Ibid., p. 3.

20 Walter Benjamin, Das Kunstwerk im Zeitalter seiner technischen Reproduzierbarkeit, quoted from Walter Benjamin, »The Work of Art in the Age of Mechanical Reproduction«, in: Gerald Mast, Marshall Cohen, and Leo Braudy (eds.), Film Theory and Criticism, 4th ed., New York, 1992, p. 672. In this es-say, the lack of direct contact between actors and au-dience is used by Benjamin as an example of loss of aura made possible by the machinery of cinema.

21 For more on the tricks of the trade, check Uta Hagen, Respect for Acting, New York, 1973.

22 Quoted in Beaumont Newhall, The History of Photography, Museum of Modern Art, New York, 1982, p. 78.

23 Magid, op. cit. (note 4), p. 32.

24 Scott McQuire, »Digital Dialectics: The Paradox of Cinema in a Studio Without Walls«, in: Historical Journal of Film, Radio and Television, 19, 3, p. 18.

25 Ron Magid, »Edit-Suite Filmmaking«, in: Ameri-can Cinematographer, vol. 80, no. 9, September 1999, p. 120.

26 David Tanaka, quoted in Ellen Wolff, »Directing in Post«, in: Millimeter, June 1999, p. 32.

27 Ken McGorry, »Optical Illusions«, in: Post, June 1999, pp. 70, 72.

28 Lev Manovich, »Cinema as Cultural Interface«, 1997, p. 10; a paper available on his website, www.manovich.net.

29 Wolff, op. cit. (note 26), p. 32.

30 Martin Heidegger, The Question Regarding Technology and Other Essays, New York, 1977, p. 134.

31 Ibid., p. 129.

32 Ibid., p. 128.

33 Ibid., p. 135.

34 Ibid., p. 131.

35 David Michael Levin, »Psychopathology in the Epoch of Nihilism«, in: Pathologies of the Modern Self: Postmodern Studies on Narcissism, Schizo-phrenia, and Depression, New York, 1987, p. 48.

36 Magid, op. cit. (note 4), pp. 26–27, 30, 32–33, 35.

37 George Lucas, narrated by Diane Sawyer, »Sixty Minutes«, CBS/KNXT, Los Angeles, March 28, 1999.

38 Marcel Hénaff, »Sade, the Mechanization of the Libertine Body, and the Crisis of Reason«, in: An-drew Feenberg and Alastair Hannay (eds.), Tech-nologies and the Politics of Knowledge, Blooming-ton, IN, 1995, pp. 232–233.

39 Heidegger, Basic Writings, op. cit. (note 6), p. 310.

40 Everybody in the business was shocked to learn that The Celebration (Thomas Vinterberg, 1999) had been shot with a camera that retailed for less than $ 2,500. Today many students have cameras more expensive than that.

41 Alexandre Astruc, »The Birth of a New Avant-Garde: La Caméra-Stylo«, in: Peter Graham (ed.), The New Wave, New York, 1968, p. 22.

42 Ibid.

43 Ibid.

44 Danny Boyle, quoted in: Cynthia Wisehart, »Prac-tical Virtues: Four Directors Discuss the Limits of Digital Production«, in: Millimeter, November 1997, p. 34.

45 Kim Reed, »DV and the Independent Filmmaker: Jon Jost Leaves Film for Digital Video« in: DV, Sep-tember 1999, p. 42.

46 This is of course Hollywood's worst nightmare: Judy Irola, ASC, for instance, noticed that on a digi-tal movie she recently shot she used four crew members as opposed to the usual fifteen. »So eleven people were out of work«, she wistfully concluded, in »Reflections on the Future«, op. cit. (note 3), p. 2.

47 The work of Max Ophüls, Miklós Jancsó, and Theodoros Angelopoulos comes to mind.

48 Mike Figgis, »Working Without a Net«, in: Film & Video, April 2000, p. 55.

49 Ellen Wolff, »Fade to Black: Mike Figgis, Director«, in: Millimeter, January 2000, p. 126.

50 Gilles Deleuze and Félix Guattari, Anti-Oedipus: Capitalism and Schizophrenia, Minneapolis, MN, 1983, pp. 244–248.

51 For a clear explanation of Benjamin's notion of phantasmagoria, cf. Susan Buck-Morss, Walter Benjamin and the Arcades Project, Cambridge, MA, 1991.

52 Figgis, op. cit. (note 48), p. 59.

53 Quoted in Stéphane Bouquet and Emmanuel Burdeau, »Dans le laboratoire de La Recherche: Entretien avec Raoul Ruiz«, in: Cahiers du Cinéma, 535, May 1999, p. 52 (my trans.).

Vinzenz Hediger: Making movies is like making cars, only more fun

1 On word-of-mouth advertising cf. Fritz Iversen's essay in Hediger, Vonderau, 2004.

2 Epes W. Sargent, »Advertising for Exhibitors«, in: Moving Picture World, vol. 11, no. 12, March 23, 1912, p. 1058.

3 »Francis X. Bushman on lecture tour«, in: Moving Picture World, vol. 15, no. 7, February 15, 1913, p. 658.

4 »Thomas H. Ince Publicity Department Launches Important National Campaign«, in: Moving Picture World, vol. 44, no. 2, April 10, 1920, p. 282.

5 »Ince Exploitation Staff Launches Three-Cornered Cooperative Drive«, in: *Exhibitors Herald*, vol. 11, no. 6, August 7, 1920, p. 39.

6 »Pictures and People«, in: *Motion Picture News*, March 10, 1928.

7 Victor M. Shapiro, »The Hollywood Scene«, in: *Motion Picture Herald*, October 6, 1934.

8 In the age of the mega-blockbuster, advertising slots in film programs featuring major box-office attractions such as *Lord of the Rings* have become a coveted commodity. While in the last three decades, trailers were already distributed free of charge to theaters, distributors are now actually paying exhibitors for the screening of trailers ahead of certain films. Estimates are that since 2001, studios have been spending up to $ 500.000 a year for agreements with cinema chains to run trailers in specific slots. Cf. Stephen Galloway, »Pay for Play?«, in: *Hollywood Reporter*, June 24–30, 2003, pp. 18–19.

9 MGM Plan Special *Teahouse Trailer*, in: *Motion Picture Herald*, vol. 205, no. 11, December 15, 1956, p. 21.

10 For the construction of authorship and authenticity claims through the film's paratext cf. also Lutz Nitsche, *Hitchcock – Greenaway – Tarantino. Paratextuelle Attraktionen des Autorenkinos*, Stuttgart / Weimar, 2002.

11 Produced by special service companies rather than by the now defunct trailer or short film departments of the studio system, the featurettes also served as springboard for aspiring young directors.

12 For an analysis of this shift cf. also Janet Staiger, »Seeing Stars«, in: Christine Gledhill (ed.), *Stardom. Industry of Desire*, London, 1991.

13 Cf. in particular Mats Björkin, »Industrial Greta. Some thoughts on an Industrial Film«, in: John Fullerton and Jan Olsson (eds.), *Nordic Explorations. Film Before 1930*, London, 1999; Manfred Rasch et al., *Industriefilm 1948–1959*, Essen 2003; Ramón Reichert, »The popularization of Productivity. The industry film of Austrian Productivity Center 1951 to 1959«, in: *Conference Proceeding. The Seventh Biennal National Labour History Conference*, Canberra, 2001.

14 Another striking example is a Vitaphone Short from 1934, entitled *A Trip Through a Hollywood Studio*, which gives a full list of all major Hollywood studios. About the Fox Studios, the commentator says: »The Fox film studios … built like a modern city. These studios employ thousands of workers with an annual payroll worth millions of dollars …« And later, about the Paramount studios: »There we see the administration buildings housing the executives, directors, writers and supervisors.«

15 »The Play Is the Thing, Motion Picture Uses«, in: *Motography. Exploiting Motion Pictures*, vol. XII, no. 7, August 15, 1914, pp. 245–248.

Frederick Wasser: The transnationalization of Hollywood

1 By »Bollywood« I mean the popular films that are regularly turned out in Bombay in a variety of languages, although I understand that Hindi dominates. These films have always had international distribution to the Indian and Arabic diaspora. Recently it is clear that distribution is attempting to cross into new territories perhaps in imitation of Hollywood. I do not mean the entire Indian film industry is Bollywood.

2 The only member of the MPPC that put much effort into feature level filmmaking was Vitagraph. They imported *The Life of Moses* in multiple reels and showed it as a weekly serial. However, their efforts were half hearted compared to the immigrant group who showed multiple reels as a complete show.

3 It should be noted that D. W. Griffith and the financiers of *Birth of A Nation* were not part of the immigrant cohort. Their success served only to point the way for Zukor et al. who were willing to invest in vertical integration.

4 Cannon film properties were absorbed into another American film studio when Crédit Lyonnais foreclosed on the bankrupt MGM in 1992. In 1996, MGM reverted to American ownership.

5 *Variety*, February 13, 1995, p 1.

6 Even in 1964, the acclaimed Italian producer, Carlo Ponti, was complaining that the French were ruining their industry by proclaiming film as an art and film directors as all-powerful artists, in: *The New York Times*, March 21, 1964.

7 This copycatting also extends to television from the 1960/70s *Til Death Do Us Part* and *Steptoe and Son* to the 2000s *Survivor* and *Big Brother*. However, at least in television the markets remain relatively confined to national audiences. Movie copies such as *Three Men and a Baby* allow Hollywood to make more money from a global audience that the French original simply did not have the marketing power to do.

8 Justin Wyatt summarizes high concept as »the look, the hook, and the book«, by which he means the look of the images, the marketing hooks, and the reduced narratives are distinguishable aspects of a high concept film, Justin Wyatt, *High Concept: Movies and Marketing in Hollywood*, Austin, TX, 1994, p. 22.

9 My comment about the return of Eisenstein to a Soviet style of filmmaking is valid despite the fact that upon his return he abandoned his original commitment to montage. Nonetheless, he worked within a national film style even if it differed now from the 1920s.

Claudia Liebrand: Negotiations of genre and gender in contemporary Hollywood film

1 This essay refers back to an anthology edited by myself and Ines Steiner, *Hollywood hybrid. Genre und Gender im zeitgenössischen Mainstream-Film*, Marburg, 2004, as well as my monograph *Gender-Topographien. Kulturwissenschaftliche Lektüren von Hollywoodfilmen der Jahrhundertwende*, Cologne 2003. Both books attempt to superimpose genre and gender theories and to bring them into a productive tension.

2 Susan Hayward, *Cinema Studies. The Key Concepts*, London / New York, 2000, p. 131.

3 Cf. Christian Metz, »The Imaginary Signifier«, in: *Screen* 16, 2, summer 1975, pp. 14–76. For a critique of Metz's conception cf. also Tag Gallagher, »Shoot-out at the Genre Corral. Problems in the ›Evolution‹ of the Western«, in: Barry Keith Grant (ed.), *Film Genre Reader II*, Austin, TX, 1995, pp. 246–260, here p. 246; Steve Neale, *Genre and Hollywood*, London / New York, 2000, p. 211 ff.

4 Only conditionally, though – early westerns are extremely self-reflective, too, as has been shown by Gallagher: »›Self-consciousness‹ is too readily assumed to have come to movies only in reaction to Hollywood's so-called ›classic codes‹ (whose existence, never demonstrated, is at least to be questioned), while such consciousness has traditionally been considered a necessary ingredient of any mature work of art and would certainly seem to be abundant in pictures of the 1930s, where style, far from being ›invisible‹, is so overwhelming. It is perhaps natural that people today, attuned to contemporary film styles and only vaguely acquainted with the past, should feel they are onto something new when in an ostentatiously revisionist film by Robert Altman (*MacCabe and Mrs. Miller*, 1971, or *Buffalo Bill and the Indians*, 1976) they perceive references to motifs and conventions from other westerns made twenty or thirty years earlier and thus cast forcibly into a ›straight man's‹ role for the revisionist's lampooning. But they forget that even those putatively naïve classics as *Stagecoach* were similarly perceived by audiences in 1939; indeed, *Stagecoach* in particular is a virtual anthology of gags, motifs, conventions, scenes, situations, tricks, and characters drawn from past westerns … A superficial glance at film history suggests cyclicism rather than evolution« (Tag Gallagher, op. cit., note 3, p. 252).

5 Cf. Tom Gunning, »The Cinema of Attractions. Early Film, Its Spectator and the Avant-Garde«, 1983, in: Thomas Elsaesser and Adam Barker (eds.), *Early Cinema: Space, Frame, Narrative*, London, 1990, pp. 56–62.

6 Neale, op. cit. (note 3), p. 219. Genre theory entered Anglo-American film studies in 1970 at the very latest, and replaced the auteur-centred way of looking at films.

7 Ibid., p. 211 ff., and p. 248 ff.

8 *Philadelphia* (USA, 1993), directed by Jonathan Demme, written by Ron Nyswaner; starring: Tom Hanks, Denzel Washington, Antonio Banderas, Jason Robards, Mary Steenburgen; director of photography: Tak Fujimoto; edited by Craig McKay; music by Howard Shore; costume design by Colleen Atwood; Tristar Pictures, Clinica Estetico Ltd. For an in-depth genre-gender reading of *Philadelphia* cf. my essay »Melodrama Goes Gay. Jonathan Demmes *Philadelphia*«, in: Claudia Liebrand and Ines Steiner (eds.), *Hollywood Hybrid*, op. cit. (note 1), pp. 171–191.

9 *The Others* (USA/F/E, 2001), written and directed by Alejandro Amenábar; starring: Nicole Kidman, Fionnula Flanagan, Christopher Eccleston, Alakina Mann, James Bentley, Eric Sykes, Elaine Cassidy; director of photography: Javier Aguirresarobe; edited by Nacho Ruiz Capillas; music by Alejandro Amenábar; costume design by Sonia Grande; Miramax Films. An in-depth reading of *The Others* can be found in my monograph *Gender-Topographien*, op. cit. (note 1), pp. 197–223.

10 The actor was also given a Berliner Bär, a Golden Globe, and an MTV Movie Award for this role.

11 Michael Walker, »Melodrama and the American Cinema«, in: *Movie* 29/30, 1982, pp. 2–38; here: p. 17; quoted after Steve Neale, op. cit. (note 3), p. 202.

12 Jeanine Basinger, *A Woman's View. How Hollywood Spoke to Women 1930–1960*, London, 1993,

p. 20. Basinger highlights the problem that arises once melodrama and woman's film are regarded as one and the same: »Eliminate more than half of the films that are concerned with women and their fates, among them Rosalind Russell's career comedies, musical biographies of real-life women, combat films featuring brave nurses on Bataan, and westerns in which women drive cattle west and men over the brink« (ibid., p. 7).

13 Neale, op. cit. (note 3), p. 186.

14 We may not be dealing with body-centred action here, but an altercation in court is as agonal as, say, a duel.

15 The reciprocative superimposing of »melodrama of action« and »melodrama of passion« may also be described as a confrontation of the increasing effeminisation of Beckett (who becomes more and more damaged, afflicted, therefore »female«) with the increasing virilisation of Joe Miller (who becomes more and more competent, confident, therefore »male«).

16 Mary Ann Doane, »The ›Woman's Film‹. Possession and Address«, in: Mary Ann Doane, Patricia Mellencamp, and Linda Williams (eds.), Re-Vision. Essays in Feminist Film Criticism, Los Angeles, 1984, pp. 67–82, here p. 79.

17 Claudia Öhlschläger has examined the striptease in a context of concepts of voyeurism and quotes Lo Duca (ed.), Das Moderne Lexikon der Erotik von A–Z. Eine reich illustrierte aktuelle Enzyklopädie in zehn Bänden, Munich/Vienna/Basel, 1963. This encyclopedia – according to Öhlschläger – describes striptease as a »›… spectacle incorporating the total undressing of a woman to a state of complete nudity, set to the rhythm of a certain music …‹ ›The striptease‹ … wants to awaken ›the man's erotic desire within the framework of a visual presentation‹, this ›spectacle‹ is based on ›the strong erotic arousal that usually occurs at the sight of the female body.‹ … One thing [states Öhlschläger] is conspicuous in this context: The striptease is in so far a gender specific matter as it ascribes certain diverging modes of behaviour to the sexes, man and woman. It is the man who, since he is meant to be the active part, directs his eyes towards the arousing female body, and it is the woman who may be moving, but who still puts her body on display, who presents that body to the spectator's look … The positions of ›observing subject‹ and ›observed object‹ may be turned around, but nothing ever changes as far as the ›gendered‹ structure of the dialectics of seeing and being seen is concerned.« (Claudia Öhlschläger, Die unsägliche Lust des Schauens. Die Konstruktion der Geschlechter im voyeuristischen Text, Freiburg im Breisgau, 1996, p. 136 and sqq.)

18 Jacques Lacan, »The Mirror Stage as Formative of the Function of the I as Revealed in Psychoanalytic Experience«, in: Jacques Lacan, Schriften 1, ed. by Norbert Haas, Weinheim, 1991, pp. 61–70.

19 Slavoj Žižek, »Das genießerische Gesetz«, in: the same author, Die Metastasen des Genießens. Sechs erotische Versuche, Vienna, 1996, pp. 145–166. The fundamental links between sexuality, »gender crimes« and judicial institutions have been highlighted by Michel Foucault in: Der Wille zum Wissen. Sexualität und Wahrheit I, Frankfurt am Main, 1983, p. 37 ff.

20 In Philadelphia, too, homosexuality is scrutinized as the obscene reverse of homosociality.

21 The fact that a female lawyer – assisted by an African-American colleague – represents Wyant, Wheeler, Hellerman, Tetlow and Brown is staged as a strategic manœuvre by the law firm intended to demonstrate its political correctness in court.

22 Beckett is also effeminized through the concept of masquerade, as such concepts play an important role in – literary and philosophical – gender discourses. Cf. Liliane Weissberg (ed.), Weiblichkeit als Maskerade, Frankfurt am Main, 1994.

23 The amount of aggression »passing« characters can trigger is depicted in a particularly impressive manner in Boys Don't Cry (USA ,1999), directed by Kimberly Peirce, or in Devil in a Blue Dress (USA, 1995), directed by Carl Franklin.

24 Cf. among others, Judith Butler, »Gender Is Burning. Questions of Appropriation and Subversion«, in: the same author, Bodies that Matter, London/New York, 1993, pp. 121–140.

25 Sirk's Imitation of Life (a remake of John M. Stahl's film of the same title from 1934) negotiates several configurations of passing; the topic is not limited to Mary Jane and her »passing for white«.

26 Quoted from Elisabeth Bronfen, Heimweh. Illusionsspiele in Hollywood, Berlin, 1999, p. 298.

27 Peter Brooks, among others, repeatedly refers to the prehistory of the cinematic melodrama: the stage melodrama, for which a manichaean battle between good and evil is characteristic: »Without wanting to go too much into the characteristics of stage melodramas, it can nevertheless be said that in its case, we are faced with an intensively emotional and ethical kind of drama which is based on the manichaean fight between good and evil.« (Peter Brooks: »The Melodramatic Imagination«, in: Michael Palm and Christian Cargnelli, eds., Und immer wieder geht die Sonne auf. Texte zum Melodramatischen im Film, Vienna, 1994, pp. 35–63, here: p. 49 ff.)

28 The Montgomery Bus Boycott of 1955 – an episode central to the American Civil Rights Movement – was sparked by the refusal of Rosa Parks to abandon her seat in one of the (segregated) buses for the benefit of a white man.

29 Later, at the office, Seidman confronts Beckett about the colour of his skin. SEIDMAN: »What's wrong with your face?« BECKETT: »What's wrong with my face? You want to know what's wrong with my face? I've got a skin condition. Next question, Bob?«

30 Carol J. Clover, Men, Women, and Chain Saws. Gender in the Modern Horror Film, New York, 1992.

31 Linda Williams, »Painful Pleasures«, review of Carol J. Clover, Men, Women, and Chain Saws. Gender in the Modern Horror Film, in: Sight & Sound 2, 4, August 1992, p. 45.

32 Splatter movies, admittedly, make references to high culture patterns, too – cf. Tromeo and Juliet, directed by Lloyd Kaufman, USA, 1996.

33 Barbara Creed, The Monstrous Feminine. Film, Feminism, Psychoanalysis, London, 1993.

Robert Blanchet: Deep impact. Emotion and performativity in contemporary blockbuster cinema

1 A similar approach has been taken by Linda Williams with her concept of the »body genre«. Linda Williams, »Film Bodies: Gender, Genre, and Excess« (1992), in : Leo Braudy, Marshall Cohen (eds.), Film Theory and Criticism: Introductory Readings, 5th ed., New York, 1999, pp. 702–707.

2 Cf. Robert Blanchet, Blockbuster. Ästhetik, Ökonomie und Geschichte des postklassischen Hollywoodkinos, Marburg 2003, pp. 204–208.

3 Cf. Michel Chion, Audio-Vision: Sound on Screen (translation by Claudia Gorbman), New York, 1994, pp. 145–148.

4 Tomlinson Holman, Sound For Film And Television, Boston, London 1997, p. 45.

5 Chion, op. cit. (note 3), p. 61.

6 Ibid., pp. 149–151.

7 Ibid., pp. 95, 109–114, 224.

8 Ibid., pp. 114–117, 223.

9 Ibid., pp. 112.

10 Cf., David Bordwell, »Die Hard – und die Rückkehr des klassischen Hollywood-Kinos«, in: Andreas Rost (ed.), Der schöne Schein der Künstlichkeit, Frankfurt am Main, 1995, pp. 194–196.

11 Cf. Barry Salt, Film Style & Technology: History & Analysis [1983], London, 2nd ed., 1992, pp. 147, 174, 214–216, 239–240, 249, 266, 283, 296; David Bordwell, Janet Staiger and Kristin Thompson, The Classical Hollywood Cinema. Film Style & Mode of Production to 1960, New York/ London, 1985, pp. 61, 304–305, 361–362.

12 Interviewed in: Prairie Miller, »Armageddon: Interview with Michael Bay«, in: Mini Reviews, A Cineman Syndicate Feature, 1998, www.minireviews.com/interviews/bay.htm.

13 Interviewed in: Prairie Miller, »Saving Private Ryan: Steven Spielberg Interview«, in: Mini Reviews, A Cineman Syndicate Feature, 1998, www.minireviews.com/interviews/spiel.htm.

14 Cf. Murray Smith, Engaging Characters: Fiction, Emotion, and the Cinema, Oxford, 1995, p. 96.

15 Ibid., pp. 85–86, 96, 102.

16 Ibid., pp. 102.

17 Ibid.

18 A subjective or semi-subjective shot which, comparable to a flight simulator, makes us feel like being in a moving object ourselves.

19 John L. Austin, How To Do Things With Words, 1965; 2nd ed., Cambridge, MA, 1999, p. 36.

20 Roger Odin, »For a Semio-Pragmatics of Film«, in: Warren Buckland (ed.), The Film Spectator: From Sign to Mind, Amsterdam, 1995, pp. 218–219.

Volker Pietsch: Body Snatchers

1 Wood isolates basic repression of drives as the difference between humans and animals, while characterizing culturally specific forms of repression as surplus repression. Cf. Robin Wood, »An introduction to the American Horror Film«, in: American Nightmare, Toronto, 1979, pp. 7 ff.

Christian W. Thomsen: Mixed realities. From HAL 9000 to *The Matrix* – computer and androids in contemporary science-fiction movies

1 For details cf. Gudula Moritz' contribution to this book.
2 Cf. Georg Seeßlen and Fernand Jung, *Stanley Kubrick und seine Filme*, Marburg, 2001, pp. 157–187. There you find comprehensive bibliographical material.
3 Cf. *IMDb*, *Tron*, trivia.
4 Cf. Hans Moravec, »The Universal Robot«, in: Karl Gerbel (ed.), *Out of Control, Ars Electronica 91*, Linz, 1991, pp. 13–28
5 Cf. Harry Harrison, *Mechanismo*, Rastatt, 1978. Good for 1970s visions of space ships and supercomputers.
6 Robert Ebert, »Johnny Mnemonic«, review in: *IMDb*, May 26, 1995.
7 William Gibson on the making of Johnny Mnemonic, in: *Wired*, June 1995, »Notes on a Process«, pp. 156–159, 204.
8 Vernor Vinge interviewed by Kevin Kelly in *Wired*, June 1995, p. 161.
9 Christian Jürgens, »Keanu im Wunderland – Ein Cybertraum. Matrix ist das Kino-Abenteuer des Jahres«, *Die Zeit*, 25, 1999.
10 There are, indeed, philosophers, who do not only believe that *Matrix* raises the same philosophical questions as classical philosophy and literature in popular form, but that it is the most philosophical film ever produced. Cf. William Irwin, (ed.), *The Matrix and Philosophy. Welcome to the Desert of the Real*, Chicago, 2002.
11 Cf. Christian Jürgens, op. cit. (note 9).
12 George Lucas, quoted in Robert Blanchet, *Blockbuster. Ästhetik, Ökonomie und Geschichte des Postklassischen Hollywoodfilms*, Marburg, 2003, 3.3. »Ereigniskino, Attraktionen, Ironie: Hollywood in den neunziger Jahren«, p. 147.
13 Excellent survey in Blanchet, op. cit., 3.3.
14 Cf. Julius Wiedemann, *Digital Beauties. 2D & 3D Computer Generated Digital Models, Virtual Idols and Characters*, Cologne, 2001.

Christian W. Thomsen: The recycling of myths in Hollywood science-fiction films exemplified by Roland Emmerich's *Stargate* (1994), Luc Besson's *The Fifth Element* (1997) and Andrew Nichol's *S1mOne* (2002)

1 Wiebke Hoheisel, in her introduction to Jan Assmann's article »Mythomotorik der Erinnerung. Fundierende und kontrapräsentische Erinnerung« (1992), in: *Texte zur modernen Mythentheorie*, Stuttgart, 2003, pp. 277–290, here: introduction, p. 277.
2 Ibid.
3 Wilfried Barner, Anke Detken, and Jörg Wesche, »Mythos und Mythentheorie«, introduction to: *Texte zur modernen Mythentheorie*, op. cit., (note 1), pp. 7–23, here: pp. 8–10.
4 Naturally, by now some film theorists have come to believe that *The Matrix* is the most philosophically profound film ever made, cf. William Irwin, (ed.), *The Matrix and Philosophy. Welcome to the Desert of the Real*, Chicago, 2002.
5 Quoted from the biographical entry for Roland Emmerich on the IMDb (Internet Movie Database).
6 Cf. Hans Blumenberg, »Arbeit am Mythos«, in: *Texte zur modernen Mythentheorie*, 1979, op. cit. (note 1), pp. 194–218.
7 Cf. Siegfried Moranz, *Ägyptische Religion*, Stuttgart, 1972, pp. 6–43.
8 Vincent Canly, »For de Mille, Moses' Egypt Was Really America«, in: *New York Times*, March 25, 1984, pp. 19 ff.
9 Hoheisel, op. cit. (note 1), p. 277.
10 Ruth Fischer in her introduction to Jean Jacques Wunnenberger: »Mytho-phorie. Formen und Transformationen des Mythos«, in: *Texte zur modernen Mythentheorie*, 1994, op. cit. (note 1), pp. 290–303, here: introduction, p. 288.
11 Ibid., p. 298.
12 Vintila Ivenceanu and Josef Schweikhardt, *Zerokörper. Der abgeschaffte Mensch*, in: Peter Engelmann (ed.), *Passagen X Media*, Vienna, 1997, p. 14.
13 Quoted from the contribution concerning sirens, in: *Antike Mythen und ihre Rezeption. Ein Lexikon*, Leipzig, 2003, pp. 229–235.
14 Barbara Vinken, »Puppe und Automat. Das fetischistische Szenario der Modefotografie«, in: Gerhard Johann Lischka (ed.), *Kunstkörper. Werbekörper*, Cologne, 2000, pp. 81–90, quote: p. 85.
15 Ibid., p. 16.

Gudula Simone Moritz: Pentagon Pictures. How Hollywood has its scripts censored by Washington

1 Peter Körte, »Wie Hollywood-Produzent Jerry Bruckheimer aus dem Krieg gegen den Terror eine Fernsehserie macht«, in: *Frankfurter Allgemeine Sonntagszeitung*, May 26, 2002.
2 Lawrence H. Suid, *Guts and Glory: The Making of the American Military Image in Film*, Lexington, KY, 2002, p. 33.
3 Ibid., p. 496.
4 Ibid., p. 499.
5 Claimed by Andrian Kreye, »Spottbilliger Jet-Set. Strubs Strategie: Das Pentagon unterstützt Hollywood – aber nur bei Filmen, die auf Linie bleiben«, in: *Süddeutsche Zeitung*, December 4, 2001.
6 Cit. from Sönke Iwersen, »Panzer für Werbefilme: Wie die US-Filmindustrie mit dem Militär zusammenarbeitet«, in: *Stuttgarter Zeitung*, March 26, 2003.
7 From a memo of June 29, 1993 from Army spokesman Lieutenant Mitchell E. Marovitz to Philip Strub, printed in: *Harper's Magazine*, November 2001.

Angela Krewani: Hollywood's new brand. Independent film production

Bernstorff, M., »Pixel Peep Holes. Sex, Lies and Videotape«, in: Frank Arnold (ed.), *Experimente in Hollywood. Steven Soderbergh und seine Filme*, Mainz, 2003, pp. 145–154.
Biskind, P., *Down and Dirty Pictures*, New York, 2004.
Chagollan, S., »Academy Embraces the Sundance Kid: Honorary Oscar: Robert Redford«, in: *Variety*, March 3, 2002, www.highbeam.com.
DiOrio, C., »Mouse Roars at B.O.: Disney, Miramax Dominate as Summer Looms«, in: *Variety*, April 7, 2003, www.highbeam.com.
Distelmeyer, J., »Drei Farben – oder: Wer hat Angst vor Gelb, Weiß, Blau? Vier Schritte zum Erfolg von TRAFFIC«, in: Frank Arnold (ed.), op. cit., pp. 225–235.
Garvin, T., »Independents Find Money Available for the Right Price«, in: *Variety*, March 2, 1998, www.highbeam.com.
Germain, D., »Sundance Celebrates 20 Years of Film«, 18, 2001, *AP Online*.
Kramer, P., »General Cinema at 75: from one Theater in 1922 to Megaplex Builder«, in: *Variety*, December 22, 1997, www.highbeam.com.
Kuschnerus, M., »Mambo mit dem Mainstream. *Ocean's Eleven*«, in: Frank Arnold (ed.), op. cit., pp. 237–250.
Levy, E, *Cinema of Outsiders. The Rise of American Independent Film*, New York, London, 1999.
LoBrutto, V., *The Encyclopedia of American Independent Filmmaking*, London, 2002.
Lyons, C., »Opposites Attract: Disney and Miramax Fill Each Other's Need, and Feed the Bottom Line«, in: *Variety*, October 27, 2003, www.highbeam.com.
Reed, K., »Steven Soderbergh's Return to Roots. Why did Soderbergh shoot *Full Frontal* on miniDV«, in: *Digital Video Magazine*, September 1, 2002, www.highbeam.com.
Roman, M., »Filmmakers get into Designers' Pants«, in: *Variety*, September 7, 1998, www.highbeam.com.
Rosenbaum, J., »Safe and Sorry«, in: *Artforum International*, January 12, 1995, www.highbeam.com.
Soderbergh, S., »Rat Pack Drowned in Ocean«, in: *Teletext.co.uk*, February 2002, in: Kuschnerus, op. cit., p. 237.
Tucker, S., »Panic in the Pentagon«, in: *The Humanist*, May 1, 1993, www.highbeam.com.
Unsigned, »Sundance Channel Announces Major Programming Inititative«, in: *Business Wire*, October 20, 1998, www.highbeam.com.
Unsigned, »Sundance Channel Distribution Increase Nearly 50% ...«, in: *Business Wire*, December 1, 2000, www.highbeam.com.
Wyatt, J. (1998), »The Formation of the ›Major Independent‹. Miramax, New Line and the New Hollywood« [Miramax Independent] M. S., in: Steve Neale, *Contemporary Hollywood Cinema*, London/New York, pp. 74–90.

1 Also cf. Frederick Wasser on this issue.
2 Cf. www.sundancechannel.com.
3 The MPPA film rating system was introduced in 1968 as an alternative to federal regulation of motion picture content. It figures as a kind of self regulatory system, controlled by the Motion Picture Association of America (MPPA). Current MPPA ratings are: G – general audiences; PG – parental guidance suggested; PG-13 – parents strongly cautioned, may be inappropriate for children under 13; R – restricted: under 17 requires accompanying parent or adult guardian; NC-17 or X – children under 17 not admitted. July 8, 2004, www.wordiq.com/definition/MPPA_film_rating_system.

Randi Gunzenhäuser: Hyperkinetic images. Hollywood and computer games

1 Since their respective effects on movies cannot be clearly differentiated, I refer to both computer and video games when I speak of digital forms of entertainment.

2 Steven Poole, *Trigger Happy: The Inner Life of Video Games*, London, 2000, p. 19 f.

3 Welf Kienast defines the action genre as hybrid in »Actionfilm«, in: *Metzler Lexikon Kultur der Gegenwart. Themen und Theorien, Formen und Institutionen seit 1945*, Stuttgart / Weimar, 2000, p. 7.

4 As early as in 2002, the German computer magazine *GameStar* took a poll on their web page gamestar.de asking for the most popular computer games in 2001. Among 1,500 participants, action games were by far the most popular genre – 31.9 % voted for ego shooters, for tactical action games 15 %. »Umfrage: Was sind die beliebtesten Computerspiel-Genres?«, in: *GameStar*, 1, 2002, p. 10.

5 Cf. Tom Gunning, »The Cinema of Attractions: Early Film, Its Spectator and the Avant-Garde«, in: Thomas Elsaesser (ed.), *Early Cinema: Space, Frame, Narrative*, London, 1990. Gunning argues that the attraction survives, in a »tamed« form, »as a component of narrative films, more evident in some genres (e.g. the musical) than in others«, p. 57. Scott Bukatman doubts that the aspect of attraction necessarily gets tamed in narrative film. Cf. his »Zooming Out: The End of Offscreen Space«, in: Jon Lewis (ed.), *The New American Cinema*, Durham, 1998, pp. 248–272, especially p. 254.

6 *Streetfighter* and its successors are still being adapted to many different gaming platforms even today. Cf. the »Retro« section of *Games*[TM], 3, 2004, p. 86.

7 Poole, op. cit. (note 2), p. 45.

8 They have been part of B-pictures, horror, and snuff movies.

9 Jonathan Clements and Helen McCarthy, *The Anime Encyclopedia. A Guide to Japanese Animation since 1917*, Berkeley, CA, 2001, p. 381.

10 For a »Mario Family Tree« cf. the »Retro« section of *Games*[TM], 3, 2004, p. 82 ff.

11 Poole, op. cit. (note 2), p. 42. With »plinth ideology", Poole quotes a concept from cognitive science and describes how ideology and symbol conflate.

12 Hartmut Winkler, *Docuverse: Zur Medientheorie der Computer*, Munich, 1997, p. 315.

13 Cf. Benjamin Maack, »Frauenrunde«, in: *Games Entertainment Education*, 2, 2004, p. 56.

14 For the spectacular looks of these female »Sexy Heroes«, as *1000 Game Heroes* calls them, cf. David Choquet (ed.), *1000 Game Heroes*, Cologne et al., 2002, pp. 504–541. The book introduces the heroines of the following games on different platforms: *Dead or Alive* (XBox, 2001), *Druuna* (PC, 2001), *Fear Effect* (Playstation, 2001), *No One Lives Forever* (PC, Playstation 2, 2000), *Perfect Dark* (Nintendo 64, 2000), *Tomb Raider* (PC, Playstation, Dreamcast, Playstation 2, 2002), *Urban Chaos* (PC, Playstation, Dreamcast, 1999). The pictures attest to the fact that these female characters have diverse origins, among which are the *femme fatale* and the hard-boiled detective novel, sexy comic books,

James Bond and science-fiction movies, and cult TV series from the 1960s like *The Avengers*.

15 Cf. my interpretation of Lara Croft, »Darf ich mitspielen? Literaturwissenschaften und Computerspiele«, in: *Jahrbuch für Computerphilologie*, 2, 2000, pp. 87–119, and http://computerphilologie. uni-muenchen.de/jg00/gunzenh/gunzenh.html.

16 Michael Allen discusses the shift in notions of realism which had to happen when new technologies which had entered cinema since the 1950s were finally taken into account by film criticism. He stresses both a »heightened sense of ›realism‹ and a bigger, more breathtaking realization of spectacle. Both of these impetuses have been realized through the development of larger, clearer, more enveloping images; louder, more multi-layered, more accurately directional sound; and more subtle, ›truer-to-life‹ colour.« Michael Allen, »From Bwana Devil to Batman Forever: Technology in Contemporary Hollywood Cinema«, in: Steve Neale and Murray Smith (eds.), *Contemporary Hollywood Cinema*, London, 1998, p. 127.

17 Cf. Martin Lister et al., *New Media: A Critical Introduction*, London / New York, 2003, pp. 141–143.

18 Donna Coco, »Creating Humans for Games«, in: *Computer Graphics World*, October 20, 1997, pp. 26–31.

19 Cf. an interview with the production manager of *Deus Ex – The Invisible War*, Harvey Smith – Bernd Graff and Markus Schulte, »Spür den Gott in dir!«, in: *Süddeutsche Zeitung*, 48, 2004, p. 14.

20 George Lucas was the first movie director to use digital technologies in *Star Wars* in 1977. About *Star Wars* and the development of digital technologies in film cf. Rob Kenner, »Hollywood!«, in: *Wired*, October, 1999, pp. 217–221.

21 Poole, op. cit. (note 2), pp. 85 ff.

22 Hartmut Winkler, »Über Rekursion: Eine Überlegung zu Programmierbarkeit, Wiederholung, Verdichtung und Schema«, 1999, www.uni-paderborn.de/~winkler/rekursio.html.

23 Accordingly, avatars in action games tend to be loners. There don't exist many love relationships between characters of computer games, especially in the action genre, the single Lara Croft being the most famous example of his. One exception to this rule is the second part of *Max Payne*, 2003.

24 Poole, op. cit. (note 2), p. 84.

25 Lister et al., op. cit. (note 17), pp. 137 ff.

26 Philip Hayward, »Situating Cyberspace: The Popularisation of Virtual Reality«, in: Philip Hayward and Tana Wollen (eds.), *Future Visions: New Technologies of the Screen*, London, 1994, p. 182, cit. in: Lister et al., op. cit. (note 17), p. 137.

27 You find screenshots of *Tron 2.0* under, www. gamers.com/game/1159401/media. Cf. the enthusiastic critical statement by Dirk Gooding, »Tron 2.0«, in: *PCGames*, 10, 2003, pp. 106–111.

28 Quoted by Jim Collins, *Architectures of Excess: Cultural Life in the Information Age*, New York / London, 1995, p. 2 (including addition).

29 Ibid., p. 5.

30 Hilary Radner, »Hollywood Redux: All About My Mother and Gladiator«, in: Jon Lewis (ed.), *The End of Cinema as We Know It: American Film in the Nineties*, New York, 2001, pp. 72–80.

31 Lister et al., op. cit. (note 17), p. 155. CGI means computer-generated imagery. As Lister et al. remind

us: »The term is commonly used to describe computer animation and special effects in film and television production«, p. 384.

32 Ibid., p. 155.

33 Ibid.

34 Jay David Bolter and Richard Grusin, *Remediation: Understanding New Media*, Cambridge, MA., 1998, London, 1999, p. 15.

Dietmar E. Fröhlich: Architecture and film. The reality play

1 Natasha Higham, »cinem(a)rchitecture: signifying the imaginary city in film«, in: *arch'it*, 01, September 1999.

2 John Ellis, *Visible Fictions: Cinema, Television, Video*, London, 1982, pp. 50, 138, cf. also: Daniel Chandler, »Notes on ›the Gaze‹«, July 8, 2004, www.aber.ac.uk/media/Documents/gaze/gaze. html.

3 Dietrich Neumann (ed.), *Film Architecture: Set Design from Metropolis to Blade Runner*, Munich / London / New York, 1999, p. 7.

4 *Minority Report* (USA, 2002), director: Stephen Spielberg, production designer: Alex McDowell.

5 *Metropolis* (Germany, 1927), director: Fritz Lang, art directors: Otto Hunte, Erich Kettelhut, Karl Vollbrecht.

6 *The Truman Show* (USA, 1998), director: Peter Weir, production designer: Dennis Gassner.

7 New Urbanism. Congress of New Urbanism founded 1993 by Peter Katz, Andres Duany, Elizabeth Plater-Zyberk, et al., advocates restructuring of public policy and development practices to support the restoration of existing urban centers and towns within coherent metropolitan regions … stand for the reconfiguration of sprawling suburbs into communities of real neighborhoods and diverse districts, the conservation of natural environments, and the preservation of our built legacy.

8 *The Fifth Element* (France / USA, 1997), director: Luc Besson, production designer: Dan Weil.

9 *Star Wars* series. *Star Wars: Episode IV – A New Hope* (USA, 1977), director: George Lucas, production designer: John Barry. *Star Wars: Episode V – The Empire Strikes Back* (USA, 1980), director: Irvin Kershner, production designer: Norman Reynolds. *Star Wars: Episode VI – Return of the Jedi* (USA, 1983), director: Richard Marquand, production designer: Norman Reynolds. *Star Wars: Episode I – The Phantom Menace* (USA, 1999), director: George Lucas, production designer: John Barry. *Star Wars: Episode II – Attack of the Clones* (USA, 2002), director: George Lucas, production designer: John Barry.

10 *The Matrix* (USA, 1999), directors: Andy Wachowski and Larry Wachowski, production designer: Owen Paterson.

11 *Dark City* (USA, 1998), director: Alex Proyas, production designer: George Liddle and Patrick Tatopoulos.

12 MVRDV (Winny Maas, Jacob van Rijs and Nathalie de Vries), *FARMAX*, Rotterdam, 1998.

13 *The Thirteenth Floor* (Germany / USA, 1999), director: Josef Rusnak, production designer: Kirk M. Petruccelli.

14 *Gladiator* (UK / USA, 2000), director: Ridley Scott, production designer: Arthur Max.

[15] Peter Greenaway with Ania Krenz, »An Interview with Peter Greenaway«, in: *arch'it*, April 27, 2003.

[16] *Citizen Kane* (USA, 1941), director: Orson Welles, art director: Van Nest Polglase.

[17] Sagi Dar Ali, *A Film Approach in Design – Spatial Experience in Film*, Montreal, 2000 (thesis).

[18] Anthony Vidler, »The Explosion of Space: Architecture and the Filmic Imaginary«, in: Dietrich Neumann (ed.), op. cit. (note 3), p. 24.

[19] Sergey Eisenstein, *Non indifferent Nature*, Cambridge, MA, 1987, p. 140, and Anthony Vidler, op. cit. (note 18), p. 22.

[20] *Berlin, Symphony of a Great City (Berlin: Die Sinfonie der Großstadt*, Germany, 1927), director: Walter Ruttmann, art director: Erich Kettelhut.

[21] *The Man with the Movie Camera (Chelovek s kinoapparatom)* (Soviet Union, 1929), director: Dziga Vertov.

[22] Gilles Deleuze, »The Brain is the Screen. An Interview with Gilles Deleuze«, in: Gregory Flaxman (ed.), *Deleuze and the Philosophy of Cinema*, Minneapolis, 2000, pp. 325–373. Interview originally published in: *Cahiers du cinema*, 380, February 1986, pp. 25–32.

[23] Greenaway, op. cit. (note 15).

[24] *Vertigo* (USA, 1958), director: Alfred Hitchcock, production designer: Henry Bumstead (uncredited).

[25] *A Beautiful Mind* (USA, 2001), director: Ron Howard, production designer: Wynn Thomas.

[26] *Spider-Man* (USA, 2002), director: Sam Raimi, production designer: Neil Spisak.

[27] *Batman* (USA/UK, 1989), director: Tim Burton, production designer: Anton Furst.

[28] *Blade Runner* (USA, 1982), director: Ridley Scott, production designers: Lawrence G. Paull and Peter J. Hampton (uncredited), visual futurist: Syd Mead.

[29] *Paris, Texas* (UK/France/West Germany/USA, 1984), director: Wim Wenders, production designer: Kate Altman.

[30] *Panic Room* (USA, 2002), director: David Fincher, production designer: Arthur Max.

[31] *Lara Croft: Tomb Raider* (UK/Germany/USA/Japan, 2001), director: Simon West, production designer: Kirk M. Petruccelli.

[32] *Superman* (UK, 1978), director: Richard Donner, production designer: John Barry.

[33] *Saving Private Ryan* (USA, 1998), director: Steven Spielberg, production designer: Thomas E. Sanders.

[34] Giovanni Battista Piranesi, *I Carceri d'Invenzione*, Rome, 1745.

[35] Celeste M. Williams, »The Architecture of Silence«, in: Malcolm Quantrill and Bruce C. Webb (eds.), *The Culture of Silence: Architecture's Fifth Dimension*, Austin, TX, 1988.

[36] *Being John Malkovich* (USA, 1999), director: Spike Jonze, production designer: K. K. Barrett.

[37] *Nostalghia* (*Nostalghiya*, Italy/France/Soviet Union, 1983), director: Andrey Tarkovsky, production designer: Andrea Crisanti.

[38] *The Scarifice (Offret – Sacrifcatio)* (Sweden/UK/France, 1986), director: Andrey Tarkovsky, production designer: Anna Asp.

[39] *Stalker* (West Germany/Soviet Union, 1979), director: Andrey Tarkovsky, production designer: Aleksandr Bojm (1977), Andrey Tarkovsky.

[40] *THX 1138* (USA, 1971), director: George Lucas, art director: Michael D. Haller.

[41] *La Notte* (Italy/France, 1961), director: Michelangelo Antonioni, production designer: Piero Zuffi.

[42] *Professione: Reporter* (*The Passenger*) (France/Italy/USA/Spain, 1975), director: Michelangelo Antonioni, art director: Piero Poletto.

[43] *Il Deserto Rosso* (*The Red Desert*) (Italy/France, 1964), director: Michelangelo Antonioni, art director: Piero Poletto.

[44] »Proposed Topics – 3« for »Cinema and Urban Remains«, Montreal, May 10–13, 2000. Conference on the renewed art of seeing and making cinema.

[45] Susan Buck-Morss, »The City as Dreamworld and Catastrophe«, in: *October*, vol. 73, Cambridge, MA., 1995, p. 8.

[46] »Proposed Topics – 2.«, op. cit., (note 44). Cf. also: Richard Sennett, *Flesh and Stone: The Body and the City in Western Civilization*, New York, 1994.

[47] »Proposed Topics – 1«, op. cit. (note 44).

[48] Thomas Forget, »Urban Editing – Cinematic Architecture in Temple Bar/Introduction« (last paragraph), June 8, 2004, www.irish-architecture.com/onsite/urban_editing/.

[49] Elizabeth Mahoney, »The People in Parentheses: Space Under Pressure in the Post-Modern City«, in: David Clarke (ed.), *The Cinematic City*, London/New York, 1997, pp 168–185.

[50] *Night On Earth* (France/Germany/USA/UK/Japan, 1991), director: Jim Jarmusch, art department: Kari Laine (set decorator, Helsinki), Johan Le Teneux (set decorator: Los Angeles), Laurent Saimond (set decorator: Paris), Neal W. Zoromski (property master).

[51] *Until the End of the World* (*Bis ans Ende der Welt*, Germany/France/Australia, 1991), director: Wim Wenders, production designers: Sally Campbell, Thierry Flamand.

[52] *Falling Down* (France/USA,1993), director: Joel Schumacher, production designer: Barbara Ling.

[53] Paul Patton, »Imaginary Cities: Images of Postmodernity«, in: S. Watson and K. Gibson (eds.), *Postmodern Cities and Spaces*, Oxford, 1995, pp. 112–121.

[54] *Badlands* (USA, 1973), director: Terrence Malick, art director: Jack Fisk.

[55] Tatooine Desert home planet of Anakin (*Star Wars*, op. cit. (note 9).

[56] Seaside, Florida. Celebration, Florida. »Celebration is an innovative, real town that successfully combines architecture, education, health and technology in ways that promote a strong sense of community. Celebration, conceived as a small southeastern town with pre-1940s architecture, is under development by The Celebration Company in northwest Osceola County, Florida. When complete, the community is anticipated to have 12,000 residents« (excerpt from the ad for Celebration, cf. www.celebrationfl.com).

[57] El Paso – Ciudad Juárez. 3,710 feet above sea level. El Paso is located in the westernmost corner of Texas, right where Texas, New Mexico, and Mexico come together. Just over 700,000 people live in El Paso, which makes it the fourth most populous city in Texas. Combined with Ciudad Juarez, Mexico, though, the metropolitan area forms the largest population center on any international border in the world. About 2.2 million live in the area, with 700,000 residents in El Paso County. The median age is 27 years. El Paso has 248 square miles in area, making it the fourth largest ‹city in Texas, and 22nd in size in the United States. It is the nation's third fastest-growing metropolitan area. El Paso is the county seat of 1,054–square mile El Paso County.

[58] *What Dreams May Come* (USA, 1998), director: Vincent Ward, production designer: Eugenio Zanetti.

[59] *Female* (USA, 1933), director: Michael Curtiz, art director: Jack Okey.

[60] *The Black Cat* (USA, 1934), director: Edgar G. Ulmer, art director: Charles D. Hall.

[61] *House on the Haunted Hill* (USA, 1959), director: William Castle, art director: David Milton.

[62] *Black Rain* (USA, 1989), director: Ridley Sott, production designer: Norris Spencer.

[63] *Grand Canyon* (USA, 1991), director: Lawrence Kasdan, production designer: Bo Welch.

[64] *The Replacement Killers* (USA, 1998), director: Antoine Fuqua, production designer: Naomi Shohan.

[65] *Rush Hour* (USA, 1998), director: Brett Ratner, production designer: Robb Wilson King.

[66] *Gattaca* (USA, 1997), director: Andrew Niccol, production designer: Jan Roelfs.

[67] *Titus* (Italy/USA/UK, 1999/2000), director: Julie Taymor, production designer: Dante Ferretti.

[68] *Brazil* (UK, 1985), director: Terry Gilliam, production designer: Norman Garwood.

[69] Gaston Bachelard, *The Poetics of Space*, New York, 1964, p. 6.

[70] Italo Calvino (*Il barone rampante*, 1957; *Le città invisibili*, 1972) uses playfully innovative structures, shifting viewpoints to examine the nature of chance, coincidence, and change.

[71] *Batman*, series 1–4. *Batman* (USA/UK, 1989), director: Tim Burton, production designer: Anton Furst. *Batman Returns* (USA/UK, 1992), director: Tim Burton, production designer: Bo Welch. *Batman Forever* (USA, 1995), director: Joel Schumacher, production designer: Barbar Ling. *Batman & Robin* (USA, 1997), director: Joel Schumacher, production designer: Barbara Ling.

[72] Marvel Comics, publisher of *Spider-Man*.

[73] Joel Sanders (ed.), *Stud: Architectures of Masculinity*, New York, 1996. »So functional for its purposes: The Bachelor Apartment in Pillow Talk«, by Steven Cohan.

[74] *Strange Days* (USA, 1995), director: Kathryn Bigelow, production designer: Lilly Kilvert.

[75] Mark Lamster, »Wretched Hives: George Lucas and the Ambivalent Urbanism of *Star Wars*«, in: Mark Lamster (ed.), *Architecture and Film*, New York, 2000, pp. 231–240.

[76] Joseph Rosa, »Tearing Down the House: Modern Homes in the Movies«, in: Mark Lamster (ed.), op. cit. (note 75), pp. 159–170.

[77] For example Georg Simmel's »The Metropolis and Mental Life«, in: Neil Leach (ed.), *Rethinking Architecture*, London, 1997, pp. 69–79.

[78] *Body Double* (USA, 1984), director: Brian de Palma, production designer: Ida Random.

[79] *L. A. Confidential* (USA,1997), director: Curtis Hansen,sproduction designer: Jeannine Claudia Oppewall.

[80] Catherine Deneuve in an interview with Charlie Rose, September 16, 2002, PBS.

[81] Anthony Vidler, »The Explosion of Space: Architecture and the Filmic Imaginary«, in: Dietrich Neumann (ed.), op. cit. (note 3), p. 14.

82 *The Lord of the Rings*. Trilogy: *The Lord of the Rings: The Fellowship of the Ring* (USA /New Zealand, 2001), director: Peter Jackson, production designer: Grant Major. *The Lord of the Rings: The Two Towers* (USA / New Zealand, 2002), director: Peter Jackson, production designer: Grant Major. *The Lord of the Rings: The Return of the King* (USA / New Zealand, 2003), director: Peter Jackson, production designer: Grant Major.

83 Douglas Garofalo in: »Interview with Douglas Garofalo«, with Matteo Zambelli, in: *arch'it*, March 31, 2002.

84 Neil Kaye, cit. in: Linda Jacobson, *Glasshouse Studio, LLC*, »When Architects Plug In«, www.glasshousestudio.com/cli_dma.html.

85 Mike Linzey, »Some Binary Architecture – Sites for Possible Thought«, in: *Interstices 4* (»architectural magazine for the electronic age«).

86 *Tron* (USA / Taiwan, 1982), director: Steven Lisberger, production designers: Jean Giraud, Syd Mead, Dean Edward Mitzner.

87 Linzey, op. cit. (note 85).

88 Lev Manovich, cit. in: Linda Jacobson, op. cit. (note 84).

89 »Walking Cities«, Ron Herron's *Walking City*, 1964, cf. also: Peter Cook (ed.), *Archigram*, New York, 1999. pp. 18–43.

90 *The Matrix Reloaded* (USA, 2003), directors: Andy and Larry Wachowski, production designer: Owen Paterson.

91 Nostromo, Ripley's spaceship in *Alien*; inspired by a novel of the same name by Joseph Conrad, 1904.

92 *Alien* (UK, 1979), director: Ridley Scott, production designers: Michael Seymour, Roger Christian.

93 *The Matrix Revolutions* (USA, 2003), directors: Andy and Larry Wachowski, production designer: Owen Paterson.

94 *Alien* series. *Aliens* (USA/UK, 1986), director: James Cameron, production designer: Peter Lamont. *Alien 3* (USA,1992), director: David Fincher, production designers: Norman Reynolds, Micheal White (uncredited). *Alien Resurrection* (USA,1997), director: Jean-Pierre Jeunet, production designer: Nigel Phelps.

95 William Cameron Menzies (1896–1957). Menzies revolutionized art direction in Hollywood, becoming the first man billed as »production designer«; *Things to Come*, 1936, *Gone with the Wind* (production design), 1939.

96 *Things to Come* (UK, 1936), director: William Cameron Menzies, art directior: Vincent Korda.

97 »The Zone«, devastated (metaphysical) space full of traps that reacts to a trespasser's mental condition; the Stalker and his company have to cross the Zone to get to the room that fulfills one's »innermost« wishes.

98 Lego / »Bionicle«, Danish toy company whose plastic building blocks' name LEGO is a combination of the Danish »leg godt«, which means to »play well«. »Bionicles« are robot-like creatures built of LEGO pieces.

99 *2001: A Space Odyssey* (UK/USA,1968), director: Stanley Kubrick, production designers: Ernest Archer, Harry Lange, Anthony Masters.

100 »Feelies«, type of movie in Aldous Huxley's *Brave New World*, written 1931, published 1932. »Feelies are the popular films.« Filmgoers sit in special chairs that allow them to feel, and to interact, with the movie. The plots are simple, and often involve sex, cf. Erica Freund, »BookRags Book Notes on Brave New World«, October 11, 2004, www.bookrags.com/notes/bnw/OBJ.htm.

101 Coop Himmelb(l)au, »Architecture Must Blaze (1980)«, in: Coop Himmelblau, *Architecture Is Now*, New York, 1983, pp.80–81.

102 Jean Nouvel, cit. in: Kester Rattenbury, »Echo and Narcissus«, in: *Architectural Design*, Profile, 112, »Architecture and Film«, London, 1994, p. 35.

103 *Impostor* (USA, 2002), director: Gary Fleder, production designer: Nelson Coates.

104 *Crime and Punishment in Suburbia* (USA, 2000), director: Rob Schmidt, production designer: Ruth Ammon.

105 Lebbeus Woods, *The New City*, New York, 1992.

106 *Twelve Monkeys* (USA, 1995), director: Terry Gilliam, production designer: Jeffrey Beecroft.

107 Michelangelo Antonioni, Carlo di Carlo, Marga Cottino-Jones and Giorgio Tinazzi, *The Architecture of Vision: Writings and Interviews on Cinema*, New York, 1996.

108 Greenaway, op. cit. (note 15).

109 *The Belly of an Architect* (UK/Italy, 1987), director: Peter Greenaway, art director: Luciana Vedovelli.

110 *The Draughtsman's Contract* (UK,1982), director: Peter Greenaway, art director: Bob Ringwood.

111 *Inside Rooms: 26 Bathrooms, London & Oxfordshire, 1985*, (UK, 1985), (documentary) director: Peter Greenaway.

112 *H Is for House* (UK, 1973), (short) director: Peter Greenaway.

113 *The Stairs: Projection*. An exhibition (celebrating 100 years of cinema) by Peter Greenaway from October 26 to November 19, 1995 in Munich, Germany. *The Stairs* (Catalogue), London, 1995.

114 Robert Venturi, *Complexity and Contradiction in Architecture*, New York, 1966.

115 Robert Venturi, Denise Scott Brown, and Steven Izenour, *Learning from Las Vegas*, Cambridge, MA, 1972.

116 Natasha Higham, in »cinem(a)rchitecture: signifying the imaginary city in film«; interview in: *arch'it*, September 1, 1999.

117 Tim Benton, »Representing Le Corbusier: Film, Exhibition, Multimedia«, in: François Penz and Maureen Thomas (eds.), *Cinema & Architecture – Méliès, Mallet-Stevens, Multimedia*, London, 1997, pp. 114–117.

118 Hans Richter (architect, artist and filmmaker) Archive at the Museum of Modern Art in New York.

119 *The City* (USA, 1939), director: Ralph Steiner and Willard Van Dyke.

120 Forget, op. cit. (note 48).

121 Higham, op. cit. (note 116).

122 Greenaway, op. cit. (note 15).

123 Higham, op. cit. (note 116).

124 Greenaway, op. cit. (note 15).

Celeste M. Williams: Cinema architecture in the United States

1 Fernando Rigon, The Teatro Olimpico in Vicenza, Milan, 1989, pp. 25–29.

2 Richard Ingersoll, »All the World's a Stage: Architecture and Spectacle«, in: *Architecture*, August 2000, pp. 78–79.

3 »The Totaltheater Proposed by Walter Gropius«, in: *Architectural Record*, April 1930, pp. 492–493.

4 Beatrix Flynn, »Losing it at the Movies: From Palace to Multiplex«, in: *Cite* (a publication of the Rice Design Alliance Houston), Houston, 1987, pp. 17–18.

5 Walter Benjamin, *Das Kunstwerk im Zeitalter seiner technischen Reproduzierbarkeit* (The Work of Art in the Age of Mechanical Reproduction), Frankfurt am Main, 1963. pp. 43–47.

6 Ingersoll, op. cit. (note 2), pp. 78–79.

7 American Multi-Cinema, Stan Durwood History, www.amctheatres.com.

8 Steve Levin, »Farewell My Lonely, The Last Days of the Single Screen Theater«, in: *Marquee*, vol. 32, no. 3, pp. 22–24.

9 Jeffrey Hardwick, *Mall Maker: Victor Gruen, Architect of an American Dream*, Philadelphia, 2004.

10 »Sector Analysis Cinemas«, in: *World Architecture*, 69, September, 1998, pp. 104–115.

11 *The Charlie Rose Show*, Interview with actor George Clooney, PBS, November 25, 2002.

12 George Lucas' THX Process.

13 Maurizio Vitta, »Cinema + Cinema – the Avalon Movie Theater in New York«, in: *L'Arca*, vol. 91, March 1995, pp. 78–81.

14 Charles K. Hoyt, »Strip Stopper – O'Neil Cinemas, Duluth Georgia: Richard Rauh and Associates Architects«, in: *Architectural Record*, January 1995, vol. 183, no. 1, pp. 78–83.

15 Frank Werner, *Covering + Exposing, The Architecture of Coop Himmelblau*, Basel, 2000, pp. 120–129.

16 »Tiefenrausch: Multi-Kinos Annenhof in Graz«, in: *Architektur, Innenarchitektur und Technischer Ausbau*, May 1998, no. 5, pp. 60–65.

17 Michael Cannell, »Jon Jerde, Neon Urbanist«, in: *Architecture*, August 2000, pp. 112–114.

18 Stephen Fox, Gerald Moorhead, and Yolita Schmidt, *Houston Architectural Guide*, Houston, 1999, p. 210.

19 Andrew White, »Downtown Six-Plex Goes Underground (Angelika Film Center)«, in: *Metropolis*, December 1989, vol. 9, no. 5, p. 20–21.

20 IMAX website.

21 Interview with Gensler Vice Presidents Michael Darner and Marty Boyko, and Gensler's theater design specialist Warwick Wicksman.

22 Gerald Levitch, »Retro-Techno Goes to the Movies – The Paramount Famous Players Theater«, in: *Canadian Interiors*, September / October, 2000, vol. 37, no. 5, pp. 40–44.

23 Edwin Heathcote, *Cinema Builders*, Chichester, 2001, p. 51.

Pamela C. Scorzin: Authentic replicas, or just like a Hollywood movie. Notes on the cinematized Las Vegas Strip

1 Cf. with regard to this topic Bob Hasenteufel / Philip Soann, *Venedig in Nevada. Traumhotel der Wüste*, TaunusFilm, ZDF, Wiesbaden, 2003; Alex Farquharson (ed.), *The Magic Hour. The Convergence of Art and Las Vegas* (Catalogue), Graz, 2001; Petra Kipphoff, »Das Original schlägt zurück. In Las Vegas eröffneten das Guggenheim Museum und die Eremitage eine Dependance. Lässt sich die

Stadt ihre simulierte Seele abkaufen?«, in: *Die Zeit*, 42, October 11, 2001, p. 47; Wolfgang Koydl, »Menschen im Hotel (V): Hinter den Kulissen des ›Venetian‹ in Las Vegas. Wenn die Kellner Gondeln tragen«, in: *Süddeutsche Zeitung*, 195, August 25/26, 2001, p. 3; Jörg Häntzschel, »Das Paradies in der Wüste«, in: Stiftung Bauhaus Dessau (ed.), *Urbane Paradiese. Zur Kulturgeschichte modernen Vergnügens*, Edition Bauhaus, vol. 8, Frankfurt am Main / New York, 2001, pp. 297–302; Rosemarie Noack, »Das Hochamt in Kopie. Was Las Vegas gerade alles unternimmt und auf die Beine stellt, um zu bleiben, was es längst ist: die Hauptstadt des Entertainment«, in: *Die Zeit*, 1, December 28, 2000, pp. 71–72; Pamela C. Scorzin, »Las Venice. ›Architainment‹ für die Fun-Gesellschaft«, in: Detlef Bluemler (ed.), *Kurzschrift – Für die Freunde der Langschrift. Texte zum kulturellen Alltag*, vol. 3, Munich, 2000, pp. 59–65; Gundolf S. Freyermuth, »Vegas, virtuelle Stadt«, March 9, 2000, available online at www://heise.de/tp/deutsch/inhalt/co/3488/1.html; Frances Anderton and John Chase (eds.), *Las Vegas. The Success of excess (= Architecture in context)*, Cologne, 1997; Hans Dieter Schaal, *Learning from Hollywood. Architecture and Film/ Architektur und Film*, Stuttgart / London, 1996.

[2] Schaal, op. cit. (note 1), p. 11.

[3] Cf. Peter Weibel, »Las Vegas. The City – A Place of Consumption in the Post-industrial Information Society«, in: Alex Farquharson, op. cit. (note 1), pp. 186–189.

[4] Silke Müller, »Traumwelt: Alexander Timtschenko«, in: *ART. Das Kunstmagazin*, 7, 1999, pp. 14–21, here p. 20.

[5] Norman M. Klein, »Vegaesthetics«, in: Alex Farquharson, op. cit. (note 1), p. 199.

[6] Gundolf S. Freyermuth, »Vegas, virtuelle Stadt«, March 9, 2000, available online at www.telepolis.de/deutsch/inhalt/co/3488/1.html.

[7] Alex Farquharson (ed.), »Some Representations«, in: Farquharson, op. cit. (note 1), p. 20.

[8] Jeremy Rifkin, *ACCESS. Das Verschwinden des Eigentums. Warum wir weniger besitzen und mehr ausgeben werden*, Frankfurt am Main / New York, 2000, pp. 208–209.

[9] Cf. Schaal, op, cit. (note 1), p. 117.

[10] Ibid., p. 122.

[11] Gundolf S. Freyermuth, »Vegas, virtuelle Stadt«, March 9, 2000, available online at www.telepolis.de/deutsch/inhalt/co/3488/1.html.

[12] Cf. Schaal, op. cit. (note 1), p. 107.

[13] »Künstliche Realitäten. Hanne Weskott im Gespräch mit Alexander Timtschenko«, in: *Tain. Magazin für Architektur, Kunst und Design*, 4, July/August 1998, pp. 54–59, here p. 55.

[14] Cf. also: Ralph Eue, »Las Vegas im Film. In Wirklichkeit ist alles ganz anders«, in: *StadtBauwelt*, 143, 36, vol. 90, September 24, 1999, pp. 2008–2013.

Bibliography

Andrew, J. Dudley, *The Major Film Theories: An Introduction*, New York, 1976.

Austin, John L., *How To Do Things With Words*, 1965; 2nd ed. Cambridge, MA, 1999.

Barsam, Richard, *Looking at Movies: An Introduction to Film*, New York, 2004.

Bart, Peter, »Too Little, Too Late«, in: *Variety*, May 24, 1993, pp. 5, 22.

Belton, John, *American Cinema / American Culture*, Boston, 2005.

Berardinelli, James, film review, 2000, www.movie-reviews.colossus.net/movies/t/requiem-dream.

Biskind, Peter, *Easy Riders, Raging Bulls: How the sex-drugs-and-rock 'n' roll generation saved Hollywood*, New York, 1998.

Björkin, Mats, »Industrial Greta. Some Thoughts on an Industrial Film«, in: John Fullerton and Jan Olsson (eds.), *Nordic Explorations. Film Before 1930*, London, 1999, pp. 263 ff.

Black, Gregory A., *Hollywood Censored. Morality Codes, Catholics and the Movies*, Cambridge, 1996.

Blanchet, Robert, *Blockbuster. Ästhetik, Ökonomie und Geschichte des postklassischen Hollywood-Kinos*, Marburg, 2003.

Bordwell, David, »Die Hard – und die Rückkehr des klassischen Hollywood-Kinos«, in: Tomlinson Holman, *Sound For Film And Television*, Boston / London, 1997.

Bordwell, David, and Kristin Thompson, *Film Art: An Introduction*, New York, 2004.

Bordwell, David, Janet Staiger, and Kristin Thompson, *The Classical Hollywood Cinema: Film Style and Mode of Production to 1960*, New York / London, 1985.

Boorstin, Daniel J., *The Image. A Guide to Pseudo-Events in America*, 1961, new ed. New York, 1987.

Brooks, Xan, »First Steps in Latin«, *The Guardian*, July 18, 2002.

Chion, Michel, *Audio-Vision: Sound on Screen*, New York, 1994.

Corrigan, Timothy, *A Cinema Without Walls: Movies and Culture after Vietnam*, New Brunswick, NJ, 1991.

Danan, Martine, »Marketing the Hollywood Blockbuster in France«, in: *Journal of Popular Film and Television*, March 23, 1995, pp. 131 ff.

De Cordova, Richard, »The Emergence of the Star System in America«, in: Christine Gledhill (ed.), *Stardom. Industry of Desire*, London, 1991, pp. 17 ff.

The Edge of Hollywood, part of the series *American Cinema*, 1995. Distributed by FoxVideo, POB 900, Beverly Hills, CA 90213.

Finney, Angus, *The State of European Cinema: A New Dose of Reality*, London, 1996.

Gabler, Neal, *An Empire of Their Own: How the Jews Invented Hollywood*, New York, 1988.

Geuens, Jean-Pierre, *Film Production Theory*, Albany, NY, 2000.

Grantham, Bill, *Some Big Bourgeois Brothel: Contexts for France's Culture Wars with Hollywood*, Luton, 2000.

Guback, Thomas, *The International Film Industry*, Bloomington, IN, 1969.

Gunning, Tom, *D. W. Griffith and the Origins of American Narrative Film. The Early Years at Biograph*, Urbana / Chicago, 1991.

Hampton, Benjamin, *History of the American Film Industry: From its Beginnings to 1931*, New York, 1931, reprinted 1970.

Haralovich, Mary Beth, »Advertising Heterosexuality«, in: *Screen*, vol. 23, no. 2, 1990, pp. 50 ff.

Haralovich, Mary Beth, »Mandates of Good Taste. The Self-Regulation of Film Advertising in the Thirties«, in: *Wide Angle*, vol. 6, no. 2, 1984.

Hediger, Vinzenz, *Verführung zum Film. Der amerikanische Kinotrailer seit 1912*, Marburg, 2001.

Hediger, Vinzenz, »L'image de l'auteur dans la publicité. A propos des stratégies auto-promotionelles de Cecil B. DeMille et Alfred Hitchcock«, in: Jean-Pierre Esquenazi (ed.), *Politique des auteurs et théories du cinema*, Paris, 2003, pp. 39 ff.

Hediger, Vinzenz, and Patrick Vonderau, *Demnächst in ihrem Kino. Grundlagen der Filmwerbung und Filmvermarktung*, Marburg, 2004.

»The Hollywood Style«, *American Cinema*, PBS series, 1995. Distributed by FoxVideo, POB 900, Beverly Hills, CA 90213.

Hoskins, Colin, and Rolf Mirus, »Television Fiction Made in USA«, in: Peter Larson (ed.), *Import / Export: International Flow of Television Fiction*, Paris, 1990.

Ilott, Terry, *Budgets and Markets: A study of the budgeting of European film*, London, 1996.

Kennedy, Joseph P., *The Story of Films*, Chicago, 1927, reprinted 1971.

Kernan, Lisa D., *Consuming Production. Documentaries About the Making of Movies*, San Francisco, 1991 (M.A. thesis).

Miller, Toby, »The Crime of Monsieur Lang: GATT, the screen and the new international division of cultural labour«, in: Albert Moran (ed.), *Film Policy: International, National and Regional Perspectives*, New York, 1996.

Nitsche, Lutz, *Hitchcock – Greenaway – Tarantino. Paratextuelle Attraktionen des Autorenkinos*, Stuttgart / Weimar, 2002.

Odin, Roger, »For a Semio-Pragmatics of Film«, in: Warren Buckland (ed.), *The Film Spectator: From Sign to Mind*, Amsterdam, 1995, pp. 218 ff.

Olson, Scott Robert, *Hollywood Planet: Global Media and the Competitive Advantage of Narrative Transparency*, Mahwah, NJ, 1999.

Rasch, Manfred, Karl-Peter Ellenbrock, and Renate Köhne-Lindenlaub, *Industriefilm als Medium und Quelle*, Essen, 1999.

Rasch, Manfred, Hans-U. Berendes, and Peter Döring, *Industriefilm 1948–1959*, Essen, 2003.

Reichert, Ramón, »The Popularization of Productivity. The Industry Films of the Austrian Productivity Center 1951–1959«, in: *Conference Proceedings. The Seventh Biennial National Labour History Conference*, Canberra, 2001, pp. 209 ff.

Rost, Andreas (ed.), *Der schöne Schein der Künstlichkeit*, Frankfurt am Main, 2001, pp. 151 ff.

Salt, Barry, *Film Style & Technology: History & Analysis*, London, 1983, 2nd. ed. 1992.

Schatz, Thomas, *The Genius of the System: Hollywood Filmmaking in the Studio Era*, New York, 1988.

Schatz, Thomas, »The Return of the Hollywood Studio System«, in: Erik Barnouw et al., *Conglomerates and the Media*, New York, 1997.

Smith, Murray, *Engaging Characters: Fiction, Emotion, and the Cinema*, Oxford, 1995.

Staiger, Janet , »Dividing Labor For Production Control. Thomas Ince and the Rise of the Studio System«, in: *Cinema Journal*, vol. 18, no. 2, 1979, pp. 16 ff.

Staiger, Janet, »Seeing Stars«, in: Christine Gledhill (ed.), *Stardom. Industry of Desire*, London, 1991, pp. 3 ff.

Talbot, Frederick A., *Moving Pictures. How They Are Made and Worked*, London, 1912.

Thompson, Kristin, *Exporting Entertainment: America in the World Film Market 1907–1934*, London, 1985.

Uricchio, William, and Roberta Pearson, *Reframing Culture: The Case of the Vitagraph Quality Films*, New York, 1993.

Vasey, Ruth, *The World According to Hollywood 1918–1939*, Madison, WI, 1997.

Vogel, Harold L., *Entertainment Industry Economics: A guide for Financial Analysis*, 3rd ed., New York, 1994.

Wasser, Frederick, »Is Hollywood America? The Transnationalization of the American Film Industry«, in: *Critical Studies in Mass Communication*, 12/4, December, 1995, pp. 423 ff.

Wasser, Frederick, *Veni, Vidi, Video: The Hollywood Empire and the VCR*, Austin, TX, 2001,

Wildman, S. S., and S. E. Siwek, *International Trade in Films and Television Programs*, Cambridge, MA, 1988.

Williams, Linda, »Film Bodies: Gender, Genre, and Excess«, in: Leo Braudy and Marshall Cohen (eds.), *Film Theory and Criticism: Introductory Readings*, New York, 1991; 5th ed. 1999, pp. 702 ff.

Williams, Michael, and Christian Mørk, »Remake Stakes are Up«, in: *Variety*, April 19, 1993, pp. 5, 8, 20.

Zettl, Herbert, *Sight, Sound, Motion. Applied Media Aesthetics*, Wadsworth, 1999.

About the authors

Robert Blanchet teaches at the seminar for cinema studies at the University of Zurich. He is the author of the book *Blockbuster: Ästhetik, Ökonomie und Geschichte des postklassischen Hollywoodkinos* (Schüren, Marburg, 2003) and editor of the online journal *cinetext* at the department of philosophy at the University of Vienna. He is currently working on a PhD thesis on film and performativity.

Dietmar E. Fröhlich studied architecture in Graz, Austria (diploma with Günther Domenig, 1984), Fulbright Scholarship and post-graduate studies in architecture at the University of Houston (M. Arch., 1986). Licensed and registered architect in Austria and the USA, worked on competitions and large-scale commercial projects in architecture offices in Washington, DC, Houston, and Graz, 1986–96. Founded Williams + Fröhlich Architects, Houston/Graz in 1996, together with Celeste M. Williams. Teaching architectural design for senior undergraduate and graduate levels, including a course on architecture and film at the Gerald D. Hines College of Architecture, University of Houston, since 1996.

Jean-Pierre Geuens holds a PhD in critical studies from the University of Southern California. He teaches film at the Art Center College of Design in Pasadena, California. His publications include a book, *Film Production Theory* (Suny Press, 2000), and many articles in *Film Quarterly*, *Quarterly Review of Film and Video*, *Film Criticism*, *Spectator*, and *LAICA Journal*.

Randi Gunzenhäuser taught American studies at Siegen University in 2003 and 2004, presently teaching at the Ludwig-Maximilians-Universität, Munich. Studied American literary and cultural studies as well as theater at Claremont Colleges, California, and at the Ludwig-Maximilians-Universität, Munich; MA and PhD at Ludwig-Maximilians-Universität, Munich, habilitation at the Technische Universität Chemnitz. In 2000–02 participation in an Americanist research project on computer games at the Technische Universität Chemnitz. Work focuses on the history and theory of the media. Publications on computer games, Gothic literature, concepts of the body, gender studies; author of *From Machine People to Cyborgs: Concepts of the Body in Print, Films, and on CD-ROMs since 1800* (2005).

Vinzenz Hediger is a professor of film studies at the Ruhr-Universität in Bochum. He has taught at the University of Zurich and the Freie Universität Berlin and has been a guest professor at the Università Cattolica del Sacro Cuore in Milan, Italy, in 2003/04. His publications include a book on movie trailers, *Verführung zum Film. Der amerikanische Kinotrailer seit 1912* (Schüren, Marburg, 2001).

Kay Hoffmann holds a PhD from the Philipps-Universität in Marburg. He works as a film historian and film journalist and has organized several film- and TV festivals as well as conferences. Since 1994 researcher at the Haus des Dokumentarfilms Euro-

päisches Medienforum Stuttgart. Furthermore he published articles on film and new media since the 1980s. His books as author and editor include: *Am Ende Video – Video am Ende?* (1990); *Natur und ihre filmische Auflösung* (1994); *Zeichen der Zeit* (1996); *Trau – Schau – Wem. Digitalisierung und dokumentarische Form* (1997); *Cinema Futures: Cain, Able or Cable? The Screen Arts in the Digital Age* (1998); *MMM: Museum – Movie – Multimedia* (2000); *Die Einübung des dokumentarischen Blicks* (2001); *Triumph der Bilder* (2003).

Angela Krewani read English and American literature and history at the Universities of Cologne and Siegen and did graduate research at Yale University, New Haven. She took her PhD on *Modernism and Femininity. American Writers in Paris* and her habilitation on *New British Cinema* with Christian W. Thomsen. They cooperated on articles, books and various artistic projects. She now teaches as a professor of media studies at the Philipps-Universität in Marburg. Frequent research visits to various universities in Canada and the United States. Angela Krewani presently works on interactive teaching methods and media arts.

Claudia Liebrand, professor of literary studies and media theory at the University of Cologne. Head of research project »Gender representations in film« at the research center »Media and Cultural Communication«. Read German, history and philosophy in Freiburg, Germany. In 1989 PhD with a thesis on the novels of Theodor Fontane. In 1995, completion of post-doctoral thesis (habilitation) on E. T. A. Hoffmann. Claudia Liebrand has published widely on European literature of the 18th and the 20th centuries. Her main focus is on classical Modernism, gender, psychoanalysis, and film. Recent publications include: *Gender-Topographien. Kulturwissenschaftliche Lektüren von Hollywoodfilmen der Jahrhundertwende* (DuMont, Cologne, 2003); *Hollywood hybrid. Genre und Gender im zeitgenössischen Mainstream-Film*, (Schüren, Marburg, 2004, ed. with Ines Steiner); *Waltraud Gölter. Langage tangage. Schriften zur feministischen Psychoanalyse, zur Autobiographie und zu Michel Leiris*, Rombach, Freiburg, 2003, ed. with Ursula Renner). Visiting professorships at the University of Pavia and at Washington University, St. Louis; many grants and fellowships, presently working on Kafka and Annette von Droste-Hülshoff.

Gudula Simone Moritz, PhD from the University of Giessen, Germany. PhD. project: »In the Shadow of the Third Reich: The image of Germany in the English novel towards the close of the 20th century«. MA in English literature, history of art, modern history (Universities of Giessen and Sunderland, Great Britain). Film specialist, editorial journalist, and reporter at the daily arts magazine »Kulturzeit« on German television ZDF/3sat since 1995. Selected recent reports: »Pentagon Pictures: How the Pentagon censors Hollywood's scripts«; »Who was Iris Murdoch?« (LiteraVison 2003: competition finalist); »Culture of fear: fearmongering and politics in America«, »Angry Old Man: Eric Hobsbawm«; »An American in Paris: Jean Pierre Melville.« Project manager of »Kulturzeit« coverage from the Berlin film

festival, reporter from the film festivals in Cannes, Venice and Moscow.

Volker Pietsch, born in 1979, student of history and German philology, first at the University of Münster, since 2003 at the Freie Universität Berlin. In the same year, joint founder of the *Galerie für Aktuelle Malerei*, a platform for professional young painters.

Karen A. Ritzenhoff teaches film theory and television production at the Department of Communication at Central Connecticut State University (CCSU). She is a tenured Associate Professor. Her Ph.D. is from the University of Minnesota and deals with the work of German documentary filmmakers after the fall of the Berlin Wall. Ritzenhoff's current research focuses on »women and film«, media literacy and the history of American cinema. She has instituted a bi-annual international women and film festival at CCSU. A German native, she began her academic training at the University of Siegen following a career in journalism. Ritzenhoff was granted a Fulbright Fellowship to complete her graduate work in the USA. She returned to Germany numerous times to conduct research and was also involved in the Sonderforschungsbereich Bildschirmmedien (special research field screen media) of the Deutsche Forschungsgemeinschaft at the University of Siegen.

Pamela C. Scorzin, born in Vicenza, Italy, read European cultural history, history, English and American literature in Heidelberg and Stuttgart; 1994 PhD at Ruprecht-Karls-Universität in Heidelberg in art history. 1995–2000 assistant professor for art history in the department of architecture at Technische Hochschule Darmstadt. 2001 habilitation in history of modern art in Darmstadt, standing-in for a chair in English and American literature at the University of Siegen in 2002, standing-in for a chair in art history at the Akademie der Bildenden Künste in Stuttgart in 2003. Lives and works as art and media theorist in Darmstadt and Milan.

Christian W. Thomsen, professor of English literature and media studies at the University of Siegen. Founder of Siegen's Media Center, co-founder of the research program for the media of the Deutsche Forschungsgemeinschaft. Teaches also architectural theory, history and design since 1982. Visiting professorships at the universities of Copenhagen, London (Bartlett School of Architecture), Jerusalem, Vancouver (University of British Columbia), Los Angeles (University of California), and Houston. Author of 26 books, editor of 55 books. 300 articles on literature, theater, architecture, film, design, and media developments in leading journals in Germany, Austria, Switzerland, Great Britain, USA, Canada, Japan. 25 documentary films. Director of stage and radio plays, organization of numerous international symposia and art exhibitions, frequent cooperation with companies of the car industry and design-oriented firms.

Frederick Wasser's book *Veni, Vidi, Video: The Hollywood Empire and the VCR* (University of Texas Press) won the 2003 Marshall McLuhan award. Worked for many years in New York and Hollywood post-production on shows ranging from the pilot for *Law and Order* to movies such as *Missing in Action* and *Nightmare on Elm Street Part IV* before becoming a professor. Also translated and published a Norwegian drama entitled *The Bird Lovers*, written by Jens Bjœrnebœ. PhD from the University of Illinois. Post-doctoral fellow at Columbia University in New York. Publication of articles in *Critical Studies in Mass Communication*, *Journal of Communication*, *Cinema Journal* and others. Currently teaching in the department of television and radio at Brooklyn College in New York.

Celeste M. Williams studied painting (BFA, 1981) and Architecture (M. Arch., 1986) at the University of Houston. Licensed architect in the USA, worked on competitions and large-scale commercial projects in offices in Washington, DC, Houston and Graz, Austria, 1986–96. Founded Williams + Fröhlich Architects, Houston/Graz in 1996, together with Dietmar E. Fröhlich. Taught architectural history at the Technische Universität Graz, assistant to guest professor Daniel Libeskind, 1995/96. Teaching architectural design for undergraduate and graduate levels, including courses on history and theory of architecture and design, and developed a course on architectural writing at the Gerald D. Hines College of Architecture, University of Houston, since 1996. PhD candidate in architectural history and theory at the Akademie der Angewandten Künste in Vienna.

Photo credits

Alexandre Astruc, *Du stylo à la caméra ... et de la caméra au stylo. Ecrits (1942–1984)*, Paris 1992
  55.3
Bionicle 168.40
Marco Dezzi Bardeschi, *Frank Llyod Wright*, Luzern
  1971 156.21
Dietmar E. Fröhlich 146.7, 171.42, 175.1, 182.6,
  183.7
Jean Pierre Geuens 51.2
The Kirkland Partnership, Inc. 183.8
Western Supply, Las Vegas, 2001 186.2
Christian Probst 166.36
Reno-Tahoe Specialty, Inc., Las Vegas 184.1
Ralph Richter 146.6
Thomas Spiegelhalter 157.24, 163.33
StadtBauwelt 143, September 24, 1999 187.4,
  188.5, 191.6
UN Studio 164.34, 165.35
Celeste Williams 178.2, 178.3, 180.4, 181.5
Die Zeit, October 24, 2002 187.3

All pictures from films and computer games are screen shots.